SUBSTANCE USE & ABUSE

Cultural and Historical Perspectives

RUSSIL DURRANT

Center for Behavioral Research in Cancer,
Cancer Control Research Institute, Melbourne, Australia

JO THAKKER

University of Waikato, Hamilton, New Zealand

SAGE Publications
International Educational and Professional Publisher
Thousand Oaks ■ London ■ New Delhi

For information:

Sage Publications, Inc.
2455 Teller Road
Thousand Oaks, California 91320
E-mail: order@sagepub.com

Sage Publications Ltd.
6 Bonhill Street
London EC2A 4PU
United Kingdom

Sage Publications India Pvt. Ltd.
B-42, Panchsheel Enclave
Post Box 4109
New Delhi 110 017 India

Printed in the United States of America

Library of Congress Cataloging-in-Publication Data

Durrant, Russil.
Substance use and abuse : cultural and historical perspectives / Russil Durrant, Jo Thakker.
    p. cm.
Includes bibliographical references and index.
ISBN 0-7619-2341-1 — ISBN 0-7619-2342-X (paper)
   1. Substance abuse—Social aspects. 2. Drug abuse—Social aspects.
I. Thakker, Jo. II. Title.
HV4998.D87 2003
306′.1—dc21

2003002400

03 04 05 06 10 9 8 7 6 5 4 3 2 1

Acquiring Editor:	Jim Brace-Thompson
Editorial Assistant:	Karen Ehrmann
Production Editor:	Sanford Robinson
Typesetter:	C&M Digitals (P) Ltd.
Copy Editor:	Pam Suwinsky
Indexer:	David Luljak
Cover Designer:	Michelle Lee

Contents

Preface   ix

Acknowledgments   xi

1. What Needs to Be Explained and
    How Should We Explain It?   1
    Introduction   1
    Levels of Analysis and the
        Multidisciplinary
        Nature of Psychoactive Drug Studies   3
    Toward an Integrated
        Model of Substance Use and Abuse   6
    Overview   11

2. The Nature and Scope of Substance Use and Abuse   13
    Introduction   13
    What Is a Drug?   14
    Who Uses Drugs?   15
    Taxonomy of Drug Use Contexts   20
    The Harm and Benefits of Drugs   23
    From Use to Abuse   26
    Summary   32

3. An Evolutionary Perspective   34
    Introduction   34
    The Nature and Role of
        Evolutionary Explanations   36
    Has Drug Use Been Selected For?   38
    Drugs and the Brain   40
    Drug Use, Sexual
        Selection, and Life History Theory   45
    From Use to Abuse   51
    An Integrated Evolutionary Model of Substance Use   54
    Summary   57

4.	**Drugs in History**	59
	Introduction	59
	What Can History Tell Us About Substance Use and Abuse?	60
	A Brief History of Drugs	63
	Early History	64
	Drugs and the Birth of the Modern World	68
	A New Order: Drugs in the Twentieth Century	79
	Summary	87
5.	**The Forces of History: Explaining Patterns of Use and Abuse**	89
	Introduction	89
	The Functions of Drugs in Historical Perspective	90
	Pharmacology	94
	New Forms, New Modes, New Substances: The Impact of Technological Change on Drug Use	95
	Availability	98
	Economic and Political Factors	100
	Legislation and Public Policy	104
	Social Factors	106
	A Complex Web: Multiple Influences on Patterns of Drug Use	113
	Summary	117
6.	**Drugs and Culture**	119
	Introduction	119
	Conceptual and Methodological Issues	121
	Indigenous Patterns of Drug Use	126
	Oceania	127
	Asia	130
	Africa and the Middle East	132
	The Americas	136
	Conclusions	140
	Drugs and Multiculturalism	142
	Ethnic Groups	143
	Migrants and Drug Use	149
	Other Cultural Groups	150
	Summary	154
7.	**The Role of Culture: Explaining Patterns of Use**	156
	Introduction	156

Drugs and Culture   157
   The Function of Drugs in Cultural Perspective   157
   Alien Poisons Versus Culturally
      Integrated Substances   160
   Production, Supply, and Availability   162
Culture and Drugs   163
   Genetic Factors   164
   Norms, Values, and Roles   166
   Beliefs, Expectations, and Concepts   169
   Socialization and Social Identity   172
Social-Structural Factors   177
   Social Organization, Social Control, and Power   177
   The Minority Experience: Marginalization,
      Poverty, Prejudice, and Social Change   179
Integrating Cultural Explanations   183
Summary   189

**8. Conceptualizing and Treating Substance Use
Problems: A Cultural-Historical Perspective**   191
   Introduction   191
   The Pre- and Early History of Addiction   192
   Treatment for Alcohol and
      Drug Problems in the Nineteenth Century   197
   The Changing Face of Drug Addiction: 1914–1960   199
   The Alcoholism Movement   202
   Contemporary Developments   204
   Culture and Classification   208
   Implications   211

**9. Prevention, Treatment, and
Public Policy: An Integrated Perspective**   216
   Introduction   216
   Prevention   217
   Assessment   223
   Treatment   225
      Biological and Psychosocial
         Treatment Approaches   226
      Cultural Issues   229
      Natural Recovery   232
      A Holistic View of Treatment   234
   Legal Sanctions, Regulations, and Restrictions   238

Harm Reduction 243
Conclusion 247

References 251

Author Index 291

Subject Index 303

About the Authors 311

Preface

Thomas De Quincey's first experience with opium in the early nineteenth century, taken to relieve the pain of a nagging toothache, was an overwhelmingly positive one. Not only did the opium assuage his pain, but, as he later related in *Confessions of an English Opium Eater*, it also opened up new vistas of "divine engagement." Later, opium became a necessity for De Quincey, but despite his warnings about its addictive properties, it is his rhapsodic eulogies to opium's mind-altering effects that tantalize the modern reader. The experience of William Burroughs with opiates in the middle of the twentieth century, related in matter-of-fact fashion in another classic in the genre of personal drug confession, *Junky*, provides a stark contrast to De Quincey's. The serenity of De Quincey's personal visions are replaced with a paranoid world of sickness, crime, and violence, populated by "junkies," "tea-heads," "feds," and "stool pigeons."

The similarities in Burroughs's and De Quincey's experiences with opiates are clear: Dependence develops, as choice, over time, becomes necessity. Yet the differences are also revealing. In the early nineteenth century opium was a valued medicinal agent, legal and freely available. Recreational use was limited, and opiates were typically consumed orally in the form of lozenges, powders, and tinctures. By the 1940s, opiate use in most Western nations was illegal, users were branded as criminals, and harsh penalties were meted out to offenders. Medicinal use was limited, and opiates were usually taken for "recreational" reasons in the form of heroin, which was injected rather than swallowed. These changes, and many others like them, were to have a profound impact on patterns of drug use in the twentieth century, with important implications for treatment, prevention, and public policy.

In this book, we set out to complement the vast literature on the biological and psychological aspects of drug use with a perspective that emphasizes the importance of cultural and historical factors.

Understanding the way that drugs have been used at different times and in different cultural contexts can provide valuable information about the nature of drug use and how a range of often neglected factors may affect patterns of use. Historians have made valuable contributions to our understanding of drug use throughout history (e.g., Courtwright, 2001; Davenport-Hines, 2001), and anthropologists and sociologists have provided a wealth of fascinating detail regarding the way that drugs are used among different cultural groups (e.g., Furst, 1990; Dobkin de Rios, 1990). Our aim in this book, however, is not only to describe patterns of drug use at different times and in different cultures but also to elucidate how cultural and historical perspectives may be integrated into a mainstream "biopsychosocial" approach in a way that can prove valuable in addressing a range of pragmatic issues relating to prevention, treatment, and public policy.

We have written this book primarily for psychologists, sociologists, and public health professionals who have an interest in drug-related issues. Although it is essential to focus on very specific concerns and issues within any academic discipline, it is also important to step outside of particular areas of expertise to consider the "larger picture." In understanding the nature of drug use and ameliorating drug-related problems, the elucidation of relevant biological and psychological mechanisms is a necessary task, but it must always be recognized that drug use occurs in a context. Moreover, the "background" against which drugs are taken can influence in important ways the experiences that individuals have with drugs, the prevalence of drug use in society, and the harms that might arise. In this book we have brought the "background" into the "foreground" by elaborating the many cultural and historical factors that influence drug use, and how such factors may be related to different patterns of use among different cultural groups over time. We have also addressed the more fundamental question of why drug use is such a ubiquitous feature of human society by exploring the evolutionary basis of drug-taking behavior. Throughout, we argue that our understanding of drug use and drug-related problems is best advanced by adopting an interdisciplinary approach.

Acknowledgments

There are many people we would like to thank for their support throughout the writing of this book. First, we would like to acknowledge Jack Schumaker, who suggested the idea for this book a number of years ago and encouraged us to pursue this project. We would also like to thank the psychology department at the University of Canterbury, and especially Garth Fletcher, for providing the time, space, and resources without which the writing of this book could not have been accomplished. Our thanks are also extended to Tony Ward, Alice Brigance, Sam Jeffries, and four anonymous reviewers who read through portions of this manuscript and provided many thoughtful comments.

The editorial staff at Sage Publications, and especially Jim Brace-Thompson, must also be thanked for their unflagging support and encouragement. Many others provided support of various kinds, particularly Lynne and Murray Wood, Darryl Forsyth, Alex McKenzie, Adrian Portis, Anthony Terry, and the volunteers at SAFE. Finally, we would like to thank Dave H. for putting everything in perspective.

1

What Needs to Be Explained, and How Should We Explain It?

INTRODUCTION

Why do humans use psychoactive drugs? This is a question that one of us (Russil Durrant) often poses to a graduate class in theoretical psychology in order to explore the topic of levels of analysis in science. Having arrived, mental loins girded, for an abstract lecture on the philosophy of psychology, the students respond to this question in enthusiastic fashion. In less than five minutes the white board is covered with various suggestions, from "to have fun" to "they make people feel better." A halt is called to proceedings, and the next task is to group the various answers according to the *kind* of explanation that they provide. Most suggestions are based on psychological and social factors: "because they feel good," "they help to remove stress," "in order to socialize," "because of peer pressure," and so on. Some students will also offer biological explanations: "because they release certain chemicals in the brain," "they activate specific brain systems." And sometimes cultural factors are invoked: "because everyone else in society does."

The question "Why do people use drugs?" is fundamental and should be the starting point for any analysis of drug-related problems.

This question leads to other, more specific, inquiries (Pandina & Johnson, 1999). The question "Why do some people abuse and become dependent on drugs?" for instance, elicits a different response from the students, although one that still involves biological and psychological factors. More specific questions tend to narrow the range of answers provided. For example, the question "Why do people in the Pacific Islands consume kava in social contexts, whereas alcohol is the prominent drug used in Western cultures?" leads to a shift in responses from biological and psychological factors to cultural and historical ones (e.g., "because of tradition"). The aim of this exercise is to illustrate to the students three key points: (1) There are *multiple levels of analysis* in science that can be brought to bear on the same phenomenon; (2) often explanations drawn from different levels of analysis will be equally relevant in furthering our understanding of the phenomenon in question; and (3) the importance of different kinds of explanation will typically vary depending on the specific question that is asked.

The broad field of psychoactive drug studies[1] embraces a wide range of specific academic disciplines, from psychopharmacology to cultural anthropology. The intellectual distance between these different academic disciplines is often immense. Consider, for example, the differences between a physiological psychologist studying a rodent model of cocaine abuse and a cultural anthropologist exploring the symbolic role of coca in an Amerindian society. They not only study very different populations, but they also use different methods, pose different questions, have different goals, use different theories, reside in different departments, publish in different journals, and obtain funding from different sources. It is highly likely that they do not read each other's work or think that each other's research is relevant to their own academic concerns. Yet they both study the same—or similar— substances and probably both consider that their own research contributes in some way to our understanding of why people use (and abuse) drugs.

Our primary aim in this book is to provide a cultural-historical approach to substance use and abuse. We believe that such an approach has much to offer in terms of enriching our understanding of why people use drugs and in elucidating the nature of substance-related problems. We also aim to demonstrate how such an approach can be integrated with a mainstream biopsychosocial perspective. To fulfill these aims, it is essential to consider how explanations drawn from different levels of analysis relate to each other. In this opening chapter we provide an overview of the nature of explanation and levels of analysis in science. We then introduce an integrated model of substance use and abuse, which is employed to further our understanding of the relations between different theoretical approaches.

LEVELS OF ANALYSIS AND THE MULTIDISCIPLINARY NATURE OF PSYCHOACTIVE DRUG STUDIES

There are many different points of view on drug-related issues. There are differences of opinion regarding why people take drugs, what the nature of substance abuse and dependence is, and what are deemed the most appropriate prevention, treatment, and policy responses to drug-related problems. Many scholars, for instance, have argued that addiction is *fundamentally* a biological phenomenon, which requires mainly biological interventions (e.g., Blum, Braverman, Holder, Lubar, Monastra, Miller, Lubar, Chen, & Comings, 2000; Kosten, 1998; Leshner, 1997). For example, Leshner (1997) suggests, "If the brain is the *core* of the problem, attending to the brain needs to be a *core* part of the solution" (p. 47, italics added). Other authors have argued that addiction is not best conceived of as a biological disorder, but is fundamentally related to individual choice and the values that people have (e.g., Peele, 1987, 1989; Schaler, 2000). Changing values, then, becomes the appropriate response to addiction:

> Appetitive behavior of all types is *crucially* influenced by people's pre-existing values, and . . . the *best* way to combat addiction both for the individual and society is to inculcate values that are incompatible with addiction and with drug- and alcohol-induced misbehavior. (Peele, 1987, p. 187, italics added)

Yet other scholars emphasize that cultural and historical variables are most important in understanding substance use and abuse (e.g., Heath, 1999; Westermeyer, 1991). Thus Westermeyer (1991) suggests that "historical and social factors are *key* to the understanding of psychoactive substance use disorders" (p. 23, italics added).

Researchers who focus predominantly on biological, psychological, or cultural explanations for substance abuse do recognize that other levels are relevant, but they intimate—either implicitly or explicitly—that their perspective is the *most* important. Who is right? We suggest that they all are—or at least all *could* be. To understand how this might be the case, we need to consider in more detail the nature of levels of analysis in science.

A *level of analysis* refers to a particular way of approaching or framing a specific research area, in terms of both the kinds of phenomena that are explained and the sorts of explanations that are offered. Different levels of analysis are typically associated with different institutional structures, sources of funding, methodological and theoretical commitments, and domains of inquiry (Bechtel, 1986; see also Darden's & Maull's, 1977, notion of scientific "fields"). Just how *many* different levels of analysis there are is a matter of some dispute, and various taxonomies have been proposed (e.g., Abrahamsen, 1987). For the purposes of this book we favor a tripartite division into biological, psychosocial, and cultural-historical levels of analysis, which captures the broad range of approaches in the social and behavioral sciences.

The biological level of analysis, fairly straightforwardly, encompasses explanations that focus on biological processes. These include genetic factors, physiological processes, neurotransmitter systems, and so forth. We also include evolutionary explanations under this level of analysis, although (in psychology at least) they are more likely to refer to psychological rather than physiological mechanisms (e.g., Buss, 1995, 1999). The psychosocial level of analysis is the traditional domain of psychological science and includes various intra- and interperson processes such as cognitions, emotions, behaviors, social interactions, and so on. Last, the cultural-historical level of analysis encompasses the range of group- and institutional-level factors such as norms, values, beliefs, and practices that delineate cultural groups and that have developed over time.

We must note that these levels are not sharply delineated and there is substantial room for approaches, or "interfield theories" (Darden & Maull, 1977), that embrace multiple levels of analysis. For example, in explaining the nature of substance abuse, researchers have variously adopted psychophysiological, biobehavioral, and sociocultural perspectives. Indeed, it is important to recognize how the processes at different levels of analysis relate to one another. Broadly speaking, psychological mechanisms and the various states and structures that they support—beliefs, desires, expectations, emotions, schemas, and so forth—can be conceived of as being *instantiated* in physiological systems (primarily the brain).[2] Organisms (with minds/brains) are embedded in social, cultural, and physical environments that are historically situated and that shape (but do not entirely determine) psychological characteristics over the course of developmental trajectories. For instance, individuals may consume drugs because the drugs give them pleasure (psychological experiences), which is the result of the drug's action on natural reward systems in the brain (physiological processes). The pleasure these individuals experience from the drug is influenced by their expectations of the drug's effects, which is related to the social learning of certain beliefs and values that may be specific to given social and cultural contexts (cultural-historical environments).

Theories or explanations drawn from different levels of analysis are rarely in direct competition with one another.[3] To say that people use drugs because the drugs activate dopaminergic neurons in the meso-limbic reward pathway, for example, is not to deny that they also generate powerful and pleasant emotional experiences, or that individuals may consume drugs because they have learned to do so and because drugs are culturally prescribed in certain contexts. More generally, theories and explanations from different levels of analysis *constrain* one another: our best biological theories of substance use and abuse should be consistent with what we know about psychological, social and cultural-historical processes (and vice versa). Theory construction should ideally proceed in a way that fosters mutual coherence between explanations drawn from different levels of analysis (see Darden & Maull, 1977; McCauley, 1996). These ideas are what lie behind the call for cross-disciplinary or interdisciplinary research. A narrow focus on specific research questions or domains, although often necessary in science, should not be pursued in the absence of an understanding of the "larger picture" and how such research coheres with inquiry in other domains.[4]

The demand for more interdisciplinary research in the field of psychoactive drug studies has been urged recently by a number of authors (e.g., Collins, Blane, & Leonard, 1999; Marshall, Ames, & Bennett, 2001; Rasmussen, Benson, & Mocan, 1998; Singer, 2001). The plea for integrative research and theory development, however, is not new. Jellinek (1960), for example, in his classic text on the disease concept of alcoholism, attempted to draw together biological, psychological, and cultural approaches to alcohol-related problems. Nonetheless, the fact that such calls for integration continue, in spite of the widespread tacit acceptance of a "biopsychosocial" model of substance abuse, suggests that there is much to be done in the way of elucidating just what such an integrated approach might look like.

Figure 1.1   An integrated model of substance use and abuse

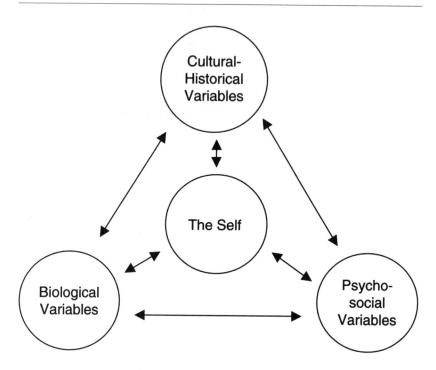

TOWARD AN INTEGRATED
MODEL OF SUBSTANCE USE AND ABUSE

In Figure 1.1 we provide an integrated model of substance use and abuse that aims to capture the relationships between the different levels of analysis that are relevant for our understanding of substance use issues (see Thakker & Durrant, 2001; Thakker, Ward, & Strongman, 1999, for the use of this model in a broader mental health context). The design of Figure 1.1 is straightforward; this model is best viewed as a way of conceptualizing different approaches to substance use and abuse rather than an explanatory framework in its own right. It is thus a "meta-model": a way of visualizing the relationships among the different levels of analysis that have been employed in other explanatory frameworks.

This model has four components: biological variables, psycho-social variables, cultural-historical variables, and the self. The first three of these components relate to the three different levels of analysis outlined previously. Explanations for drug use and drug-related problems have variously favored biological, psychosocial, and cultural-historical factors. These components, moreover, can be unpacked to reveal many different theories and approaches. For instance, in Chapters 5 and 7 we describe a number of different historical and cultural explanations of drug use. Biological and psychosocial levels also contain a similar variety of "intralevel" approaches (e.g., West, 2001). Many explanatory accounts also *combine* these three variables to create interlevel theories of substance use. For instance, a number of etiological models of substance use disorders include the role of biological (e.g., genetic) and psychosocial (e.g., expectancies, life stress, peer influences) factors (Pihl, 1999). The way that different levels of analysis may be combined to provide theoretical explanations is illustrated by the inclusion of double-headed arrows between pairs of the three components.

The role of the self in drug use is also critical. Regardless of what level of analysis (or combination of levels) is emphasized, what ultimately needs to be explained is why individuals choose to initiate drug use, continue to use drugs, give up, or start using drugs again after a period of abstinence. Many may balk at the use of the term "choice" here; after all, a number of approaches to drug abuse and dependence focus on the loss of control over drug-taking behavior. However, regardless of how *impaired* an individual's capacity for choice is (e.g., as the result of prolonged exposure to drugs), or how limited their choices might be (e.g., as the result of adverse social conditions), the self as an executive agent is still involved. People, at some level, still make decisions to use or not to use drugs, even if those decisions are influenced by a myriad of factors that may or may not be in an individual's power to change. All theories of drug use, therefore, whether implicitly or explicitly, involve the notion of selfhood. By placing the self at the center of the model in Figure 1.1, we also wish to highlight the importance of meaning and purpose in understanding substance use. Meaning is constructed in multiple ways from biological, psychosocial, and cultural-historical components, but comes together uniquely for each individual. The combination of the self with the biological, psychosocial, and cultural components may be referred to as the "self-system."

Although theories from different levels of analysis may be integrated into overarching frameworks, often explanations drawn from one level of analysis will be privileged over those from other levels,

Table 1.1   Key Questions

Broad Domain	Question
1. Use	(a) Why do people use drugs? (b) Why are some drugs used more frequently and in different ways than are other drugs? (c) Why do some people use drugs more frequently and in different ways than do other people? (d) Why does the use of drugs vary in different social, cultural, and historical contexts?
2. Abuse	(a) Why do problems such as abuse and dependence sometimes arise from the use of drugs? (b) Why do some individuals develop drug-related problems? (c) Why does the level of abuse and dependence vary depending on the drug that is employed? (d) Why does the nature and incidence of drug-related problems (including dependence) vary over time and among different social and cultural groups?
3. Course	(a) Why do patterns of drug use change over the course of the life span? (b) Why do some individuals manage to reduce or eliminate their drug-related problems while others do not?
4. Intervention	(a) How should we develop effective prevention, assessment, classification, and treatment initiatives? (b) What sort of policies should be developed that can best address the range of issues that arise from patterns of substance use and abuse?

depending on what is being explained. Explanation is in part pragmatic in nature (van Fraassen, 1985)[5]: how we go about explaining a phenomenon depends on the nature of the questions that we ask, which in turn are guided by individual interests and concerns. Consider a sample of questions that are relevant to our global understanding of drug-related issues (depicted in Table 1.1). These different inquiries are likely to elicit different kinds of explanations drawn from different levels of analysis and are motivated by different concerns and interests.

For most of the questions depicted in Table 1.1, explanations can, and have been, drawn from multiple levels of analysis. How should we evaluate such alternative perspectives? One fruitful approach for addressing this important question draws on the ideas of the philosopher

Peter Railton. Railton (1981) has argued that ideally we should be striving for complete explanations in science that can elucidate the full panoply of causal (and noncausal) connections that obtain between phenomena. However, the world is a complex place, and such an account is unlikely to be forthcoming. Instead, individual scientists (and other scholars) exert their intellectual labors in illuminating particular portions of this ideal causal story and are influenced by pragmatic concerns. The ideal explanatory text determines what is *relevant* in a particular case, while *salience* is driven by more pragmatic considerations. We suggest that in answering the range of questions provided in Table 1.1, explanations drawn from all three levels of analysis—biological, psychosocial, and cultural-historical—will be *relevant*, but some explanatory accounts will be more *salient* than others depending on the precise form of the question and who is posing it.

Take, for instance, a more fine-grained form of Question 1(d): Why has the consumption of alcohol—especially wine—declined in countries of southern Europe over the past thirty years or so (Gual & Colom, 1997; Pyörälä, 1990; Sulkunen, 1989)? In France, levels of alcohol consumption have dropped from 17.7 liters per capita in 1961 to 11.5 liters in 1993. This decline is especially noticeable for wine, with France halving its consumption over the same time period from 126.1 liters to 63.5 liters per capita (Gual & Colom, 1997). Given the association between per capita alcohol consumption and various indices of health (Norström, 2001; Ramstedt, 2001), providing a satisfactory explanation for these changes is an important task. Moreover, although motivated by somewhat different concerns, individuals with vested interests in the wine industry will also be keen to obtain an explanation for these trends. Clearly, explanations drawn from a biological level of analysis will provide little in the way of epistemic relief: nothing in the physiological constitution of southern Europeans has changed over the past thirty years. However, psychological and cultural-historical explanations—in terms of the impact of new beverages, marketing initiatives, public health policies and modernization, on social norms and individual beliefs, values, and expectations—will prove more satisfying (Gual & Colom, 1997; Simpura, 1998).

If, by contrast, to take a more specific form of Question 2(b), we wish to explain why one strain of selectively bred mice is more likely to become dependent on alcohol than is another strain of mice (e.g., Crabbe, Belknap, & Buck, 1994), explanations drawn from different levels of analysis become more important. Cultural-historical explanations are not likely to be of much help, but genetic and neurophysiological accounts will prove more valuable. Clearly, cultural-historical accounts are more salient in explaining declining alcohol consumption in southern European countries, and biological accounts are more salient for accounting for variations in alcohol use among different strains of mice.

In many cases, of course, determining what the most salient explanation is will not be as clear-cut as in the two examples outlined here. If we wish, for instance, to explain why tolerance to the effects of alcohol occurs with regular use, theories that draw on biological components appear to be the most salient—tolerance is, after all, a physiological process. However, individuals may experience tolerance in different ways depending on their beliefs, expectations, and values. And, as we discuss in Chapter 8, how tolerance is viewed (whether positively or negatively) will depend on specific cultural contexts (Room, Janca, Bennett, Schmidt, & Sartorius, 1996). Thus, psychological and cultural approaches to tolerance will also be relevant. In some cases all four components may be equally salient (or relevant) in addressing specific questions. For instance, to fully understand gender differences in the prevalence of alcohol abuse and dependence, we need to integrate biological (evolutionary, physiological), psychosocial (social roles, beliefs, expectations), and cultural-historical (cultural norms, social sanctions) accounts (e.g., Wilsnack, Vogeltanz, Wilsnack, & Harris, 2000). Different components or combinations of components will also be more salient depending on what aspects of drug use we wish to explain. Certain factors, for instance, will be more salient in explaining the initiation of drug use; other variables will be more important in accounting for drug dependence.

We draw on this analytic framework for understanding the relations among explanations at different levels of analysis throughout the book, although our focus is primarily directed at elaborating the salience of cultural-historical accounts. By paying more attention to the details of what needs to be explained, the relative salience of different explanatory accounts can be assessed in a way that can, in part, reconcile the divergent views on the nature of substance use and abuse. Although not all approaches may be "right" or even "equal" in their explanatory or predictive power, the value we place on any perspective depends crucially on what we wish to explain.

OVERVIEW

In this opening chapter we have provided a broad analytical framework for understanding the relations among explanatory accounts drawn from different levels of analysis. This framework allows us to understand the role of different kinds of explanation in answering questions relating to substance use and abuse. In Chapter 2 we examine some fundamental issues in the field of alcohol and drug studies. We outline what a drug is (for the purposes of this work); who uses what kinds of drugs in what contexts; what constitutes substance abuse and dependence; and what the harms (and benefits) of substance use (and abuse) are to individuals and society. In Chapter 3 we engage the central question of why the use of psychoactive drugs has been so prevalent across cultures and throughout history. We argue that the most salient level of analysis from which to address *this* specific question is an evolutionary one, and discuss how the evolution of psychological and physiological mechanisms can plausibly underpin drug-taking behavior in a wide variety of cultural contexts. The heart of the book is contained in the next five chapters, in which we explore historical and cultural approaches to substance use and abuse. In Chapters 4 and 6 we provide predominantly descriptive accounts of the way that drugs have been used throughout history and across cultures. These accounts are followed, in Chapters 5 and 7 respectively, by details of the way that historical and cultural factors can be employed to *explain* patterns of drug use and drug-related problems. Our focus in these four chapters will embrace both substance use and abuse. However, in the final two chapters, issues relating to abuse and dependence become more prominent. In Chapter 8 these issues are explored from historical and cultural perspectives: how has our understanding of drug abuse and dependence changed over time, and are such concepts cultural universals or do they differ in important ways in different cultural contexts? In Chapter 9 we examine various ways of responding to substance use problems, including prevention, treatment, and policy initiatives with an emphasis on the role of cultural approaches to these various strategies.

The primary aim of this book is to encourage more interest in the cultural and historical determinants of substance use and abuse, and we hope that this work will provide a useful source of ideas for those interested in pursuing these perspectives. We also aim to provide an understanding of how a cultural-historical perspective might be integrated into a mainstream biopsychosocial framework for understanding substance use and drug-related problems. In particular, we wish to illustrate how a cultural-historical approach proves relevant in addressing important clinical and policy issues. Last, in a field beset with more than its fair share of acrimonious disputes, we aim to offer an analytical framework that can further our understanding of the source of these disagreements—if not necessarily provide a way for their resolution.

NOTES

1.   This field is typically referred to as "alcohol and drug studies." However, this designation tends unnecessarily to reinforce the separation of alcohol from other psychoactive substances (see Chapter 2 for a more detailed discussion of this issue). We thank an anonymous reviewer of this manuscript for the alternative label that we employ here.

2.   The idea that mental processes are *instantiated* or *realized* in brain systems reflects a central strand of thought in functionalist philosophies of mind. Essentially, each mental experience is also a physical experience; however, there is no simple reduction of mind states to brain states, for the relationship is not a lawful one (the same mental state, for example, can be realized in the brain in different ways by different people at different times) (see Sterelny, 1990).

3.   There are some exceptions here. For example, differences between certain Asian and European cultural groups in levels of alcohol dependence have been variously explained in terms of differences in genetics *or* cultural norms. Plausibly, either one of these explanations might offer the whole story; although as it turns out both genetic *and* cultural factors appear to be relevant (see Chapters 7 and 9).

4.   See Maxwell (1984) for an excellent critique of "specialism" in science.

5.   There is, however, more to scientific explanation than pragmatics. Interested readers are referred to the work of Kitcher (1985, 1989) and Salmon (1985) for a more detailed discussion of the nature of explanation in science.

2

The Nature and Scope of Substance Use and Abuse

INTRODUCTION

Most people will use drugs at some time in their lives. Indeed, the consumption of psychoactive substances is a daily ritual for the majority of individuals in Western society. The most frequently consumed drug is caffeine, in the form of coffee, tea, cocoa, chocolate, and soft drinks, but alcohol and tobacco are also regularly employed. Illicit substances such as cocaine, cannabis, and heroin are far less frequently used, although about half of the American population reports that they have ingested an illegal drug at least once in their lives (Substance Abuse and Mental Health Services Administration, 2001). In addition, there is a myriad of psychoactive drugs—benzodiazepines, amphetamines, anxiolytics, antidepressants, and so forth—that are prescribed by physicians and used in therapeutic contexts, although many of these substances also make their way into *non*-prescribed patterns of use.

An understanding of why people use—and sometimes abuse—psychoactive drugs requires us to consider the nature and scope of substance use in some detail. We need to clarify just what *counts* as a drug, and *who* uses *what* drugs in *what* contexts. The relationship between substance use and substance abuse also needs to be considered, and the prevalence of abuse and dependence outlined. Finally, we need to evaluate the harms and—somewhat controversially—the *benefits* of substance use to individuals and society. In this chapter we provide a broad overview of these issues. We begin by addressing the most fundamental conceptual issue: What is a drug?

WHAT IS A DRUG?

The term "drug" has multiple meanings. A standard dictionary definition draws the distinction between "1. A medical substance"; and "2. A narcotic, hallucinogen, or stimulant, especially one causing addiction" (Oxford Encyclopedic English Dictionary, 1991).[1] This definition captures the two common uses of the term *drug* in Western contexts: as medicinal agents and as substances that exert various psychological effects. However, although most medical substances are not psychoactive, they may be stimulants, narcotics, or hallucinogens. They may also cause addiction. We shall define the word *drug*, for the purposes of this book, as "any substance, whether natural or artificial in origin, which, when taken into the body in sufficient quantities, exerts a non-negligible effect on a person's perception, cognition, emotion, and/or behavior" (cf. Giancola & Tarter, 1999, p. 2; Julien, 1998, p. xi). This definition captures the idea of a *psychoactive* drug, although the words *drug* and *substance* are typically employed without this prefix. We use the terms "drug" and "substance" interchangeably in this book, although in many respects the notion of a "substance" better captures the range of entities that are consumed that have psychoactive effects. For example, substances like glue, gasoline, coffee, tea, and even alcohol are not typically referred to as "drugs," although they are all consumed (in part) for their effects on cognition, emotion, and behavior.

Some authors have suggested that the study of *all* ingested substances, whether "drug," "medicine," or even "food," be unified under a single methodological and conceptual framework (e.g., Hunt & Barker, 2001). This proposal is based on the recognition that in many cultural contexts there is simply no sharp dividing line between these different categories. Alcohol in many cultures, for example, is considered a substance with important nutritional value and is therefore categorized as a "food." And, historically, many familiar illicit drugs such as opium, cannabis, and cocaine have played important roles in medicinal contexts. However, we shall restrict our focus to those substances that fall within the boundaries of our definition presented here.

We make no special distinctions, therefore, between alcohol and other psychoactive substances and argue against the separation implied in the label "alcohol *and* drug studies" as though alcohol is not *also* a psychoactive substance (see Hunt & Barker, 2001). The tendency to make a special case for alcohol is illustrated by Jonnes (1996) in her otherwise excellent history of illicit drugs in American society, when she states, "The fact is that drugs are very different from alcohol—and far more dangerous" (p. 10). Alcohol is clearly not *less* dangerous than (all) other drugs. Gable (1993), for example, in a thorough comparative overview of the dependence potential and acute toxicity of different substances, identified alcohol as being more toxic and having a greater potential for dependence than cannabis, LSD, caffeine, or psilocybin.

It is important to recognize, nonetheless, that different psychoactive substances have reliably different effects (although moderated by psychosocial and cultural-historical factors), with different implications for drug-related harm. Caffeine and cocaine, for instance, are related to very different levels of harm in Western society, due in part to their different actions on the central nervous system. However, the focus in this book is more on the context in which drugs are employed than on their psychopharmacological properties. A focus on the social and cultural context of consumption moves attention away from the nature of the substance itself to the way that it is employed—from "what drugs do to people" to "what people do with drugs" (Hugh-Jones, 1995, pp. 47–48).

WHO USES DRUGS?

Any discussion of drug-related issues must begin with information about levels of substance use in society. In the United States, two large annual surveys—the Monitoring the Future study (MTF) and the National Household Survey on Drug Abuse (NHSDA)—provide information on drug use by eighth, tenth, and twelfth grade students and the general population respectively. Although these sources are by no means perfect, they do provide regular and reliable data on what drugs are used, how regularly they are consumed, and what individuals in society use them. Information on the prevalence of drug use in other countries is not as comprehensive; Australia, New Zealand, Canada, and Great Britain all have fairly regular household surveys or

Table 2.1   Per Capita Consumption of Alcohol per Adult Aged 15 Years and Over by Geographic Region

Region	Consumption (L)	Range	Percentage of Population Covered
AFRO	1.37	0.02–7.72	34
AMRO	6.98	1.66–14.03	95
EMRO	0.30	0.05–10.00	19
EURO	8.60	0.85–15.12	45
SEARO	1.15	0.004–8.64	67
WPRO	5.54	0.340–18.39	93

SOURCE: World Health Organization (2001)
Key:
 AFRO = African Region
 AMRO = Region of the Americas
 EMRO = Eastern Mediterranean Region
 EURO = European Region
SEARO = Southeast Asian Region
WPRO = Western Pacific Region

questions on drug use in other surveys, and less frequent studies have assessed substance use in other countries. For alcohol and tobacco, fairly reliable estimates can be obtained on per capita use based on sales, and these can provide the basis for establishing a global picture of consumption. However, cross-national comparisons for illicit substances are more problematic. We focus in this section, then, predominantly on patterns of use in the United States, although we supplement this information with data from other countries where relevant.

After caffeine, alcohol is the most widely and regularly consumed psychoactive substance in the world. However, levels of use vary substantially across cultures. As illustrated in Table 2.1, per capita consumption of alcohol is highest in European regions, followed by the Americas and the Western Pacific region (predominantly Australia and New Zealand). Levels of use are significantly lower in the Eastern Mediterranean region (due presumably to the influence of Islam) and in Southeast Asian countries. In most Western nations, the majority of individuals consume alcohol at some time in their lives. In the United States, New Zealand, and Australia, more than 80% of individuals surveyed reported lifetime alcohol use (Miller & Draper, 2001; New Zealand

Table 2.2   Percentage Reporting Past-Month Alcohol Use, "Binge"
Alcohol Use, and Heavy Alcohol Use in the United States,
2000 (Persons Aged 12 and Older)

	Any Alcohol Use	"Binge" Alcohol Use	Heavy Alcohol Use
Gender			
Male	53.6	28.3	8.7
Female	40.2	13.5	2.7
Age			
12–17	16.4	10.4	2.6
18–25	56.8	37.8	12.8
26 or older	49.0	19.1	4.8

NOTE: "Binge" alcohol use is defined as drinking five or more drinks on the
same occasion on at least one day in the past 30 days. Heavy alcohol use is
defined as drinking five or more drinks on the same occasion on each of five
or more days in the past 30 days.

SOURCE: Substance Abuse and Mental Health Services Administration (2001)

Health Information Service, 2001; Substance Abuse and Mental Health
Service Administration, 2001). Indeed, because the lifetime prevalence
of alcohol use is so high in most Western countries, fine-grained
measures of drinking quantity and frequency prove to be more informative in providing a picture of alcohol consumption. As illustrated in
Table 2.2, 53.6% of men and 40.2% of women reported having consumed alcohol in the last month in the United States, whereas a much
lower proportion reported "binge drinking" (five or more drinks on
the same occasion on at least one day in the past 30 days) and heavy
alcohol use (five or more drinks on the same occasion on each of five
or more days in the past 30 days). In New Zealand, 87% of the population aged between 14 and 65 reported that they had consumed alcohol
in the last 12 months, with the average frequency about four times a
week for men and two to three times a week for women (New Zealand
Health Information Service, 2001). Taken at face value and ignoring
differences in the frequency of consumption based on age, gender, and
ethnicity, these statistics indicate that drinking is a normative activity
in most Western cultures.

The same could also be said for the use of tobacco, although rates
of use have been steadily falling in most Western nations during the
past 50 years. As with alcohol, the majority of individuals report

Table 2.3   Prevalence (%) of Reported Lifetime, Past-Year, and Past-Month Illicit Drug Use in the United States, 2000 (Persons Aged 12 and Over)

Drug	Lifetime	Past Year	Past Month
Any illicit drug	38.9	11.0	6.3
Cannabis	34.2	8.3	4.8
Cocaine	11.2	1.5	0.5
Heroin	1.2	0.1	0.1
Hallucinogens	11.7	1.6	0.4
Inhalants	7.5	0.9	0.3

SOURCE: Substance Abuse and Mental Health Services Administration (2001)

having tried tobacco at least once in their lives. In the United States, 66.5% of individuals surveyed in 2000 reported lifetime tobacco use (Substance Abuse and Mental Health Service Administration, 2001), and similar prevalence rates are found in Australia and New Zealand (Miller & Draper, 2001; New Zealand Health Information Service, 2001). Current smokers in the United States, Australia, and New Zealand represent about a quarter of the population of each country respectively, and rates of use are similar for men and women (Miller & Draper, 2001; New Zealand Health Information Service, 2001; Substance Abuse and Mental Health Service Administration, 2001). The prevalence of tobacco use, however, does vary dramatically across cultures: from more than 60% of men in the Russian Federation, Latvia, and the Republic of Korea, to less than 25% in Paraguay, Sweden, and Bahrain (Ramström, 1997). Although in many countries, levels of tobacco consumption have declined due to concerted efforts to reduce use, in most places in the world smoking is still a fairly common activity.

The use of alcohol and tobacco in Western cultures provides an interesting contrast to the prevalence of *illicit* drug use. In Table 2.3 we provide lifetime, past-year, and past-month prevalence data for a range of illicit drugs in the United States. As can be seen, the reported lifetime prevalence for the use of *any* illicit drug in the United States is substantially lower than for either alcohol or tobacco. This difference between licit and illicit drugs is particularly noticeable in reported patterns of recent drug use. For instance, individuals are more than seven times more likely to report the use of alcohol in the past month than they are for all illegal drugs combined. By far the most common illicit substance used in the United States is cannabis. The use of other substances, such as cocaine, heroin, and hallucinogens, is much less frequent; fewer than 1% of the population report using any one of these substances in the past month.

A similar picture can be established by examining the use of illegal drugs in Australia, New Zealand, and Europe. Again, by far the most commonly reported substance employed is cannabis. In Australia, in 1998, 39% of individuals aged 14 or older reported having tried cannabis at least once in their lives (Miller & Draper, 2001), while the lifetime reported prevalence of cannabis use in New Zealand and Great Britain was 50% (for individuals between the ages of 15 and 45) and 27% (for individuals between the ages of 16 and 59) respectively (New Zealand Health Information Service, 2001; Ramsay, Baker, Goulden, Sharp, & Sondhi, 2001). Lifetime prevalence rates for no other illicit substance in Australia, New Zealand, or Great Britain exceeded 16%. Building up an accurate *global* picture of illicit drug use is problematic, as few non-Western countries provide regular information on basic prevalence levels. From what information we do have, however, it is clear that levels of use vary dramatically in different cultural contexts.

These overall prevalence levels for substance use mask many individual differences based on demographic characteristics such as ethnicity, gender, and age. We discuss gender and ethnic differences in substance use in Chapters 3 and 8, respectively. However, the most dramatic differences in levels of drug use are found by comparing substance use in different age groups. As illustrated in Table 2.2, individuals in the United States between the ages of 18 and 25 are far more likely to report both binge alcohol consumption and heavy alcohol use than are individuals in younger or older age categories. Age differences in the reported consumption of illicit substances are even more striking. For instance, in the United States 15.9 % of individuals aged 18 to 25 reported that they had used an illicit drug in the past month, compared to 4.2% of persons aged 26 or older (Substance Abuse and Mental Health Service Administration, 2001). Of course, cross-sectional data cannot tell us whether these age differences reflect maturational or cohort effects. Most research suggests that adolescence and young adulthood is the peak period for—especially illicit—drug use, which then declines as individuals get older and take on new roles and responsibilities (e.g., Bachman, Johnston, O'Malley, & Schulenberg, 1996). In one longitudinal study, for instance, it was found that virtually no one began their use of any substance after the age of 29, and that drug use in general declined from around the mid-twenties (Chen & Kandel, 1995). However, it should also be recognized that levels of use do vary significantly as a function of cohort. Substance use among American adolescents, for instance, declined from the late 1970s and early 1980s, although recent trends show an increase in use (O'Malley, Johnston, & Bachman, 1999).

In summary, after caffeine, alcohol and tobacco are the most widely and regularly used psychoactive substances in Western cultures. Illicit substances, in comparison, are used far less frequently, although this pattern differs somewhat depending on demographic factors such as age and ethnicity. Cannabis is by far the most frequently used illegal drug, and most individuals in Western countries have *not* tried cocaine, heroin, hallucinogens, or other illicit substances. The basic prevalence figures presented in this section, it should be noted, are relatively uninformative regarding how and in what contexts such substances are employed. Indeed, as Hunt and Barker (2001) note, there is a surprising paucity of studies that examine non-problematic substance use. We believe that although it is important for clinical purposes to distinguish use from abuse (see following), there is also a need to examine the "normal" role of substance use in people's lives and to explore the place of drugs in society in a way that embraces multiple different patterns of use, be they harmful or not.

TAXONOMY OF DRUG USE CONTEXTS

It is important to pay attention to the *context* in which drugs are used. The idea of a "drug use context" embraces both the *reasons* that individuals give for using drugs and the *functional* significance of substance use at individual, social, and cultural levels. We suggest, based on our cultural and historical review of substance use (see Chapters 4 and 6), that six broad categories of drug use can be discerned. As depicted in Table 2.4, these are (1) medicinal, (2) recreational, (3) social, (4) pragmatic, (5) ritual-religious, and (6) dietary. These different categories should not be viewed as necessarily mutually exclusive, as a given instance of drug use might well be classified into two or more drug use contexts. We discuss each of these six categories in turn.

Psychoactive substances have been widely used in *medicinal* contexts throughout history and across cultures. In contemporary Western

Table 2.4   Taxonomy of Drug Use Contexts

Functional Context	
Medicinal	The prescription of drugs for mental health problems; or the use of drugs to reduce stress, relieve withdrawal symptoms, or to cope with mental illness
Recreational	The use of drugs for pleasure or entertainment
Social	The use of drugs in social contexts, to delineate membership in social groups, or to demarcate social status
Pragmatic	The use of drugs in order to facilitate certain desirable psychological or behavioral states
Ritual-religious	The use of drugs in ceremonial or religious contexts
Dietary	The use of drugs for nutritional reasons

society, medicinal contexts include the use of prescription drugs to relieve pain, induce sleep, relieve depression, reduce anxiety, or to treat substance dependence. A subset of medicinal contexts involves the use of drugs for *self*-medication (e.g., Khantzian, 1997). Examples of self-medicinal drug use include the consumption of alcohol to reduce stress and tension (Greeley & Oei, 1999; Rhodes & Jason, 1990), the use of heroin to relieve withdrawal symptoms, and the consumption of cocaine, heroin, alcohol, and other drugs by prostitutes to cope with the psychological stress associated with their occupation (El-Bassel, Schilling, Irwin, Faruque, Gilbert, Von Bargen, Serrano, & Edlin, 1997; Young, Boyd, & Hubbell, 2000). A number of authors have also speculated that the comorbidity of substance use disorders with other mental health problems may also reflect, in part, patterns of self-medication (e.g., Pomerleau, 1997).

Drugs are also widely employed in *recreational* contexts. This is probably the most frequent—or at least the most studied—drug use context in Western societies. People use drugs for pleasure, to have fun, for entertainment, or simply out of curiosity. Individuals engage in many activities for recreational reasons—from playing chess to climbing mountains—and the use of drugs is one available option out of many. The recreational use of drugs often overlaps with *social* drug use contexts. Alcohol, for example, is prominent at many social occasions that people attend primarily for recreational reasons. The social use of drugs encompasses such familiar examples as the consumption of alcohol at parties and the use of coffee during work breaks, which are played out with different substances in different cultures throughout the world (see Chapter 6). The social category of drug use also includes the consumption of particular substances in order to demarcate status hierarchies—as occurs in the kava ceremony in Pacific Island cultures—and to delineate membership in social groups (Chapters 6 and 7).

Drugs are also used in *pragmatic* contexts. Psychoactive substances are, and have been, extensively employed because of their capacity (or belief in their capacity) to facilitate certain desirable mental and behavioral outcomes. Coffee, tea, coca, betel nut, and tobacco have all been used, for example, to relieve fatigue and hunger and to promote work. Coffee, for instance, has been ingested by graduate students and religious devotees alike for its ability to increase mental alertness and to stave off fatigue and sleep. Pragmatic drug use contexts can be distinguished from medicinal and self-medicinal domains in that they involve the use of drugs to *enhance* performance, rather than to relieve states of distress and suffering.

The use of drugs in *ritual-religious* contexts has been prominent across cultures and throughout history, although it is less common in contemporary Western societies. Drugs have often been, and continue to be, employed in order to facilitate communion with the spirit world, in coming-of-age and other rituals, and as offerings to the gods (see Grob & Dobkin de Rios, 1992; Dobkin de Rios, 1990). The use of sacramental wine in Catholic religious ceremonies is one example of ritual-religious drug use more familiar to Western readers, and attitudes toward drugs and the way that they are employed are often influenced by their status in such contexts.

Lastly, psychoactive substances have also been consumed in *dietary* contexts—as foods, liquids, or sources of nutrients. Alcohol is the most obvious example, and its nutritional value has been clearly established (Forsander, 1998). Alcohol is also widely consumed for its taste and for its thirst-quenching properties (Mäkelä, 1983). In many cultures alcohol is considered as a food substance (Heath, 2000), and historically the scarcity of potable water has contributed to alcohol's role as an important source of fluids (Vallee, 1998). Mäkelä (1983) suggests that alcohol is the only intoxicant that has dietary value (Mäkelä excludes psychoactive but non-intoxicating substances like coffee, tea, and cocoa), and certainly it is the only substance that has been *primarily* consumed in dietary contexts. However, other psychoactive substances such as coca and qat (Brooke, 2000) may also have nutritional value that contributes to their importance in certain cultural contexts.

Paying attention to the context of drug use can be valuable in a number of ways. Social attitudes and policy responses, for instance, vary depending on the context in which drugs are employed. A substance when consumed in medicinal contexts may be legally sanctioned and viewed as beneficial, whereas when it is employed for recreational reasons it becomes—or is perceived as—a harmful social problem that needs to be addressed with strict legal measures. Surprisingly little research has been directed at the context in which drugs are employed and the reasons for use (although see Williams & Parker, 2001). Although we have a wealth of data on the prevalence of drug use and drug use disorders, it is also essential to elucidate the roles that drugs play in people's lives.

THE HARM AND BENEFITS OF DRUGS

Pharmakon, the Greek word for "drug," could be used to refer to either a remedy or a poison, reflecting the dual role of drugs in classical Greek society (Porter, 1997, p. 4). Throughout history and across cultures psychoactive substances have been employed in therapeutic contexts. Moreover, many people have taken drugs because of their role in producing pleasurable emotional, psychological, and social experiences. However, the use of drugs has also been related to manifold harms. Drugs are, as the Greeks fully comprehended, ambiguous substances with potential for both good and ill. In most contemporary discourse, the harm caused by drugs—outside of the narrowly circumscribed domain of medicine—is given full weight, and perhaps this is a reasonable, pragmatic response to the problems that are related to the use of drugs in society. It is important to recognize, nonetheless, that the use of psychoactive drugs may also have benefits that need to be considered if we are to reasonably evaluate the place of such substances in society.

MacCoun and Reuter (2001) in their recent book *Drug War Heresies* provide an excellent taxonomy of drug-related harm, and we draw on their framework in the following discussion. Four categories of harm are delineated by MacCoun and Reuter: health; social and economic functioning; safety and public order; and criminal justice.[2] These can be further evaluated according to three main dimensions: the nature of the harm; who bears the harm; and the primary source of the harm.

Many of the costs of alcohol use, for instance, are health-related and are primarily born by the user of alcohol. Long-term heavy alcohol consumption increases the risk of stroke, liver cirrhosis, alcohol dependence, and cancer (Anderson, 1995). Changes in per capita alcohol consumption, for example, have been shown to be positively related to both the prevalence of liver cirrhosis (Ramstedt, 2001) and all-cause mortality (Norström, 2001; Rehm & Sempos, 1995). Indeed, the World Health Organization (2001) estimated that in 1990 more than 750,000 deaths could be attributed to alcohol use worldwide, leading to almost 20 million years of life lost.

The costs associated with alcohol use are also related to safety and public order, and alcohol is implicated in traffic accidents, occupational injuries, violence, and homicide (Romelsjö, 1995). For instance, in a study of 14 European nations, it was found that changes in aggregate alcohol consumption were positively related to mortality from traffic and other kinds of accidents, although the nature of this relationship varied cross-nationally (Skog, 2001a, 2001b). There are also substantial social, economic, and criminal justice costs associated with the use of alcohol, which are born by users, intimates, employers, neighborhoods, and society (e.g., Godfrey, 1997; Devlin, Scuffham, & Bunt, 1997). For example, by combining the different costs associated with production losses, excess unemployment, reduced work efficiency, absenteeism, premature death, incarceration, health care, and criminal justice expenditure, Devlin et al. (1997) calculated that the annual cost to New Zealand society from alcohol use was in the region of $1–$4 billion. More generally, studies suggest that the costs of alcohol use are roughly equivalent to 2–5% of a nation's GDP (see Godfrey, 1997).

Most of the harm associated with alcohol arises directly as the result of the effects of consumption on the human body. Many of the costs associated with illicit substances like cocaine, cannabis, and heroin are also health-related. For example, the negative health consequences of chronic heavy cocaine use are well recognized (e.g., Chen, Scheier, & Kandel, 1996), and in the United States the use of cocaine in the year 2000 was associated with approximately 5,000 deaths and 175,000 emergency room visits (Substance Abuse and Mental Health Services Administration, 2000). However, for illegal drugs, the primary source of some kinds of harm arises *because* of the drugs' illicit status. These costs include the expenses relating to enforcement, which are born by society; costs to users in terms of criminal records, jail sentences, and loss of civil liberties; and harm to neighborhoods stemming from the systemic violence associated with drug dealing (MacCoun & Reuter, 2001).

Although it is essential to evaluate the harm associated with the use of drugs, it is important to evaluate the potential benefits as well. One obvious way in which at least some people benefit from the use of drugs is financially. Whether through the profits and taxes garnered from the sale of legal drugs such as alcohol and tobacco, or the income generated from the cultivation, transportation, and sale of illicit substances, many individuals benefit in economic terms from the use of drugs. The other obvious way in which drug use benefits individuals and society occurs in medicinal contexts. Large numbers of a range of psychoactive substances are prescribed by physicians for a diverse array of physical and mental ailments, which have positive effects for individuals and society. Non-prescribed substances may also have positive health effects. Individuals who use alcohol in moderation, for example, have been shown in a number of studies to have a reduced risk of cardiovascular disease when compared to those who abstain from alcohol use, although these benefits may be limited to middle-aged and older individuals (e.g., Doll, 1998; Doll, Peto, Hall, Wheatley, & Gray, 1994; McElduff & Dobson, 1997; Yuan, Ross, Gao, Henderson, & Yu, 1997). These findings have found their way into some national statistics on drug-related mortality. For instance, in Australia it was calculated that the "modest consumption of alcohol averted the deaths of 5,624 people" in 1998 (Miller & Draper, 2001, p. 37). However, some research has failed to find a reduced risk of heart disease among moderate users of alcohol (e.g., Hart, Smith, Hole, & Hawthorne, 1999), and there is a suggestion that many studies have failed to control for ex-drinkers and individuals with health problems among those who abstain from alcohol use (e.g., Fillmore, 2000; Puddey, Rakic, Dimmitt, & Beilin, 1999). More generally, there is a growing recognition that the *pattern* of alcohol consumption (rather than average weekly or monthly use) is an important variable that needs to be considered in evaluating potential health benefits (McElduff & Dobson, 1997; Puddey et al., 1999).

The potentially positive *psychological* benefits of moderate alcohol use also need to be considered. These benefits include positive effects on mood, stress reduction, increased sociability and social integration, and improvement in mental health (Peele & Brodsky, 2000). Although Peele and Brodsky in their review of the benefits of alcohol use could draw on a diverse body of data, comprehensive evaluations of similar benefits for other drugs, such as cannabis, cocaine, hallucinogens, and heroin, have yet to be undertaken. However, given that most individuals, most of the time, consume such substances presumably out of choice, they must at least *perceive* that there are benefits to be had, at least in the short term.

Although it seems that benefits can be derived from the use of drugs, weighing such benefits against the manifest harm of drug use is a difficult task. The costs and benefits of substance use are unequally distributed. Many subsistence-level farmers in developing nations, for example, may benefit substantially from the cultivation of opium and coca, while the harm clusters predominantly in Western countries such as the United States.[3] Moreover, both costs and benefits are influenced by the licit status of drugs in significant, although often difficult to quantify, ways. Cost–benefit analyses are also sensitive to the cultural-historical context in which drugs are employed. The use of opiates in contemporary Western societies, for instance, is related to a plethora of problems including dependence, crime, and the spread of HIV and other diseases. These harms are likely to outweigh whatever benefits accrue (at least to users). In the early nineteenth century in Britain and America, by contrast, it is probably fair to suggest that the medicinal value of opium, which was employed in a variety of contexts (see Chapter 4), outweighed whatever costs were entailed by its use.

FROM USE TO ABUSE

As the prevalence figures outlined earlier in this chapter illustrate, most people use psychoactive substances at some time in their lives. At what point can we consider that this drug *use* becomes drug *abuse*? This is a surprisingly difficult question to answer. The formal criteria employed by the two widely used systems for psychiatric diagnoses— the *Diagnostic and Statistical Manual of Mental Disorders* (DSM) and the *International Classification of Diseases* (ICD)—allow us, in principle, to demarcate substance-related disorders from non-pathological patterns of drug use. However, many discussions of drug abuse completely ignore the criteria laid down by the DSM and ICD and assume that *all* illicit patterns of substance use are evidence of abuse. For instance, although mainly concerned with detailing prevalence patterns, the "National Household Survey on Drug *Abuse*" carried out in the United States clearly signals this "problem inflation" orientation in its title. Another unambiguous example of this point of view is provided by

DuPont (1997) when he states, "Alcohol use by anyone under the legal drinking age of 21 and any use of any illicit drug are evidence of an addiction problem . . ." (p. 323).

In contrast to these points of view, we argue that use of psychoactive substances—whether licit or illicit, "hard" or "soft"—does not necessarily constitute abuse in any clinically or even socially well-grounded sense. Of course some patterns of drug use are clearly problematic, and these need to be satisfactorily demarcated from instances of non-problem drug use. Furthermore, there may always be gray areas between what is considered non-harmful substance use and what counts as substance abuse. However, it is both unhelpful and inaccurate to describe the consumption of a glass of wine with a meal by a sixteen-year-old or the occasional use of cannabis, cocaine, or ecstasy as necessarily constituting an "addiction problem," as DuPont (1997) suggests. We therefore endorse the point of view offered by Schuckit (1996a) when he states, "It is essential to not use the term 'abuse' as a substitute for 'use of an illegal substance,' or as a way of indicating some problems that do not necessarily meet the criteria set forth in any standard diagnostic manual" (p. 469).

The two current, widely used classification systems—the DSM-IV and the ICD-10—provide diagnostic criteria that, in principle, can help to distinguish instances of at least certain kinds of "problem" drug use from other kinds of use. Two main diagnostic categories are employed in these classification schemes for drug-related problems:

1. Alcohol and drug dependence (DSM-IV and ICD-10)

2. Alcohol and drug abuse (DSM-IV); Harmful use (ICD-10)

An overview of these criteria is provided in Tables 2.5 and 2.6. As can be seen, whereas the concept of drug dependence is predominantly the same in the DSM-IV and the ICD-10, the categories of "drug abuse" and "harmful use" diverge in that the latter does not include harm that arises from *social reactions* to substance use (Room, 1998a). However, despite these differences, there appears to be fairly good statistical agreement in the use of these two classification schemes, although concordance seems to be higher for diagnoses of drug dependence than for drug abuse or harmful use, as might be expected (Langenbucher, Morgenstern, Labouvie, & Nathan, 1994a). Whether or not agreement between the two systems holds up cross-culturally, however, is an interesting question that we explore in Chapter 10.

Table 2.5   DSM-IV and ICD-10 Diagnostic Criteria for Substance Dependence

DSM-IV[a]	ICD-10[b]
A maladaptive pattern of substance use, leading to clinically significant impairment or distress as manifested by three or more of the following occurring at any time in the same 12-month period:	Three or more of the following have been experienced at some time during the previous year:
(1) Need for markedly increased amounts of a substance to achieve intoxication or desired effect; or markedly diminished effect with continued use of the same amount of the substance	(1) Evidence of tolerance, such that increased doses are required in order to achieve effects originally produced by lower doses.
(2) The characteristic withdrawal syndrome for a substance or use of a substance (or closely related substance) to relieve or avoid withdrawal symptoms.	(2) A physiological withdrawal state when substance use has ceased or been reduced as evidenced by: the characteristic substance withdrawal syndrome, or use of a substance (or a closely related substance) to relieve or avoid withdrawal symptoms
(3) Persistent desire or one or more unsuccessful efforts to cut down or control substance use.	(3) Difficulties in controlling substance use in terms of onset, termination, or levels of use.
(4) Substance use in larger amounts or over a longer period than the person intended.	(4) Progressive neglect of alternative pleasures or interests in favor of substance use; or a great deal of time spent in activities necessary to obtain, to use, or to recover from the effects of substance use.
(5) Important social, occupational, or recreational activities given up or reduced because of substance use.	(5) Continued substance use despite clear evidence of overtly harmful physical or psychological consequences.

(Continued)

Table 2.5   (Continued)

DSM-IV[a]	ICD-10[b]
(6) A great deal of time spent in activities necessary to obtain the substance, use the substance, or recover from its effects.	(6) A strong desire or sense of compulsion to use substance
(7) The substance use is continued despite knowledge of having a persistent or recurrent physical or psychological problem that is likely to have been caused or exacerbated by the substance.	

SOURCE: [a]Reprinted with permission from American Psychiatric Association, *Diagnostic and Statistical Manual of Mental Disorders*, 4th ed.
[b]Reprinted with permission from World Health Organization, *The ICD-10 Classification of Mental and Behavioral Disorders*.

The current concept of "drug dependence" has evolved over time and differs in important ways from earlier classification schemes (Room, 1998a; Chapter 10). In its current guise, it owes much to the concept of the "alcohol dependence syndrome" forwarded by Edwards and Gross (1976). Key features of this diagnosis involve tolerance and withdrawal, which together comprise *physiological* dependence; impaired control and compulsive use; disproportionate amount of time spent in drug-related activities; and continued use despite problems (Grant & Dawson, 1999). One important change over earlier classification systems is the broadening of the concept of dependence to include psychological and behavioral aspects in addition to physical dependence. This move does not appear to have impaired the validity of the classification scheme (e.g., Carroll, Rounsaville, & Bryant, 1994), although given that only three criteria are required to meet a diagnosis of "drug dependence," multiple subtypes comprising different combinations of these criteria are possible.

Although the term "dependence" is currently favored in classification schemes, the older concept of "addiction" is still widely employed,

Table 2.6   DSM-IV and ICD-10 Diagnostic Criteria for Substance
Abuse/Harmful Use

DSM-IV (Substance Abuse)[a]	ICD-10 (Harmful Use)[b]
[A] A maladaptive pattern of substance use leading to clinically significant impairment or distress, as manifested by one (or more) of the following occurring within a 12-month period.	[A] A pattern of substance use that causes damage to health. The damage may be physical or mental. The diagnosis requires that actual damage should have been caused to the mental or physical health of the user.
(1) recurrent substance use resulting in a failure to fulfill major role obligations at work, school, or home.	[B] No concurrent diagnosis of the substance dependence syndrome for same class of substance.
(2) recurrent substance use in situations in which use is physically hazardous.	
(3) recurrent substance-related legal problems.	
(4) continued substance use despite having persistent or recurrent social or interpersonal problems caused or exacerbated by the effects of the substance.	
[B] The symptoms have never met the criteria for substance dependence for the same class of substance.	

SOURCE: [a]Reprinted with permission from American Psychiatric Association, *Diagnostic and Statistical Manual of Mental Disorders*, 4th ed.
[b]Reprinted with permission from World Health Organization, *The ICD-10 Classification of Mental and Behavioral Disorders*.

and some authors have argued that it captures the behavioral aspects of drug use disorders more effectively and should be reinstated (e.g., Maddux & Desmond, 2000). We use the terms "addiction" and "dependence" interchangeably throughout this book, and both refer to the criteria outlined for substance dependence in the two diagnostic systems discussed.

Although the criteria that are used to classify substance abuse and dependence are clear, there remain important issues regarding the best way to conceptualize the relationship among drug use, drug abuse, and drug dependence. One perspective is to view the use of drugs on a continuum: from non-harmful, moderate patterns through to the increasingly deleterious forms of use characterized by abuse and dependence. According to this view, drug abuse and dependence simply reflect different *kinds* of use, mainly relating to the frequency and quantity of consumption and the various harms that such use entails. However, an alternative view is to conceptualize drug abuse, and particularly drug dependence, as *qualitatively* different from drug use per se. For instance, Leshner (1999a) states, "Drug use and addiction are not simply poles of a single gradient along which one slides in either direction over time. Once addicted, one appears to have moved into a different state" (p. 1). Although we do not deny that prolonged exposure to drugs may result in important—perhaps qualitative— changes at a physiological level, a considerable body of evidence suggests that individuals can and do move in and out of states of dependence over time, with or without treatment (see Booth, 1990; Drew, 1990; Miller, 1998a; Price, Risk, & Spitznagel, 2001; Sobell, Sobell, & Toneatto, 1991). It is hard to reconcile these findings with the view that drug dependence is *qualitatively* different from regular, non-problematic substance use; although, as in many such debates, deciding what is to *count* as a qualitative difference is often the major source of disagreement. Regardless of these thorny conceptual issues, there is clearly a need to demarcate use from abuse and dependence, if on pragmatic grounds alone.

One of the most important questions for those working in the field of psychoactive drug studies is why some individuals have—generally speaking—*problems* with the use of drugs while others do not. We review cultural-historical, biological, and psychosocial attempts to answer this question at various places in this book, but it is important first to establish what the levels of substance abuse and dependence are in society. In the United States, lifetime prevalence rates for drug dependence (using DSM-III-R diagnostic criteria) were assessed in the National Comorbidity Study carried out in the early 1990s (Anthony, Warner, & Kessler, 1994; Kessler, McGonagle, Zhao, Nelson, Hughes, Eshleman, Wittchen, & Kendler, 1994). The results of this study indicated that the lifetime risk for dependence was greatest for tobacco (24.1%), followed by alcohol (14.1%) and cannabis (4.2%). These three substances were also the ones most likely to have been used at least once in the respondents' lives. If we examine the history of dependence among lifetime users, we find that the risk of qualifying for a diagnosis of drug dependence for individuals who report using a given substance at least once is greatest for tobacco (31.9%), followed by heroin (23.1%), cocaine (16.7%), and alcohol (15.4%).

Important gender differences were also found in this study. Lifetime prevalence rates for dependence on both alcohol and other drugs (excluding tobacco) in men (20.1% and 9.2% respectively) were much higher than they were for women (8.2% and 5.9% respectively) (Kessler et al., 1994). Rates of dependence also varied in different age groups. For alcohol, cannabis, cocaine, psychedelics, and inhalants, dependence among users was highest in the 15–24 age group; heroin dependence among users was greatest in the 35–44 age group; and dependence on analgesics and anxiolytics was highest in those aged 45 and over (Anthony et al., 1994). The lifetime prevalence of any substance use disorder (including alcohol and drug abuse, but excluding tobacco use disorders) was 26.6%. Putting these results another way, most individuals who try drugs do not abuse or become dependent upon them. This is the case for all substances, although there is some variation in the likelihood of dependence given use, depending on the drug in question.

SUMMARY

In this chapter we have briefly explored some important conceptual issues relating to the use of drugs and outlined the nature and extent of substance use and abuse in Western cultural contexts. Drugs are widely employed in such societies, and their use occurs in a variety of different contexts. Most individuals who use psychoactive drugs do not fulfill the diagnostic criteria for either substance abuse or dependence. However, in the United States at least, these disorders are more prevalent than other mental health problems (Kessler et al., 1994). Even though we agree that it is important to consider the manifold harms that arise from substance use and to distinguish drug use from abuse and dependence, we also urge a more inclusive framework for viewing the use of drugs in society. Drugs are used in a variety of different ways, only some of which might be considered harmful. Moreover, the concept of harm itself is influenced in important ways by the social and cultural context in which drugs are used—a point that we come back to in later chapters. People also obtain benefits from the use of drugs;

although generally these have attracted only a limited amount of research attention.

Ideally, these different facets of drug use should be included under one conceptual framework, although it is not surprising that research is primarily directed at the problems that arise from the use of drugs. Nonetheless, a better understanding of drug-related harms may be achieved by examining the context in which drugs are employed and engaging the fundamental question of why people choose to use (as oppose to abuse) psychoactive substances. In Chapter 3 we address this question by drawing on the resources of evolutionary theory.

NOTES

1.   The second meaning of the word *drug* listed here is of fairly recent origin. Parascandola (1995) suggests that the association of the word *drug* with abuse did not really occur until the early part of the twentieth century, and that prior to this the medicinal concept of *drug* prevailed.

2.   No doubt others could be included here. One important kind of harm relating to the use of drugs, for example, is environmental in nature. The cultivation and production of both licit substances such as tobacco and illicit drugs such as coca can have deleterious effects on ecosystems (Courtwright, 2001, pp. 60–64).

3.   The production of illicit substances in developing nations can of course also wreak local damage on social, political, and environmental systems.

3

An Evolutionary Perspective

INTRODUCTION

The earliest concrete evidence of human drug use dates back more than 5,000 years. Recipes for beer appear in Mesopotamian clay tablets dated to 3000 B.C.E. (Katz & Voigt, 1986), and recent excavations at Godin Jepe in modern-day Iraq suggest that both beer and wine were distributed to soldiers in Mesopotamian armies 5,500 years ago (Bower, 1994). The earliest written record of opium appears in Sumeria in 3400 B.C.E., where it is referred to as *hul gil* or "joy plant," hinting at its use in recreational contexts (Booth, 1996). The early use of other psychoactive substances such as cannabis, coca, coffee, betel, and hallucinogens is also well documented (e.g., Dobkin de Rios, 1990; Rudgley, 1993), and if some speculations are correct, drug taking may well have been an integral part of human life at the very emergence of our species some 120,000 years ago (e.g., Lewis-Williams & Dowson, 1988). Drugs are also widely used across cultures. Although the particular choice of drug and the use to which it is put varies from culture to culture, drug taking is—with isolated exceptions—a cross-cultural universal.[1] Furthermore, the use of drugs, as documented in Chapter 2, is also widespread within cultures. Although there are some individuals who abstain entirely from all forms of drug use, drugs are employed at some time and in some manner by most members in society.

The ubiquity of drug use prompted Baron Ernst von Bibra (1855), in his classic monograph *Plant Intoxicants*, to suggest, "The enormous numbers [of drug users] just cited demonstrate the paramount importance these substances have for the human race, since there exists no people on the Earth that fails to consume one or another of these dainties, which I have subsumed under the name 'pleasure drugs.' There must therefore exist a deeper motive, and the notion of fashion or the passion for imitation cannot be applied here" (p. xv). The "deeper motive" that von Bibra alludes to in this quote suggests that drug use might reflect basic human tendencies that are anchored in the evolutionary history of our species. As anthropologist Donald Brown (1991) argued in his book *Human Universals*, features of human behavior that are found across all cultures often suggest the existence of evolutionary factors that underpin their universality.

As we note in Chapter 1, the question of why people use psychoactive substances has been addressed from multiple theoretical perspectives: from detailed accounts of neurotransmitter functions in the brain to elaborate discussions of social, developmental, and cultural factors. In our attempts to answer this question, however, we must also examine the *origins* of the basic human tendencies that underlie drug-taking behavior. It is important to consider the *ultimate* as well as the *proximate* causes of substance use (see Hill & Newlin, 2002, for a discussion of this distinction in relation to drug use). That is, we need to engage the fundamental question of just *why* mind-altering substances have been so widely sought after in virtually every culture throughout history. Are humans innately predisposed in some way to seek out and consume psychoactive substances? Is there something about *Homo sapiens* as a species that can account for the ubiquity of drug-taking behavior? We propose that an evolutionary approach can shed light on these important questions.

We begin this chapter by briefly outlining the nature and role of evolutionary explanations in psychology. Specifically, we discuss the importance of identifying psychological adaptations and reflect on the possibility that drug taking may best be conceptualized as a *byproduct* of adaptive mechanisms. We then examine various different evolutionary approaches to drug use, including the possibility that drug use may have been specifically selected for. These various evolutionary accounts are then integrated into a more general model of substance use, which reflects the multiple ways in which drugs might influence human cognition and behavior. Although we primarily focus on possible evolutionary explanations for substance *use* in this chapter, we conclude by discussing some implications for our understanding of substance abuse and dependence.

THE NATURE AND ROLE OF EVOLUTIONARY EXPLANATIONS

Evolutionary psychology is an emerging perspective within the behavioral sciences that explains human cognition and behavior in terms of the processes of natural and sexual selection. More specifically, evolutionary psychologists argue that the human mind is composed of a large number of psychological mechanisms that have evolved in ancestral environments because of their ability to promote survival and reproductive success (see Buss, 1995, 1999; Durrant & Ellis, 2002, for general introductions to evolutionary psychology). Evolutionary psychologists, therefore, offer *ultimate* explanations of human characteristics in terms of phylogeny and adaptation. These kinds of explanations are best seen as complementary to, rather than competing with, the more *proximate* explanatory accounts typically offered by psychologists. In addressing the evolutionary origins of drug taking in humans, the first question that needs to be considered is whether or not such behavior reflects the operation of mechanisms that have evolved *specifically* for drug consumption. That is, we need to consider whether drug use is a biological *adaptation*.

Adaptations are inherited and reliably developing characteristics of species that have been selected for because of their causal role in enhancing the survival and reproductive success of the individuals that possess them (Buss, Haselton, Shackelford, Bleske, & Wakefield, 1998; Williams, 1966). Evolutionary psychologists usually employ a number of different methods in identifying adaptations (Durrant & Haig, 2001; Tooby & Cosmides, 1990). The importance of *special design* features such as economy, efficiency, complexity, precision, and functionality are often emphasized (Williams, 1966). One hallmark that a trait is the product of natural selection, for example, is that it demonstrates adaptive complexity—that is, the trait is composed of a number of interrelated parts or systems that operate in concert to generate effects that serve specific biological functions (Dawkins, 1986). The vertebrate eye is one textbook example of such a trait: it is composed of a number of parts—lens, iris, cornea, and retina—which operate in a precise and coordinated fashion to produce a specific functional outcome: vision.

However, evolutionary forces do not perfectly tune organisms to their surrounding environments. Not all aspects of an animal's behavioral repertoire are likely to be the direct product of natural selection. Wherever natural selection generates adaptations it also generates byproducts of adaptations (Buss et al., 1998). A simple example will help to clarify this point. The human heart has the evolutionary function of pumping blood, for that is the reason it was selected: blood-pumping hearts contribute to the survival and reproductive success of those individuals that possess them. Hearts also have other properties, such as their color and the noise they make while pumping. These properties of hearts, however, have not been *directly* selected for, but rather are *byproducts* of the selection process with no specific function.

Furthermore, biological adaptations that have evolved to serve specific functions may become utilized in the production of novel behaviors without any specific evolutionary purpose (see Gould, 1991). For example, consider the seemingly suicidal "flame-seeking" behavior of moths, which apparently drives them toward candle flames and fires to their ultimate demise. This behavior is clearly maladaptive. However, in a world before naked flames were common, small bright sources of light would have represented escape holes from hollow logs or caves, or celestial bodies at optical infinity (Dawkins, 1982). Thus, although "flame-seeking" behavior itself has no evolutionary function, it may well be explained by reference to behavior that does.

In a similar fashion, the human predilection for the sweet sugary concoctions widely on offer in contemporary society is undoubtedly maladaptive in that consumption of such products leads to a variety of negative health consequences. Our sweet tooth, however, probably reflects selection for olfactory and gustatory preferences that would have signaled the presence of nutritious food sources, such as fruit, in ancestral environments. Mismatches between modern environments and what has been termed the Environment of Evolutionary Adaptedness, in which biological traits were selected, can result in dysfunctional behavior. As Steven Pinker (1997) in his book *How the Mind Works* summarizes, "[The mind] is driven by goal states that served biological fitness in ancestral environments, such as food, sex, safety, parenthood, friendship, status, and knowledge. That toolbox, however, can be used to assemble Sunday afternoon projects of dubious adaptive value" (p. 524).

In addressing the evolutionary origins of drug taking in humans, the first question that needs to be considered is whether or not such behavior reflects the operation of mechanisms that have evolved *specifically* for drug consumption. That is, we need to consider whether drug use is a biological adaptation. The universal nature of drug taking by humans throughout history and across cultures may, however, not reflect specific adaptations *for* drug taking per se. Rather, drug use may be the result of mechanisms that *do* have evolutionary functions, but that are exploited in the context of drug use. We may well be, like the moths in the example, ineluctably drawn to the experiences that drugs provide, satisfying innate needs, but often getting burnt in the process. Most of the evolutionary accounts of human drug use that we discuss in this chapter adopt the view that drug consumption reflects basic evolved psychological and physiological processes, but which are not specifically designed for the use of psychoactive drugs per se. However, we begin by considering the possibility that at least some aspects of drug use have been specifically selected for.

HAS DRUG USE BEEN SELECTED FOR?

There are a number of ways, as Smith (1999) outlines, that drug use might have enhanced fitness in ancestral environments. Stimulants, such as coca, coffee, and tobacco, have the ability to reduce fatigue, suppress appetite, and increase wakefulness. Sedative-hypnotic substances such as alcohol can be employed to reduce anxiety and relieve insomnia. And analgesics, like opium, can serve to alleviate pain and generate euphoric states. Certainly these uses of psychoactive substances might well have been adaptive in terms of improving personal well-being. The critical question, however, is whether they would have also increased survival and reproductive success.

One recent evolutionary account of drug use that outlines how substance seeking in humans might have been specifically selected for has been offered by Sullivan and Hagen (2002). The starting point for their theory is the long co-evolutionary relationship between humans (and our hominid and mammalian ancestors) and plant chemicals. Before the advent of highly refined drugs such as cocaine and heroin, all psychoactive substances consumed by humans would have been directly obtained from plants.[2] Plants, however, have an evolutionary interest in preventing predation by herbivores and have as a consequence evolved a variety of toxic defenses to deter their consumption. The evolution of plant chemicals that interact with mammalian nervous systems by mimicking the structure of endogenous neurotransmitters like serotonin, dopamine, and acetylcholine are examples of such defense systems. By altering physiological, cognitive, perceptual, and behavioral processes, these chemicals can deter feeding and thus increase the reproductive success of the plants that possess them. Indeed, almost all of the psychoactive plants consumed by humans have been shown to possess analogs of endogenous neurotransmitters.

The evolution of chemical defense systems in plants, however, sets up counter-selection pressures on organisms that consume plants for food. Many animals, for instance, have evolved specific physiological adaptations for ingesting and processing otherwise toxic plant substances. Monarch butterfly caterpillars, for example, have evolved enzymes that allow them to feed on plants of the milkweed family without being poisoned. Sullivan and Hagen (2002) argue that the presence of chemical defenses in plants that mimic endogenous neurotransmitter systems creates conditions that are ripe for counter-exploitation. The synthesis of neurotransmitters such as serotonin and dopamine requires the consumption of food products that provide the precursors to these endogenous substances. "Substance seeking," Sullivan and Hagen (2002, p. 395) suggest, "evolved to alleviate these constraints on brain-signaling processes." By consuming plants that provided essential neurochemicals directly, time and effort spent in foraging could be reduced. Substance seeking may have been specifically triggered during times of stress when levels of neurotransmitters were depleted, somewhat analogous to the seeking and ingestion of clay and salt by many animal species to enhance digestion and make up for mineral deficiencies.

Although plausible, the account offered by Sullivan and Hagen (2002) leaves several questions unanswered. First, were psychotropic plants widely enough available in the environments of ancestral hominids in East and Southern Africa to allow for the evolution of substance-seeking mechanisms? Second, and more important, what could the nature of these psychological and physiological mechanisms be? Presumably they would involve some kind of olfactory or gustatory preferences. However, given the diversity of psychoactive substances in the environment—plant leaves, roots, mushrooms, berries, and so forth—it is not clear what feature of these substances such mechanisms could pick out. Of course once they had been consumed and the desired effects obtained, they could be sought out again, and knowledge of the relevant plants could be transmitted to other members in the population. However, the mechanisms required for this process are general, not specific in nature, and operate for *all* food substances. Despite these queries, the ideas developed by Sullivan and Hagen (2002) are novel, testable, and should provide the basis for further study.

The consumption of at least one psychoactive substance—ethyl alcohol—however, has clearer links with evolved taste preferences (Dudley, 2000, 2002). Dudley has argued that as part of our primate legacy as frugivores we have inherited a preference for ripe fruits that contain significant quantities of ethanol, which would have signaled the presence of energy-rich sugars. Indeed, in many cultures throughout history alcohol has been considered a "food" and viewed as an important source of calories (Barr, 1995; Heath, 2000). Dudley (2000) suggests, therefore, that "natural selection has acted on human ancestors to associate ethanol with nutritional reward, promoting rapid identification and consumption of ethanol-containing fruit resources" (p. 8). This idea is supported by comparative evidence that demonstrates that a wide variety of animal species, including vervet monkeys (Ervin, Palmour, Young, Guzman-Flores, & Juarez, 1990), butterflies (Miller, 1997), and elephants (Siegal & Brodie, 1984), will all consume overripe fruits high in ethanol content, which lead to behavioral manifestations of intoxication. Human alcoholism, however, reflects a maladaptive pattern of behavior arising from innate preferences for ethanol coupled with (among other factors) virtually unlimited access to alcoholic beverages, only possible in more recent times (Dudley, 2000, 2002).

It is plausible, therefore, that preferences for alcohol and other psychoactive substances may have been specifically selected for. The evolutionary benefits, in ancestral environments, may have included a cheap source of valuable neurochemicals and, for alcohol, an important supply of nutrients. In modern environments, where psychoactive substances are readily available and in more potent forms, these evolutionary advantages are more obscure. In order to understand how more maladaptive patterns of use might arise we need to consider in more detail the action of drugs on evolved brain systems.

DRUGS AND THE BRAIN

Perhaps the most obvious answer to the question, "Why do people take drugs?" is simply that drugs make them *feel* good. Why do drugs have this capacity to generate positive emotional and psychological states, at least in the short term? One suggestion is that psychoactive drugs effectively short-circuit mechanisms that have evolved to signal positive and negative experiences (Nesse, 1994; Nesse & Berridge, 1997; Smith, 1999). The evolutionary function of emotions is to motivate organisms to pursue adaptive and avoid maladaptive experiences (Nesse, 1990). Positive, fitness-enhancing events, such as the consumption of food, sexual activity, and positive social relations, bring pleasure to those who experience them or alleviate negative emotional states. In contrast, fitness-decreasing experiences, such as social rejection, physical pain, and sexual betrayal, are linked to emotions and feelings that are subjectively experienced as unpleasant in nature. These emotional experiences, furthermore, are underpinned by specific mechanisms in the brain, associated with particular neurotransmitter systems.

People take drugs, according to this view, because they activate endogenous reward systems in the brain that have evolved to signal the presence of evolutionarily beneficial stimuli and experiences (Nesse & Berridge, 1997). Furthermore, by alleviating the unpleasant and aversive experiences associated with pain, guilt, anxiety, and fear, drugs serve to block the realization of negative emotions. The universality of drug consumption by humans, therefore, can be explained in terms of the ability of psychoactive drugs to stimulate specific mechanisms in the brain that have evolved for other, more adaptive, purposes. Just as humans are predisposed to enjoy the unhealthy offerings of fast-food outlets and candy stores, because foods high in fat and sugar would have offered fitness benefits in ancestral environments, so too are we inclined to pursue the powerfully rewarding experiences that many psychoactive drugs offer—often to similar maladaptive ends. The interaction of drugs with specific brain systems has been extensively investigated by neuroscientists and forms a voluminous and highly technical literature (see Goldstein, 1994; Koob, Caine, Hyytia, Markou, Parsons, Roberts, Schulteis, & Weiss, 1999; Wise, 1998, for reviews). We focus here, however, only on the relevance of this research for the evolutionary perspective on drug use outlined.

The reward systems in the brain that have been implicated in understanding the effects of psychoactive drugs were first discovered by psychologists James Olds and Peter Milner (Olds & Milner, 1954). It was found that laboratory rats responded in specific ways when certain parts of their brain were electrically stimulated. When the rats had implants fitted to their brains that allowed self-stimulation after pressing a lever, they would reliably continue pressing the lever to the point of exhaustion. Olds and his colleagues appeared to have found an area in the brain that was responsible for generating rewarding experiences, and that presumably served an adaptive function in the normal context of an animal's life. Subsequent research has revealed that a diverse range of psychoactive drugs also activate these so-called natural reward systems in the brain. An enormous body of literature has demonstrated that a variety of different animal species will do considerable work (typically in terms of bar-pressing) in order to receive a range of psychoactive drugs such as cocaine, heroin, and alcohol. It appears that such drugs, by stimulating reward systems in the brain, operate as powerful primary reinforcers.

The critical brain circuit implicated in the rewarding effects of many psychoactive drugs connects areas of the frontal cortex with the nucleus accumbens and the ventral tegmental area, in the limbic system of the brain. This brain circuit—the mesolimbic reward pathway— is served by a variety of neurotransmitters, although the most critical one appears to be dopamine. Psychoactive drugs act on the central nervous system by mimicking or blocking a range of specific, endogenous neurotransmitters. For example, opioids, like heroin, act on natural opioid receptors (Akil, Owens, Gutstein, Taylor, Curran, & Watson, 1998), caffeine blocks adenosine receptors (Daly & Fredholm, 1998), and cannabis exerts its effects on recently discovered endogenous cannabanoid systems (Childers & Breivogel, 1998; Gardner, 1999). However, the rewarding effects of a wide range of psychoactive substances appear to result from their action—directly or indirectly—on dopaminergic neurons in the mesolimbic reward pathway. Thus, there seems to be a common physiological basis for many drugs of abuse (Wise, 1998; Picciotto, 1998). Cocaine and amphetamines, for example, operate as powerful dopamine agonists by blocking the reuptake of this neurotransmitter, and hence increasing the levels of dopamine available at the synapse. Delta-9-tetrahydrocannabinol (THC)—the active ingredient in cannabis—functions in a similar fashion, inhibiting the reuptake of dopamine in the nucleus accumbens (Gardner, 1999). Other psychoactive drugs, such as nicotine, alcohol, and opiates, also increase levels of dopamine in reward pathways in the brain, although their rewarding effects probably also involve the stimulation of other important neurotransmitter systems (Picciotto, 1998).

The rewarding effects of psychoactive drugs probably operate in two different ways. First, by stimulating natural reward systems they act as powerful primary reinforcers. Second, by relieving pain caused by drug withdrawal or for other reasons, they also operate as negative reinforcers (Koob & Le Moal, 1997). These two mechanisms of action—positive and negative reinforcement—may well be served by anatomically distinct systems in the brain (Wise, 1988). This suggestion is supported in the psychological literature on motivations for drug use, which indicates that drug taking can be employed to regulate either positive or negative emotions (e.g., Cooper, Frone, Russell, & Mudar, 1995). It is unlikely, however, that the brain systems implicated in the rewarding effects of psychoactive drugs have evolved specifically *for* the ingestion of such drugs. Rather, these systems are implicated in the generation of positive emotional states that are linked to stimuli in the world that *do* have survival and reproductive relevance for the organism. For example, the release of dopamine in relevant mesolimbic portions of the brain is strongly associated with feeding and sexual behavior (Phillips, Blaha, Pfaus, & Blackburn, 1992).

The effectiveness of drugs as primary reinforcers is illustrated by the way that previously neutral stimuli acquire special significance in relation to drug taking, and may trigger drug-like and drug withdrawal-like responses in drug dependent individuals (Self & Nestler, 1998). For example, individuals may experience craving when exposed to drug-related stimuli such as needles and pipes, and specific drug-taking environments. Self and Nestler propose that the neural process underlying this type of phenomenon involves the activation of the mesolimbic dopamine system via the hypothalamo-pituitary-adrenal axis. The evolutionary function of this kind of conditioned reinforcement is clear: organisms that respond in specific ways to stimuli that are *associated* with fitness benefits (or costs) will be at a selective advantage because the range of relevant stimuli has been enlarged. The often detailed rituals and elaborate paraphernalia that accompany all kinds of drug use—from the preparation of tea, to the injection of heroin—plausibly reflect cultural elaborations of conditioned responses.

Although the account outline here provides a plausible evolutionary basis to why people use drugs, there is some dispute regarding the functions of the mesolimbic dopaminergic system. For instance, it has been argued that this brain system may mediate incentive salience or "wanting," rather than (or in addition to) reward or "liking" (Robinson & Berridge, 2001). In order to steer behavior into adaptive channels, certain stimuli in the world become imbued with special significance—they demand attention and become the focus of appetitive behavior. The mesolimbic dopaminergic system, therefore, may be specifically implicated in the prediction, expectation, and seeking of rewarding consequences generated by activities such as feeding, drinking, and sex (Schultz, Dayan, & Montague, 1997). According to this view, with repeated drug use the neural substrate that mediates incentive salience becomes sensitized, resulting in compulsive drug-seeking behavior. In short, drugs and, through classical conditioning, drug-related stimuli take on special significance and are sought out at the expense of other activities.

This perspective helps to explain why drugs continue to be used even though they no longer provide positive hedonic experiences. It also accounts for the peculiar features of compulsion and "loss of control" that characterize drug addiction. In addition, drugs may be employed initially even though they produce aversive rather than pleasurable states, and there appears to be no simple correlation between the pleasure induced by drugs and their addiction potential (Lende & Smith, 2002). These facts are difficult to explain from a perspective based purely on the rewarding consequences of drug use, but can be accounted for by the incentive salience view presented here. It seems plausible, however, that the reward and salience theories can be integrated: drugs have multiple effects on neurotransmitter systems, including the generation of pleasurable and the alleviation of negative emotional states, and the triggering of incentive salience and appetitive behavior. The relative importance of these two effects may vary depending on the drug in question and the stage of drug use (initiation, regular use, or dependence).

The perspectives outlined in this section go a long way toward explaining the cross-cultural and historical ubiquity of drug consumption by humans, as well as their addictive potential. Drugs, by virtue of their specific chemical properties, operate on brain mechanisms that have evolved for other purposes. Because the evolved function of these systems relate to adaptively meaningful stimuli such as food, sex, and social relations, drugs can take on special meaning and significance. Drug consumption per se, according to this view, has not been selected for, but the mechanisms that drugs activate have. Clearly, more work needs to be done before we can establish just how drugs interact with endogenous brain systems, what the evolutionary function of those systems is, and how they may be altered through repeated use of psychoactive drugs (e.g., see Gerald & Higley, 2002; Lende & Smith, 2002; Newlin, 2002; Panksepp, Knutson, & Burgdorf, 2002, for further alternatives, refinements, and implications of the general approach outlined in this section).

DRUG USE, SEXUAL SELECTION,
AND LIFE HISTORY THEORY

As well as addressing the basis of drug use and addiction, evolutionary accounts can also help us to explain the demographic patterns of use that are found in society.

One striking finding that emerges from epidemiological research on the use and abuse of drugs is the difference between men and women. Men are more likely to use, abuse, and be dependent on a wide range of both licit and illicit psychoactive substances. For example, results from the 1992 National Longitudinal Alcohol Epidemiological Survey indicated that the prevalence of lifetime alcohol use in the United States for men was 78.3%, whereas for women it was 54.7% (based on consumption of 12 or more drinks during any 12-month period). Figures for the lifetime prevalence of heavy alcohol use show a similar pattern: 35.6% of men and 12.1% of women reported average daily consumption of more that 1 ounce of ethanol during their period of heaviest drinking (Grant, 1996; Grant & Dawson, 1999). These differences are significant even taking into account differences in body size between men and women. The use of other drugs reveals a similar pattern of sex differences, although the magnitude of the difference varies by drug considered and population sampled (Grant & Dawson, 1999). These differences are consistent with research findings in other countries such as Australia, New Zealand, and Great Britain (Miller & Draper, 2001; New Zealand Health Information Service, 2001; Ramsay, Baker, Goulden, Sharp, & Sondhi, 2001).

Another consistent finding is that levels of substance use and abuse are generally higher in adolescents and young adults than among older individuals, although again, this varies somewhat by the type of drug considered. For instance, in the United States the percentage of respondents who reported past-month use of any illicit drug was four times higher among 18 to 25 year olds than it was for adults aged 26 and over (Substance Abuse and Mental Health Services Administration, 2001; see Grant & Dawson, 1999; Kandel, 1998; Chapter 2 for more details). Finally, drug use is related to education and socioeconomic status. Individuals with less education and lower socioeconomic status typically have higher rates of illicit drug use and substance use problems (e.g., Midanak & Room, 1992).

What sort of factors can account for these demographic differences in patterns of substance use and abuse? A number of possible explanations have been suggested. The importance of gender roles, for example, has been offered as one explanation for sex differences in rates of substance use and abuse (e.g., Heath, 2000; Neve, Lemmens, & Drop, 1997; Room, 1996). The relative social disapproval of female drug use, its incompatibility with traditional female roles and responsibilities, and positive attitudes toward (certain aspects of) male drug use all no doubt play an important role in accounting for gender discrepancies in substance use and abuse. The higher prevalence of substance use and abuse among adolescents and young adults has also received considerable scholarly attention (e.g., Bachman, Johnston, O'Malley, & Schulenberg, 1996; Grob & Dobkin de Rios, 1992; Kandel, 1998; Schedler & Block, 1990; Schulenberg, O'Malley, Bachman, Wadsworth, & Johnston, 1996). Adolescence and young adulthood are times of considerable change and upheaval, as transitions are being made into the adult world with all its attendant freedoms and responsibilities. An increased propensity for general reckless behavior and novelty seeking (Arnett, 1992), lack of experience in drug use, greater freedom (but often limited responsibility), and peer influence have all been proposed as potential explanations for heavy drug use among adolescents and young adults. A consistent finding is that as the transition to adulthood is made, most individuals tend to "mature out" of abusive patterns of drug taking, as new responsibilities such as employment, marriage, and parenthood are taken on (Bachman et al., 1996). Both age and sex differences in patterns of substance use, therefore, can be explained in terms of a number of proximate social and psychological explanations, such as social roles, changes in lifestyle, and peer influence.

The demographic profile of drug use outlined is also consistent with the ideas of sexual selection and life history theory. Sexual selection arises not from a struggle to survive but rather from the competition over mates and mating (Andersson, 1994). Traits such as the male peacock's gaudy tail or the red deer's vast branching antlers are selected for because they attract more mates or are employed in intrasexual contests over mates. They thus increase their owner's reproductive success relative to other individuals with less developed versions of the same trait. The relative importance of sexual selection on males and females of a species will depend on differences in *parental investment* and variance in mating success. Parental investment, according to Trivers (1972), is "any investment by the parent in an individual's offspring chance of surviving ... at the cost of the parent's ability to invest in other offspring" (p. 132). In humans, for example (as in all mammalian species), women bear the obligatory costs of pregnancy, childbirth, lactation, and nursing, whereas a teaspoon full of sperm may be all the resources that a male contributes (although of course male investment is usually substantially more than this—see Geary, 2000). Because of these differences, the reproductive success of men is primarily constrained by the number of fertile females that they can inseminate. Females, by contrast, are constrained by the number of eggs that they can produce and the number of viable offspring that can be raised. Selection favors males that compete successfully with other males, or who have qualities preferred by females that increase their mating opportunities. Conversely, selection favors females who choose mates who have good genes and (in paternally investing species) are likely to provide external resources such as food or protection to the female and her offspring (Durrant & Ellis, 2002; Trivers, 1972).

Life history theory is primarily related to tradeoffs that occur during different developmental periods. All organisms have finite resources, and decisions have to be made whether to invest more effort into survival, growth, current reproduction, or future reproduction (Chisholm, 1993). Important trade-offs include those between survival (e.g., foraging, avoiding predation, and so on), reproduction (e.g., attracting and retaining a mate), and parenting (caring for offspring). Which choices prove to be most effective in furthering reproductive success will depend critically on such factors as age, sex, and environmental circumstances. For instance, in highly unpredictable or impoverished environments where survival prospects are uncertain, it pays to engage in risky behavior. Simply put, when your prospects are diminished you have less to lose (Hill & Chow, 2002; Hill, Ross, & Low, 1997).

What has all this got to do with the demographics of substance use? One prediction of both sexual selection and life history theory is that young men (and young males of many species) should be most prone to engage in risky, dangerous, and costly behavior of all kinds, including the reckless use of psychoactive substances (Wilson & Daly, 1985). The reason for this is that the fitness payoffs for such behavior in terms of increased status, resources, and mating success, relative to costs incurred, is the greatest in this developmental period. Young, unmarried men, in contrast to both women and older men, simply have less to lose and the most to gain (in evolutionary terms) from such risk-taking behavior. The suggestion that young men are prone to engage in risky exploits is amply supported by a wide range of findings that indicate that young men are more likely to be involved in automobile accidents, die in homicides, engage in risky sexual behavior, pursue dangerous leisure activities, and of course experiment in risky ways with a range of psychoactive drugs. As Wilson, Daly, and Gordon (1998) summarize, "Several lines of evidence about life-span development support the idea that young men constitute a demographic class specialized by a history of selection for maximal competitive effort and risk-taking. Young men appear to be psychologically specialized to embrace danger and confrontational competition" (p. 514).

Risky and competitive behavior by young men is likely to reflect, from an evolutionary perspective, the effects of both *intra-* and *inter*sexual selection. That is, such behavior is not only the result of competition *between* males in accruing resources and establishing status and dominance hierarchies, but males also engage in behaviors for "display" purposes, to demonstrate their fitness to potential reproductive partners. This latter form of selection—via mate choice—has led to the specific suggestion that the consumption of drugs by young males may be one manifestation of "sexual display." According to the *handicap principle* (Zahavi & Zahavi, 1997), individuals can display their biological fitness by engaging in costly behaviors or bearing costly ornaments (such as the peacock's tail). Members of the opposite sex will favor such individuals in mating contexts because they have traits that can be maintained *in spite* of their harmful consequences, thus honestly signaling the fitness of their bearers. Diamond (1992) has suggested that the use of drugs may reflect one aspect of such costly display. This idea is summarized by Zahavi and Zahavi (1997) in their book *The Handicap Principle*: "Showing off by consuming harmful chemicals like alcohol, tobacco, betel nut, opium, and the like is common among humans. In some societies, men even demonstrate their vigor by drinking naptha.... One who can drink quantities of alcohol without apparent ill-effect shows reliably his or her good physical condition ..." (p. 160).

Heavy drinking by young men is viewed in many countries, such as Australia and New Zealand, as a badge of masculinity or manhood (Heath, 2000). Excessive alcohol consumption is also often common in many coming-of-age rituals (Heath, 2000), as is the use of various other psychoactive substances (Grob & Dobkin de Rios, 1992). A specific example of apparent "fitness evaluation" occurs in many sub-Saharan African countries where prospective grooms are engaged by their future bride's male relatives in prolonged bouts of heavy drinking over a period of several months (Heath, 2000). Furthermore, as noted earlier, youthful patterns of heavy drinking and drug use are often significantly reduced once individuals marry and have children (Bachman et al., 1996). From an evolutionary perspective, the benefits of such activities are less likely to outweigh the costs involved once stable relationships are formed and there are dependent children to care for.

According to life history theory, environmental factors should also influence decision making and risky behavior in important ways. As mentioned previously, levels of education, socioeconomic status, and income are all—inversely—related to patterns of harmful substance use. Individuals from relatively deprived environments simply have less to lose from risky behavior and this manifests in many forms, including the harmful use of drugs. In support of these ideas, a study by Hill et al. (1997) found that individuals with greater future unpredictability and who had shorter lifespan estimates were also more likely to report engaging in risky behavior. The association of smoking with lower socioeconomic status (Schelling, 1992) and the relative ineffectiveness of anti-smoking campaigns directed at youth which emphasize long-term health consequences (Goldman & Glantz, 1998) are good examples of demographic differences in the tendency to discount the future which can be explained from the perspective of life history theory.

However, demographic differences in patterns of drug use are unlikely to reflect selection specifically *for* drug-taking behavior. Rather, it seems more plausible to suggest that adolescence and young adulthood (especially for men) is a time when evolved mechanisms relating to such things as risk taking and novelty seeking are most in evidence. Substance use and abuse may reflect one manifestation of more general patterns of behavior that are linked in theoretically coherent ways to age and gender-specific traits. Although drug-taking behaviors are not specifically the result of sexual selection, the mechanisms that relate to such behaviors probably are.

The most important psychological mechanism in this context appears to be *sensation seeking*, which has been described by Zuckerman (1994) as "a trait defined by the *seeking* of varied, novel, complex, and *intense* sensations and experiences, and the willingness to take physical, social, legal, and financial risks for the sake of such experiences" (p. 27). A plethora of studies have examined the relationships between the psychological trait of sensation seeking and a wide range of behaviors, including the use and abuse of psychoactive drugs. The findings of these studies indicate that sensation seeking appears to be positively related to a wide range of risky activities, including dangerous sports, criminality, sexual behavior, gambling, reckless driving, heavy drinking, and substance abuse (Zuckerman, 1994; Zuckerman & Kuhlman, 2000).

Moreover, men score consistently higher than women in measures of sensation seeking. Sensation seeking also appears to peak in late adolescence and early adulthood, and declines as individuals get older (Zuckerman, 1994). The common finding that males are more likely to engage in risky behaviors than females (see Byrnes, Miller, & Schafer, 1999) appears to be almost entirely mediated by sensation seeking, or more specifically *impulsive* sensation seeking (Zuckerman & Kuhlman, 2000). The mechanisms underlying sensation seeking, we suggest, are in part the product of sexual selection for traits that are involved in competition over mates and mating. More generally speaking, sensation seeking can be conceptualized as a trait that is related to the seeking of novel situations with all the attendant rewards and risk that this might bring (Zuckerman & Kuhlman, 2000). Given the greater variance in reproductive success for men compared to women, and the greater costs for women in engaging in risky behavior, we should expect risk taking to demonstrate both age and gender differences—which it does. Experimenting with a wide range of drugs and engaging in heavy and abusive patterns of drug use can be considered, in part, as one consequence of the evolved mechanisms underlying novelty seeking and risk taking.

The psychological trait of sensation seeking appears to be instantiated in basic physiological mechanisms that are involved in approach and reward. As we have seen, the critical brain system implicated in reward seeking and appetitive behavior is the mesolimbic dopaminergic pathway. It seems plausible to suggest, therefore, that a highly reactive dopamine system may be a factor that instantiates high levels of sensation seeking and greater risk for substance abuse (Zuckerman, 1995). "Dopamine," as Zuckerman and Kuhlman (2000) state, "is the accelerator in the drive to risky behavior, particularly in the area of drug use and abuse" (p. 1021). In support of this idea, a recent study (Perkins, Gerlach, Broge, & Grobe, 2000) found that nonsmokers high in the experience-seeking and disinhibition subscales of sensation seeking experienced greater sensitivity to the subjective effects of nicotine (administered via a nasal spray) than individuals low in these traits.

Summarizing the key ideas in this section, we have suggested that differences in parental investment between males and females have resulted in sexual selection for traits involved in risk taking, impulsivity, and novelty seeking, which for young males in ancestral environments would have correlated with greater reproductive success. These behaviors are mediated by the psychological trait of sensation seeking, which is instantiated, in part, in dopaminergic reward systems in the brain. Tendencies for novelty seeking and risk taking take many forms, one of which is the use and abuse of a wide range of psychoactive substances. These mechanisms, although adaptive in ancestral environments, in contemporary contexts often result in less beneficial outcomes. As Zuckerman and Kuhlman (2000) suggest, "Modern forms of human sensation seeking such as drug use, reckless driving, mountain climbing and parachuting are not adaptive. They are merely a testimony to the persistence of traits produced by the selective pressures of the distant evolutionary history of our species." (p. 1025).

The ideas that are presented in this section, we should note, although plausible, are still tentative in character and require further conceptual and empirical elaboration. A number of qualifications are also in order. First, although young males are at a *greater* risk for substance abuse and dependence, older men and women of all ages also both use and abuse drugs. Therefore, although the mechanisms underlying sensation seeking may have different levels of activation in men and women of different ages (as a result of sexual selection pressures), they represent more basic human traits. Second, the suggestion that substance use and abuse—especially by young males—may have an evolutionary basis in no way implies that such patterns of drug use are either inevitable or need be harmful in character. As Grob and Dobkin de Rios (1992) have argued, drug use by adolescents in many cultures is not viewed as problematic, as it is managed in ways that minimize harm and serves as part of the passage to adulthood. Indeed, even in Western cultures, drug use, as opposed to drug abuse, is associated with psychological adjustment in adolescents and young adults (Shelder & Block, 1990). Moreover, as the trait that has been selected for is sensation seeking and not substance use per se, there are likely to be less harmful ways of allowing this trait expression. Third, social and cultural factors can significantly modify patters of drug use by men and women in all age groups (e.g., see Waldron, 1991) suggesting that the age and sex differences in drug use outlined at the beginning of this section are by no means inevitable.

FROM USE TO ABUSE

In this chapter we have discussed some plausible evolutionary explanations for the important question of why the use of psychoactive substances is virtually ubiquitous across cultures and throughout history. This analysis may seem far removed from the concerns of practicing clinicians treating heroin addiction in the downtown clinics of large urban centers, or the dilemmas facing policy makers in their attempts to formulate the most effective ways of reducing drug-related problems. However, although detailed discussions of treatment and policy are reserved for later chapters, we offer some provisional suggestions here as to how an evolutionary approach can contribute to our understanding of how drug use may result in various drug-related problems, such as substance abuse and dependence.

The first question to consider is whether drug abuse and dependence might themselves be the product of evolutionary processes. Alexander (1990), in his adaptive model of addiction, for instance, has argued that it is these apparently harmful modes of drug taking that represent biological adaptations to adverse circumstances. Specifically, Alexander suggests that addiction is an adaptive response to "integration failure," which occurs when individuals are unable to obtain valued social roles within society. Addiction, according to this model, operates as a form of coping that enables individuals to bear the negative consequences of their social isolation and to achieve new patterns of meaning in their lives. Certainly we agree that even apparently harmful patterns of substance use may be functional in terms of providing self-medication in intolerable life circumstances (see Khantzian, 1997). Moreover, there is a well-established relationship between substance use problems and other psychological disorders, hinting at the role of drugs in the management of mental health problems (e.g., Strakowski & DelBello, 2000; Swendsen & Merikangas, 2000).[3] However, for a number of reasons, it is unlikely that addictive patterns of drug use reflect mechanisms that have evolved specifically *for* this purpose. First, the reproductive benefits of such mechanisms are obscure, especially when the costs of addiction are factored in. Second, although our ancestors in East Africa over 100,000 years ago may well have consumed psychoactive drugs, it is extraordinarily unlikely, given the way drugs are typically employed in hunter-gatherer societies, that these substances would have been available in sufficient quantities, and in appropriate forms, to support addictive patterns of consumption. Generally speaking, it is important to emphasize that demonstrating the usefulness of drug use should not be confused with claims that there are specific evolved mechanisms that have been selected *for* such use.

Mental health problems, including substance use disorders, can, however, be fruitfully addressed from an evolutionary perspective. In recent years, a number of evolutionary explanations of human mental disorders such as depression, autism, and sociopathy have been advanced (see Baron-Cohen, 1997). From an evolutionary perspective there are two ways of conceptualizing mental disorders (Murphy & Stich, 2000): as a result of malfunctions in specific evolved psychological mechanisms, or in terms of a mismatch between the evolved functions of the mind and novel environmental circumstances. Substance abuse and dependence can be conceptualized in both of these ways. The various psychological and physiological adaptations that we have outlined in this chapter as implicated in substance use—olfactory and gustatory preferences, evolved brain systems, and sensation-seeking traits—all were probably adaptive prior to the advent of potent and regularly available psychoactive drugs. But, with such substances always at hand and in novel forms, these mechanisms can lead to abusive patterns of drug use. In short, there is a discrepancy between our evolved psychological mechanisms and the current environment that contributes to drug-related problems.

It has also been suggested that some individuals have a genetic predisposition to develop what has been termed "reward deficiency syndrome" (Blum, Cull, Braverman, & Comings, 1997). According to Blum et al. (1997), some people possess a "biochemical inability to derive reward from ordinary, everyday activities" (p. 132). This deficit, it is argued, underlies a number of addictive and compulsive behaviors, including substance abuse, binge eating, and gambling problems. Furthermore, the excessive consumption of psychoactive drugs may result in changes in brain systems, which alter adaptive mechanisms relating to reward and the experience of positive and negative affect. Robinson and Berridge (2001) have suggested, for example, that repeated exposure to drugs results in the sensitization of reward systems related to drug "wanting," making drug use increasingly more alluring. Additionally, prolonged exposure to drugs may lead to a change in the "set-point" of the reward system, such that individuals find it difficult to obtain normal pleasures from life and drugs take on an even more prominent role in their lives (Koob & Le Moal, 1997). Drug abuse and dependence may reflect, therefore, genetically based or self-induced malfunctions of specific adaptive systems.

AN INTEGRATED EVOLUTIONARY
MODEL OF SUBSTANCE USE

The starting point for any analysis of why humans consume plant products for their psychoactive effects must begin with the question of why humans consume plants at all. The answer to this question may seem rather obvious: Plants are ingested because they are an essential part of our dietary requirements. This is of course not the only role that plants play in human lives, as they are also employed for medicinal, material, and consciousness-altering purposes. However, the predominant use of plants by people around the world, and no doubt by early hominids, was for food. Humans, like many other primate species are omnivores: we obtain the energy required to maintain vital bodily functions by consuming a wide array of plant and animal products. Omnivores in general, and primates in particular, typically exploit an extraordinarily wide array of plant and animal products. Howler monkeys, for example, will forage from more than 109 different plant species over the course of a year (Milton, 1987). Contemporary hunter-gatherers also exploit an enormous variety of different plants, as no doubt would have early hominids.

In order to be able to utilize such a plethora of different plants, humans must possess a rich and detailed knowledge of the flora in their environment. Indeed, the Kalam people of New Guinea can distinguish more than 1,400 plant and animal species by name (Diamond, 1993). Similar extensive knowledge is found among indigenous people throughout the world. For example, more than 1,000 plants are employed in the various preparations used in traditional Indian medicine (Dev, 1999). This extensive knowledge base is anchored, argues E. O. Wilson (1984) in his book *Biophilia* (see also Kellert & Wilson, 1993), in the innate human tendency to relate in motivational, cognitive, and affective terms with the natural biological world. The so-called biophilia hypothesis states that humans possess a collection of specialized learning rules that guide the acquisition of knowledge pertaining to living organisms. One such putative cognitive adaptation that has received support from anthropological research is the apparent ability of humans everywhere to classify plant and animal species in hierarchical fashion, in the same way that trained biologists do (see Atran, 1990; Berlin, Breedlove, & Raven, 1973). It would seem, on the basis of these findings, that humans possess an innate natural history intelligence that guides their exploration of the biological world around them.

This knowledge of the natural world serves specific pragmatic ends. Plants that offer significant nutritional benefits are retained by foraging groups. Moreover, combinations of plants are experimented with and combined in novel ways to produce nutritionally balanced diets (Dunbar, 1991). This capacity of human cultures to combine different types of foodstuff together in a nutritionally balanced fashion, probably reflects, Dunbar argues (1991, 1995), the operation of relatively general intellectual abilities, which enable humans to understand relevant cause and effect relationships in the world. Although humans have some innate taste preferences, such as a liking for sweet food and an aversion to bitter food, food selection appears to be strongly influenced by sociocultural factors (Rozin, 1996). Knowledge of food items and food combinations that prove beneficial are retained and transmitted from generation to generation within the cultural group. Such transmission of ideas is greatly facilitated by language and the ability to teach—themselves evolutionary adaptations—allowing the accumulation of knowledge over time, in a manner unprecedented in scope among other species.

The starting point for our integrated evolutionary model of substance use begins with these basic innate motivational, cognitive, affective, and sensory mechanisms that guide human exploration of the botanical world (see Figure 3.1).

The fruits of this exploration are further assessed via a collection of general and specific intellectual abilities that lead to the retention of some and the rejection of other plants as part of a culture's shared knowledge base. As well as unearthing plants that play a role in a culture's cuisine, these explorations of the natural environment also lead to the discovery of plants and plant products that serve other important functions. For example, plant products are utilized for important medical purposes throughout the world. They also serve as the basis for material culture, as they are used for building, ship making, binding, weaving, and so forth. Plants are also employed in other domains, such as in the production of dyes and arrow poisons (Balick & Cox, 1996).

Of course, some plants have additional properties, which in interaction with the human nervous system create changes in psychological functioning: plants are also employed for their psychoactive effects. Accordingly, we illustrate in our model how the human tendency to explore the flora in their environment leads to the discovery of plants that possess nutritional, psychoactive, medicinal, and other properties. These various categories of plant use should not necessarily be considered

Figure 3.1   An integrated evolutionary model of substance use

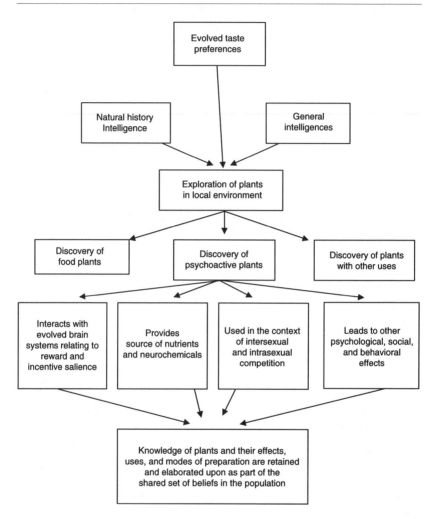

mutually exclusive in nature. Many plants and plant products can serve multiple functions and are variously employed as medicine, food, intoxicant, and for ritual and religious reasons. Further on in the model we can see how psychoactive plants can generate a variety of effects. They can, as detailed earlier, interact with evolved brain systems in ways that promote their use. Mechanisms evolved in the context of sexual selection may lead some individuals to explore the effects of psychoactive plants in various ways. Psychotropic plants also produce other effects, such as mental alertness and behavioral stimulation. Thus, drugs like caffeine and coca may be employed for their ability to promote physical and mental endurance, relatively independently of their other effects. The use of hallucinogens is also widespread across cultures and often serves important ritual-religious functions (Dobkin de Rios, 1990). Although these substances certainly operate on endogenous neurotransmitter systems, they are rarely employed in a compulsive way, and their widespread use is probably best interpreted in terms of interaction with indigenous cultural values and beliefs.

These various kinds of effects are not necessarily mutually exclusive, but rather reflect overlapping categories. For example, tobacco has been employed for its ability to produce positive effects on mood and cognition in some contexts (Pomerleau, 1997); while in others it generates profound shifts in consciousness that have specific religious significance (Goodman, 1993). Additionally, nicotine may activate natural brain reward systems (producing intrinsically pleasurable experiences), be employed as a way of medicating mental health problems such as depression, or be used in the context of youthful experimentation and risk taking.

SUMMARY

To reiterate, adopting an evolutionary approach to substance use is best seen as complementary to, rather than competing with, perspectives from other levels of analysis. Indeed, as Nesse (2002) points out, an evolutionary framework provides a useful starting point for *integrating* a diverse range of approaches. Our understanding of the psychological experiences generated by the use and abuse of drugs, for instance, can be informed from research on the evolved function of brain systems that provide the physiological basis of drug effects. Furthermore, although substance use might be influenced by innate sensory preferences, the knowledge of drugs and drug effects is essentially a cultural product and is shaped by norms, beliefs, and expectations. The interaction between culture and biology can be viewed as reciprocal in nature. For example, the spread of cultural practices relating to brewing and drinking beer is influenced by sensory preferences, nutritional considerations, and the effects of alcohol on the central nervous system. These practices, in turn, create selective environments that favor the evolution of physiological mechanisms for metabolizing alcohol and which ultimately influence patterns of subsequent use (see Dudley, 2000, 2002; Katz & Voigt, 1986). The precise nature of these dynamic relations between culture and biology will hinge on just how long humans have been consuming psychoactive drugs, which at our present state of knowledge remains unknown.

We suggest that there is no *single* evolutionary basis for substance use. Instead, the use of psychoactive drugs reflects the operation of a constellation of evolved mechanisms, some general and some more specific in nature. Indeed, drug use itself represents a heterogeneous class of behaviors. Furthermore, it is the interaction of these evolved systems with aspects of culture that dictate which drugs are employed and what purposes they serve. An evolutionary perspective on drug use suggests that the use of psychoactive substances is likely to be a part of our future as it has been an important part of of our past. In our attempts to alleviate the various problems that drugs can cause in contemporary societies, we must be mindful of the functions that drugs offer in people's lives and *why* the use of drugs is so appealing. An evolutionary approach offers some insights to these issues and provides the most salient level of analysis for addressing the question of why drug use is virtually ubiquitous throughout history and across cultures.

NOTES

1.   To the best of our knowledge, the only two cultural groups (prior to contact with Western culture) that did not use psychoactive drugs were the Inuit and the Maori.

2.   This is not entirely correct, as non-plant psychoactive substances such as hallucinogenic mushrooms have also been employed by traditional cultural groups.

3.   The causal relationship between substance use disorders and other mental health problems, however, has yet to be satisfactorily elucidated. Drugs may be employed to self-medicate pre-existing problems, they may cause or precipitate such problems, or both substance use and other mental disorders may be the result of other factors.

4

Drugs in History

INTRODUCTION

If you were to take a stroll along the main street of practically any city in the Western world, you would sooner or later come across an establishment devoted to the sale of a potent psychoactive drug. That drug is, of course, alcohol, and the assorted places that it may be found are variously termed "bars," "inns," "taverns," "pubs," "lounges," and "liquor stores." If you were then to enter this establishment, you would find the drug *ethyl alcohol* displayed in all its myriad forms. Propped up along the bar counter you might find a number of patrons, in various stages of intoxication, quaffing their favored variety of alcohol. Some of these individuals may be holding little white sticks trailing smoke, thus consuming another popular and potent psychoactive drug—tobacco. Perhaps also, depending on the nature of the establishment, there might be a harried *barista* in a corner churning out steaming cups of black liquid, representing a third ubiquitous psychoactive substance in Western society—coffee.[1]

None of this will strike the average reader as unusual, out of place, dangerous, or morally pernicious. But drawing back from our immersion in the present for a moment, we can ask the interesting and important question of why this triad of mind-altering substances—alcohol, tobacco, coffee—out of the dozens of potential candidates, are the accepted, legal drugs of choice in contemporary Western society. Alcohol, for sure, has been part of Western civilization for thousands of years (Sournia, 1990; Vallee, 1998), but so too have opium and cannabis (Abel, 1980; Booth, 1996). However, shops devoted to their sale and use would seem out of place, not to mention illegal, in most Western cities. Coffee and tobacco are, by contrast, relative newcomers to the Western drug scene; their regular use dates back only to the sixteenth century (Courtwright, 2001; Matthee, 1995). Why have these drugs dominated in Western culture, rather than other psychoactive substances such as kava, qat, betel, datura, and peyote? Furthermore, our use of these and other substances has changed dramatically over the course of the last two millennia: rates of consumption have risen and fallen, and so too have levels of abuse and dependence. Some drugs such as alcohol have been outlawed in several countries only to become legal again. Others, such as opium and cocaine, were once legal, but now are prohibited. And others still, like tobacco, although currently licit, are being slowly chivvied out of existence. What factor or factors can explain these patterns, and how do such factors contribute to our understanding of the way that drugs are used and abused in contemporary society? In the next two chapters, our aim is to answer these questions by drawing on the resources that history has to offer.

Interpreting the past, however, is no easy task; it lends itself at times to broad generalizations rather than to narrow testable hypotheses. In this chapter, therefore, we begin by discussing both the benefits and dangers of adopting a historical perspective and discuss the sorts of questions that can be fruitfully addressed at an historical level of analysis. We then provide a brief history of drugs and drug use, predominantly focusing on Western cultural contexts. Condensing 2,000 years of history into a single chapter naturally necessitates paring away many important details.[2] However, we aim to pick out some of the key ideas and developments and provide a backdrop for subsequent discussions on the ways that drugs have been used over the course of human history, and the various factors that are related to these patterns of use.

WHAT CAN HISTORY TELL US ABOUT SUBSTANCE USE AND ABUSE?

The study of the past can have social relevance in dealing with the problems and issues that we face in the present, as well as those that we might have to cope with in the future. In an oft-quoted remark, the philosopher George Santayana noted that "progress, far from consisting of change, depends on retentiveness. . . . Those who do not remember the past are condemned to repeat it." One of the roles of history is a kind of collective memory, which can inform us of what paths to avoid and which ones might be best to take (Marwick, 1989; Tosh, 1991). In short, the past cannot be ignored; the study of history is not a luxury but a necessity: Because the past "pervades the present—we'd better understand it" (Marwick, 1989, p. 17). History can enrich our understanding of the human condition in a number of important ways (see Tosh, 1991).

First, an analysis of history alerts us to the full range of human variability and thus the scope of possibilities that we have at our disposal. The different ways that drugs have been employed across history, for example, remind us that even such heavily abused drugs as heroin and cocaine are derived from substances—opium and coca—that have been employed to serve important therapeutic ends at different times in history. Second, the study of history also reminds us that there are multiple ways of responding to situations, each with its own advantages and disadvantages. For instance, the levels of alcohol use in society (and the problems associated with this use) have been reduced by increasing price, by controlling supply, by outright prohibition, and through the dissemination of health-related information (Edwards, 2000a; Hanson, 1999; Spring & Buss, 1977). Third, the study of history allows us to draw on precedents and make plausible predictions about future occasions. For example, it should by now be obvious that draconian penalties for drug use, by themselves, have a limited if not negligible impact on reducing levels of substance use and abuse (MacCoun & Reuter, 2001). Fourth, the study of history promotes an understanding of "what is enduring and what is ephemeral in our present circumstances" (Tosh, 1991, p. 18). That is, it encourages us to consider what features of human behavior and society are more or less open to change. It should be clear, for example, that the use of psychoactive substances is an enduring feature of human society, but the way those drugs are used and the relative benefit and harm that their use engenders are more malleable features of our cultural landscape. Fifth, history allows us to trace the origins and patterns of particular institutions, commodities, and ways of living, and thus allows us to see how the ways of the present are derived from patterns in the past. Attention to history, for instance, allows us to understand the rich cultural embeddedness of alcohol use as a social intoxicant in Western societies, or the use of kava as a way of delineating social hierarchies in various islands of the Pacific—and thus why such use may be difficult to alter. It should not be forgotten that the past leaves an indelible mark on present situations and circumstances. Last, and most generally, by drawing back from our understanding of drug use at the beginning of the twenty-first century and looking across the vast span of history, we can discern the influence of a range of forces that might not be so immediately apparent. A historical perspective can remind us of the complexity of the factors that underlie present trends and developments.

Despite the many benefits that can accrue from historical research, studying the past has its problems, and there are limits to the value of historical inquiry. The central limitation in historical research of any kind is a methodological one: How should we cope with the quantity and quality of the evidence that is available? Issues relating to the limitations of evidence, moreover, run in two seemingly opposite directions: sometimes there is not enough evidence and sometimes there is too much. Historians who study the remote past labor under the first difficulty—there is a dearth of relevant evidence from which to reconstruct past events. Inferences about the past sometimes have to be made on the basis of fragmentary evidence and limited sample sizes. For example, an archaeological find of a 14-year-old girl's skeleton in a burial tomb in Jerusalem dated to 315–392 C.E. provides suggestive evidence for the early medicinal use of cannabis (Zias, Stark, Sellgman, Levy, Werker, Breuer, & Mechoulam, 1993). On the basis of the girl's position and the skeletal remains of a full-term fetus in her pelvic area, she appears to be in the final stages of pregnancy or perhaps giving birth at the time of her death. Forensic analysis of the carbonated material in the abdomen area of the skeleton revealed the presence of cannabis, suggesting the use of this drug as an inhalant to facilitate the birth process. However, claims based on this isolated finding that the use of cannabis in medicinal contexts was widespread in the Middle East 1,500 years ago must be viewed as conjectural at best and need to be corroborated by other sorts of evidence.

In contrast to the paucity of evidence facing the historian who studies the distant past, those who research modern history are often overwhelmed with a plenitude of potentially relevant information. As the historian J. M. Roberts (1999) notes in the introduction to his history of the twentieth century, the central difficulty facing the contemporary historian is what to select for inclusion and what to leave out. Should we, for example, in pursuing the issue of medicinal cannabis, focus exclusively on controlled scientific studies using synthetic cannabinoids such as donabinol and nabilone, or should we also pay attention to the numerous anecdotal accounts of the efficacy of marijuana in relieving suffering in various medical contexts?

In making decisions about what material to include and what to omit, there lies the ever-present danger of selecting episodes and evidence that support one's own ideas, beliefs, expectations, and theories at the expense of conflicting findings. Those who champion the introduction of marijuana in medicinal contexts may, for example, place great emphasis on personal testimonies of its efficacy and ignore or downplay negative evidence from controlled scientific studies. As Tosh (1991) notes, the problems and concerns of the present can guide the sorts of *questions* that can be asked of the past, but they should not dictate the *answers* that are received. "The responsibility of historians," Tosh avers, "is clear: it is to provide a historical perspective which can inform debate rather than to serve any particular ideology" (p. 26). Given the often heated controversy that accompanies the subject of drugs, this is certainly sound advice.

In many respects, historical approaches to substance use and abuse lie at the margins of the broad, sprawling field of psychoactive drug studies—used more commonly as a way of introducing a topic rather than as a means to develop theories or to test ideas. However, a number of non-historians have made more thorough use of the rich historical literature, and historians themselves have made valuable contributions to our understanding of the multiple factors that shape the use (and abuse) of psychoactive drugs. The journal *Addiction* regularly includes articles of a historical nature, and many comprehensive handbooks of substance use and abuse contain chapters that explore historical perspectives (e.g., Galanter & Kleber, 1999). Given the vast intellectual terrain of global history and the numerous drugs that have been employed in varying contexts, we can at best provide a broad overview, picking out major themes, issues, and processes, while inevitably missing some details that a more fine-grained analysis might be able to discern. However, we believe that due attention to the history of substance use and abuse can advance our understanding of drugs and drug-related problems in many important ways.

A BRIEF HISTORY OF DRUGS

Throughout history and across cultures, humans have employed a vast repertoire of psychoactive substances. William Emboden (1979) in his book *Narcotic Plants*, for example, provides a list of more than 120 such plants, ranging from the familiar—cannabis, coffee, and coca—to the exotic—mandragora, iboga, and betel. Add to this list the cornucopia of drugs that have streamed forth from the laboratory in the past 200 years or so, and the range of psychoactive substances on offer is truly immense. However, despite these impressive resources, the widespread use of psychoactive drugs in Western society over the past 500 years is limited to a handful of substances. Excluding synthetic drugs, this list includes alcohol, cannabis, coca (and its derivatives, cocaine and crack), tobacco, opiates (opium, morphine, and heroin), and various caffeinated beverages (predominantly coffee, tea, and cocoa). We shall focus our discussion in this section primarily on the use of these substances in Western society. The use of other drugs, in various different cultural contexts, is described in more detail in Chapter 6.

Early History

The use of alcohol, in the form of beer and wine, was prominent in early Egyptian and Mesopotamian civilizations more than 6,000 years ago (Katz & Voigt, 1986; Newman, 2000; Vallee, 1998). As noted in Chapter 3, recipes for beer appear in early Sumerian texts, and beer played an important role in Mesopotamian cultures. Beer not only provided a valued source of nutrients, but it was also used as a medicine, social intoxicant, and as a substance imbued with religious significance (represented in the Sumerian pantheon by Ninkasi, the goddess of beer and brewing). Wine was also consumed in early Egyptian and Mesopotamian cultures, although it was viewed more as a luxury item consumed by the noble classes (Newman, 2000). Egyptian papyri dating to 1700 B.C.E. contain numerous references to alcoholic beverages and outline strict regulations for their use. Early alcohol-control measures were also employed. For instance, in response to a period of heavy alcohol consumption in Egyptian society around 1100 B.C.E., heavy taxes were levied on alcoholic drinks (el-Guebaly & el-Guebaly, 1981). Strict regulations relating to alcohol use were also laid down in 1800 B.C.E. by the Babylonian king Hammurabi, who, for example, decreed death by drowning for tavern owners who degraded the quality of their drinks.

Wine was a prominent feature of early Mediterranean cultures more than 2,000 years ago, and for the Greeks the drinking of wine was equated with happiness, well-being, and virility. Wine was employed in Greek cultures in a diverse range of contexts: as a social lubricant, an anesthetic, solvent, coolant, and disinfectant (Sherratt, 1991). The dangers of wine, however, were not unknown in classical times, and heavy drinking and drunkenness were frowned upon in Greek society, except on specific occasions. In general, wine was viewed as a "neutral spirit," capable of generating good or evil depending on the way it was used and the context of its consumption (Sherratt, 1991; Sournia, 1990). It appears as though patterns of alcohol use varied considerably over time in classical civilizations. Jellinek (1976), for example, traces the rise and fall of alcohol consumption in ancient Roman culture from periods of relative moderation (600 B.C.E.) to times of excess (around 100 C.E.). Jellinek suggests that "alcoholism" as we know it was widespread during this latter period, as contemporary authors such as Pliny (c. 23–70 C.E.) recognized many of the prominent features of alcohol dependence, like hand tremors and alcoholic blackouts. Furthermore, periodic calls for temperance suggest concern about excessive alcohol consumption in Roman society (Vallee, 1998).

Alcohol was not the only psychoactive substance familiar to individuals in the ancient world, as both opium and cannabis—among other substances—were also employed. Although the exact origins of the opium poppy remain unclear, archaeological evidence from Neolithic sites in Switzerland suggest that opium poppies were cultivated in this region more than 6,000 years ago (Booth, 1996). Ancient Egyptian hieroglyphs mention poppy juice as an important analgesic and sedative used, among other purposes, to quieten obstreperous infants (Davenport-Hines, 2001). The opium poppy was also well known from the earliest periods in Greek history and played an important role in both Greek and Roman medicine. The first reference to opium in Greek literature appears in Homer's *Odyssey*, where the drug is described as one that can "quiet all pains and quarrels" (Scarborough, 1995). Indeed, the juice of the opium poppy, as documented by Dioscorides (c. 70 C.E.) in his medical text *Materia Medica*, was employed in treating a wide range of ailments, including insomnia, pain, coughs, hysteria, and conditions of the digestive system (Scarborough, 1995). The extent of opium abuse and dependence is hard to gauge from the historical record, but Scarborough (1995) declares that the habit-forming properties of opium and its ability to generate tolerance were well recognized by Greek and Roman physicians, and prescription of the drug was suitably modified by this knowledge. The dangers of opium overdose were also well understood—a fact recognized by those wishing to employ opium as a poison (Davenport-Hines, 2001).

The origin of the cannabis plant probably lies in regions of Central Asia, and its cultivation and use extends back at least 6,000 years in China, where remains of hemp fibers have been found in archaeological sites (Peters & Nahas, 1999). It is likely that hemp was primarily cultivated in China—initially, at least—for its strong and versatile fiber rather than for its mind-altering capacities. Chinese medical texts also suggest that cannabis was employed in a diverse array of therapeutic contexts, including the treatment of gout, rheumatism, malaria, and "menstrual fatigue" (Abel, 1980). The use of cannabis in India is well documented from at least 4,000 years ago; it was employed in both medicinal and religious contexts (Abel, 1980). The use of cannabis for its psychoactive effects is also mentioned by Herodotus (446 B.C.E.), who describes a Scythian purification ritual where hemp seeds are tossed onto hot stones inside a closed tent to give off intoxicating vapors that moved the occupants to "howl with pleasure" (Sherratt, 1995, p. 27). This account is supported by archaeological evidence unearthed in Siberia, where burial mounds have been found accompanied with wooden frame tents, stones, and hemp seeds. Sherratt (1995) suggests that "the practice of burning cannabis as a narcotic is a tradition which goes back in this area [Romania and the Caucasus] some five or six thousand years and was the focus of social and religious rituals of the pastoral people of central Eurasia in pre-historic and early historic times" (p. 27).

The use of alcohol, opium, and cannabis for various purposes was thus well recognized in the major centers of civilization—Mesopotamia, Egypt, the Mediterranean, India, and China—from at least 6,000 years ago. Moreover, the development of trade routes—by both land and sea—connecting these cultures facilitated the spread of knowledge regarding the use of these substances. To what extent drugs were a "problem" in the ancient world is difficult to ascertain. Certainly, as noted previously, harmful patterns of use were recognized and various policies implemented to control drug use. However, alcohol, opium, and cannabis were all employed in social, medicinal, and ritual-religious contexts, and their use (in specific cultures at least) was generally accepted.

In Europe the use of opium and cannabis was limited in the Middle Ages, while alcohol remained the most common psychoactive substance employed. As urban centers grew and expanded across Europe, finding clean and uncontaminated sources of water became increasingly difficult. Alcohol, therefore, in the form of ale, beer, or wine, was not just a social and recreational intoxicant but also a valued source of uncontaminated fluids and much-needed calories (Spring & Buss, 1977; Vallee, 1998). While the rise of Islam in Near and Middle Eastern cultures in the seventh century ushered in the prohibition of alcohol in these regions, throughout most of Europe drinking was an integral part of daily life. As Warner (1992) summarizes, "Indeed, with the exception of the very poor, the population of medieval Europe drank alcohol steadily throughout the day, starting at breakfast and continuing well into the night" (p. 409). Little concern, however, was shown toward alcohol, although excessive drunkenness was condemned—becoming an offense under civil law in England in the sixteenth century (Edwards, 2000a). Given its integration into all parts of daily life, alcohol itself was as little to blame for excessive intoxication as food was for gluttony.

The use of cannabis and opium, although limited in European contexts, flourished elsewhere in the world during the first millennium. The opium poppy and its various uses spread via Middle Eastern trade routes to Europe, India, and Asia. Opium was widely employed in Arabic cultures during this period. The tenth-century poet and physician Avicenna (980–1037), for instance, extolled the praises of opium as a medical agent, valuable in treating pain, dysentery, diarrhea, eye disease, and other ailments (Booth, 1996). Between the ninth and thirteenth centuries, the use of cannabis spread widely throughout Arab cultures, aided perhaps by Islamic injunctions against the consumption of alcoholic beverages (Page, 1999). As in Chinese and Indian cultures, cannabis was employed in a wide variety of different contexts. The Sufis used cannabis as an aid to attaining mystical insight and religious ecstasy; Arab physicians exploited its medicinal properties; and it was also used in more secular contexts as a popular recreational intoxicant (Abel, 1980). From Islamic cultures in the Middle East and North Africa, cannabis spread down the east coast of Africa in the fourteenth century, and from there to central and southern regions. Its use remains widespread among various African people, including the Bantu, Bushmen, and Hottentots, where it is employed in a variety of social and ritual-religious contexts (Abel, 1980).

Although the use of cannabis was limited in Europe during the Middle Ages, it was certainly not unknown during this period. The strong, durable fibers of the cannabis plant (typically referred to as "hemp" in this context), for instance, were exploited in the manufacture of ropes, clothes, canvas, and paper. The importance of hemp as a commodity is illustrated by King Henry VIII's decree that all English farmers must set aside a percentage of their arable land for its cultivation.

References to cannabis as a medicinal agent also periodically occurred throughout the Middle Ages and early modern period. Robert Burton (1621) recommended that it be tried for depression, and many books about plants (known as "herbals"), such as *Culpepers* in the seventeenth century, prescribed cannabis for headaches, jaundice, diarrhea, and rheumatic pain (Crawford, 2002). The use of cannabis in recreational and social contexts, however, was—with isolated exceptions—virtually unknown in Western cultures until the twentieth century. The use of opium, by contrast, was becoming increasingly widespread in Western nations from the seventeenth century on, although by this time a number of other important psychoactive substances were also being integrated into European society, including coffee, tea, tobacco, and coca.

Drugs and the Birth of the Modern World

The coffee tree is native to Ethiopia in East Africa, and coffee has been an important part of Ethiopian culture since at least the tenth century (Topik, 2000; Pendergrast, 1999). By the late fifteenth century, coffee had spread across the Red Sea to Yemen, where it was employed by devotees of the Sufi religious order to enable them to stay awake during their long devotional exercises. From Yemen the use of coffee unfurled along Near Eastern trade routes in the sixteenth century: to Mecca, Cairo, Damascus, and Constantinople. In 1645 the first European coffeehouse opened in Venice, and by 1661 London had more than a dozen of these new establishments. Throughout the eighteenth century, European imperial interests spread the growth of coffee to their various newly acquired dominions: the Dutch in Java, the French in Haiti, the Portuguese in Brazil, and the Spanish in South and Central America (Matthee, 1995; Pendergrast, 1999; Smith, 1995). Consequently, with more widespread cultivation and falling prices, European consumption of coffee increased dramatically over the course of the eighteenth century: from an estimated 2 million pounds to more than 120 million pounds per annum (Goodman, 1995).

However, the spread of coffee in the Near East and its integration into European society was not universally welcomed. The consumption of coffee throughout the Ottoman Empire in the sixteenth and seventeenth centuries was a highly social affair. Groups of (typically) men would gather in coffeehouses to talk, play chess, listen to live music, and of course to imbibe coffee (and often other psychoactive substances) (Hattox, 1985). The impact of coffee on social habits in the Near East, however, was subject to criticism by those who perceived that coffee was a threat to social order in Islamic society. Subsequently, attempts to repress coffee in the sixteenth century included raids on coffeehouses, temporary prohibitions on coffee consumption, and vigorous debate. Such concerns might seem odd to the modern reader, but as with any drug it is important to pay attention to the wider context of consumption. Worries over coffee use in Islamic lands in the sixteenth century arose not so much because of the putative harmful effects of coffee itself—although there were such concerns—but rather due to the manner of its use. In particular, concern was voiced over the role of coffeehouses in encouraging idleness and promoting social discourse of a political, potentially revolutionary, nature. More broadly, the social ethic of Islamic society emphasized sobriety, moderation, and a proper sense of decorum—values that coffee and coffeehouses appeared to challenge (Hattox, 1985).

Similar apprehensions regarding coffee and coffeehouses arose in Europe in the seventeenth century. In England, for example, a group of women, piqued at the time their men folk were spending in these newly opened and exclusively male establishments, organized a petition against coffee in which they asserted, "[Why do our men] trifle away their time, scald their Chops, and spend their Money, all for a little base, black, thick, nasty bitter stinking, nauseous Puddle water?" (cited in Pendergrast, 1999, p. xv) Continuing their attack where it could be assumed to most hurt, they further suggested, "Excessive use of that Newfangled, Abominable, Heathenish Liquor called *Coffee*, which . . . has so *Eunucht* our Husbands, and *Crippled* our more kind *gallants* . . . they come from it with nothing *moist* but their snotty Noses, nothing *stiffe* but their Joints, nor *standing* but their Ears" (cited in Pendergrast, 1999, p. 13). In response, King Charles II issued a proclamation in 1675 calling for the closure of coffeehouses. This demand, however, in response to heated protest, was withdrawn in ten days. By the eighteenth century, as coffee use became more widespread, dissension diminished. Part of the reason for this growing acceptance was coffee's purported medicinal benefits, but perhaps more important, coffee was promoted as a substance that encouraged sobriety and respectability and was thus seen as an important antidote and alternative to excessive alcohol consumption (Goodman, 1995; Schivelbusch, 1992; Smith, 1995). Moreover, as cultivation, production, and distribution of coffee increased throughout the eighteenth century, it became an important source of revenue, and thus any concerns over its use were tempered by economic interests.

In many respects, tea played a secondary role to coffee among European interests in the early modern period. Although tea had been valued in its native China since the Han dynasty period (206 B.C.E.–221 C.E.) (Evans, 1992), it wasn't until 1658 that it was offered for sale in London coffeehouses (Weisburger & Comer, 2000). However, by the eighteenth century the consumption of tea in England had become a ritual, social affair—especially for women, who were excluded from the male domains of tavern and coffeehouse. Under British colonial rule, tea was cultivated in earnest in India and Ceylon in the nineteenth century, ensuring a steady supply to Britain and her colonies—although still supplemented by imports from China. With the exception of the Netherlands, tea was less popular in Continental Europe and, after the Boston and Charleston "tea parties," it played a limited role in American society as well. The consumption of tea, however, has remained important in China and Japan, where it developed into an elaborate ritualized practice.

The introduction of coffee and tea to Europe in the early modern period wrought important changes in the social and economic fabric of Western society. Both substances were not only valued for their capacity to promote sobriety and industry during a time of social and political reform, but also generated substantial revenues, thus providing an impetus for the colonial aspirations of European nations. However, it was two drugs—coca and tobacco—"discovered" in the New World in the early sixteenth century that were to ultimately have a more lasting impact on our current understanding of drugs and drug-related problems.

Archaeological evidence suggests that coca has been employed in various regions of South America for over two millennia. Dried coca leaves have been found in Peruvian mummy bundles dated to 2,000 years ago, and ancient pottery vessels depict men with distended cheeks—the characteristic feature of the coca chewer. It is likely that coca in these cultures was used for various pragmatic, medicinal, and ritual-religious purposes, such as to reduce fatigue, suppress appetite, and to facilitate trance-like states employed by shamans for divination and healing (Dobkin de Rios, 1990). These functions of coca are still found in many regions of South America, such as among the Barasana in Northwest Amazonia (Hugh-Jones, 1995). Given the relatively low levels of cocaine extracted from coca leaves via traditional methods of consumption, it is likely that very few problems arose from such use.

Although the use of coca was restricted to specific cultural groups in South America prior to European contact, tobacco was widely employed throughout the Americas. Tobacco is derived from plants of the genus *Nicotiana*, of which there are at least 60 species. These are predominantly found in North and South America, but are also native to Australia and the South Pacific (Goodman, 1993). Two widely diffused varieties subsequently cultivated by Europeans are *Nicotiana tabacum* and *Nicotiana rustica*, both of which are hybrids of species native to South America. By the time Columbus set foot in the New World in 1492, the cultivation and use of tobacco was widespread among the native people of both North and South America and was employed in a diverse array of contexts (Goodman, 1993; von Gernet, 1995). As Goodman (1993) summarizes, tobacco's "uses ranged from the purely symbolic to the medicinal; from its role as a hallucinogen in shamanistic practice and ritual to ceremonial and formal social functions; from profane to religious use; from its identification with myth and the supernatural to the formal ritualism of social experiences" (pp. 24–25).

Tobacco's role in medicine was especially prominent; it was employed for treating asthma, chills, fever, coughs, headaches, and virtually any other ailment that might arise (Goodman, 1993). Although little has been written on the topic of tobacco dependence among Native Americans, the ubiquity of tobacco use (especially among males) clearly indicates that tobacco addiction was fairly widespread. For example, von Gernet (1995) reports that at the time of European contact, Iroquoian- and Algonquian-speaking people (the men at least) were rarely seen without a pipe in their mouths, and every man carried a pipe and tobacco pouch with him at all times. Shamans attributed the craving for tobacco to the "hunger pangs of the spirits," indicating that widespread use also probably entailed significant levels of dependence (Goodman, 1993).

The use of tobacco spread rapidly across the globe in the sixteenth and seventeenth centuries. First employed by sailors and soldiers, the tobacco habit was taken up by the English in the sixteenth century, who introduced it to Russia in the 1560s. By the last half of the sixteenth century, tobacco was cultivated in England, Belgium, Spain, Italy, and Switzerland. And by the early seventeenth century, via Dutch and Portuguese traders, it had spread to Africa and Asia (Goodman, 1993; Matthee, 1995). As production increased and the price of tobacco dropped, it was rapidly transformed in the seventeenth century from a luxury item to a commodity of mass consumption. For example, in England in 1603, 25,000 pounds of tobacco were imported, a figure that had ballooned to 38 million pounds by 1700. The revenue opportunities from this transformation were quickly seized upon, as the relatively inelastic demand for tobacco proved an important source of income, via taxation, for England, France, Spain, and other European nations (Price, 1995).

Economic interests, therefore, certainly played an important role in the global spread of tobacco, as did tobacco's ability to produce dependence (without obvious intoxication) and the relative ease with which it could be cultivated and transported. However, this trend of rising tobacco use in the seventeenth century must also be understood in terms of prevailing medical beliefs. Tobacco was lauded as the "panacea of panaceas" in Western medicine (Stewart, 1967); a "holy herb" or "sacred weed" with manifold therapeutic possibilities (Goodman, 1993). In her exhaustive survey of the medicinal use of tobacco between 1492 and 1860, Stewart (1967) identified no less than 254 diseases and other conditions—including aches, pains, gout, madness, syphilis, and even the plague—for which tobacco was employed as treatment. Indeed, tobacco's putative role as a prophylactic against the Black Death was so widely recognized that in 1665 Eton schoolboys were *required* to smoke and were whipped for not complying (Walker, 1980).

However, opinions on tobacco use, although on balance favorable in the sixteenth and seventeenth centuries, were by no means unequivocally so. A fierce debate raged in Elizabethan England over the virtues of tobacco, and King James I in his *Counterblaste to Tobacco*, published in 1604, made his distaste clear, as he fulminated:

A custome lathsome to the eye, hateful to the nose, harmefull to the braine, dangerous to the lungs, and the blacke stinking fume thereof, nearest resembling the horrible Stigian smoke of the pit that is bottomlesse. (James I, 1616/1971, p. 222)

Tobacco received similarly critical responses in other parts of Europe. It was, for example, prohibited in Russia during parts of the seventeenth century, and beatings and exile awaited those who failed to comply. Smoking bans were also enacted in various regions of present-day Germany and Austria. And in Lüneberg in 1691, persons found smoking tobacco within the city walls could be put to death (Proctor, 1997). Part of the reason for this opprobrium resided in the very real fire risks posed by tobacco consumption, but concern was also voiced over the health effects and moral propriety of smoking. In 1726, for example, Cotton Mather, a physician and clergyman from

Massachusetts, claimed that snuff was a "leader to the coffin" (cited in Stewart, 1967, p.243), while Benjamin Rush, better known for his views on alcohol, also warned against the dangers of tobacco consumption.

In 1828 the pharmacologically active alkaloid in tobacco was isolated by the German physician Wilhelm Posselt and chemist Karl Reimann and named "nicotine" after the Frenchman Jean Nicot, who had enthusiastically promoted tobacco in the sixteenth century. The role of tobacco, and its newly discovered alkaloid, nicotine, declined in therapeutic contexts in the late eighteenth and nineteenth centuries. The use of tobacco in social and recreational contexts, however, continued unabated. Indeed, the introduction of cigarettes in the nineteenth century, accompanied by aggressive and innovate marketing techniques, pushed tobacco consumption even higher. In the United States, for example, 54 cigarettes were consumed per capita in the year 1900, while by 1963 this figure had climbed to more than 4,000 (Slade, 1989).

While tobacco made rapid inroads into European society from its introduction in the sixteenth century, little interest was shown in coca until some three centuries later. The Spanish were initially ambivalent toward the indigenous use of coca. Spanish missionaries deplored its use because they were of the opinion that it impeded the advance of Catholicism and the conversion of the "natives." Coca was described as "a useless object liable to promote the practices and superstitions of the Indians" (cited in Lewin, 1924/1974, p. 239), and efforts were made to suppress its use. Pious concerns over the fate of Indian souls, however, were fairly easily put to one side as the pecuniary advantages of coca use became apparent. Not only could coca production be taxed, providing valuable revenue, but its use also promoted hard labor in the newly discovered silver mines, such as at Potosí in Bolivia. The native miners were ill fed, ill housed, and worked long hours in difficult conditions, but they were liberally supplied with coca leaves, which helped to reduce fatigue and stave off hunger (Karch, 1998).

Nicholas Monardes of Spain provided a description of coca in his text on medical plants of the New World in 1574 (translated into English in 1596). However, this description sparked little interest in Europe. Partly, it would seem, because coca leaves simply do not travel well, and their active ingredients tend to lose their potency over the course of the long ocean journey from South America. European interest in coca, however, grew rapidly in the latter half of the nineteenth century. This was due, in no small part, to the isolation of cocaine—the active alkaloid in the coca leaf—in 1859 by Albert Niemann, a graduate student at Göttingen (Freud, 1884; Karch, 1998). The effects of cocaine, once isolated from the coca leaf and produced in sufficient quantities, were now clearly manifest.

The putative benefits of cocaine were made available to the wider public in 1868 in the form of Vin Mariani, a coca-based wine developed and enthusiastically marketed by the Corsican Angelo Mariani (Karch, 1998). Others, such as Mark Twain, delighted by his personal experiences with the drug, longed to open up a trade in coca to the world, and Robert Louis Stevenson completed his novel *The Strange Case of Dr Jekyll and Mr Hyde* in six cocaine-fueled days and nights (Plant, 2000). By the late 1880s, commercial quantities of cocaine were readily available and were employed in various wines, tonics, medications, and beverages (Courtwright, 1995; Karch, 1998; Musto, 1991). The story of Sigmund Freud's brief and unpropitious flirtation with cocaine is well known. In *Über Coca*, published in 1884, Freud was enthusiastic about the manifold possibilities that cocaine had to offer. Not only did cocaine reduce fatigue and promote physical vigor, Freud averred, but it could also be used for digestive disorders of the stomach, asthma, as an aphrodisiac, and most ironically to the modern reader, in the treatment of morphine and alcohol addiction. Freud clearly rejected the possibility that cocaine itself might result in dependence, as he stated, "The treatment of morphine addiction with coca does not, therefore, result merely in the exchange of one kind of addiction for another—it does not turn the morphine addict into a *coquero*; the use of coca is only temporary" (Freud, 1884/1974, p. 71). On the basis of this confidence about the curative powers of cocaine, Freud prescribed liberal doses to his friend and colleague Ernst von Fleischl-Marxow, who was dependent on morphine. Fleischl-Marxow rapidly became dependent on cocaine, by 1885 was injecting a gram daily (Musto, 1974), and ultimately died of cocaine poisoning in 1891. Ironically, the most important medical application of cocaine in the nineteenth century—as a local anesthetic—was only alluded to in passing by Freud. This application was subsequently taken up by Carl Koller, who demonstrated cocaine's efficacy as a local anesthetic in the context of eye, nose, and mouth surgery (Karch, 1998).

Although cocaine was rapidly becoming incorporated into Western medicine in the late nineteenth century, undoubtedly opium had been the most important therapeutic drug employed in Western society in the preceding three centuries. The use of opium was widespread in both Britain and America during this period and was employed for a variety of medicinal purposes: as a sedative, painkiller, anti-malarial agent, for dysentery and diarrhea, and for coughs and respiratory ailments. Opium was administered in various forms, such as cakes, lozenges, tinctures, and wines (Berridge & Edwards, 1981). Laudanum, a combination of alcohol and opium devised by the English physician Thomas Sydenham (1624–1689), was a particularly popular source of opium, and was in widespread use until well into the nineteenth century. Given the paucity of effective treatments at this time, opium was understandably a valued commodity in the physician's limited medical armory. In particular, the ability of opium to relieve diarrhea—a common and life-threatening complaint in an era of dysentery and cholera—probably saved many thousand of lives. Given the alternative treatments in vogue, such as bloodletting, cupping, blistering, and so forth, opium must have been viewed as a valuable palliative for physician and patient alike (Berridge & Edwards, 1981; Booth, 1996).

Medicinal use of opium in Britain during this time was not restricted to prescription by physicians. Instead, for most of the population—who could not afford the luxury of doctors—the use of opium was a normal part of relieving personal pain and distress, much as taking aspirin is today. Opium, in different forms and preparations, was readily available for purchase throughout Britain for much of the nineteenth century. As Berridge and Edwards (1981) state, "The corner shop, and not the doctor's surgery, was the center of popular opium use" (p. 30). This pattern of use reflects a long history of opium as a folk remedy in Britain, usually taken in the form of poppy-head tea. The craze in patent medicines in the second half of the nineteenth century, in both Britain and America, served to extend opium's reach, as both opiates and cocaine were frequent and undisclosed ingredients in many a "magical" elixir—even found in putative *cures* for opiate dependence (Musto, 1999).

A number of important developments in the use of opium occurred in the nineteenth century, which contributed in significant ways to patterns of use and dependence. In 1803 an alkaloid was first isolated from crude opium by the German pharmacist's assistant Friedrich Setürner, which he termed "morphium" after Morpheus, the Greek god of sleep and dreams. Although this discovery was initially ignored, morphium, morphia, or morphine, as it was variously called, began to be used in Europe and America in the 1820s by physicians, who recognized its superior analgesic properties. Other alkaloids of opium, such as codeine, narvaine, and thebaine, were also isolated in the nineteenth century. In 1853, the hypodermic syringe was introduced into medicine. Physicians quickly recognized that morphine administered via injection could alleviate pain and distress far more rapidly than opium taken orally. In 1878 the German pharmaceutical firm Bayer and Company first marketed a preparation created from morphine: diacetylmorphine, or heroin. Originally marketed as a cough suppressant and even touted as a non-addictive cure for morphine dependence, heroin is a substance three times more potent than morphine. Furthermore, when injected, heroin produces a powerful and euphoric "rush" because of its ability to rapidly cross the blood brain barrier (Julien, 1998).

These new technological developments, coupled with the ready availability of opiates, contributed to rising levels of dependence in both Britain and America in the nineteenth century. As early as 1700, John Jones (1645–1709), in his book *Mysteries of Opium Reveal'd*, recognized the possibility of opium dependence and described in detail the pattern of withdrawal that occurred after cessation of chronic opium use (Davenport-Hines, 2001). Opium dependence occurred at all levels of British society, although it was among the wealthier classes, to whom opium was prescribed by physicians, that it was most frequently encountered. Given that opiates were employed in treating a diverse array of problems—pain, diarrhea, neuralgia, malaria, asthma, bronchitis, and even masturbation and nymphomania—it is hardly surprising that the primary cause of opiate dependence during this period was iatrogenic in nature. Patients were even given take-home doses of morphine and syringes with which to inject them. As a consequence of these various factors, levels of opiate dependence in the United States rose from 0.72 individuals per thousand in 1842 to 4.59 per thousand in the 1890s (Courtwright, 1982).

As the nineteenth century drew to a close, the harmful effects of cocaine were also becoming increasingly recognized. Reports of dependence on cocaine became more widespread, and by 1891 at least 13 deaths in the United States could be attributed to cocaine poisoning. By 1910 President William Taft had proclaimed cocaine as public enemy number one, and patterns of use had shifted, in large part, from medical to recreational. The level of use during this period increased dramatically—some 500% between 1893 and 1903—forming what Courtwright (1995) has termed "America's first cocaine epidemic." The use of cocaine at the end of the nineteenth and beginning of the twentieth centuries was also increasing elsewhere: in Canada, Germany, and the United Kingdom (Courtwright, 1995; Spillane, 1998). However, in England, despite the literary role model of Sherlock Holmes, cocaine use remained at relatively low levels until after the First World War, when a fashion for cocaine emerged as part of a craze for "all things American" in the 1920s (Berridge, 1988; Kohn, 1992).

The use of opiates in recreational and social contexts did not become widespread until the twentieth century, and thus only a small percentage of opiate dependence arose from non-medicinal use. Opium certainly was employed as a recreational intoxicant by the working classes in Britain in the nineteenth century (Berridge & Edwards, 1981). The recreational use of opium in early nineteenth century Britain was also associated with such figures as Samuel Taylor Coleridge, John Keats, and Thomas De Quincey. It was De Quincey's *Confessions of an Opium Eater*, published in 1822, that brought this pattern of opium use to a wider audience, and helped to fuel a small but notable group of users for whom opium use was both a means for consciousness expansion and a badge of social identity. From the middle of the nineteenth century, with a large influx of Chinese immigrants into the United States, the practice of opium smoking became prevalent in some areas. Opium smoking by Chinese was a highly social affair, carried out in a communal place, and served, in part, as an affirmation of cultural identity. From about 1870 opium smoking was also taken up by a new type of user: young white males, typically of working-class origin. For this type of user, opium smoking was very much recreational in character, although due to the laborious, almost ritual nature of opium smoking, it was also a social affair and served as a marker of social identity. Courtwright (1982) summarizes these patterns of use: "In virtually all particulars—peer reinforcement, exclusive membership, common argot, and shared rules of appropriate behavior—opium smoking anticipated the pattern of the various twentieth-century drug cultures" (p. 74). Unlike the use of opium for medicinal purposes, opium smoking was considered a vice with no therapeutic value. This belief was partly fueled by racist attitudes toward Chinese immigrants, who were portrayed as corrupting young European men, and especially women, with their opium dens and foreign ways. As a consequence, various cities passed ordinances penalizing opium smoking in the 1870s, although these did little to curb the practice (Courtwright, 1982).

Alcohol, although more firmly entrenched in the cultural milieu of Western society, was not immune to the kind of criticism that was being directed at opium and cocaine at the end of the nineteenth century. Indeed, concerns over alcohol use had been building throughout the eighteenth and nineteenth centuries. Heavy drinking was the norm in Britain in the early modern period, and this pattern of consumption was readily transported with colonists and convicts to various regions around the world. The use of alcohol, for example, was pervasive in early American society. As in England, alcohol was an accepted, even essential substance, while excessive consumption and drunkenness were condemned (Rorabaugh, 1979). In Australia, founded predominantly by convicts and jailors, rum was both an important form of currency and a favored recreational intoxicant (Hughes, 1987; Ward, 1992). Early drinking patterns in Australia have been described as the heaviest anywhere in the world at any time, reaching 4 1/2 gallons per capita annually in New South Wales by the 1830s (Dingle, 1980). Given the cultural transplantation of heavy drinking patterns from Britain into a harsh and unforgiving new environment with little to offer in the way of leisure or diversion, this was hardly surprising.

Various concerns over the effects of alcohol consumption had been voiced at numerous points throughout history, but it was in the nineteenth century in Britain, America, Australia, and elsewhere that such fears were to find more widespread acceptance. Important texts on alcohol abuse by the Englishman Thomas Trotter (1760–1832) and the American Benjamin Rush (1743–1813) clearly outlined the manifold harm that alcohol could cause and urged for abstinence or at least moderate consumption. This sea change in attitudes toward alcohol was most clearly manifest in the proliferation of temperance societies in the nineteenth century. In 1826, the American Temperance Society was born, and by the late 1830s there were more than 800 such organizations with a combined membership of more than 1.5 million individuals (Hanson, 1999; Sournia, 1990). Initially, the focus of these groups, as their name implies, was directed at encouraging moderation in drinking habits. Following Rush's "moral thermometer," which outlined the harm that various kinds of alcoholic beverages would bring, spirits were particularly targeted as agents of disease, while moderation in the consumption of other alcoholic beverages was accepted. From the middle of the nineteenth century, however, calls for temperance had escalated into cries for abstinence, as societies like the Washingtonians urged individuals to take the pledge and renounce alcoholic beverages entirely. And with some success: By 1843 more than a million converts had pledged their allegiance to teetotalism (Pegram, 1998). Other abstinence societies, such as the Women's Christian Temperance Union (1873) and the anti-saloon league (1893), emerged in the second half of the nineteenth century, by which time *any* alcohol use was beginning to be viewed as problematic (Hanson, 1999). Calls for the prohibition of alcohol increased in intensity throughout the nineteenth century; however, it was changes in the legal status of various other substances that were to profoundly shape attitudes toward drugs in the twentieth century.

A New Order: Drugs in the Twentieth Century

The early decades of the twentieth century were to prove formative in shaping modern attitudes toward drugs. The transformation of opiate use from medical necessity to criminal act clearly illustrates these changes. Although opium smoking was commonly viewed as a vice, the medical use of opium and morphine was also increasingly called into question. For example, various anti-morphine laws were enacted in the United States in the 1890s, as public awareness of the dangers of morphine use increased (Musto, 1999). In Britain, the Poisons and Pharmacy Act, which put restrictions on who could sell opium and how, was enacted in1868. This act, however, did not cover the lucrative patent medicine industry until 1892. In the United States, the Pure Food and Drug Act, which demanded the accurate identification of opiates (and other "narcotics") in all patent medicines, was introduced in 1906. With reliable labeling, the public could make their own choices about whether they wanted to carry on using such nostrums, and as a consequence the sale of patent medicines containing opiates and other drugs such as cocaine dropped by a third (Musto, 1999). Three years later, in 1909, the Smoking Opium Exclusion Act was passed, which outlawed the importation of opium for other than medicinal purposes and made the possession of opium for smoking a criminal offense. In 1911, the first international conference on opium at The Hague brought the question of opiate control into the international spotlight. Signatories at this convention agreed to restrict opium consumption to legitimate purposes, although they left the details of implementation to individual nation states. The transformation in the legal status of opiates and cocaine in the United States was made complete in 1914, when the Harrison Narcotics Act was passed, criminalizing all use and sale of opiates and cocaine outside of legitimate medical channels. By 1920, after two further international opium conferences, Britain had passed the Dangerous Drug Act, which effectively criminalized all use of opiates except by physician's prescription (Booth, 1996).

Thus in both Britain and the United States the use of opium was gradually but firmly taken from the hands of the populace and placed under medical and legal control in the first few decades of the twentieth century. There were a number of reasons for this transformation in the status of opium. First, as we noted earlier, there was growing concern over opiate dependence and the harm caused by opiates during the second half of the nineteenth century. Second, important changes in medicine itself were occurring at this time. New medical agents and treatments were being introduced, such as aspirin, vaccinations, and public health measures, which reduced the need for opium and morphine as therapeutic agents (Acker, 1995; Courtwright, 1982; Porter, 1997). In line with new developments in medical theory, drugs were being developed that could purportedly target specific disorders and conditions—the days of opium (and morphine) as panaceas were thus drawing to an end. Changes in the role of physicians in society also played a role in modifications to the use of opiates, as doctors were gaining more and more control over who could take what drugs and for what reasons. Physicians were also becoming acutely aware of their role in increasing levels of opiate dependence, and as a consequence, by 1910, had dramatically cut their prescription of these substances (Acker, 1995).

Although the use of cannabis in the United States in recreational contexts was limited, in the spirit of the times legal restrictions on its use were also put into place. In 1915 the importation of cannabis to America was outlawed except for medical purposes, and by the 1930s a number of states had banned cannabis use entirely. A raft of critical articles emerged during this period, testifying to the dangerous consequences of cannabis use. One notable example was produced by Narcotic Commissioner Harry Anslinger and Courtney Cooper (1937) and given the alarmist title "Marihuana: Assassin of Youth." In this article, the dangers of cannabis use were spelled out in lurid detail:

> The sprawled body of a young girl lay crushed on the sidewalk the other day after a plunge from the fifth story of a Chicago apartment house. Everyone called it suicide, but actually it was murder. The killer was a narcotic known to America as marijuana, and to history as hashish. It is a narcotic used in the form of cigarettes, comparatively new to the United States and as dangerous as a coiled rattlesnake. (p. 19)

Legislation reflected such emerging concerns, and in 1937 this had culminated in the Marihuana Tax Act, which by levying a $100 per pound tax on all (non-medicinal) supplies of cannabis, effectively outlawed its supply and use, which by now were illegal anyway in many states (Jonnes, 1996).

By 1920 the transfiguration of drug use in American and British societies had been completed. This transformation, Courtwright (1982) suggests, entailed changes in both the typical pattern of opiate use—from medicinal to primarily social and recreational—and also in the *type* of user encountered. In the United States, throughout the nineteenth century, the modal kind of individual dependent on opiates (whether opium or morphine) was female, white, middle-class, and over 30. These individuals were likely to have become dependent on opiates as a consequence of prescription by a physician for some medical complaint. By 1920, this kind of user and pattern of use had virtually disappeared. The typical pattern now observed was marked by recreational and social use, and by users who were overwhelmingly young, white, lower-class, and male. Heroin—whether snorted or injected—was, by 1920, becoming the opiate of choice for such users. Similar developments occurred with cocaine, as medicinal use gave way to recreational consumption early in the twentieth century. In sum, the legal, social, and political developments that occurred in the first three decades of the twentieth century were to profoundly shape future attitudes toward a wide range of psychoactive substances.

Alcohol, which had been subject to vigorous attack by temperance societies throughout the nineteenth century, also became a prominent target of legislative reform. By 1855, 13 states in America had instigated prohibition (Edwards, 2000). Following World War I, when abstinence from alcohol was linked to patriotism and concerns over drunkenness heightened, America initiated prohibition on a national scale, coming into effect on January 16, 1920. Although Prohibition is sometimes portrayed as a period where alcohol *use* was criminalized, in fact possession of alcohol was not an offense, nor was it illegal to brew one's own beer or to make wine. It was illegal, however, to manufacture, sell, and transport alcoholic beverages—although some beverages were exempt, such as cider and "near beer" (less than 0.5% alcohol content). In the Twenty-First Amendment, on December 5, 1933, Prohibition was subsequently repealed—although a number of states retained the restrictions.

Scholars have spent much time debating whether Prohibition was a "success" or a "failure" (see Pegram, 1998; Tyrell, 1997). However, for a number of reasons, no simple verdict can be reached. There are multiple measures of what constitutes success or failure. Certainly alcohol consumption declined during this period: Americans were drinking some 2.4 gallons of absolute alcohol per capita in 1915, which fell to less than 1 gallon throughout Prohibition, and remained at lower than pre-Prohibition levels until 1970 (Hanson, 1999; Rorabaugh, 1979). Cirrhosis deaths also dropped considerably from pre-Prohibition levels, in line with the reductions in overall alcohol consumption (Edwards, 2000). It is not clear, however, that such reductions were entirely a *result* of the new legislation or were more generally a *reflection* of changing social attitudes, which of course were responsible for the instigation of Prohibition in the first place. The harm that Prohibition purportedly caused included the rise in organized crime, the sale of contaminated alcohol, and increased levels of alcohol abuse as a result of encouraging rapid consumption of high-proof alcoholic beverages (Hanson, 1999). Certainly, if Prohibition was intended to *eliminate* alcohol problems in America, as some pundits optimistically averred, it was an unmitigated failure (Pegram, 1998). However, others have suggested that the rise in organized crime that Prohibition supposedly ushered in has been greatly exaggerated, and that during the 1920s at least, there was substantial public support for the new legislation (Tyrell, 1998).

The rise of temperance societies in the nineteenth century and subsequent changes in alcohol legislation were not confined to America. Finland, Sweden, and Norway all witnessed the emergence of temperance movements and experimented with prohibition in the early decades of the twentieth century (Edwards, 2000). In Australia and New Zealand, calls for temperance culminated in the birth of the infamous "six o'clock swill": an hour of heavy drinking in crowded bars, squeezed in between the end of work and the new six o'clock closing time (Olsen, 1992; Phillips, 1980). Initially such measures were part of an emerging culture of restraint, self-denial, and self-sacrifice, brought about by the start of the First World War. Australians were urged to "follow the king" (Phillips, 1980, p. 251), a reference to King George V's pledge of abstinence. In New Zealand, many hotels were closed, the minimum drinking age was hoisted to twenty-one, and a raft of other restrictive measures were enacted (Olsen, 1992). As in America, calls for temperance in Australia and New Zealand were very much influenced by concerns over crime, social unrest, and the relaxation of moral standards. "Drink was identified and condemned as the cause of crime, disease, insanity, marriage breakdown, poverty and a host of other social problems which threatened to undermine the moral foundations upon which this way of life was built" (Dingle, 1980, p. 239).

Attitudes toward alcohol use following Prohibition in America changed in important ways. With the emergence of Alcoholics Anonymous and the influential Yale Center for Alcohol Studies in the 1930s, a revival of the disease concept of alcohol was initiated (see Chapter 6). This was to have a profound influence not only on the prevention and treatment of alcohol problems, but also on attitudes toward alcohol itself. This so-called alcoholism movement focused to a large extent on medical issues relating to, and arising from, the excessive consumption of alcohol. What Dwight Heath (1989) has called "the new temperance movement," however, has highlighted the social issues relating to alcohol use and abuse. In particular, growing concern over drunk driving, and the formation of various organizations, such as MADD (Mothers Against Drunk Driving) and SADD (Students Against Drunk Driving), have contributed to various changes in alcohol legislation such as raising drinking ages and increasing penalties for drunk driving offenses (Heath, 1989). These changes emphasize how acceptable levels of drinking are very much influenced by cultural and historical contexts. Medieval patterns of alcohol consumption, for example, although not raising substantial concerns at the time, would be difficult to sustain in a world of cars, machinery, and a rigorous work ethic.

Whereas concern over alcohol in the latter half of the twentieth century was primarily directed at how it was used, attitudes toward other drugs, such as heroin, cocaine, and cannabis, were shaped by fears over *any* kind of use. After World War II, supplies of heroin were on the increase, with the aid, as McCoy (1992) has demonstrated, of the CIA. With the Communist "menace" at the forefront of American political agendas in the 1950s, the CIA were actively involved in supporting anti-Communist groups, even if that meant aiding them in the trafficking of illegal substances such as heroin. From the 1950s through to the 1970s, CIA alliances with French anti-Communist groups drawn from the Corsican underworld contributed to the development of Marseilles in France as one of the major ports in global heroin trafficking. Opium grown in Turkey and Lebanon was shipped to Marseilles, where it was refined and smuggled to the United States and elsewhere in the world. Later in the century, CIA involvement in Southeast Asia (especially Vietnam, Laos, and Myanmar), Afghanistan, and South America was to assist heroin trafficking in these various regions, ensuring a constant supply of heroin to Western nations (McCoy, 1992).

Prior to the 1960s, heroin use in the United States was primarily restricted to specific subcultures—predominantly African American hipsters, jazz musicians, and the urban poor (see Jonnes, 1996). By the early 1960s, however, the use of heroin in America had spread from the comparatively narrow confines of these social groups to the wider population (Jonnes, 1996; Musto, 1999). In particular, white middle-class youth were increasingly represented among Americans who were addicted to heroin. This rise in heroin use occurred in spite of increasingly harsher penalties for the possession and sale of heroin and other drugs. The Hale Boggs bill was passed in 1951 and mandated for the first time minimum sentences for narcotic offenses. In 1956, the Boggs Daniel bill increased minimum penalties even further—including the death penalty as an option for the sale of heroin to individuals less than 18 years of age (Musto, 1999). The Vietnam War exposed an even larger section of predominantly young men to heroin. It has been estimated that 10–25% of enlisted men used heroin in Vietnam; however, only a small number of these men (less than 1%) continued their use after returning to the United States (Jonnes, 1996; Musto, 1999; Robins, Helzer, Hesselbrock, & Wish, 1998).

The 1960s was, of course, also a time when the recreational use of a wide range of psychoactive substances became prominent. The use of hallucinogens such as LSD played an important role in hippie subcultures; however, the most significant rise in drug use occurred with cannabis. Cannabis use spread rapidly and widely throughout many Western countries in the late 1960s and early 1970s. While youthful members of the emerging "counterculture" amused themselves by watching reruns of the 1930s anti-marijuana film *Reefer Madness*, policy makers were discussing various liberal reforms in cannabis legislation. The British Wooten report in 1968, for example, reached the conclusion that cannabis, if used in moderation, was a relatively harmless substance. It also recommended changes in the law: Cannabis possession should be subject to small fines in the manner of a civil misdemeanor, rather than to criminal prosecution. The American-instigated Shafer Commission reached a similar conclusion in 1972, and at this time cannabis had reached its "zenith of acceptance . . . as a relatively safe drug" (Iverson, 2000, p. 248).

The backlash, however, was quick to come. A strong anti-cannabis movement emerged in the United States in the mid-1970s, led by concerned parents who mobilized into effective lobbying groups such as PRIDE (Parents Resource Institute for Drug Education) and research scientists such as Gabriel Nahas, who published books such as *Marihuana—Deceptive Weed* (1973), and *Keep Off the Grass* (1978), which focused—as their titles suggest—on the dangers of cannabis use. This critical movement reached its peak in Reagan's much satirized "Just say no" campaign in the 1980s. Many teenagers in America were apparently doing just this, as those who reported ever having used cannabis fell from 60.4% of high school seniors in 1979 to 50.9% in 1986 (Bachman, Johnston, O'Malley, & Humphrey, 1988). Bachman and colleagues argue that this decline was related to an increase in the perceived risks and disapproval associated with regular cannabis use during this time period. More recently, levels of cannabis use have been on the rise in the United States (Bachman, Johnston, & O'Malley, 1998), legal reforms have been enacted in many nations decriminalizing cannabis use, and there is a tentative but emerging consensus about the importance of adopting a harm-reduction approach to cannabis use (e.g., Abel, 1997; Lenton, 2000; Swift, Copeland, & Lenton, 2000).

Although cannabis use in the United States was widespread in the 1970s, a gradual reduction in heroin use and dependence occurred during this period (Jonnes, 1996). McCoy (1992) suggests that the number of people addicted to heroin declined from some half-million in the late 1960s to fewer than 200,000 by the mid-1970s. Similar reductions occurred in the number of overdoses from heroin and in the number of heroin-related arrests (Jonnes, 1996). A number of factors were implicated in this decline, including reductions in the supply and purity of heroin, an increase in street-level prices, more active law enforcement, and a surge in the range and availability of treatment facilities. This reduction also occurred at a time when the use of cocaine was becoming more prominent.

What has been termed "the second cocaine epidemic in American history" ran from around 1970 to the late 1980s (Courtwright, 1995) and has features similar to, but also different from, the first epidemic, which had ended just under half a century ago. The National Survey Results on Drug Use from the Monitoring the Future Study revealed that in 1975, 9% of graduating high school seniors had tried cocaine; by 1985 this figure had almost doubled to 17.3% (Johnston, O'Malley, & Bachman, 1996). In the early 1970s cocaine emerged as the drug of choice among the glitterati of American culture. Given its exorbitant price tag and ego-enhancing effects, cocaine represented an attractive option for displays of power, status, and resources. Cocaine was also viewed as a relatively safe, non-addictive substance, and claims to the contrary were dismissed as misinformed propaganda. As Jonnes (1996) summarizes, "The words and especially the images of the time promoted cocaine as a safe, classy, and purely pleasurable drug historically used by brilliant, creative, and powerful people because it made you feel smart, energetic, and sexy" (p. 306). It is no wonder that cocaine use skyrocketed throughout the 1970s.

Other factors also contributed to this rise in the use of cocaine. Restrictions on amphetamines—previously cheap and easily available—and a demographic bulge characterized by a large number of 18–25-year-olds (whose levels of all drug use typically exceed that of any other age bracket) were also important (Courtwright, 1995). Supplies of cocaine, fueled by burgeoning demand, increased substantially in the 1970s and '80s. Drug smugglers like Zachary Swan realized that margins of profit could be greatly enhanced by switching from the bulky and easily detectable marijuana to more compact and less noticeable substances such as cocaine (Sabbag, 1976). Important changes in the way cocaine was processed and used also occurred during this period. The smoking of concentrated cocaine paste had emerged in Andean cities in the 1970s. By the end of the decade freebasing cocaine was becoming more common in America, and in the early 1980s the practice of smoking crack cocaine had surfaced. These methods of cocaine use lead to shorter and more intense "highs," increasing the likelihood of abuse and dependence (Julien, 1998). The affordability of crack cocaine in particular, it has been argued, also contributed to increased levels of use among poorer sectors of society and especially among African Americans and Hispanics (Ma & Shive, 2000; although see Caulkins, 1997).

Cocaine use by white middle-class individuals, however, had declined significantly by the late 1980s, and the potential dangers of cocaine were more widely appreciated. As Bachman, Johnston, and O'Malley (1990) have documented, increases in the perceived risks and dangers of cocaine are inversely related to the levels of cocaine use—the greater the perceived risk, the lower the use. Bachman et al. (1990) argue that realistic information about the dangers of cocaine were instrumental in reductions in use, even as reported availability of cocaine did not change. However, as MacCoun and Reuter (2001) note, these declines in use are moderated by sociodemographic characteristics. Increases in cocaine use in the 1970s were relatively unrelated to factors such as education; by 1990 there was a strong negative relationship between education and cocaine use.

While the image of cocaine as the glamour drug for young middle-class users became tarnished in the wake of emerging health costs and the crack epidemic of the 1980s, heroin surfaced as the drug of choice among a new generation of users (Fernandez, 1998; Jonnes, 1996). Although there remained a sizeable number of people addicted to heroin among the poor and marginalized, it was a new kind of user—elegant, fashionable, and middle-class—that raised concerns over heroin addiction. Waif-like models epitomized this new aura of "heroin chic," and fashion moguls were rebuked for conveying the association of glamour with heroin. Several important factors were responsible for this change in heroin's image among a new group of users. Most important, the purity of heroin available in the United States had increased dramatically: from less than 10% in 1973 to more than 60% in 1998 (Frank, 2000). New smuggling operations, such as those from South America, had created a competitive black market for heroin that had driven down prices and increased purity. The AIDS epidemic, which hit Western nations in the 1980s, had made heroin use via intravenous injection an increasingly risky affair, and thus decreased the popularity of heroin as a recreational drug. The higher purity of heroin meant that consumption via sniffing, snorting, or smoking could produce similar effects to injected heroin, but with comparatively less risk. As a consequence, heroin sniffing and smoking have gradually become the methods of choice among a new generation of users in the United States (Frank, 2000), Ireland (Smyth, O'Brien, & Barry, 2000), Australia (Maxwell, 2001), and elsewhere (see Strang, Griffiths, & Gossop, 1997). In the decade between 1988 and 1998, for example, intravenous heroin use had declined from 71% to 39% in the United States, while consumption via inhalation had risen from 25% to 59% (Maxwell, 2001). Heroin's image had once more been transformed: from a drug used only by the most disaffected and marginal members of society to a popular recreational intoxicant for young middle-class users.

SUMMARY

The status of drugs in society is subject to often rapid changes. As this brief history of substance use illustrates, there is clearly nothing inevitable about our current relations with psychoactive drugs, and an understanding of contemporary attitudes and patterns of use can only be fully understood in an historical context. All of the drugs that we have described in this chapter have been subject to vigorous criticism at some points in time and praised as medical marvels at others. The legal status of drugs has also undergone important changes. Cocaine and opiates, for instance, were legal and readily available just over 100 years ago but are now strictly outlawed. Cannabis use, although illegal in most Western countries for much of the twentieth century, has been decriminalized under a number of jurisdictions in the past 30 years. Tobacco, although still legal and freely available (for adults, at least), has been subject to increasing restrictions in many Western nations and may join the list of controlled substances in the near future. Even alcohol, the social and recreational drug of choice in Western cultures for the past two millennia, has been subject to prohibition. Elucidating the historical factors that relate to changing patterns of use, attitudes toward drugs, and policy responses is an important task. Understanding what factors might be historically related to higher levels of drug problems, for instance, can inform contemporary debates and policy responses. The reasons for such changes, however, are inevitably complex and multifaceted. In Chapter 5 we explore a number of factors that can individually, and in combination, explain many of the important developments in drug use over the course of history that we have outlined here.

NOTES

1.   Coffee represents a convenient stand-in here for the host of substances containing caffeine—such as tea and soft drinks—that are widely consumed in Western cultures.

2.   The sheer volume of material relating to the global history of drug use has deterred many, and good single-volume overviews are few and far between. Two excellent recent monographs on drug use during the past 500 years or so are Courtwright (2001) and Davenport-Hines (2001). A number of more popular accounts have also been published (Escohatado, 1996; Rudgley, 1993; Schivelbusch, 1992). Two edited volume collections, *Consuming Habits: Drugs in History and Anthropology* (1995) and *Drugs and Narcotics in History* (1995) offer an array of more detailed analyses on specific drugs and time periods.

5

The Forces of History:
Explaining Patterns
of Use and Abuse

INTRODUCTION

In an influential book, Norman Zinberg (1984) argued that the effects
of a drug are determined by three different factors: drug, set, and
setting. Zinberg's work was important in that it demonstrated how the
same pharmacological substance might exert quite different effects on
users depending upon users' beliefs, expectations, and mental state
and on the social context in which the drug is taken. All three of these
factors—drug, set, and setting—have changed over time in a number
of ways. Different drugs and different forms of drugs have been introduced and developed; people's beliefs and expectations regarding
drug effects have changed; and the social context of drug use has
varied tremendously. For instance, a young adult in the early twenty-first
century who prepares to inject heroin purchased illegally from a street
dealer in a large urban center will have a drug experience (and drug
career) in many ways different from a similar-aged counterpart prescribed laudanum by an eighteenth-century physician. Not only has
the form of the drug changed, but so too has its mode of use, understanding about its effects, and the social context of consumption. Given

such changes over time, it is not surprising that the way that drugs have been employed and the extent of drug-related problems have varied substantially over the course of history.

In this chapter we provide an overview of the various factors that can explain the patterns of drug use throughout history that we outlined in Chapter 4. Specifically, we address three key questions:

1. How have the functional contexts of drug use changed over time, and what are the implications of these changes for drug-related problems?

2. What factors can explain changes in the levels of drug use and drug-related problems in society over time? More specifically, why do patterns of substance use appear to reach epidemic proportions at some points in history, only to virtually disappear at others?

3. Why have changes in attitudes toward drug use and their legal status in society occurred, and how are these related to patterns of use?

As we shall see, there are no simple answers to these important questions. However, if we draw on the history of substance use, many relevant themes begin to emerge and a number of plausible explanatory accounts can be advanced.

THE FUNCTIONS OF DRUGS
IN HISTORICAL PERSPECTIVE

In Chapter 2 we suggested that drugs are employed in six (non-mutually exclusive) contexts: medicinal, recreational, social, pragmatic, ritual-religious, and dietary. What is perhaps most noticeable about the way that drugs have been used throughout history is that all six substances described in Chapter 4 have been employed in all six functional contexts (with the possible exceptions of coffee and tobacco as dietary agents).[1] This finding underscores an important point: Drugs can be employed for a diverse array of reasons and in sometimes quite different functional contexts. Of course, there has been much overlap in the different contexts of use of these substances in any particular time or place. Opium, for example, was used by working-class people in nineteenth century England as a recreational agent, a form of self-medication, and for pragmatic and dietary reasons (Berridge & Edwards, 1981).

The importance of different functional contexts has changed in various ways over time. For instance, new substances are typically employed initially as medicinal agents in therapeutic contexts (Courtwright, 2001). Before the emergence of the idea of "therapeutic specificity" in the nineteenth century—that is, that specific drugs can be used to treat specific medical problems—substances were often looked upon as *general* medical agents with wide ranging indications. Opiates, tobacco, coffee, distilled liquor, cannabis, and cocaine have all been used as therapeutic substances in a plethora of different medical contexts—from treating gout to preventing the plague. New drugs, or new forms of drugs, have been seized upon as potential panaceas that can be pressed into service in the treatment of a wide variety of health problems. Over time, patterns of use tend to shift from medicinal to recreational and social contexts. Opiates, cocaine, distilled liquor, and to a lesser extent, cannabis were all initially prominent in medical contexts, but subsequently (with the possible exception of morphine) have been replaced by recreational and social patterns of use. New drugs such as amphetamines, which were developed in the 1930s, were also originally employed in medical domains only to be transformed into secular substances utilized widely in recreational contexts.

The transition from medical to recreational and social patterns of use impacts on drug-related problems in a number of ways. First, outside of medical domains, drugs are often used in a less controlled fashion, increasing their liability for harm and dependence (Westermeyer, 1991). However, problems can also arise from the legitimate medical use of drugs. Indeed, as outlined in Chapter 4, dependence on opiates in the nineteenth century was primarily iatrogenic in nature. Furthermore, the widespread prescription of amphetamines, barbiturates, and benzodiazepines in the twentieth century has also created many problems. Second, when drugs are employed in non-medical contexts, their use is often *viewed* as a problem and they typically become subject to various regulations. The transformation in the status and role of physicians in the late nineteenth and early twentieth centuries (Acker, 1995) served only to sharpen the boundaries between licit, acceptable, and safe medical use and illicit, dangerous, and unacceptable social and recreational use. As the power and prestige of physicians increased, they sought—implicitly or explicitly—to be the sole guardians of who could and who could not use psychoactive substances.[2] Once drugs have crossed the border between medical and recreational use, they rarely return. The struggle to reaffirm cannabis as a substance with legitimate medical uses clearly illustrates this point, although some drugs, like amphetamines, have a place in both medical and recreational contexts.

In general, although the use of drugs in recreational contexts has a long history, this pattern of use has become especially prominent in the twentieth century. A wider menu of psychoactive substances to choose from, increases in leisure time and disposable income, and more extensive knowledge of drugs and drug effects have all contributed to the increasing use of a more diverse range of drugs in recreational contexts. Social patterns of use also have a long history and continue to be prominent in contemporary society. The social functions of drug use can be illustrated by a number of examples from history. Cannabis, for instance, played an important role among the members of the *club de haschischins*—a group formed in Paris in the 1840s and which counted among its circle such luminaries as Honoré de Balzac, Eugéne Delacroix, Théophile Gautier, and Victor Hugo. For this clique of self-styled bohemians, drug use was a means of affirming group identity and rebelling against mainstream middle-class values (Davenport-Hines, 2001). The poly-drug explorations of the "hippies" in the 1960s were driven by similar motives, and the use of drugs in these contexts took on a wider symbolic significance. Of course the use of many substances such as coffee, tea, and alcohol are intimately connected to their role in social contexts. Indeed, coffee in particular has been attributed an important role in *transforming* the nature of social relations after its introduction in the Near East and Europe in the sixteenth and seventeenth centuries (Hattox, 1985; Schivelbusch, 1992). Westermeyer (1991) suggests that social contexts may encourage controlled use if norms foster moderate consumption or if use is restricted to specific occasions. If the rationale for the group, by contrast, resides for the main part in drug use, then group norms might encourage excessive and harmful patterns of use.

In general, the use of drugs for ritual-religious reasons is likely to result in low levels of harm because patterns of use are usually rigidly controlled by powerful social norms (Dobkin de Rios & Smith, 1977; Westermeyer, 1991). The low level of alcohol abuse among Jewish people is one prominent example here (Straussner, 2001c), as is the controlled use of peyote by members of the Native American Church. Part of the reduced risk for drug-related problems in such contexts arises because such use is deemed legitimate and acceptable by relevant social groups. Drug use in ritual-religious contexts, however, is not immune from harmful effects. Ritual tobacco use by Native Americans, for instance, would not have precluded risks related to long-term regular consumption. We explore the ritual-religious context of drug use in more detail in Chapters 6 and 7, but it is worth noting that this pattern of use has been rather less prominent in Western cultures—certainly in regard to the six substances discussed in Chapter 4.

Drugs have also been used in dietary and pragmatic contexts throughout history. With the exception of alcohol, the dietary role of most drugs has been quite limited, although we should not ignore the important role of tobacco, coffee, coca, and opium in suppressing appetite—a valuable attribute in times where sufficient quantities of food have not been readily available. The pragmatic function of drugs in people's lives has been somewhat neglected by researchers, but emerges as an important theme in historical context. Substances such as coca, coffee, and tobacco, as well as suppressing appetite, also reduce fatigue and increase the capacity for mental and physical work. These drugs have been employed for such reasons in numerous contexts: from the use of coca to stave off fatigue by indigenous people working in the silver mines in Bolivia to the use of coffee and tea as aids to meditation. Rather less benignly, substances such as LSD and other hallucinogens were investigated as potential mind control agents by the CIA in the 1950s and 1960s (Lee & Shlain, 1985), and amphetamines were doled out to soldiers in World War II to reduce fatigue and to enhance their performance in battle contexts (Courtwright, 2001).

As we have argued elsewhere, it is important to attend to the functions of drug use, and a historical perspective highlights the multiple ways in which drugs have been employed across time. It is difficult to quantify, however, just how different contexts of use are related to patterns of abuse and dependence. Certainly drugs used in medicinal contexts tend to be under greater control, which reduces their liability for harm. However, the widespread dependence on opiates and cocaine in the nineteenth century was predominantly the result of medicinal use, and recreational use of other substances, such as alcohol, have been associated with health benefits, blurring any obvious relation between functional context and drug-related harm. More clearly, when drugs are employed in social and recreational contexts they are *viewed* as problematic, and the use of many substances in such contexts has been criminalized in the twentieth century.

PHARMACOLOGY

Although the focus in this chapter is the role of historical factors on patterns of substance use and abuse, it is important not to ignore the nature of the substance itself. That is, in explaining patterns of drug use across history we need to pay attention to the pharmacology of psychoactive substances. The importance of alcohol, tobacco, coffee, and opium in Western society, while other psychoactive substances such as kava, qat, and betel are virtually unknown, is due, in part, to differences in pharmacology.

Many drugs initially produce an unpleasant reaction on naïve users—kava, for example, has an appalling taste, and mescal buttons and other hallucinogens often induce nausea and vomiting. Moreover, the psychological effects of many drugs may be disturbing to novices. This is especially true of the wide array of hallucinogens, such as ayahuasca, ololiuqui, datura, and psilocybe mushrooms, that have been employed in various different cultures. Many psychoactive substances also have unpleasant and deleterious physical effects: betel chewing leads to stained and rotting teeth; coca users develop distended faces; and habitual consumers of qat can suffer from extreme constipation, insomnia, and psychological problems. All of these factors may have deterred would-be European users from making these substances a regular part of their daily lives. By contrast, coffee, tea, and tobacco produce relatively subtle shifts in cognition and emotion and can be easily incorporated into pre-existing patterns of daily life. The interaction of pharmacology with belief systems is also important. Coffee, tea, and tobacco produced effects commensurate with early modern European values of sobriety, respectability, and industry. Hallucinogens, such as datura and psilocybe mushrooms, by contrast, posed a threat to Christian ideals, especially as their indigenous use was so firmly integrated into so-called primitive ritual-religious contexts (Courtwright, 2001).

The ability of a substance to be transported long distances with its pharmacological power intact is another important factor influencing patterns of historical distribution. Coca's introduction into Western cultures was, as we have seen, retarded by its loss of potency over time, and a similar problem has probably prevented the widespread use of qat, which also loses its psychoactive potency if left unused after being harvested. In contrast, tobacco, coffee, and tea all retain their psychoactive properties and are relatively easy to cultivate and transport.

The capacity of a substance to generate psychological and physical dependence is of course also relevant. Tobacco, coffee, alcohol, and opium have an advantage in this respect over hallucinogens like peyote, psilocybin, and datura, partly accounting for their more widespread distribution. The role of pharmacology in accounting for historical patterns of substance use also helps to make sense of the dramatic impact that new substances, new forms of old substances, and new modes of consumption have had on patterns of use and drug-related problems.

NEW FORMS, NEW MODES, NEW SUBSTANCES: THE IMPACT OF TECHNOLOGICAL CHANGE ON DRUG USE

One of the most prominent themes that emerges from the history of drugs is how new substances, new forms of old substances, and new modes of consumption have impacted on patterns of use and abuse. As a number of scholars have noted, the effect of these changes is almost always to increase the levels of drug-related harm (Courtwright, 2001; Edwards, 2000; Sherratt, 1995; Westermeyer, 1991). Schivelbusch (1992) describes a process of "acceleration" in the use of drugs across history as more potent and rapidly rewarding versions of familiar substances become introduced into society. Certainly, in the past 500 years there have been dramatic changes in the nature and scope of drugs available, with important implications for substance-related problems.

For example, the use of opiates has undergone a number of changes throughout history. Prior to the introduction of tobacco and tobacco pipes, opium was exclusively taken via oral routes. However, the practice of smoking opium, particularly in China, gradually replaced traditional modes of administration in the seventeenth and eighteenth centuries and contributed to rising levels of opium dependence in Chinese society (Booth, 1996). The isolation of morphine and the development of heroin in the nineteenth century also increased levels of opiate dependence, as these substances provide more potent and rapid effects—especially when administered via the newly introduced hypodermic syringe. More recently, with the availability of heroin of greater purity, the sniffing and smoking of heroin has become more prevalent; a change which has led to a shift in the demographic profile of users. A similar story, of course, can be told regarding the transformation of the relatively benign substance coca into its considerably more dangerous derivatives—cocaine and crack.

The widespread diffusion of distilled alcohol in Europe in the sixteenth and seventeenth centuries also wrought changes in the potential harms that alcohol consumption could cause. Although known to the Greeks and developed by the Arabs in the eighth century, the practice of distillation and the consumption of distilled spirits made an impact on European societies only from the latter half of the sixteenth century (Comer, 2000; Matthee, 1995; Vallee, 1998). With the sobriquet "Aqua Vitae," or water of life, distilled alcohol was evidently valued for its role as a therapeutic agent, and it was employed in various medicinal contexts. However, given distilled liquor's higher alcohol content (more than three times the familiar ales, beers, and wines), it also presented increased liability for drunkenness and abuse—concerns that were to reach an apogee during the English gin epidemic between 1720 and 1751 (see A Complex Web later in this chapter).

The impact of technology on tobacco use has perhaps been as dramatic as that of any drug, but has taken somewhat different forms. In the late nineteenth and early twentieth centuries, a series of technological developments were to accelerate the levels of tobacco consumption, with ultimately devastating effects. Before the middle of the nineteenth century, procuring a light for one's pipe or cigar involved either an open fire or a supply of flint, steel, and tinder—one reason why snuff was so popular in the eighteenth century. With the invention of safety matches in 1844 and the wheel action lighter in 1909, "lighting up" was accomplished with much greater ease. And the introduction of the Bonsack machine in 1884 greatly accelerated the production of cigarettes. Previously limited to 3,000 a day by hand rolling, the new invention could churn out more than 120,000 in the same amount of time. Finally, the development of flue- and air-cured tobaccos between 1840 and 1870 resulted in a sweeter, less irritating, and easier to inhale substance that greatly enhanced smoking pleasure (Goodman, 1993; Slade, 1989; Walker, 1980). In combination, these developments contributed to rising rates of tobacco use in the twentieth century, with well-recognized effects on health and mortality.

In the nineteenth and twentieth centuries, the most visible impact of technological change on drug use was the proliferation of synthetic substances with a diverse array of pharmacological effects. Chloral hydrate, for instance, was introduced in the second half of the nineteenth century and was employed as an anesthetic and treatment for insomnia, depression, and opiate addiction. However, problems soon arose as overdoses and cases of dependence emerged. Other newly introduced substances in the nineteenth century included amyl nitrites, ether, arsenic, and chloroform, all of which were initially employed in medical contexts but also made their way into recreational patterns of use (Davenport-Hines, 2001). Amphetamines, barbiturates, benzodiazepines, anesthetics, inhalants, and various "psychedelic" substances have also made a considerable impression on patterns of drug use in the twentieth century, and have vastly increased the repertoire of substances that can be abused. Consider, for example, the history of amphetamines. First introduced as decongestants in the 1930s and readily available in the form of Benzedrine inhalers, amphetamines were employed in a variety of medical contexts (Courtwright, 2001). However, given that amphetamines have similar pharmacological effects to cocaine, recreational patterns of use soon emerged, and the long-term harm of amphetamine abuse is now well recognized.

There are a number of reasons why technological developments in the form and mode of drug consumption across history have had predominantly deleterious effects.[3] First, purified substances such as cocaine and heroin are simply more *potent* than the substances from which they have been derived. They therefore generate more rapid and intense positive psychological and emotional states, which encourage more compulsive patterns of use and increase the risk for drug-related harm such as overdose and dependence. Similarly, individuals can become intoxicated far more rapidly when drinking distilled spirits in comparison to the consumption of wine, beer, and cider, increasing the risk for a variety of harms. Changes in the mode of consumption have similar effects. More of a substance is absorbed more rapidly as the route of administration changes from oral ingestion to smoking, sniffing, and intravenous injection. For example, the mastication of a wad of coca leaves results in a 45–90-minute "high" some 5–10 minutes after ingestion, with the release of 20–50 mg of cocaine. Smoked crack cocaine, in contrast, produces a 5–10-minute "high" within 10 seconds of consumption with a dose of 250–1000 mg of cocaine (Julien, 1998, p. 123). Because the consumption of crack cocaine leads to more rapid and intense psychological effects that dissipate rapidly, the likelihood of repeated, compulsive use is much greater than for coca leaves, with obvious implications for drug-related harm. Empirical research supports these suggestions. Several studies have shown that cocaine when smoked or taken intravenously is related to higher levels of dependence and more severe physical, psychological, and social problems (Gossop, Griffiths, Powis, & Strang, 1992, 1994; Hatsukami & Fischman, 1996).

Second, as changes are wrought in the form of drugs and their mode of consumption, individuals lack knowledge (initially at least) about the short- and long-term effects of these new substances. Consumption occurs, therefore, in the absence of specific social and cultural norms regarding appropriate patterns of use, and information about potential drug-related harm is not as readily available. In short, new substances and forms of consumption lack a cultural history, and they are often experimented with in ways that increase the risks for abuse and dependence. An appreciation of drug harm can be slow to emerge as individual differences in drug effects, the nature of drug combinations, and other factors that affect drug actions are only apparent after a period of use. The attraction of new products of any kind, emerging fads for specific drugs, the seemingly endless chemical permutations, and the substantial profits to be made from drug development (both licit and illicit) ensure that issues relating to new drugs and forms of drugs will remain important in years to come and should be carefully monitored.

AVAILABILITY

People cannot use—and therefore abuse—drugs if drugs are not available. The availability of psychoactive substances, therefore, should influence levels of use, and this should be reflected in the historical record. Certainly drug historians have emphasized this point. Courtwright (1982, 1995, 2001), for example, has accentuated the importance of availability in explaining patterns of drug use over time for a variety of substances, and Jonnes (1996) unequivocally states, "Availability is fundamental, for wherever there are drugs to be had, use and addiction will *always* rise" (p. 11). Our overview of the history of drugs in Chapter 4 tends to support these claims, although we argue that the impact of availability on drug use is moderated by a host of other factors. Crucially, availability must be coupled with sufficient demand to generate increases in levels of drug use.

The history of opiates perhaps most vividly illustrates the importance of availability. Levels of use and dependence in China, Southeast Asia, Europe, and North America all have been influenced by fluctuations in the supply of opiates. The gunboat diplomacy of Britain in the nineteenth century, which sought to retain lucrative opium exports to China despite the resistance of the Chinese government, ensured a constant flow of opium into Chinese territory, with concomitant high levels of local opium dependence. In a similar fashion, the emergence of sophisticated heroin smuggling operations in the twentieth century, aided by CIA complicity, has guaranteed an enduring—if somewhat irregular—supply of heroin to American users (McCoy, 1992). Disruption to supply, as occurred in the early 1970s, led to declines in use, but the market has rebounded numerous times as new sources of heroin have been established. Likewise, the burgeoning supply of cocaine from South America in the early 1970s coincided with dramatic increases in American cocaine use. And the decline in cocaine use in the 1920s and 1930s can be attributed, to a considerable extent, to reductions in supply brought about by new legal restrictions (Spillane, 1998). Further support for the importance of availability in determining levels of use comes from studies that indicate there is a direct relationship between levels of opiate dependence and proximity to opium-producing areas (Westermeyer, 1981; see also Baridon, 1973). Pakistan, for example, experienced a dramatic surge in heroin use between 1980 and 1983 as a result of burgeoning local supply. In the four years between 1975 and 1979, the cultivation of opium poppies increased tenfold: from fewer than 3,000 to more than 30,000 hectares (Farrell, 1998). This resulted in a substantial increase in users—from an estimated 5,000 to some 1.3 million individuals dependent on heroin (Jonnes, 1996).

A similar story holds for licit substances as well. With the expansion of world trade routes and the colonial aspirations of European nations in the sixteenth to nineteenth centuries, the transportation of substances such as coffee, tea, tobacco, and alcohol was more easily achieved. The result was to expose a wider proportion of European society to these substances, with commensurate increases in use (Matthee, 1995). The rise in gin consumption in Britain in the eighteenth century can also be linked, in part, to increases in supply and falling prices brought about by grain surpluses. Similarly, the increase in whiskey drinking in the United States in the last decade of the eighteenth century was due in no small measure to increased availability (Rorabaugh, 1979). Globalization in the twentieth century and the development of even more rapid transportation and communication links have served only to accelerate this process.

Although restrictions in supply tend to reduce the prevalence of drug use, they can also, paradoxically, increase the levels of drug-related harm. The enactment of National Prohibition in the United States, to use the most obvious example, although reducing the total amount of alcohol consumed, also had several unintended consequences: it increased the consumption of distilled spirits, encouraged the consumption of harmful products containing alcohol, and created a climate in which organized crime could flourish (Miron & Zweibel, 1995). A similar pattern of events occurred in response to alcohol prohibition in Russia—for instance, more than 10,000 Russians died in one year from methanol and related poisonings after the introduction of strict alcohol controls in 1985 (Courtwright, 2001). In general, policies that make substances illegal or reduce their availability tend to encourage the production and consumption of higher-potency drugs, which can lead to increased levels of abuse and drug-related harm (Thornton, 1998). A focus on reducing the supply of illicit drugs has certainly been the cornerstone of American drug policy in the twentieth century and appears to be commensurate with our historical understanding of the effects of availability on levels of use. However, such attempts have generally been unsuccessful: no more than 10% of any illicit drug crop has been eradicated in a given year, and farmers, suppliers, and distributors rapidly adapt to such strategies by employing new methods, shifting locations, and cultivating new drug crops (Farrell, 1998). The effects of the availability of psychoactive substances, then, are tempered by many other important factors. Although declines in supply are generally related to reductions in drug use and drug-related harm, negative consequences must also be taken into account. Policies that focus predominantly on reducing supply while ignoring other factors will generally prove ineffective.

ECONOMIC AND POLITICAL FACTORS

In a recent review of the "economics of substance abuse," Rasmussen, Benson, and Mocan (1998) note, "Economic considerations play virtually no explicit role in the discussion of drug abuse by criminologists, psychologists, psychiatrists, sociologists, and social workers" (p. 575). Economic (and political) factors, however, loom large when patterns of substance use and abuse are examined over the course of history. Indeed, many of the familiar licit substances on the Western psychoactive scene—tobacco, tea, coffee, and alcohol—owe their global diffusion to the twin forces of colonialism and mercantilism in the early modern period.

The benefits to governments via the taxation of psychoactive drugs were clearly recognized early in the global careers of substances like tobacco, coffee, opium, and alcohol and were welcomed at a time when burgeoning military and administrative expenditure was sapping the financial resources of many European states (Goodman, 1995; Matthee, 1995). The revenues accrued via what are now termed "sin taxes" were often considerable, and played an important role in encouraging the consumption of substances like tobacco and coffee, whose place in society was a matter of sometimes heated debate. For example, during the mid-seventeenth century, amid disputes over tobacco's health effects, duties on American tobacco alone represented as much as 5% of the English government's total revenue (Courtwright, 2001; see also Price, 1995). Even more dramatically, more than 70% of the state's revenue in New South Wales in 1830 came from duties on alcohol and tobacco (Walker, 1980). As Walker notes, "These commodities could be severely taxed as luxuries in the sure knowledge that consumers would still buy them as necessities" (p. 283).

The importance placed on the revenue earned via taxation is one factor that has promoted the use of drugs throughout history. Conversely, raising taxes and therefore drug prices is one method governments have used to *reduce* demand for psychoactive substances. As Spring & Buss (1977) have demonstrated, increases in duties on alcoholic beverages are related historically to reductions in demand. A similar theme emerges from Warner et al.'s (2001) more fine-grained analysis of gin consumption in the eighteenth century. Consumption initially declined in response to rises in the taxes on gin; however, these demand-reducing effects were only temporary in nature. More generally, patterns of consumption are related to broader economic trends, with the use of such substances as alcohol decreasing during depression years and increasing in times of prosperity (Dingle, 1980; Spring & Buss, 1977).

To what extent drug consumption is sensitive to price changes is an important question, as the putative effect of legislative moves to curb the availability of (especially illegal) drugs is to raise prices and thus reduce demand. Some research has suggested that the demand for drugs, because of their addictive nature, is fairly inelastic—that is, increases in price have limited effects on levels of use. However, more recent studies indicate that the demand for drugs—whether alcohol, tobacco, or heroin—is sensitive to changes in price (see Caulkins & Reuter, 1998, for a recent review). For example, in a historical study of the opium market in the Dutch East Indies between 1923 and 1938, Van Ours (1995) found relatively high long-term price elasticities for opium of about -1.0.[4] In a somewhat different kind of study, Caulkins (2001) discovered that fluctuations in the price of cocaine and heroin between 1978 and 1996 could account for a significant portion of the variance in the mention of cocaine and heroin in emergency department visits during the same period: as prices rose, emergency department visits declined. Clearly price matters. Although to what extent reductions in demand for one drug, as a result of increases in price, are offset by rising demand for other drugs is an interesting question and a matter for further research. Moreover, the persistent demand for substances such as cannabis, which is literally worth its weight in gold, and for cocaine and heroin, which are *orders of magnitude* more expensive than gold by weight, is testimony to their enduring appeal despite substantial monetary costs.

The importance of economic factors in influencing patterns of substance use extends beyond the money earned via taxation or the costs imposed on consumers. In fact there is a complex network of individuals who cultivate, manufacture, transport (smuggle), distribute, and sell drugs who have a vested interest in maintaining consumer interest in their products, licit or otherwise. When you consider that the net farm income per hectare for coca is $1,940, compared to $907 for coffee and $157 for bananas (Farrell, 1998), it is not surprising that the cultivation of drug plants is an attractive option, especially for individuals in developing nations. The economic benefits to be derived from the commerce in psychoactive substances become even more lucrative further along the chain of distribution, and entrepreneurs engaged in both legal and illegal practices can benefit substantially.

Drugs have also been used extensively throughout history as trade items. Many vivid examples illustrate this perennial relationship, from the exchange of furs and skins for rum by Native Americans with early settlers, to sex for crack transactions by some prostitutes in contemporary society (e.g., Goldstein, Ouellet, & Fendrich, 1992; Mancall, 1995; Sterk, Elifson, & German, 2000). Rum, itself a product of Caribbean slave labor, was widely used as an item of barter with Native Americans in the seventeenth and eighteenth centuries (Frank, Moore, & Ames, 2000; Mancall, 1995). Rum and tobacco were used for similar purposes by Australian settlers in their negotiations with indigenous Australians (see Dingle, 1980; Hughes, 1987; Saggers & Gray, 1998; Walker, 1980), and psychoactive drugs in general have been intimately connected with colonial activities throughout history. These transactions served a number of purposes: they integrated indigenous people into the web of European commerce; they were an important means by which Europeans obtained the commodities they wanted; and they encouraged demand for substances that could be used—implicitly or explicitly—as agents of control. Unlike other products, the demand for alcohol and tobacco did not wane, and as European colonists controlled the production and distribution of these substances, their exchange could be made on favorable terms (from a European perspective, at least).

Patterns of drug use have also been influenced by a variety of political factors. The British involvement in illegal opium exports to China in the nineteenth century and the CIA's complicity in the global trafficking in heroin and cocaine in the twentieth century stand out most vividly here, but numerous other examples could be used to illustrate this theme. The belief that LSD constituted a valuable mind control agent and was thus of military importance, for example, helped launch in the 1950s the CIA operation MK-ULTRA, whose mandate was to develop chemical and biological agents during the Cold War. The U.S. military, fearful of hallucinogens as agents of warfare, dosed thousand of GI "volunteers" in the 1960s with LSD and other even more powerful agents such as BZ (quinuclidnyl benzilate), in order to accustom them to their effects (Lee & Shlain, 1985).

More generally, social and political elites have long been concerned with the potentially disruptive role of psychoactive substances on social stability. As we have seen, the emergence of coffeehouses in the Near East in the sixteenth century generated concern over disruptions to the social and political status quo, and similar worries have accompanied various other drugs such as gin in the seventeenth century, cannabis in the 1960s, and crack cocaine in the 1980s. Any psychoactive substance that might be seen (correctly or otherwise) to destabilize social arrangements and thus threaten the interests of elites is likely to attract attention and foster—sometimes punitive—control (see Szasz, 1985). Economic and political factors, as Rasmussen et al. (1998) indicate, are often neglected by psychologists and sociologists, but attention to historical patterns of drug use underscores their relevance. In particular, it is important to recognize the vested economic and political interests that various groups have in psychoactive drugs (be they cultivators, dealers, or governments) and how patterns of drug use are shaped by a range of economic and political forces.

LEGISLATION AND PUBLIC POLICY

Perhaps the most obvious way in which governments can affect patterns of drug use is through legislative means. The price of drugs can be raised via taxation, controls can be enacted limiting supply and availability, and the sale and use of psychoactive substances can be prohibited and enforced with strict penalties. All of these measures, and more, have been employed by social, religious, and political elites over the last 2,000 years or so. But just how effective have such measures been? Evaluating the impact of divergent policies is a complex task because their efficacy, as we discuss, is influenced by a raft of social and cultural factors that are unique to specific times and places. However, drawing on our overview of the history of drug use in Chapter 4, some important themes do begin to emerge.

One such theme is that punitive measures, by themselves, have a surprisingly limited impact on patterns of use over time. Various examples of draconian penalties for drug use are presented in Chapter 4: virtually all psychoactive substances at some time or place have been prohibited and punished with harsh penalties. Thus, tobacco smokers in seventeenth-century Lüneberg could be executed, snuff takers in Russia could have their noses torn off, opium sellers in eighteenth-century China were condemned to death by strangling, and users of cocaine, heroin, and cannabis in America in the twentieth century have been subject to lengthy jail sentences. Although quantitative data are not available for all of these examples, there is general agreement that such severe policies are relatively ineffective at curbing levels of drug use. Why should this be the case? Who would want to risk lighting up a cannabis joint, snorting a line of cocaine, or dropping a tab of LSD when they could face a lengthy and life-changing jail sentence as a result? As MacCoun and Reuter (2001) summarize, the effectiveness of drug laws depends on three factors: severity, certainty, and celerity. The most important factor appears to be the *certainty* of prosecution. Most drug users, most of the time, are unlikely to be caught. For example, MacCoun and Reuter (2001) calculate that a regular cannabis user has an annual risk of being arrested of about 3%, and that the risk per episode of drug use is negligible.

This is not to say that legislation is never effective in reducing drug use and drug-related harm. The 1914 Harrison Narcotic Act, for example, did contribute to the decline in opiate and cocaine use in American society, especially among specific demographic groups. And the new laws enacted in the early part of the twentieth century to control the patent medicine industry's use of psychoactive substances were equally effective in reducing overall levels of use (Jonnes, 1996; Musto, 1999; Spillane, 1998). Often, however, the positive effects of law changes on reducing drug use are of a temporary nature. Consumption of gin, for instance, declined following each of the various gin acts introduced in Britain in the eighteenth century, but soon rebounded to former levels (Warner et al., 2001). Likewise, the recent introduction of severe penalties for drunk driving in various nations has tended to have an immediate positive effect that wears off over time (MacCoun & Reuter, 2001, pp. 79–81).

Changes in the law designed to reduce drug problems can also have unintended consequences that actually increase the levels of drug-related harm. The introduction of harsher penalties for cannabis cultivation, sale, and use in the United States in the early 1970s, for example, coupled with restrictions on the availability of amphetamines, encouraged the development of trafficking in cocaine. Similarly, more punitive punishments for opium sale and use in Southeast Asia in the 1950s and 1960s encouraged the production and use of heroin, which is less bulky and easier to conceal. Levels of overall opiate dependence increased as a result. Even a fairly simple change in the law, such as the introduction of six o'clock closing in Australia and New Zealand, can have the effect of altering patterns of drug use in deleterious ways—in this case by encouraging the rapid consumption of alcohol and thus increasing levels of intoxication and acute alcohol-related problems.

Perhaps the most important lesson that can be drawn from the history of legislative changes in the status of psychoactive substances is that such changes are most likely to be effective when they are accompanied by commensurate modifications in social attitudes toward drug use. Drug use, as Warner et al. (2001) assert, is often woven into the tapestry of people's lives, so that effecting changes in patterns of use via modifications to the law will impact on many aspects of daily life. Therefore, for legal sanctions to be successful in reducing drug-related harm they must be accompanied by informal social and cultural proscriptions that reinforce legislative moves and encourage compliance (Westermeyer, 1996a). The prohibition of alcohol use in Islamic societies, for example, is effective because it is accompanied by little demand for alcoholic beverages and has substantial long-term cultural and religious support. Ideally, laws should *reflect* rather than dictate socially shared beliefs, norms, and attitudes. Moreover, they should be sensitive to local cultural variations in patterns of drug use. An historical perspective suggests that legislation and public policy initiatives can be effective in reducing levels of substance use and abuse and in ameliorating drug-related harm, but they have to be located within the sphere of wider cultural beliefs.

SOCIAL FACTORS

Many individuals deliberately engage in risky and potentially dangerous activities. Base jumping, professional boxing, mountaineering, and—more prosaically—simply driving to work all entail some level of non-negligible risk. Most people do not pursue such activities with the belief that they will come to harm. That is, people are sensitive to the costs and benefits of their actions.[5] The same is true for the consumption of psychoactive substances: Beliefs about the harms and benefits of drugs impact in important ways on levels of use. Moreover, as such beliefs fluctuate over time, we should also expect parallel changes in patterns of substance use. Our historical overview in Chapter 4, in general, supports these suggestions. However, it is only with more recent data sets that the effects of attitudes, beliefs, and norms relating to drugs and drug use can be rigorously evaluated.

The relatively rapid and widespread diffusion of coffee, tobacco, and distilled liquor from the sixteenth to the eighteenth centuries was due, in part, to the therapeutic value placed on these substances. Although, as we have seen, the use of all three substances received strident criticism from some quarters, they were also energetically praised in other circles and were widely employed in medicinal contexts. Individuals who had already incorporated these substances into their daily lives could thus draw upon learned opinion as to their health-promoting virtues. Although coffee's role in medicinal contexts had disappeared by the twentieth century, no serious challenges to its use have emerged, and it remains an extremely popular drug. By contrast, changing beliefs about the harmfulness of tobacco as a result of the widespread dissemination of scientific research demonstrating its causal role in the development of cancer and heart disease have had a huge impact on patterns of use.

Beliefs regarding the harm of tobacco use have a long history, and possible connections with cancer were noted as early as the eighteenth century. By the middle of the nineteenth century, a number of anti-smoking and anti-tobacco leagues had emerged in the United States, Britain, and Australia (Goodman, 1993; Walker, 1980), and in 1908 a bill prohibiting the sale of tobacco to children was passed in the United States (Brandt, 1990). However, it was the carefully controlled studies of Doll and Bradford Hill (1954; see also Le Fanu, 1999) and accumulating evidence from a variety of other sources that led to the first American Surgeon General's warning issued in 1964. The public's response to these new developments was swift. In the quarter of a century between 1964 and 1989, levels of smoking had declined in the United States from 42% to 26% of the population. These dramatic changes were brought about almost entirely by the dissemination of ideas regarding the harms of smoking. Indeed, consumption patterns closely track the development of putatively less harmful tobacco products. In the 1950s, filter cigarettes were introduced and, by virtue of promotions that emphasized their safety, rapidly cornered the tobacco market. A similar effect occurred with the introduction of low-tar brands in the 1960s, and tobacco companies continue their search for a "safe" cigarette (Slade, 1989; Warner, 2001). Although a residue of smokers have ignored health warnings, emerging evidence regarding the harm of secondhand smoke in the 1980s has placed smoking under even greater critical attention at the end of the twentieth century, and *social norms* regarding tobacco use are clearly changing (Brandt, 1990).

The decline in tobacco consumption (in Western nations, at least) in the second half of the twentieth century is perhaps the clearest example of how beliefs about the harm of a substance can affect patterns of use. The history of alcohol use also reflects the powerful role that beliefs, attitudes, and norms can play in influencing patterns of consumption. Heavy drinking in medieval and early modern Europe was an accepted practice; however, by the end of the nineteenth century drinking was viewed by many as a vice. Temperance societies played an important role in this transformation as they promulgated claims about the harms of alcohol use. By 1900, for instance, virtually every state in America had passed laws that required that children be taught in schools that alcohol was a poison (Pegram, 1998). Not surprisingly, alcohol use declined during this period. More recently, research suggesting that moderate alcohol consumption serves as a prophylactic against heart disease and other health problems (e.g., Doll, 1998) could well affect future patterns of use.

David Musto (1999) has argued that cycles of drug use in American society occur as experiences with harmful substances lead to increased knowledge about their dangers, and consequently to reductions in consumption. As this knowledge is lost with subsequent generations, old substances are rediscovered and widely used until their harms once again become apparent. This model, as Courtwright (2001) indicates, appears to best fit the pattern of heroin and cocaine use in the United States. Certainly *one* factor in the decline in cocaine use in the early part of the twentieth century was a growing awareness of its potential harms. The resurgence of cocaine use in the 1970s was also accompanied by beliefs about its non-addictive, harmless nature, until its dangers once more became apparent and use started to decline. As Bachman et al. (1990) have demonstrated, declines in cocaine use among young adults between 1976 and 1988 correlate with increases in the perceived risk and disapproval of cocaine. A similar relationship between the perceived risk and disapproval of cannabis and levels of cannabis use has also been demonstrated as patterns of use have fluctuated over the past 20 years (Bachman et al., 1998).

The impact of beliefs about the harms of drugs on patterns of use, however, is moderated by various social factors. For example, the dangers of tobacco smoking are widely known, but the impact of this knowledge on patterns of use has been greatest for middle-class users (Schelling, 1992). The effects of knowledge about drug harm will depend on how much an individual has to lose by using dangerous drugs, the availability of alternatives to drug use, networks of social support, and other such factors. Beliefs about the effects of drugs, as well as influencing *levels* of use, may also impact on the nature of the drug experience itself. For example, Becker (1953) argued that adverse responses to cannabis in the 1920s and 1930s were a result of *expectations* about possible negative effects derived from the media. As individuals became more experienced with using cannabis, these negative reactions declined. A similar pattern of events seems to have occurred with LSD in the 1960s, as the incidence of "bad trips" actually declined when use became more widespread (Zinberg, 1984).

Given the impact of beliefs regarding drug-related harm on patterns of use, there is a special onus on health professionals and the media to provide accurate, unbiased information to the public. The widespread promulgation of the dangers of cannabis use in the 1930s, for example, had the unintended effect of fostering mistrust for government information regarding drugs as a new generation in the 1960s discovered that it wasn't the "killer weed" that it was made out to be. Recent media attention directed toward the dangers of ecstasy amid widespread regular use among some social groups may be having a similar effect (Parker, Aldridge, & Measham, 1998).

Drug-related harm can also be inappropriately discounted. The tobacco industry, for example, is currently attempting to change the evidential requirements for science and the standards of proof as it deploys the concepts of "junk science" and "sound science" in ways that protect its economic interests (see Ong & Glantz, 2001). The interrelationships between science and society are, inevitably, complex and multifaceted, especially as the results of scientific inquiry are typically refracted through the distorting lenses of the media to the public at large. However, attention to providing accurate and objective information regarding drugs and drug-related harm is crucial in reducing such harm in society and providing a sound platform for effective policy initiatives.

The beliefs, attitudes, and norms regarding the putative costs and benefits of drugs are just one important way that social factors have impacted on patterns of use across time. Another important avenue for social influences arises from the association of drug use with specific social groups. At various times in history, apparent widespread use of specific drugs, coupled with social problems, has precipitated "moral panics," typically directed at specific groups of users. For instance, reactions toward opium, and in particular opium smoking, in Western nations such as the United States, England, Canada, and Australia were often highly emotive and driven by prejudicial attitudes toward immigrant Chinese. Indeed, laws against opium *smoking* were enacted far in advance of laws against other forms of opium consumption (Manderson, 1993, 1999; Musto, 1999). "Opium," Manderson (1993) notes, "was seen as a pollutant, moral as well as physical; it was tainted by the environment of its consumption and by its connection with the Chinese themselves" (p. 23).

Likewise, laws enacted against cannabis and cocaine use in the United States in the early twentieth century and the characterization of these substances as "demon drugs" were a result, in part, of their connection with racial minorities—Mexicans and African Americans, respectively. Cannabis in the United States during the early part of the twentieth century was primarily associated with Mexican immigrant laborers. Fears were voiced about the spread of cannabis to American youth and concerns raised over cannabis-fueled crime sprees by immigrant Mexicans. Laws against cannabis—some 29 states banned its sale and use outside of medical contexts between 1914 and 1931—reflected these beliefs, and culminated in the Marihuana Tax Act in 1937 (Musto, 1999).

Similarly, the use of cocaine in the early part of the twentieth century was widely associated with crime and violent behavior, especially as perpetrated by African Americans (Courtwright, 1995). Indeed, the public was unnerved and frightened by reports of cocaine-crazed "Negroes" running amok, raping white women, and causing general mayhem. "Cocaine," asserted Hamilton Wright, who was influential in the forming of American drug policy early in the twentieth century, "is often the direct incentive to the crime of rape by the Negroes of the South and other sections of the country" (cited in Helmer, 1975, p. 47). There was little in the way of evidence to support these claims, but such beliefs contributed to the lynching of African Americans across the southern states in 1919 and helped to usher in laws against the use of cocaine (Musto, 1999).

Manderson (1999), in a review of racism in drug history, highlights the way that substances take on symbolic value that transcends their pharmacological reality. Through the processes of metaphor and metonymy, drugs emerge as scapegoats on which racial fears and prejudices can be expediently hung. Drugs, and their association with specific social groups, therefore, often take the blame for wider, more complex social problems.[6] Perceived social unrest in eighteenth-century England, for example, could be conveniently blamed on gin consumption by the poor (Warner, 1994a). And, more recently, the so-called American crack epidemic of the 1980s provided an easy target for political "solutions" to wider, more intractable problems in American society (Reinarman & Levine, 1997). In short, numerous historical examples illustrate how drugs have become the target of "moral panics," as groups of users are marginalized, typecast, and blamed for specific social problems (see Cohen, 1980; Ben-Yehuda, 1986, on the sociology of moral panics). Such panics often follow a familiar pattern. First, actors or practices are identified that threaten mainstream social values. These individuals or behaviors are portrayed via the media in a distorted fashion. Public concern is aroused, and—sometimes drastic—solutions are proposed and may be implemented. Then, finally, the panic subsides. Both the gin epidemic in eighteenth-century England and the more recent crack scare provide good illustrations of this process.

What emerges as the most crucial insight from the history of drug use among specific social groups is that *who* uses drugs and for what *reasons* are profoundly important factors in determining patterns of use and societies responses to drug-taking behavior. The transformation of opiate and cocaine users in the late nineteenth and early twentieth centuries from predominantly middle-class individuals who used these drugs in therapeutic contexts to marginalized individuals who took the same (or similar) drugs for recreational, social, and self-medicinal purposes exerted a huge impact on subsequent social policy. As Courtwright (1997b) suggests:

> Jailing sick-old-lady addicts or patients whose prescriptions happened to contain certain drugs would have made no moral sense. . . . However, punishing junkies and crackheads and potheads (all pejorative terms of twentieth century coinage) seemed morally dramatic and satisfying. . . . (p. 242)

Clearly, one important area of research that emerges from a historical perspective on drug use is the role of social and cultural groups in influencing patterns of drug taking, and in affecting social and political responses to drugs and drug-related problems.

Social factors that are *specific* to the use of (often particular) drugs can influence patterns of use in a number of ways. In addition, more general social and cultural variables are also relevant to understanding patterns of substance use throughout history. Such factors include, but are not restricted to, urbanization, industrialization, advances in technology, demographic changes, and vacillations in general beliefs, values, norms, and expectations.

Changes in the forms of transportation, the European "discovery" of new lands, and the subsequent expansion of global trade routes from the sixteenth century onward have, together, dramatically affected the flow of psychoactive substances around the world. Such familiar substances as coffee, tea, and tobacco owe their ubiquity in modern Western society (in part) to such developments. More recently, the accelerating pace of globalization and radical transformations in transport and communication technologies over the course of the past century have facilitated even more complex global networks of drug cultivation, production, and distribution. Technological developments, however, have not only assisted the global trade in psychoactive drugs, but they have also wrought changes in the way such substances can be acceptably employed and in the very definitions of substance abuse. The regular consumption of alcoholic beverages throughout the day caused little harm in the pre-industrial world and was an accepted social practice that could be combined with work. However, in an environment of exacting and dangerous machine work, even relatively small amounts of alcohol may prove harmful and impede production. Similarly, what counts as inappropriate or excessive alcohol use has been transformed by the widespread introduction of the motor car (Courtwright, 2001; Gusfield, 1991; Westermeyer, 1991).

Demographic changes can also profoundly affect patterns of substance use in society. Cohort effects are essentially historical in nature. That is, they reflect patterns of use in a given historical period with its collection of specific social, economic, political, and cultural circumstances. Because most individuals who use drugs—illicit or otherwise—begin their drug-taking careers during adolescence or young adulthood (Kandel & Chen, 1995) and tend to reduce consumption as they mature (Kandel & Yamaguchi, 1999; Price, Risk & Spitznagel, 2001), the availability and popularity of specific drugs at particular times and places becomes especially important. The skewed age distribution arising from the postwar baby boom, for example, resulted in a relatively disproportionate number of individuals entering adolescence and early adulthood during the 1960s—one important factor in the burgeoning use of drugs in this period (Courtwright, 2001). Changes over time regarding the age that people enter parenthood and get married are also likely to be relevant, as taking on adult roles and responsibilities is related to declines in substance use (Bachman et al., 1996). Although we know of no systematic research that has explored these relationships over long time periods, the extended period of young adulthood that is emerging in modern Western societies and the deferment of adult roles (Arnett, 1998) may well contribute to longer drug-taking careers.

Changes in drug use over time are also influenced by prevailing patterns of general beliefs, norms, values, and expectations. Tobacco, coffee, tea, and cocoa, for example, rapidly became popular substances in European cultures in part because they were commensurate with an emerging ethic of self-restraint, discipline, and individual responsibility. In contrast to the use of alcohol, the consumption of these relatively new substances did not result in intoxication and unruly behavior, but rather promoted sobriety and respectability (Goodman, 1995; Matthee, 1995; Schivelbusch, 1992). Likewise, attitudes toward alcohol in American society, and subsequent levels of use, have been profoundly influenced by predominant beliefs, values, and norms regarding self-discipline, health, and morality. Temperance movements tend to flourish in an environment where beliefs about the value of self-control and propriety dominate, and ideas regarding health and morality are intertwined (Gusfield, 1997). As the nature and predominance of religious beliefs and liberal ideas have changed over time in American culture, so too have attitudes toward the use of alcohol and other drugs. More generally, Buchanan (1992) has argued that substance use in American society reflects "a wrenching tension between conflicting ideals of liberation and communal obligation" (p. 33). Consequently, Buchanan avers that substantial increases in drug use have occurred during periods of national crisis such as the American Revolution, the Civil War, and the 1960s, as drug use becomes linked to independence and the forging of new social identities. Reactions to these periods of excess, however, are quick to occur as communal ideals come to the fore and drug use declines.

Although there is much merit in Buchanan's analysis and other attempts to explain broad patterns of substance use over time (e.g., Musto, 1999), it must always be recognized that the way drugs are used at any given time and place is affected by a myriad of different factors, which may themselves be causally related. Changes in prevailing ideological and religious beliefs, fluctuations in norms and values, transformations in technology, and demographic shifts have all affected drug use in important—although often difficult to quantify—ways. This suggests that it is essential to pay attention to the "culture at large" in understanding patterns of drug use and drug-related problems.

A COMPLEX WEB: MULTIPLE
INFLUENCES ON PATTERNS OF DRUG USE

In the preceding sections we have treated the range of factors that have impacted on patterns of substance use across time in a predominantly independent fashion. However, explanations for historical changes in drug use are naturally more complex than such an analysis implies. The use of drugs is always affected by combinations of these factors, which themselves often interact in complex ways. Moreover, the relative importance of each factor varies from case to case. In short, each historical episode in which drug use has been examined is unique in its details, even if more general similarities can be extracted.

Sometimes the interactions between relevant factors and substance use can be illustrated in a relatively simple and straightforward

Figure 5.1   The effects of prohibition on drug potency and drug-related harm

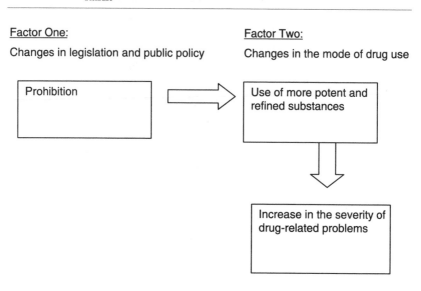

fashion. For example, Thornton's (1998) suggestion that when a drug is prohibited, it leads to the use of more potent forms of the substance and hence increases its liability for abuse, dependence, and other drug-related harm can be easily depicted (see Figure 5.1). This interaction captures important features of a number of episodes in history, including National Prohibition in the United States and the rise in heroin use in a number of Southeast Asian countries in the 1950s and 1960s. Typically, though, other factors will be at work that moderate these relationships, and the interactions among factors will be substantially more complex.

An illustration of the way that multiple factors interact to influence patterns of substance use is provided by the so-called British gin epidemic of the eighteenth century (see Figure 5.2). Permission was first granted by Parliament to set up distilleries in England in 1689 (Edwards, 2000). Distilled liquor thus represented a novel—and more potent—variation on a familiar substance. Five years later, the total British annual consumption of spirits was about 800,000 gallons. Less than half a century later, in 1736, this figure had risen dramatically to some 6 million gallons (Matthee, 1995; Warner et al., 2001). Given a long cultural history of heavy drinking in England, the popularity of spirits was not surprising. Indeed, the consumption of beer remained static during this period, indicating that the use of spirits was in *addition* to an already considerable alcohol intake. Dramatic rises in gin consumption were fueled by a surplus of grain, reductions in cost, and repressive social conditions that favored drunkenness as a cheap and convenient form of escape. Concerns over excessive gin drinking, although real enough, were fueled by fears of social unrest, crime, and loss of control (Warner, 1994a). Originally a drink of middle- and upper-class origin, by 1720 gin was very much an intoxicant of the lower classes. It was convenient, therefore, to saddle the blame for social unrest, rises in crime, and moral infractions on gin rather than more complex and less tractable social causes. Rum, too expensive for the poor, was exempt from the attack on spirits, and so too was beer, ale, and cider. Indeed, brewers enthusiastically supported the gin reforms—although as noted, consumption of beer did not actually drop during this period.

Responses to the problem were varied and included depictions in the media of the harms of gin, gin taxes, and restrictions on places of sale and consumption. Hostile attitudes toward gin were immortalized in Hogarth's famous engravings, "Beer Street" and "Gin Lane." The happy folk of "Beer Street" were depicted as honest, industrious, and merry as they hoisted great foaming tankards of beer, with only the pawnbroker's shop in disarray. The unfortunate residents of "Gin Lane," however, cavorted in a debauched fashion amid crumbling buildings (except for the now-profitable pawnbroker), with a depraved, bare-breasted woman at the center of the picture carelessly dropping her wailing infant to its probable demise. The gin epidemic also represented the earliest example of systematic intervention by the government in the control of alcohol (Warner et al., 2001). Between 1700 and 1770 there were no fewer than 11 interventions by the state, the most important being the gin acts of 1729, 1736, and 1757. The first two acts attempted to control the consumption of gin by levying taxes to raise prices and by demanding that retailers be licensed—for a substantial fee. These regulations proved all but unenforceable, as gin was sold in such a variety of places—from cellars to street corners, from barges to back rooms—that effective policing (at a time before an effective police force) was impossible. As Warner et al. (2001) have shown, consumption of gin did decline in the year following each act but soon rebounded to former levels. The gin act of 1757 actually banned the

Figure 5.2   Factors involved in the English gin epidemic of the eighteenth century

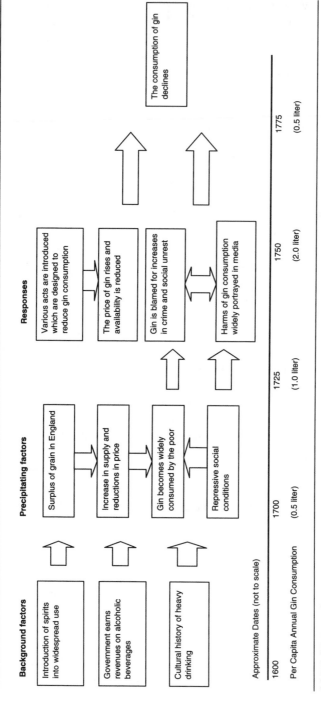

SOURCE: Based on Warner et al. (2001).

production of distilled spirits entirely, but this was more a response to poor grain harvests than uncontrolled gin consumption, and the ban was lifted in 1760. Altogether, gin consumption increased by more than 400% between 1700 and 1745, but declined gradually thereafter to stabilize at a higher than pre-epidemic level, but which was substantially less than that found at the peak of the epidemic (Warner et al., 2001).

The lesson to draw from this example for contemporary patterns of use and drug-related problems is that any systematic policy initiative cannot be based on the alteration of single factors. Rather, efforts to reduce the harms that arise from the use of drugs must target the full range of relevant variables and be sensitive to the way that such factors might interact with one another. The history of drug use provides some guides to the way that different factors might be involved, although we should add that each specific episode will be unique, and unexpected interactions may well arise.

SUMMARY

Much of our current discourse on drugs centers on the harm that these substances can cause for both individuals and society, and how such harm can be reduced or eliminated. This focus is entirely understandable: many individuals suffer as a result of their drug taking, and the costs of substance use on society are considerable. Examining the way that drugs have been employed at other times, however, reminds us both of the diverse ways that such substances have been used and the equally diverse responses to such use that have occurred. Returning to Zinberg's elucidation of the role of drug, set, and setting on the effects of psychoactive substances, we suggest that these three factors are equally important in understanding the history of drugs. Changing rates of drug problems and views of drugs *as* problems have been influenced in profound ways by the nature and mode of the substance consumed; beliefs, attitudes, and expectations regarding drugs; and the sociocultural contexts in which use has occurred. Our overview of the historical factors that have influenced patterns of drug use highlights some important theoretical linkages among biological, psychosocial, and cultural-historical levels of analysis. The appeal of drugs, generally speaking, lies in their ability to generate certain psychological states as a result of their interaction with evolved brain systems (see Chapter 3). However, to what extent drugs are used and the problems that they cause depend to a large extent on individual norms, values, beliefs, and expectations, which are in turn shaped by cultural-historical environments.

The history of drug use is, of course, open to multiple interpretations (e.g., compare Courtwright, 1998, with Szasz, 1998, on the implications of history for drug legislation). However, by taking a historical perspective on substance use, attention can be more closely focused on the rich economic, political, social, and cultural contexts of use. In particular, a historical perspective allows us adequately to address a range of specific questions—such as why levels of use have changed over time, and why some substances are licit while others are not—in a manner that other perspectives cannot.

NOTES

1.   As we note in Chapter 2, substances like coffee and tobacco may be used to suppress appetite even though they have not been employed (as far as we know) for their nutritional value. Of course, both substances are taken, in part, because users enjoy their "taste."

2.   Alcohol is the interesting exception to these general points, and the only potentially dangerous *intoxicating* substance (we exclude tobacco and caffeine here, as their effects on emotion and cognition are more subtle) that is licit and widely available in Western countries. The cultural embeddedness of alcohol in Western society has insulated it, with the obvious exception of brief national prohibitions, from strict medical and legal control.

3.   Not all such developments, however, are necessarily harmful. The introduction of methadone and the development of nicotine patches and chewing gum are two examples of new forms of drugs that have served to ameliorate drug-related problems.

4.   "The price elasticity of demand" is defined as "the percentage change in consumption associated with a 1% increase in price" (Caulkins, 2001, p. 1446). Commodities with price elasticities under 1% are considered relatively inelastic in nature, so the use of opium in the Dutch East Indies was fairly sensitive to price changes: increases in price resulted in commensurate reductions in use.

5.   Of course, as many studies have demonstrated, people may not assess such costs and benefits *accurately*, and under many circumstances costs may be discounted, especially if they are distal in nature (see Hernstein, 1990; Hill, Ross, & Low, 1997).

6.   In making these points we do not, in any way, deny that drugs are responsible for, and related to, many social problems. Rather, they can rarely be viewed as the sole or even principal cause of such problems.

6

Drugs and Culture

INTRODUCTION

At the headwaters of the Amazon River, in eastern Bolivia, lives a group of people known as the Camba. The Camba, thanks to more than 30 years of anthropological research by Dwight Heath and others (Heath, 1991a, 1991b, 1994), are renowned for their extraordinary patterns of heavy drinking. Alcohol made from sugar cane, containing a startling 89% pure ethanol, is imbibed in large quantities in the context of frequent fiestas and other social events. The drinking of this potent form of alcohol is a ritualized affair. Individuals, one at a time, make a toast to another participant, down their glass of alcohol, and pass the glass on to the person whom they have just toasted, who does the same, and so on. These drinking bouts may last for several days—until the alcohol runs out, or the participants have to go back to work. The remarkable finding from Heath's early research was that, despite these regular episodes of what might be termed "binge drinking" and the drunkenness that accompanied them, "aggression and sexual license are conspicuously absent. . . . Moreover, there is no evidence whatsoever of individual instances of dependence upon alcohol comparable to alcoholism or addiction as it is known in the United States" (Heath, 1991b, p. 65). Drinking in Camba society, Heath concluded, played at integral role in the development and maintenance of social relations, and caused few if any problems.

The role of alcohol in Camba society and similar reports of the "socially integrative" function of drinking from other cultural groups (e.g., Field, 1991; Lemert, 1958) offer a stark contrast to alcohol use and alcohol-related problems in Western society. Perhaps, as MacAndrew and Edgerton (1969) suggested in their pioneering book *Drunken Comportment*, the behavioral problems that arise from alcohol consumption are the result of social learning processes rather than a direct consequence of alcohol's physiological effects. Significant cultural variation in the use and abuse of alcohol and other drugs is also prominent *within* Western societies. In the United States, for example, there are important differences between various ethnic groups in the prevalence of substance use, levels of abuse and dependence, frequency of drug-related emergency room visits, and criminal arrests for drug possession and sale (e.g., Kandel, 1995). Patterns of drug use and drug-related problems are also related to other sociodemographic characteristics such as age, gender, socioeconomic status, and various lifestyle variables. For example, in Great Britain, frequency of visits to nightclubs and participation in the "rave music scene" is positively associated with the consumption of drugs such as ecstasy and LSD (Ramsay, Baker, Goulden, Sharp, & Sondhi, 2001).

The aim of this chapter is to provide an overview of the relationship between drug use and culture, focusing on the patterns of drug use that are found among different cultural groups. However, the relations between culture and substance use are not straightforward. Indeed, the very concepts of "race," "ethnicity," and "culture" are fraught with multiple interpretations, and are measured and employed in various ways. We begin, therefore, by providing an overview of some important conceptual and methodological issues in the study of culture and drug use. We then provide a review of "indigenous" or "traditional" patterns of substance use. An examination of the ways that drugs are employed in different cultural contexts provides an interesting contrast to more familiar patterns of drug use in Western society. Finally, we outline how patterns of drug use and drug-related problems vary in important ways *within* Western society as a function of membership in specific ethnic and social groups. One important question that arises from this review is, What factor or factors can explain these differences in the way that drugs are used across cultures and between different ethnic and social groups? Providing a satisfactory answer to this question is important not only in advancing our theoretical understanding of drug-taking behavior, but also in the development of effective prevention, treatment, and policy initiatives. We argue that a cultural-historical perspective is the most *salient* level of analysis from which to address this important question, and in Chapter 7 we review various explanations for the pattern of findings discussed in detail in this chapter.

CONCEPTUAL AND METHODOLOGICAL ISSUES

Before we can effectively elucidate the relationship between culture and drug use, it is important to clarify the concepts of "culture," "race," and "ethnicity." As sociologists and anthropologists are quick to point out, there are numerous definitions of *culture*, which although similar in some respects, also vary in important ways. At the heart of most concepts of culture, however, are the opposing notions of similarity and difference: a cultural group is one that *shares* a set of norms, values, concepts, beliefs, and practices, which, in part, *differentiates* them from other cultural groups. An important distinction can also be made between the *products* that identify cultural groups and the *process* by which they are acquired, although both features are typically bound up in definitions of culture. Through the process of what has been variously termed "social learning," "socialization," or "enculturation," members of a cultural group take on the characteristics (beliefs, values, norms, practices, and so forth) that define that group and distinguish it from others. In what follows, we shall use the term "cultural group" to characterize a collection of individuals who tend to share a set of values, norms, beliefs, concepts, and practices. The idea of a cultural group does not imply *uniformity* in these attributes; instead, it captures the idea that groups can be distinguished from each other, in part, on the basis of such characteristics.

One important kind of cultural group, which forms the basis for much of our discussion on the relations between culture and drug use, is an "ethnic group." The idea of "ethnicity" has largely replaced the older concept of "race," which, as Ashley Montagu (1964) unequivocally asserted, "is nothing but a whited sepulchre, a conception . . . [that] is utterly erroneous and meaningless, and . . . should be dropped from the vocabulary of the anthropologist, for it has done an infinite amount of harm and no good at all" (p. 3). The idea of race has been roundly attacked by sociologists, anthropologists, psychologists, and biologists alike as a social construct with no grounding in biological reality (e.g., Cornell & Hartmann, 1998; Jenkins, 1997; Lewontin, Rose, & Kamin, 1984; Montagu, 1964; Phinney, 1996; Winant, 2000). Winant (2000), for example, claims, "There is no biological basis for distinguishing human groups along the lines of race, and the sociohistorical categories employed to differentiate among these groups reveal themselves, upon serious examination, to be imprecise if not completely arbitrary" (p. 172). Although we might cavil at the claim that the notion of race is *completely arbitrary*, it is, as Winant suggests, imprecise, and thus of limited descriptive, explanatory, or predictive value.

The notion of "ethnicity," however, has its own problems, and does not necessarily cover the same conceptual ground as that of "race" (Cheung, 1990–1991; Cornell & Hartmann, 1998; Jenkins, 1997). The concept of "race," as it has been typically applied, refers to the delineation of particular groups primarily on the basis of *physical* criteria, like skin color, and is usually a label thrust on groups by others. The idea of "ethnicity," by contrast, tends to reflect the shared cultural history of groups of individuals who are usually also bound by common descent. Ethnic groupings may be assigned by others or arise from within the group itself. In practical terms, however, there appear to be multiple ways of cashing out the concept of ethnicity, depending on who is employing the concept and for what reasons (see Heath, 1990–1991).

These conceptual issues are not only of theoretical importance; they also have implications for our understanding of many social problems, including ones that arise from the use and misuse of psychoactive substances. Whatever the difficulties in delineating the boundaries of ethnic groups, it is clear that patterns of drug taking, and consequently drug-related problems, differ in a number of ways as a function of ethnicity. Providing appropriate ethnic categories and suitable measures of ethnic identity, therefore, is crucial in furthering our understanding of these important differences. Too often, as Trimble (1990–1991) has pointed out, "descriptions of ethnic and cultural groups tend to rely on the use of broad 'ethnic glosses,' superficial, almost vacuous, categories which serve only to separate one group from another" (pp. 152–153).

The use of such "ethnic glosses" can often mask considerable within-group heterogeneity (Cheung, 1990–1991; Phinney, 1996; Trimble, 1990–1991). The label "Native American," for instance, obscures as it embraces the rich cultural diversity of more than 2 million individuals and more than 500 different tribal affiliations (Castro, Proescholdbell, Abeita, & Rodriguez, 1999). Similarly, the term "Asian," as it is sometimes employed in the United States, covers a diverse range of different cultural groups: Japanese, Chinese, Filipino, Korean, Hmong, and so forth, who differ not only on important demographic characteristics (e.g., Waters & Eschbach, 1995), but also in regard to patterns of drug use. The problems that arise from the use of broad labels for heterogeneous groups of individuals are compounded by changes in ethnic identities over time as a result of immigration, acculturation, and so on. Crucially, it is important to recognize that ethnic groups are not static, monolithic entities, but rather are dynamic and fluid in nature, and are subject to often rapid cultural change.

There is thus a need to recognize that ethnicity is not a straightforward categorical variable (Lock, 1993; Phinney, 1996). Rather, it is a complex, multifaceted concept that encompasses notions of identity, meaning, and social-structural relations (Jenkins, 1997). It is essential, therefore, to "unpack" the idea of ethnicity (Phinney, 1996) and to move beyond descriptive analyses, to embrace "culturally competent theory that captures significant aspects of the *experience* of ethnicity . . ." (Castro et al., 1999, p. 500; emphasis added). As we shall see over the course of the next two chapters, such variables as degree of acculturation, ethnic identification, immigration status, and so forth play important roles in understanding cultural differences in patterns of substance use and abuse. Furthermore, in a clinical context, there is a need to treat clients as individuals rather than in terms of cultural stereotypes, and to establish their experience of culture over and above basic demographic categorization (e.g., Huriwai, Robertson, Armstrong, & Huata, 2001).

An "ethnic group" is one important kind of cultural group, but it is not the only one. Individuals can belong to what might be termed "social groups"—collections of people who share certain interests, beliefs, values, and practices, but who are not necessarily tied by common descent or "deep" cultural roots. Social groups may be relatively ephemeral—such as members of an animal rights group or adherents of "dance culture," or they may be more enduring. Individuals may belong to multiple social groups or change their group identity over time. Furthermore, the nature of the group itself may also evolve in important ways. One kind of social group that has been the subject of much discussion in sociological circles is captured by the concept of "subcultures." A "subculture," as it has been typically employed, refers to a group of individuals bound by a specific set of beliefs, values, and practices that differ from those in the mainstream culture of which they are a part. The concept of a "subculture," however, is often a pejorative term that connotes rebellion against the values of the wider cultural group; thus we prefer to use the more neutral idea of a "social group."

In exploring cultural differences in patterns of substance use, there is a need to recognize both the benefits and limitations of various methodological approaches. Much of our information about cultural differences in rates of drug use within multicultural societies such as the United States, Australia, and Great Britain is based on large-scale surveys employing self-report measures. Despite attempts to minimize reporting biases, there will always be some limitations on the use of such measures, especially regarding behaviors like drug use, which may be illicit in nature. However, the important question is whether these problems are likely to vary in systematic ways depending on membership in specific cultural groups. For example, will ethnic minorities underestimate their drug use because of the social stigma and discriminatory responses that often accompany their drug-taking behavior? Are there systematic ethnic differences in response rates to surveys that might skew results? Do most surveys miss a greater proportion of some cultural groups by not sampling certain populations, such as prison inmates or the homeless? Are there different cultural interpretations of what counts as a "drink," or a drug-taking episode, that might bias results? These are important questions that need to be addressed. Although there is some attempt to minimize bias arising from these sources, more research is needed to explore potential ways that ethnic differences might manifest in survey responses, and which might obscure the "true" nature of drug use (see Collins, 1995; Kandel, 1995; Wallace, Bachman, O'Malley, & Johnston, 1995, for a discussion of these issues, and Dawson & Room, 2000; Room, 2000, for general issues relating to the measurement of alcohol use).

An illustration of the kinds of problems that can arise from standard survey methods is provided by Strunin's (2001) qualitative analysis of alcohol consumption by African American and Haitian adolescents. The results of this study suggest higher rates of alcohol use than previously recognized using standard survey instruments. Moreover, it transpired that what counted as a "drink" or "drinking" for these participants suggested problems with standard questionnaire methods. "Sips" and "tastes" of alcohol, frequently reported by individuals, did not count as "drinking" for them, and some drinks favored by Haitians, such as "kremas" and "likay," which often contain rum, were not recognized as alcoholic beverages. Moreover, the conceptualization of time, crucial to most survey research, differed from what might be expected: a small but significant number of participants reported that they had not consumed alcohol in the past six months, but that they had in the past month, suggesting that they perceived the past month as separate from the past six months. Strunin (2001), on the basis of this research, concluded, "The use of ethnographic interviewing and other qualitative methods in assessing alcohol use among different racial and/or ethnic groups of adolescents reveal drinking patterns that would otherwise be concealed by survey methods" (p. 224) (see also Medina-Mora, Borges, & Villatoro, 2000; and Obot, 2000, for measurement issues relating to alcohol use in other cultural contexts).

The use of time-consuming qualitative methods, of course, would simply not be practical with the large sample sizes employed by national surveys such as the National Household Survey on Drug Abuse, which, despite their limitations, still provide valuable information about cultural differences in patterns of drug use. Perhaps the best recommendation should be to adopt a stance of "resolute methodological pluralism." That is, to avoid drawing conclusions based on research employing uniform methods, and to explore multiple methodological avenues for investigating cultural differences in drug use patterns. Such an approach necessitates cross-disciplinary research, which draws on the particular skills and methods that are fostered within different academic disciplines, such as anthropology, sociology, psychology, economics, and epidemiology.

Despite considerable interest in drug use across such interdisciplinary boundaries, Hunt and Barker (2001) in their recent overview of sociocultural approaches to alcohol and drug research, suggest a number of avenues for further research. Little is known, for example, about the culture of qat, betel, and even cannabis use. There is also a striking lack of research on middle-class users, who after all, are influenced by cultural factors. There is also a need, it is suggested, to explore the rich social interrelations of production, distribution, and consumption, rather than focusing on drug *use* alone. Such research, Hunt and Barker (2001) claim, would contribute to a better understanding of the social context of drug use and how it is embedded in a network of political, economic, familial, and community relations. More generally, there has been a call to explore the "political economy of drugs" (Singer, 1986, 2001) and to locate drug use within the broader issues arising from the flow of wealth, production, and political interests. Intrusive political agendas, for example, have thwarted national funding for syringe exchange programs in America, despite overwhelming evidence as to their value in reducing drug-related problems, such as the transmission of HIV (Singer, 2001).

Cultural approaches to substance use and abuse are valuable in a number of important ways. They allow us, as we have noted, to address questions relating to differences in patterns of drug use between different cultural groups. Providing explanations for such differences is also relevant in the development of effective and culturally sensitive intervention initiatives. By adopting a cultural perspective, we are able to step outside of familiar Western frameworks for categorizing, describing, and explaining drug use and drug-related problems. For example, are the problems associated with drug use in Western society an inevitable feature of the cultural landscape, or are there other ways of thinking about our relations with drugs that can minimize or even eliminate such problems? Cultural approaches also encourage the development of alternative methods that can complement quantitative and experimental approaches with detailed ethnographies rich in "thick description" (Room, 1984), which use qualitative methodologies (e.g., Strunin, 2001).

INDIGENOUS PATTERNS OF DRUG USE

As we have noted previously, the use of psychoactive substances is almost universal across cultures. Drugs that are more familiar to Western readers, such as alcohol, cocaine, and cannabis, form a small part of the rich repertoire of such substances traditionally employed by diverse cultural groups around the world. In this section we provide a brief overview of indigenous or traditional patterns of drug use. This begs the question of just what *counts* as "traditional" or "indigenous." Given the often rapid nature of cultural change and the way that drugs can diffuse quickly to different geographical regions, it is not always easy to discern the traditional from the novel. What looks like a long-standing indigenous practice may in fact turn out to be of more recent origin, or have been influenced in important ways by contemporary developments. These points remind us that cultures, whether exposed to Western ideas and practices or not, are not static entities, but rather change and develop over time. However, we will not be too concerned with certifying the traditional authenticity of the drug use we describe, but rather offer this section as a complement to our discussion of the history of drugs in Western cultures provided in Chapter 4. As such, we describe drug use in various places as it occurred prior to contact with Western cultures, as well as outlining contemporary patterns of use. Space precludes an exhaustive discussion of drug use in different cultures;[1] however, we hope to provide enough detail to enable a picture to be drawn of the way that different drugs are used in a diverse array of cultural contexts.

Oceania

Indigenous Australians, prior to European colonization, used a number of different psychoactive substances, including various species of native tobacco, alcohol, and pituri (Brady, 1991; Dobkin de Rios, 1990). About 13 species of native tobacco have been identified in Australia; these were mixed with ash and usually chewed rather than smoked. Various alcoholic beverages were also made from indigenous flora. It is suggested, however, that given limitations in supply, storage, and transportation, the use of these alcoholic beverages was neither widespread nor of major cultural significance (Brady, 1991).

By far the most important psychoactive substance used by indigenous Australians was pituri, the local name for plants of the *Dubiosia* genus, of which there are three species (Dobkin de Rios & Stachalek, 1999). The pituri plant is a shrub that grows to about 4 meters in height, and the leaves and stem of the plant are dried, mixed with ash, and usually consumed in the form of a wad. The primary alkaloids responsible for pituri's psychoactive effects are hyoscine (a form of scopolamine), hyoscamine, and, in some varieties, nicotine. Pituri was employed in a variety of different contexts. It was consumed, for instance, for pragmatic reasons such as to alleviate thirst, pain, and hunger—valuable attributes in a predominantly hot and dry continent. Pituri was an important item of trade and was transported long distances along a series of trails known as the "pituri roads" in order to barter for other commodities. Pituri was also used in social contexts and on ceremonial occasions. Its use in male initiation rites, which involved genital circumcision and subincision, was especially important. Pituri served multiple functions in these contexts: as an anesthetic, amnesic,[2] and, by inducing states of suggestibility, as a way of inculcating cultural beliefs and values (Dobkin de Rios, 1990; Dobkin de Rios & Stachalek, 1999). The functional role of pituri is summed up by Dobkin de Rios and Stachalek (1999): "It is clear that hallucinogenic plants like pituri were used to create states of consciousness, particularly hypersuggestible ones, in order to enculturate adolescents with a special consciousness state that contributed to the survival success of the community" (pp. 160–161). It is claimed that because the pituri plant was in fairly limited supply and its use was controlled by adults, levels of abuse were negligible or nonexistent (Dobkin de Rios & Stachalek, 1999).

While indigenous Australians exploited the psychoactive properties of the pituri plant, various native tobacco species, and on occasion alcohol, the most common mind-altering drug traditionally employed throughout the Pacific was (and still is) kava. Kava is a beverage made from the roots of the kava plant, *Piper methysticum*—the "intoxicating pepper." This perennial shrub thrives in warm, moist conditions and grows to a height of about 6 meters, although it is usually harvested when it is about 2 1/2 meters tall (Singh, 1992). Kava is prepared by processing the roots and infusing them with water to make a cloudy, astringent-tasting beverage. The traditional method of preparation in many cultures—much to the disgust of Christian missionaries—involved chewing the kava roots, spitting out the masticated pulp, and then adding water to the mixture before straining the residue into a bowl (Lebot, Merlin, & Lindstrom, 1992; Singh, 1992).

The cultivation and consumption of kava is widespread in Pacific Island cultures, and it plays an important role in a variety of different contexts: social, medicinal, recreational, and ritual-religious. Kava is particularly valued for its role in social contexts. Kava is a substance that is intimately associated with peace, sociability, and amiable relations between people, and is rarely consumed outside of a social setting. Kava's traditional role in social contexts takes on many forms. It is used, for example, as an important item of social exchange among island people. The offering of kava or the gift of a kava plant or the roots of the plant are often indicated in many important contexts such as weddings, initiation ceremonies, and funerals. Kava also takes on an important role in the welcoming of visitors, especially those high in status. For example, the Tongans brought out a gift of kava on their canoes for Captain Cook as a mark of friendship and good will when his ships arrived in their waters. This practice still remains in many Pacific Islands, and visiting dignitaries to Tonga, Samoa, and Fiji are welcomed with a traditional kava ceremony (Lebot et al., 1992; Singh, 1992). The kava ceremony, especially as practiced in Fiji, Tonga, and Samoa, also serves to demarcate important social boundaries and to maintain political hierarchies within island communities. The order in which kava is served is of special importance, with the highest-ranking individuals drinking first, in strict order of hierarchical status. Kava drinking in Polynesia is usually the sole prerogative of males, with women's consumption of kava typically forbidden. However, this varies somewhat in different cultures, and the use of kava by women has become more acceptable in recent years (Lebot et al., 1992; Pollock, 2000).

The use of kava is also prominent in ritual-religious contexts in many Pacific Island cultures. Although the effects of kava may be relatively subtle in nature compared with other psychoactive substances, they still entail altered states of consciousness that are deemed valuable in certain contexts. The kava experience is used, for example, because of the belief that it can facilitate communion with the gods or ancestors. Kava is also used in many therapeutic settings. Indeed, kava appears to be the central ingredient in the pharmacopoeia of Pacific Island societies, and is used in the treatment of gonorrhea, urinary tract problems, menstrual difficulties, headaches, insomnia, skin diseases, and so on (see Lebot et al., 1992, pp. 112–118 for a summary). It is interesting that the therapeutic value of kava, especially its putative anxiolytic effects, is becoming increasingly recognized in the West (e.g., Kilham, 1996).

One important question concerning the use of kava is to what extent it is a drug of abuse in Pacific Island societies. Traditionally, sanctions, regulations, and norms regarding the use of kava limited the possibility of extensive abuse. Kava drinking in almost all societies was restricted by a number of factors, such as sex, age, social status, and time of day. Moreover, because the use of kava was intimately bound up in specific ritual-religious contexts, the potential for abuse was limited. However, even though these factors must have restricted kava's potential for abuse in traditional settings, problems arising from kava's use were not unknown, and early European accounts of excessive kava consumption in some Pacific Island communities with the attendant problems of skin lesions, poor health, and apathy were noted (Brunton, 1989). More recently, cultural changes in the Pacific Islands appear to have affected patterns of kava use with a concomitant increase in kava-related problems (McDonald & Jowitt, 2000).

European colonization of Australia and the Pacific in the eighteenth century has, not surprisingly, changed the social ecology of drug use in these regions. Although kava is still widely employed in Pacific Island cultures, the use of pituri by indigenous Australians is now virtually unknown. Most significant, many new substances, such as alcohol and tobacco, were introduced with overwhelmingly harmful consequences (see Marshall, 1987, 1991). Alcohol problems, in particular, are prominent among indigenous Australians and are also common in some Pacific Island communities (Dernbach & Marshall, 2001; Lemert, 1964; Saggers & Gray, 1998). Kava abuse has also been reported among communities of indigenous Australians (e.g., Gregory & Cawte, 1988), although the introduction of kava has been viewed by some as an antidote to alcohol problems and levels of use may be comparable to those found in Pacific Island cultures (see Cawte, 1986; Clough, Burns, & Mununggurr, 2000).

Asia

A variety of psychoactive substances have a long history of use throughout the diverse cultural environments of Asia. Some of these drugs, such as alcohol, opium, tea, and cannabis, are familiar in Western contexts, whereas others, such as betel, are virtually unknown. We have already briefly mentioned the use of opium, tea, and cannabis in India, China, and Southeast Asia in Chapter 4, and these substances have been employed in these regions for several millennia. Opium and tea in particular both have an extended association with Chinese culture, but alcoholic beverages such as rice wine and millet beer have also long been employed (Comer, 2000). Although opium, cannabis, and, to a lesser extent, alcohol have been employed in Asian cultures for more than 1,000 years, the oldest, most popular, and most widespread psychoactive substance in Asia is betel.

Betel, or as it is sometimes inaccurately referred to, "betel nut," is the seed of the areca palm (*Areca catechu*), which is usually mixed with slaked lime and encased in the leaf of the betel plant (*Piper betle*), formed into a wad, and chewed (Rooney, 1993). It is estimated that some 10% of the world's population are consumers of betel, making it the fourth most popular psychoactive substance after nicotine, ethanol, and caffeine (Hirsch, 1995). Betel consumption is widespread: from Tanzania and Madagascar in the east, to the Indian subcontinent, Southeast Asia, New Guinea, and Melanesia in the west. It also has a long history. A skeleton found in caves in the Philippines, for example, dating to 2680 B.C.E., possessed the characteristic stained teeth that accompany habitual betel consumption, and remains of *Areca catechu* dating to 10,000 B.C.E. have been found in caves in northern Thailand (Rooney, 1993; Rudgley, 1993).

The appeal of betel lies in its ability to suppress hunger and fatigue and to promote feelings of well-being. As such, it is used to enhance both work and social activities. It is also reputed to be an aphrodisiac and imparts a pleasant odor to the user's breath. Nine alkaloids have been identified in the typical betel nut wad, the most significant being arecoline, a stimulant with nicotine-like properties. Indeed, the way that betel is used resembles the use of tobacco or coffee in Western cultures, as it is consumed throughout the day with little or no restrictions on age or sex. Betel therefore is employed predominantly in pragmatic and social contexts, although it is also a substance with significant economic and symbolic value and is exchanged in the context of marriage negotiations (Rooney, 1993). Surprisingly little research has been carried out on the potential harm of betel consumption, especially considering the large number of regular users. However, there is a suggestion that long-term chronic use may contribute to the development of oral cancers, and that excessive consumption may lead to psychomotor agitation and psychotic symptoms (Cawte, 1985). More recently, there are some indications that betel use might actually *reduce* both the negative and positive symptoms of schizophrenia (Sullivan, Allen, Otto, Tiobech, & Nero, 2000). Clearly more research is needed on the contextual and medicinal implications of betel use.

Whereas the use of betel in Asian cultures is largely unproblematic and of little concern to Western interests, the cultivation and use of other substances such as opium and cannabis is viewed less benignly. Opium poppies, for instance, are intensively cultivated in the region known as the "The Golden Triangle," which encompasses the hilly northern areas of Thailand, Laos, and Myanmar. In Myanmar alone it was estimated that more than 146,000 hectares of illicit opium were cultivated in 1994—about as much as all the other major opium producing regions combined (Farrell, 1998). The *use* of opium is also widespread in these regions in a variety of contexts, from recreational to medicinal, and the prevalence of opium dependence is often high (Westermeyer, 1981). For instance, it was estimated that there were more than 300,000 individuals dependent on heroin in Myanmar in 1998, around half the number found in the United States (Cherry, 2002a). Opium also has a long history of use in India, where it has been employed in medicinal, social, and recreational settings since at least the ninth century C.E. (Sharma, 1996). Chowdhury (1995) has argued that in harsh desert regions such as Rajasthan the use of opium plays an important role in enabling the inhabitants to cope with adverse social and environmental stresses, and attempts at intervention and control should be sensitive to these facts (see also Ganguly, Sharma, &

Krishnamachari, 1995; Gossop, 1995). However, concern has also been raised over the *harm* caused by opium in these communities, especially as more traditional patterns of opiate use are being replaced by the use of heroin and synthetic opioids such as buprenorphine (Rugh, 2002; Westermeyer, 1995a).

The use of cannabis, in various forms, is also widespread in many Asian cultures, especially India. Although there are important regional variations in the use of cannabis, it is seen by many as a customary practice and is consumed in social, medicinal, and ritual contexts (Rugh, 2002). Substance use in India is strongly shaped by religious and caste affiliations. Traditionally, Hindus are forbidden to consume alcohol, but are permitted to imbibe bhang, a beverage made from cannabis (Sharma, 1996). As Carstairs (1954) has observed, the consumption of either bhang or alcohol has served to demarcate membership in specific cultural groups. However, in contemporary Indian society, although "caste, religion, and local customs play a major role in promoting and controlling substance-using behavior" (Sharma, 1996, p. 1709), drug use is widespread among different castes and religious affiliations. Indeed, in many Asian cultures, what might be termed "traditional" patterns of drug use have been substantially transformed by a combination of factors: modernization, changes in the form of drugs and their mode of administration, and the flourishing of a lucrative global black market in illicit substances.

Africa and the Middle East

A number of both familiar and less widely known psychoactive substances are employed by a diverse range of cultural groups in Africa and the Middle East. In Islamic countries alcohol is proscribed; however, both opium and cannabis have a long history of use (Baasher, 1981). In African cultures, both cannabis and alcohol are widespread. As discussed in Chapter 4, the use of cannabis spread with Arab traders into African cultures more than 500 years ago (Abel, 1980), and it has been employed by various cultural groups in medicinal, social, and ritual-religious contexts. More recently, cannabis has become a valuable cash crop in some regions—notably Malawi, Mozambique, Zambia, and South Africa. Indeed, South Africa is reported to be the largest producer of cannabis in the world after Mexico and Morocco (MacDonald, 1996). The consumption of alcohol is also widespread in sub-Saharan African cultures, predominantly in the form of homebrew beer made from a variety of plant products including millet, sorghum, maize, manioc, and cassava. Beer plays an integral role in the social and ritual life of many African cultures, and is also an important part of the diet. Indeed, some cultural groups classify beer as something that can be "eaten," clearly indicating its role as a valuable source of calories (Heath, 2000; Netting, 1964; Suggs, 2001).

Two substances less known to Western readers but widespread in some regions are qat and kola. Qat (or khat, chat, or ghat, as it is variously spelled) is the name for the evergreen shrub or tree *Catha edulis*, which grows to a height of about 10 meters. Qat is grown over a wide swathe of territory—from South Africa to Turkistan—but it is most intensively cultivated and consumed in Yemen and various East African countries, such as Somalia, Kenya, and Ethiopia (Brooke, 2000; Cassanelli, 1986). The leaves of the qat plant are typically chewed, but they must be consumed within 48 hours of being picked in order to retain their psychoactive effects. These effects are often compared to those experienced after a low dose of amphetamine, and include feelings of elation, sociability, an increase in self-esteem, and alleviation of hunger and fatigue (Kalix, 1992). The main active alkaloid in qat is *Cathinone*, which, not surprisingly given qat's psychological effects, is structurally similar to amphetamine (Pantellis, Hindler, & Taylor, 1989).

Qat is used in a number of different contexts. It is widely consumed for its stimulant and fatigue-alleviating properties by workers in various professions, from long-distance truck drivers to judges, and as an aid to prayer by religious men, especially in the month of Ramadan (when Muslims are expected to fast between dawn and dusk). Qat also has a long history of use in medicinal contexts. In Ethiopia, for example, qat is believed to cure more than 500 different diseases, and it is reputed to be effective in treating such diverse medical problems as malaria, asthma, and rheumatism (Cassanelli, 1986). The use of qat in ritual-religious and ceremonial contexts is also firmly established; it is consumed during such occasions as births, circumcisions, and marriages. In contemporary contexts, qat is an integral component of social gatherings. The regular afternoon qat party, for instance, is a familiar feature of the social landscape in places like Yemen (Kennedy, 1987). Guests typically arrive at these parties in the late afternoon and stay for 2–3 hours, chewing on wads of qat leaves, smoking tobacco, and drinking tea and soft drinks. The consumption of qat is a central component of these social occasions and encourages both sociability and solidarity. Membership and participation at qat parties reflects social divisions of labor in Yemeni society, and the seating arrangements may indicate one's position in the social hierarchy.

The consumption of qat, although firmly entrenched and socially integrated among various cultural groups, is not without its problems. Long-term chronic use of qat may result in a number of complaints, such as stomach problems, insomnia, and anorexia. Patterns of use may also reflect *dependence* on qat, although there has been little systematic evaluation of this possibility.[3] There is also some suggestion that heavy qat use might precipitate a qat-induced psychosis (paralleling psychological problems associated with heavy amphetamine use), although in traditional contexts, at least, this appears to be rare (Kalix, 1992; Pantellis et al., 1989). The spread of qat with East African migrants to Western nations has also recently become an issue of concern (e.g., Griffiths, Gossop, Wickenden, Dunworth, Harris, & Lloyd, 1997; Kalix, 1992). We discuss the use of qat outside of its traditional borders in more detail later in the chapter. However, even within its historically normal geographical boundaries, qat use has been of concern to elites, and it was banned in Somalia in 1983. This prohibition, though, probably had as much to do with qat's association with disaffected elements in Somali society, rather than, as the government claimed, economic and health concerns (Cassanelli, 1986). Rapid social change in places like Yemen, and an increasing flow of refugees from East African countries to Western cultures, has created new contexts for qat consumption that are likely to influence the way it is used and its potential for harm in a number of ways.

Another widely used stimulant that has a long and rich history in various African cultures is kola (or cola) nuts, which Lovejoy (1995) refers to as the "coffee of the Central Sudan." Kola nuts are obtained from two species of tree (*Cola nitida* and *Cola accuminata*), which grow predominantly in West Africa. The bitter nuts are typically chewed, although they may be made into a beverage. The psychological effects are similar to coffee—not surprising given that kola nuts contain caffeine, along with theobromine and kolatine, which are all central nervous system stimulants. Kola nuts, like coffee in the West (and betel in the East), are therefore used for their ability to reduce fatigue and alleviate hunger. These attributes have led to their consumption to combat weariness at work, and they have also been distributed to soldiers before battle (Lovejoy, 1995).

Kola nuts are also employed in social contexts, much as coffee and tea are in Western cultures. Given the proscription on alcohol and most other drugs in many Muslim countries, kola nuts are especially prized and are the most important psychoactive substance in use. This importance also reflects their role in therapeutic contexts: traditional Arab medicine, for instance, has listed more than 40 physical and psychological problems for which kola nuts are prescribed (Lovejoy, 1995). Although grown predominantly in West Africa, kola nuts have been an important source of trade between cultures in Central Africa for more than 1,000 years, and the value attributed to them in places like Sudan is due, in part, to their traditional scarcity (Abaka, 2000; Lovejoy, 1995). Indeed, the consumption of kola nuts is one way of displaying social status in such cultures, and they also have symbolic value in the context of courtship, marriage, and other ceremonial occasions (Drucker-Brown, 1995).

Given the popularity of coffee, tea, and tobacco in Western cultures, it is somewhat surprising that kola nuts have played a fairly limited role in Western contexts. Despite a brief period in the late nineteenth century, when kola tonics, sodas (including the original coca-cola), and chocolates were in vogue, cheaper sources of caffeine have restricted kola's use predominantly to West and Central African cultures. Little has been written on the potentially deleterious effects of kola consumption. However, it is unlikely that regular use generates any more problems than does the consumption of tea or coffee in Western cultures.

Along with the widespread use of drugs like cannabis, alcohol, kola, and qat, there are also substances used in more localized cultural contexts in Africa and the Middle East. The use of the hallucinogen *Tabernathe iboga* by the Fang people of Gabon is one such example that highlights the ritual-religious significance of drug taking in many traditional cultures (Dobkin De Rios, 1990; Fernandez, 1990). Eboka, the Fang name for *Tabernathe iboga*, is a bush that is common to the understory of equatorial forests in Africa and grows to a height of several meters. The roots of this plant, which contain the alkaloid ibogaine, are consumed after being grated, ground into a powder, and soaked in water. The effects of eboka vary, depending on the amount consumed and the context of consumption. Small doses, usually taken in the context of ceremonies, reduce fatigue and enable participants to stay awake late into the night. Eboka is also consumed in much larger quantities several times in an individual's life, in the context of initiation rituals or for a specially delineated spiritual purpose, such as to make contact with the ancestors. In the past 100 years the use of eboka has been associated with the *Bwiti* cult, which derives from a confluence of traditional spiritual beliefs and Christian influences (Fernandez, 1990). When taken in large quantities, eboka induces an altered state of consciousness that "enables men to pass from the familiar village to the mysterious forest, which harbors the secrets of the dead" (Fernandez, 1990, p. 246).

According to Fernandez, the use of eboka is strictly regulated by Bwiti cult leaders, and eboka abuse, he suggests, is unheard of. However, the death of initiates due to eboka use is not unknown, and at higher doses the threshold for toxicity can be surpassed. Recently, ibogaine (the active alkaloid in eboka) has emerged as a possible drug therapy for heroin addiction. Anecdotal evidence and the results of a few small-scale clinical trials suggest that ibogaine might reduce both withdrawal symptoms and subsequent craving for heroin (Alper, Lotsof, Frenken, Luciano, & Bastiaans, 1999; Fernandez, 1998, pp. 167–173). It may also help, suggest ibogaine's supporters, by generating a profound psychological experience that encourages heroin addicts to examine their lives from alternative perspectives. Despite a number of studies on nonhuman animals, however, the efficacy of ibogaine has yet to be evaluated in large-scale clinical trials, and some authors have urged caution (Edwards, 2000a). Further elucidation of the use of *Tabernathe iboga* in traditional ritual-religious contexts may contribute to an understanding of its effects and potential uses in other domains.

The Americas

The "New World" is home to an extraordinary variety of psychoactive plants that have been exploited by diverse cultural groups for thousands of years. Indeed, significantly more psychoactive plants have been employed in Amerindian cultures than in the Old World (Schultes, 1990).[4] Space precludes anything like a comprehensive review of the use of these substances here. We restrict ourselves, therefore, to a brief overview of the range of substances employed and examine in more depth the use of drugs within the context of ancient Aztec society.

Hallucinogenic plants have been used by various cultural groups in diverse areas of the world, from New Guinea highlanders to the reindeer herdsmen of Siberia (Dobkin de Rios, 1990). However, the traditional use of hallucinogens has been especially prevalent in New World cultures (Schultes, 1990). Various *Datura* species, for instance, played an important role in ritual-religious contexts among a number of Indian groups in North America (Dobkin De Rios, 1990). For example, the Algonquian Indians of East America exploited the psychoactive properties of jimson weed (*Datura stramonium*) in the context of male initiation rites (Schultes, 1990), and the use of datura extends south to many different cultural groups in South America. Numerous members of the cactus family also played a prominent role in the rich pharmacopoeia of Amerindian cultures. Peyote, for instance, is used by the Huichol Indians of Mexico (Furst, 1990), and has become a central component of the Native American Church. San Pedro cactus plays a similarly important role in the context of traditional Peruvian folk healing and is used to facilitate trance states that enable the *curandero* to diagnose and treat a variety of illnesses (Sharon, 1990). Other hallucinogenic substances that have been widely employed include various species of mushrooms (e.g., Wasson, 1990), water lilies (Emboden, 1981), and a variety of intoxicating snuffs (De Smet, 1985). The Yanomamö, for example, use a fine green powder made from the bark of the *yakowana* tree (among others), collectively known as *ebene*, which is blown up the nostrils and is used to facilitate contact with the spirit world. In some villages, ebene is consumed on a daily basis, and consumption is sometimes related to aggression and violence (Chagnon, 1997).

One important hallucinogen that is used by a number of different cultural groups is obtained from the rain forest vine *Banisteriopsis caapi* and forms part of potent preparations variously known as yajé, ayahuasca, and hoasca (McKenna, Luna, & Towers, 1995; Reichel-Dolmatoff, 1990). The Matsigenka of the Peruvian Amazon, for instance, use the *Banisteriopsis caapi* vine in combination with other plants to make a thick paste, which is used to enhance well-being, heal or diagnose illness, and improve hunting skills. It has also been proposed that these mixtures are effective in alleviating depression and other symptoms of psychopathology (Grob et al., 1996; Shepard, 1998). A number of other psychoactive substances are employed by the Matsigenka in ritual-religious, medicinal, and pragmatic contexts. Shepard (1998) summarizes these various functions:

Psychoactive plants play a central role in the medical system of the Matsigenka. Powerful hallucinogens provide shamans with a direct link to the spirit world. Mildly psychoactive plants are used to rein in socially disruptive emotions and to optimize the performance of men and women (and even dogs) in their respective social roles as hunters and farmers, weavers and mothers. Psychoactive plants act to restore harmonious relations in the realm of human society while fostering positive relationships with the invisible society of the spirits who control matters of life and death in the cosmos. (p. 330)

A number of non-hallucinogenic substances are also used in Amerindian cultures. Without doubt tobacco was the most widespread psychoactive substance utilized by Amerindian people throughout North and South America prior to European colonization. As we discussed briefly in Chapter 5, tobacco played an integral role in ritual-religious, medicinal, social, and pragmatic contexts (Goodman, 1993). Moreover, tobacco remains an important substance among many cultural groups, like the Waroa Indians of Venezuela, whose shamans employ it to facilitate trance states and to engage in spiritual healing (Wilbert, 1990). Coca, however, is probably the most familiar example of a South American indigenous drug, and it is still chewed today by large numbers of individuals across diverse cultural groups. Among the Barasana in Western Amazonia, for instance, coca is used in pragmatic, social, and ritual-religious contexts, and it is a revered substance with important cultural and social functions (Hugh-Jones 1995). Other substances employed include alcohol, cocoa (from the tree *Theobroma cacao*), and maté, a beverage containing caffeine made from the shrub *Ilex paraguayensis* and widely consumed throughout Argentina.

Drugs have played a prominent role not only among indigenous hunter-gatherer groups in North and South America, such as the Yanomamö and the Matsigenka, but also in the renowned ancient civilizations of the Maya, Inca, and Aztecs (Dobkin de Rios, 1990). The Aztecs of Mexico, for instance, are known both for their rich and complex civilization, epitomized in their magnificent lake city Tenochtitlan, which fell to the Spaniards in 1521, as well as for their less appealing culture of human sacrifice (Clendinnen, 1991). They are also, asserts Dobkin de Rios (1990), "one of the most interesting hallucinogenic-drug using societies for which there are data" (p. 137).

The Aztecs employed four primary hallucinogenic substances in predominantly ritual-religious contexts whose use was strictly controlled by elites. Various species of mushrooms were used (of Stropharia and Psilocybe genuses), which were collectively termed *teonanacatl*, or "God's flesh," which induced euphoria, visions, and general inebriation. A number of datura species were also used, along with peyote and the seeds of the morning glory plant, known as *ololiuqui*. These various substances were consumed primarily in ritual-religious contexts for the purpose of divination, communion with the gods, and for divine healing. The use of these drugs, however, was typically restricted to the priestly castes, although they were also employed more widely on specific ceremonial and festive occasions (Dobkin de Rios, 1990).

Psychoactive drugs also played a prominent role in Aztec medicine. As outlined in the *Codex Badianus* (1552) (see Furst, 1995), peyote was used to heal cuts, scratches, and wounds;[5] datura was employed in numerous therapeutic contexts such as the alleviation of pain; morning glory seeds were reported to cure gonorrhea, among other uses; and tobacco, as in many Amerindian cultures, had wide-ranging indications. Two other psychoactive substances of importance to the Aztecs were cacao and *pulque* or *octli*. The use of pulque—the fermented juice of the maguey cactus—was restricted to specific groups of individuals (the aged and sacrificial victims) and to specific occasions (such as marriage ceremonies), although its use may have been more widespread (Clendinnen, 1991; Paredes, 1975). Consumption of pulque, and especially drunkenness, outside of these specific ceremonial contexts was strictly forbidden and harshly punished. As described by Paredes (1975):

> The macehual [commoner] found intoxicated for the first time had his head shaven and was exposed to public derision. If he was a recidivist, he was beaten with wooden canes until he died. His dead body was then exhibited to others as an example of what would happen to the intemperate. If the drunkard was a nobleman, he was killed after the first offence. . . . (p. 1143)

It is hard to judge just how effective these social controls were, although they clearly were in place to reduce any social disruption brought about by heavy drinking and intoxication. The most sought after beverage in Aztec society, however, was chocolatl. This drink was made from the beans of the cacao tree (rich in caffeine and theobromine), which were beaten into a froth and drunk with the addition of honey and maize gruel. Chocolatl too was restricted to specific individuals (such as the priestly nobility) on specific ritual occasions, and played an important role in the context of marriage ceremonies (Clendinnen, 1991).

This discussion of Aztec drug use raises a number of interesting points. First, the sheer range and variety of psychoactive substances employed highlights the determined exploration of the botanical environment and the value placed on the psychological states induced by these plants. Second, the role of hallucinogenic plants in both ritual-religious and medicinal contexts—widespread in Amerindian cultures—suggests complex relationships among drugs, healing, and spiritual beliefs. The contrast with contemporary Western cultures is interesting. In the West, there is a fairly clean distinction between religious and medicinal contexts, and although drugs are widely used in the latter, they typically differ from the ones that individuals "want" to take for their psychological effects. Third, the control of psychoactive drugs in Aztec society suggests the role that social stratification (as clearly evident in Aztec culture) might play in encouraging elites to control the emotional, cognitive, and behavioral states of the population, to their own ends.

Contemporary patterns of drug use in the Americas have of course been shaped by 500 years of European colonization and the various global developments in drug use, which we described in Chapter 4. Alcohol problems, as in many places in the world, are prevalent among indigenous people, especially in North America (French, 2000). In recent decades, the practice of smoking coca paste has also become more common in many countries, such as Colombia, where coca has been traditionally used, with concomitant increases in dependence and other drug-related harm (Cherry, 2002b; Morales, 1990–1991). Problems with other substances, such as glue, which is cheaper than food in some places, is especially prominent among street children in countries such as Honduras and Brazil (Forster, Tannhauser, & Barros, 1996; Wittig, Wright, & Kaminsky, 1997), and clearly the *traffic* in illicit substances has major social repercussions in many countries (e.g., Clawson & Lee, 1996).

Conclusions

What can we conclude from this rapid global tour of indigenous patterns of drug use? A number of important themes emerge. First, the sheer variety of psychoactive drugs employed by cultural groups around the world highlights some of the ideas developed in our evolutionary model of substance use in Chapter 3. Wherever human populations exist, they explore the botanical resources within their environment. Many of the plants that they experiment with become incorporated into medicinal and dietary contexts. Others, by virtue of their psychoactive effects, become valued commodities used in various domains. Many of the cultural groups we describe, for example, use drugs in pragmatic contexts to enhance work and to alleviate hunger and fatigue. The use of betel, coca, qat, kola, and pituri are just some examples that we have discussed, and there are obvious parallels to the use of coffee, tea, and tobacco in Western cultures.

Drugs are also widely used in cross-cultural contexts for social reasons. The way that kava and qat are employed, for example is similar to the use of alcohol in Western contexts (although without the often overt ritual significance). Perhaps what is most striking, though, and largely absent from Western contexts, is the use of psychoactive plants—especially hallucinogenic ones—in ritual-religious ways. Substances like peyote, iboga, pituri, and ahayuasca form an integral part of the spiritual life of the many cultural groups by which they are employed. By contrast, the use of hallucinogens in Western cultures typically occurs in the absence of culturally informed beliefs and values, and is best described as recreational in nature.

The use of drugs in traditional contexts for medicinal and ritual-religious reasons is related to their capacity to generate altered states of consciousness (ASC). Indeed, a large body of anthropological research has demonstrated a relationship between ASC and healing (e.g., Jilek, 1989; Field, 1992; Shaara & Strathern, 1992; Winkelman, 1990). Although the methods of generating ASC vary considerably from culture to culture, from the use of powerful hallucinogenic drugs such as Ayahuasca (Andritzky, 1989) to fasting, stimuli bombardment, repetitive drumming, and chanting (Ward & Kemp, 1991), the function of ASC appear to be strikingly similar. Specifically, ASC are employed to generate positive psychological states and to eliminate negative ones, via appropriate cultural channels. Of course, ASC have also been a mainstay of various Western psychotherapies (see Field, 1992) and have been employed in the contexts of both psychological and physiological healing. Indeed, in explaining the efficacy of ASC, theoretical links can be drawn between psychosocial, biological, and cultural processes (see Winkelman, 2001).

ASC may be therapeutically effective via tension reduction, the generation of restorative emotional experiences (Field, 1992), and by increasing suggestibility and thus the enhancement of placebo effects (Winkelman, 1990). ASC are also associated with specific physiological changes in the body and brain, such as the release of endorphins

(Prince, 1982) and the lowering of blood pressure and heart rate, which contribute to their therapeutic efficacy. Furthermore, ASC occur in specific cultural contexts and allow for the development of experiences that are commensurate with a culture's worldview (see La Barre, 1990; Winkelman, 1990). One avenue, therefore, for the therapeutic effects of ASC is through the increased sense of meaning and self-worth associated with the generation of powerful feelings of social affiliation. The adaptive value of ASC, whether induced by drugs or other methods, has even been placed in an evolutionary context (Schumaker 1990, 1991, 1995; Weil, 1986). Schumaker, for instance, suggests that our capacity to experience ASC reflects an evolutionary adaptation to the potentially harmful consequences of self-awareness. When employed in culturally appropriate contexts, drugs, rather than "disintegrating the self" or "obliterating reality" (Schumaker, 1995, p. 168), as they often do in other more secular contexts, serve to reconstruct the self and provide an adaptive integration of self and world.

More generally, it is important to consider the integral role of drugs in a range of culturally prescribed contexts, and there is a need to evaluate both the costs *and* benefits of drug use among cultural groups. This point needs to be taken seriously in the context of Western attempts to control, suppress, and eradicate drug use in other cultures. Of course, as we have mentioned earlier, cultural groups are not static entities, but instead are open to change—a fact made even more salient by the rapid pace of globalization in the late twentieth and early twenty-first centuries. Just how different cultural groups respond to such change, and the impact such changes have on patterns of traditional drug use, deserves close attention.

DRUGS AND MULTICULTURALISM

If one were to arrive at a Caucasian middle-class party to find the guests sitting cross-legged in a circle, chatting amiably and plucking shiny green leaves from a heap of branches in the middle of the room and putting them in their mouths to chew, one would, to say the least, be a little surprised. If, however, you realized that you had accidentally entered the wrong house and this was the Somali family next door, things might seem a little more normal. Although there have been connections between various cultural groups for thousands of years, the process of globalization only really took off with the development of long-distance ocean transport and the commercial interests of European nations in the sixteenth and seventeenth centuries. This process, which continues apace in the modern world, entails, among other things, the diffusion of products and people across previously restricted geographical boundaries. Within large multicultural societies, a diversity of different psychoactive substances are employed by different cultural groups in different social contexts. It may be normal for Somali immigrants in Australia or the United States to chew qat leaves, but not for most middle-class individuals of European origin (or indeed African Americans, Hispanics, or indigenous Australians). Moreover, the use of more familiar substances such as tobacco, alcohol, cocaine, and cannabis varies considerably among different cultural groups. There are also important and substantial differences in levels of substance-related problems such as drug dependence, medical problems, and (for illicit drugs) arrests and imprisonment. In this section we describe these differences in terms of kinds of cultural groups that may be found in multicultural societies, mainly focusing on patterns of drug use in the United States.

Ethnic Groups

The use of drugs varies in important ways among the different ethnic groups that are found in the United States. In Table 6.1 we display the lifetime, past-year, and past-month prevalence rates for the use of any illicit drug for individuals age 12 and over in the United States (Substance Abuse and Mental Health Services Administration, 2001). Overall, Native Americans have the highest prevalence rates, followed by people of more than one ethnic group, Caucasians, African Americans, Hispanics, and Asians. The differences among these ethnic groups are often quite substantial. Caucasians, for example, are more than twice as likely as Asians to have reported the use of an illicit drug at least once in their lives, and Native Americans are twice as likely to report the use of an illicit drug in the past month as Caucasians or African Americans.

As noted earlier in this chapter, the use of labels such as "Hispanic" and "Asian" often obscures many important within-group differences in patterns of drug use. As illustrated in Table 6.2, the prevalence of reported drug use for different subgroups within these broad ethnic categories varies considerably. Among Asians, Japanese and Koreans have the highest prevalence rates, whereas Chinese have the lowest.

Table 6.1   Lifetime, Past-Year, and Past-Month Use of Any Illicit Drug
Among Persons Aged 12 or Older in the United States, by
Ethnic Group Membership (%)

Ethnic Group	Lifetime	Past Year	Past Month
Caucasian	41.5	11.2	6.4
African American	35.5	10.9	6.4
Hispanic	29.9	10.1	5.3
Asian	18.9	5.2	2.7
Native American or Alaska native	53.9	19.8	12.6
More than one ethnic group	49.2	20.6	14.8

SOURCE: Summary of findings from the 2000 National Household Survey on
Drug Abuse (Substance Abuse and Mental Heath Services Administration,
2001)

Indeed, Koreans are almost seven times more likely to report having
used an illicit drug in the past month than are Chinese. Similar differences emerge among subgroups of Hispanic people. Puerto Ricans, for
example, have higher prevalence rates for all three time periods
compared to other Hispanic groups. Examining these within-group
differences is important because they point to specific differences in the
experiences of individuals from different ethnic groups that might
otherwise be ignored.

Prevalence rates for alcohol and cigarette use reveal generally similar findings as those for illicit drugs, as illustrated in Tables 6.3 and 6.4.
Caucasians have the highest frequency of reported past-month alcohol
use, followed by Native Americans, people of more than one ethnic
group, and Hispanics. Binge and heavy alcohol use, by comparison,
was more frequently reported by Native Americans, followed by
Caucasians. And Asians reported the lowest rates of alcohol use in all
three categories. These differences are quite substantial. Caucasians,
for example, are more than four times more likely to report heavy
alcohol use in the past month than are Asians. Once more, these patterns are likely to be more nuanced than depicted in Table 6.3. Dawson
(1998b), for example, using data from the 1992 National Longitudinal
Alcohol Epidemiological Survey, found that the differences between
broad ethnic groupings are as large as those within them. Interestingly,

Table 6.2   Lifetime, Past-Year, and Past-Month Use of Any Illicit Drug Among Persons Aged 12 and Older, by Ethnic Subgroup (%)

Ethnic Subgroup	Lifetime	Past Year	Past Month
Hispanic			
Mexican	30.5	10.3	5.5
Puerto Rican	41.3	16.3	10.1
Central or South American	25.8	8.2	4.1
Cuban	23.8	8.1	3.7
Asian			
Chinese	14.5	3.6	1.0
Filipino	24.7	6.1	2.7
Japanese	29.3	8.3	5.0
Asian Indian	13.3	4.2	2.1
Korean	29.2	9.5	6.9
Vietnamese	17.8	6.7	4.3

SOURCE: Annual averages based on summary of findings from the 1999 and 2000 National Household Survey on Drug Abuse, (Substance Abuse and Mental Health Services Administration, 2001)

there were significant differences between Caucasians depending upon their European place of origin. Those who originated from Southern and Eastern Europe, for example, reported less frequent heavy drinking and less alcohol consumed daily than did those of Northern or Central European origin. This finding suggests that the well-recognized drinking differences between "wet" and "dry" cultures (although see Room & Mäkelä, 2000) can persist for some time in different geographical (and cultural) contexts. The use of cigarettes follows a similar pattern to that of alcohol. As depicted in Table 6.4, Native Americans report having the highest lifetime, past-year, and past-month rates of use, followed by Caucasians, African Americans, and Hispanics. Again, Asians have the lowest reported rates of use in all three categories.[6]

Ethnic differences in patterns of drug use in the United States, however, tell a somewhat different story once we move beyond basic prevalence rates to various measures of drug-related harm, such as rates of dependence, emergency room visits, and drug-related arrests. Estimates for ethnic differences in levels of drug dependence vary somewhat depending on the sample and measures employed; however,

Table 6.3   Past-Month Alcohol Use, "Binge" Alcohol Use, and Heavy
Alcohol Use Among Persons Aged 12 and Older, by Ethnic
Group: 2000 (%)

Group	Any Alcohol Use	"Binge" Alcohol Use	Heavy Alcohol Use
Caucasian	50.7	21.2	6.2
African American	33.7	17.7	4.0
Native American or Alaska native	35.1	26.2	7.2
Asian	28.0	11.6	1.4
Hispanic	39.8	22.7	4.4
More than one ethnic group	41.6	17.5	5.2

SOURCE: Summary of Findings from the 2000 National Household Survey
on Drug Abuse (SAMHSA, 2001)

NOTE: "Binge" alcohol use is defined as drinking five or more drinks on the
same occasion on at least one day in the past 30 days. Heavy alcohol use is
defined as drinking five or more drinks on the same occasion on each of five
or more days in the past 30 days.

some general patterns can be discerned. Caucasians and Native
Americans tend to have the highest levels of nicotine dependence
among ethnic groups in the United States (Anthony, Warner, & Kessler,
1994; Breslau, Johnson, Hiripi, & Kessler, 2001; Kandel, Chen, Warner,
Kessler, & Grant, 1997). Alcohol dependence is highest among Native
Americans, followed by Caucasians and Hispanics; whereas Asians
have the lowest levels (Anthony et al., 1994; Kandel et al., 1997;
Straussner, 2001b). African Americans, however, have higher rates of
cocaine dependence (among individuals who have ever used) than
either Hispanics or Caucasians (Kandel et al., 1997).

Data from emergency room visits and drug-related deaths in the
United States also display important ethnic differences. Hispanics and
especially African Americans are over-represented among drug abuse
episodes and drug abuse deaths (see Table 6.5). For instance, the prevalence of drug-related emergency room visits for African Americans is
more than twice that for Caucasians and almost three times greater for
drug-related deaths. There are also important ethnic differences in
the kind of drugs that are most frequently associated with emergency
room visits. The most common drug mentioned for Caucasians is

Table 6.4   Lifetime, Past-Year, and Past-Month Use of Cigarettes Among
Persons Aged 12 and Older, by Ethnic Group: 2000 (%)

Group	Lifetime	Past Year	Past Month
Caucasian	71.4	30.2	25.9
African American	54.9	26.7	23.3
Native American or Alaska native	72.8	45.7	42.3
Asian	38.8	18.8	16.5
Hispanic	54.0	26.1	20.7
More than one ethnic group	62.3	36.1	32.3

SOURCE: Summary of Findings from the 2000 National Household Survey
on Drug Abuse (Substance Abuse and Mental Health Services
Administration, 2001)

alcohol-in-combination (32.7%), followed by cocaine (17.86%), and
marijuana/hashish (14.64%). Cocaine, however, is the drug most
commonly reported by emergency departments in relation to African
Americans (56.73%), followed by alcohol-in-combination (40.21%), and
heroin/morphine (23.37%). Remarkably, of 174,896 emergency department mentions for cocaine in 2000, 43.39% were for African American
individuals, compared to 34.2% for Caucasians and 13.56% for Hispanics
(Substance Abuse and Mental Health Services Administration, 2000).
What is especially noteworthy about this finding is not only that African
Americans make up less than 12% of the population, but that their lifetime
prevalence rates for cocaine and crack combined are slightly *less* than
those for Caucasians, although their past-year and past-month rates are
marginally higher (Ma & Shive, 2000).

Perhaps the most dramatic ethnic differences in drug-related statistics, however, relate to arrests, prosecutions, and sentences for drug
possession and sale. African Americans are more likely to be arrested
on drug-related charges, receive longer sentences, and are more likely
to receive mandatory minimum sentences than are Caucasians
(Lusane, 1994; Tonry, 1994). More than two-thirds of admissions to
state prisons for drug offenses in 1994, for example, were African
Americans, despite their constituting fewer than 12% of the national
population (MacCoun & Reuter, 2001). The most recent statistics
underscore these findings—African Americans represented 34.5% of

Table 6.5   Drug Abuse Episodes (2000) and Drug Abuse Deaths (1999) in the United States, by Ethnic Group

	Caucasian	African American	Hispanic	Other
Total number of drug episodes	334,985	133,776	68,282	5,160
Prevalence (per 100,000)	206.64	538.16	296.63	-----
Total number of drug deaths	7,042	3,023	1,286	167
Prevalence (per 100,000)	4.34	12.16	5.58	-----

SOURCE: Based on Drug Abuse Warning Network Annual Medical Examiner Data 1999 (Substance Abuse and Mental Health Services Administration, 2000). Prevalence rates are calculated based on estimated number of individuals in each ethnic group for 1999 provided by the National Household Survey on Drug Abuse (Substance Abuse and Mental Health Services Administration, 2001).

all arrests for drug abuse violations in 2000. By contrast, African Americans are under- or about equally represented for arrests relating to drunkenness (13.7%), driving under the influence (9.6%), and violation of liquor laws (10.6%) (Federal Bureau of Investigation, 2000). Again, what is remarkable about these findings is that the prevalence rates for illicit drug use (as represented in national surveys, at least) are similar or lower for African Americans and Hispanics than for Caucasians, but they are grossly overrepresented in the prison system for drug-related arrests. Moreover, Lusane (1994) argues that there is little evidence that either African Americans or Hispanics engage in more drug trafficking or selling than Caucasians, although reliable data on this issue are difficult to obtain.

The various statistics that we report in this section should be treated with some caution, for as we note in Chapter 5 there are various ways in which they might fail to be truly representative. However, a fairly clear pattern does seem to emerge from the multiple lines of evidence reviewed here. Prevalence rates for the use of alcohol, tobacco, and illicit drugs tend to be highest for Native Americans, followed by Caucasians, African Americans, Hispanics, and Asians, although there are some drug-specific variations here. Levels of alcohol abuse, alcohol dependence, and nicotine dependence also appear to be highest for Native Americans and Caucasians and lowest again for Asians. On virtually all other measures of drug-related harm, however, African Americans and Hispanics are over-represented. Numerous explanations have been advanced to account for these apparent paradoxes: methodological artifacts; choice of drugs; differences in norms, values, and beliefs regarding drug use; and social-structural factors such as discrimination, marginalization, and poverty (Kandel, 1995). We discuss these various explanations in detail in Chapter 7; however, we suggest that it is likely that multiple factors need to be invoked to satisfactorily explain the important differences outlined here.

Migrants and Drug Use

Although most research has been carried out on ethnic groups in multicultural societies who make up a significant portion of the national population, important issues also arise for "minority minorities" whose numbers are often too small to stand out in large national surveys. Of particular relevance is the use of drugs by immigrants and migrants (Westermeyer, 1996c). As Westermeyer (1996b) notes, immigrants have an increased risk for just about all psychological disorders, including substance abuse and dependence. Refugees are at an even greater risk for psychological disorders, including substance-related ones, as they may have experienced profound trauma in their country of origin and are often cut off from family members and other forms of social support.

Traditional patterns of drug use, however, can serve as important markers of social and cultural identity for some migrants, although the way that these drugs are used may take on different forms in novel contexts. For example, social and political unrest in Somalia and other East African countries has led to a stream of refugees into Western countries such as Italy, Great Britain, and Australia. These refugees are often keen to continue their traditional use of qat (described earlier), which not only serves to maintain cultural identity but is also an integral component of social occasions (Griffiths et al., 1997; Kalix, 1992; Nabuzoka & Badhadhe, 2000; Stevenson, Fitzgerald, & Banwell, 1996). The use of qat by East African refugees in places like England, however, appears to differ from traditional patterns of use: More qat is consumed by a wider range of individuals and sometimes outside of traditional social contexts. As a result, it is believed that the consumption of qat causes more problems than is the case in traditional contexts

(Griffiths et al., 1997; Nabuzoka & Badhadhe, 2000). It is likely that the stress associated with refugee status, often-poor living conditions, and the exposure to a wide range of other drugs contributes to these different patterns of use. Questions regarding qat's legal status in many Western countries are likely to contribute to these difficulties. As Stevenson et al. (1996) emphasize, however, in their study of East African communities in Melbourne, Australia, the cultural importance of qat to East African refugees should not be underestimated. Although some authors have voiced concern about the spread of a potentially harmful new substance to Western users (e.g., Kalix, 1992), policy and clinical intervention initiatives should be made in full awareness of the role that qat plays within the context of East African cultural groups.

Since economic, political, and environmental perturbations in many parts of the world are likely to increase in the twenty-first century, it is inevitable that Western nations will continue to be home for a wide range of refugees from diverse cultural groups. The use of traditional and novel substances by these individuals is thus an important area of research, and both clinicians and policy makers need to be sensitive to the special needs of these groups and to develop their intervention strategies appropriately.

Other Cultural Groups

In a recent issue of *Granta* ("Confessions", 2001), an anonymous author penned an article with the striking title: "Confessions of a Middle-Aged Ecstasy Eater." What makes the title work, apart from its obvious allusion to De Quincey, is the conjunction of "middle-aged" with "ecstasy." "Confessions of a Young Ecstasy Eater" raises no eyebrows, nor does "Confessions of Middle-Aged Gin Drinker." Clearly, middle-aged individuals are not expected to take ecstasy, whereas a substantial portion of young people are. In fact, ecstasy use is strongly associated not just with "youth culture" in general, but with "dance" or "rave culture" in particular. The use of ecstasy in Western societies, it seems, is strongly patterned by membership in specific social groups.

Numerous examples of the relationship between social groups and drug use could be employed, and we have discussed some of these in previous chapters. We focus here, however, on two somewhat different social groups that can be found within Western society: dance culture and Alcoholics Anonymous (AA) culture. The first, as we shall see, is clearly associated with the use of a wide array of drugs, including ecstasy, whereas the second is identified with a rejection of drug use, especially alcohol. Both groups have certain features that maintain their distinction from the mainstream culture and that encourage very specific patterns of drug-taking (or not taking) behavior.

In the late 1980s in Britain, Europe, and the United States, large numbers of predominantly young individuals were gathering at events variously called "raves" or "house parties," which took place in factories and warehouses, and later in clubs and other venues. These gatherings centered on an emerging form of music known variously as *dance* or *rave*, but which has subsequently spawned multiple sub-genres such as *techno, trance, jungle, house,* and *hardcore* (Collin, 1997; Measham, Parker, & Aldridge, 1998; van de Wijngaart, Braam, deBruin, Fris, Maalsté, & Vergraeck, 1999). The emergence of dance culture was coupled with the growing use of MDMA and MDMA-analogs, popularly known as ecstasy, although a wide variety of other drugs such as amphetamines, LSD, cannabis, ketamine, and nitrous oxide are also often employed.

To what extent is the use of ecstasy specifically associated with dance culture per se? As Parker et al. (1998) have clearly demonstrated for Britain, the use of a wide range of drugs by young people in general has increased substantially over the course of the past decade. Is ecstasy use, therefore, part of "youth culture" at large rather than being specifically associated with the dance scene? Although drug use is more prevalent among young people in general, the evidence that we review, although tentative, is commensurate with the idea that the use of drugs in general and ecstasy in particular is specifically associated with dance culture. In a large sample of 1,121 participants at 10 house parties in the Netherlands, for example, it was found that 81% of individuals interviewed reported consuming ecstasy at least once in their lives, and 64% of participants had taken ecstasy that evening (van de Wijngaart et al., 1999). The lifetime prevalence of ecstasy use in this sample differs dramatically from the 1.9% found in the general Dutch population (Spruit, 1999). In short, participation at a dance culture event increases the likelihood of having consumed ecstasy 40 times, compared to the population at large. Similarly high rates of ecstasy use among individuals who participate in dance culture have been found in other studies in Australia, Scotland, and Norway (Forsyth, 1996; Lenton, Boys, & Norcross, 1997; Pederson & Skrondal, 1999). Moreover, this relationship seems to be specific to involvement in dance culture: Young people who report liking rave music are more likely to have tried a wide range of drugs, including ecstasy (Forsyth, Barnard, & McKeganey, 1997; Pederson & Skrondal, 1999).

It is important, of course, to compare the use of ecstasy and other drugs by participants in dance culture with that of individuals from the same age group who do not participate in the dance scene. In Britain, for instance, the prevalence rates for the use of any "hallucinant" (which includes LSD, magic mushrooms, ecstasy, and nitrous oxide) is highest in the 20–24 age bracket, with 36% of participants reporting lifetime use and 11% reporting use in the past year (Ramsay et al., 2001). Comparable figures were found by Measham et al. (1998) in a longitudinal study of adolescents: 14% of 17-year-olds had tried ecstasy, 21% LSD, and 23% nitrites. Although these figures are significantly higher than those found in the general population, they are also substantially lower than those reported by similar-aged individuals who participate actively in dance culture. Pederson and Skrondal (1999), in their Norwegian sample, also found that for individuals who had not used any illegal substance in the past year, only 3.7% had attended a house party, whereas 40.6% of those who had consumed amphetamines and ecstasy had. It seems as though the experience of belonging to dance culture and engaging in dance culture events is intimately connected to the use of specific drugs—particularly ecstasy, but also other substances such as LSD, amphetamines, ketamine, and nitrous oxide (e.g., French & Power, 1998; Jansen, 2000). Other drugs, like alcohol and heroin, by contrast are not consistently related to involvement in dance culture.

In order to establish the potential harm of ecstasy use and to develop appropriate policy responses, it is essential to take into account the cultural context in which ecstasy appears to be predominantly consumed. The notable differences in patterns of use found in participants in dance culture compared to the general, or even youth, culture at large highlight the importance of attending to the sociocultural factors that encourage use in some populations and not others. This issue is of particular importance given recent suggestions that dance culture is rapidly expanding to encompass youth culture at large, and that the use of illicit drugs by youth in general (in Britain at least) has essentially become normalized (Measham et al., 1998; Parker et al., 1998).

A rather different kind of social group that is associated with abstinence from drug use is found within the cultures of treatment and recovery. As Westermeyer (1999) explicitly outlines:

> *Recovery subcultures* are substitute social groups and networks that can foster early recovery. . . . Such subcultures may have their own jargon, values, customs, symbols, status markers, and/or social organizations. A subculture of therapists, therapy groups, and self-help groups can guide the individual towards health and stability. (p. 81)

Perhaps the most obvious example of a culture of recovery is found in Alcoholics Anonymous (AA) and other twelve-step facilitated (TSF) treatments. Antze (1987), for example, has developed the theme that AA facilitates a totemic religious conversion experience, and others have explicitly labeled TSF groups as cults, religious orders, or social movements (see Schaler, 2000; Ragels, 2002). Whether or not such organizations should be branded as cults is a matter of some debate (e.g., Khantzian, 1995), especially given the overwhelmingly pejorative overtones of such a designation. However, it is clear that TSF groups like AA are fairly clearly delineated cultural groups that have specific norms (e.g., the rejection of any drinking), beliefs (that alcoholism is a disease; that alcoholics are powerless to control their drinking), and practices (abstinence, regular meetings, the use of rituals). Moreover, these groups entail the development of new social networks, employ role models, and (sometimes) encourage the rejection of former social ties. In short, organizations like AA offer an alternative worldview that involves the "resocialization" of the individual participant (Wallace, 1999). AA members, for instance, clearly pledge their allegiance to their new cultural group with their opening statement: "My name is _____ and I am an alcoholic."

Although these aspects of AA and other TSF groups have been the subject of criticism from some authors (e.g., Ragels, 2002; Schaler, 2000), it is probably these features that contribute to their efficacy (if indeed they are efficacious). Just as membership in dance culture encourages certain ways of using psychoactive substances—as normal components of dance and other experiences—membership in AA and other treatment groups fosters drug abstinence and beliefs about the dangers of drugs. It seems likely that these rather different groups achieve their different results in similar ways: through peer reinforcement, role models, group-level norms, values, and beliefs, and social-structural features associated with group participation. In fact, there are numerous different kinds of social groups that are often intimately associated with the use of, or abstinence from, a range of specific drugs.

Understanding how participation in these different cultural groups affects drug taking and how such influences may be moderated by various factors such gender, degree of group identification, and so forth, is an important avenue for further research.

SUMMARY

Understanding cultural differences in rates of substance use and substance-related problems is important for a number of reasons. Critically, it allows us to gain insight into the range of cultural factors that influence drug use, and to develop culturally appropriate prevention and treatment initiatives. However, in developing cultural explanations, attention must be paid to the way that cultural groups are both defined and measured. The development of more fine-grained categories of ethnicity, and the inclusion of measures that assess such important factors as acculturation status, degree of ethnic identification, and immigration status, should improve the explanatory and predictive value of cultural approaches. It is crucial to recognize that ethnic and cultural groups are not homogeneous and static collections of individuals, but rather are variable, fluid, and open to change.

Over the course of this chapter we have explored the use of a myriad of different drugs by a wide range of different cultural groups. We first described the traditional use of a variety of psychoactive substances among cultural groups around the world. This review highlighted the ubiquity of drug use and the way that various different kinds of substances become integrated in specific cultural contexts. We also elaborated on the use of drugs in an array of different cultural groups *within* multicultural societies. Importantly, the nature and severity of drug-related problems were shown to be strongly patterned by cultural group membership. The material reviewed in this chapter raises some important questions: Why is the ritual-religious use of hallucinogens common in many cultural groups around the world, but predominantly absent in Western cultures? Why do Native Americans have more alcohol-related problems than any other ethnic group in the United States? Why are African Americans overrepresented in drug-related emergency room and crime statistics? Why are ravegoers more likely to use ecstasy? More generally, we need to explain why the use of drugs and the nature of drug-related problems vary among different cultural groups. In Chapter 7, we review a number of different cultural explanations that can address these issues.

NOTES

1. There is a paucity of comprehensive book-length overviews of cultural patterns of drug use. Knipe's (1995) *Culture, Society, and Drugs* is perhaps the best introduction to this field, and is firmly anchored in social science methodology and theory. Richard Rudgley's (1993) *The Alchemy of Culture* also provides an interesting and readable introduction to drug use across cultures, as does William Emboden's (1979) *Narcotic Plants*. Two excellent overviews of the cross-cultural use of hallucinogens are provided by Furst (1990) and Dobkin de Rios (1990), and Jonathan Ott's (1993) encyclopedic *Pharmacotheon* provides a comprehensive survey of the botany, chemistry, and history of what he terms "entheogenic drugs" (those that are used in shamanic or religious contexts). The recent volume edited by Straussner (2001c) offers an excellent overview of treatment issues for different cultural groups, and Klingemann and Hunt (1998) provide a good review of treatment systems in different countries.

2. The alkaloid hyoscine is a form of scopolamine that is known to be capable of generating profound amnesia, and is found in a large number of psychoactive plants such as datura, mandrake, and deadly nightshade (Julien, 1998). Hyoscine was used in North America up to the 1940s as an anesthetic during childbirth (Dobkin de Rios & Stachalek, 1999).

3. Most authors indicate that although *psychological* dependence on qat is clearly evident in some users, there is little evidence of marked tolerance or withdrawal (Nencini & Ahmad, 1989; Pantellis, Hindler, & Taylor, 1989).

4. Why this is the case is a matter of some speculation. Schultes (1990) suggests the reason is unlikely to reflect botanical differences, but rather, as La Barre (1990) has argued, is the result of cultural differences in the nature and use of ritual-religious experiences and the important role played by hallucinogenic substances within shamanistic ideology.

5. There is some efficacy in this practice, given the presence of antibiotic chemicals effective against a wide range of bacteria (Furst, 1995).

6. It is worth noting that the prevalence figures we cite here vary in important ways by age and to some extent by the use of specific drugs (see Substance Abuse and Mental Health Services Administration, 2001, for further details).

7. However, it is likely that Hispanics and African Americans may be overrepresented among low-level street dealers whose operations are more visible, and perhaps more targeted by police than are clandestine operations.

7

The Role of Culture: Explaining Patterns of Use

INTRODUCTION

The concept of culture has been employed in many different ways when explaining patterns of drug use and drug-related problems. Many of these accounts make reference to the role of norms, beliefs, values, and expectations in influencing drug-taking behavior. There is also an extensive literature relating to the process of socialization or enculturation and its impact on substance use and abuse. The symbolic and functional role of drugs in society has also been highlighted, especially by anthropologists. Finally, a number of social-structural accounts have been advanced, often relating to the different experiences of cultural groups in economic, social, and political terms. At times these various kinds of cultural explanation are in direct competition with one another. For example, we can legitimately inquire whether the high rates of alcohol abuse found among Native Americans are the result of specific culturally based norms, beliefs, and values regarding the nature of alcohol and its effects, or whether they arise as a consequence of social, economic, and political marginalization. Testing these different alternatives, however, is not easy; it is hard to disentangle the different causal contributions for factors that themselves are likely to be related to each other in important ways. Typically speaking, it is necessary to invoke multiple contributing factors in order to account for cultural patterns in substance use and drug-related problems (see Hunt & Barker, 2001).

Bearing these points in mind, in this chapter we consider different kinds of cultural explanation in isolation, and then draw them together to provide a sketch of the way such factors interact to produce the observed patterns in drug use among different cultural groups. We first discuss the place of drugs within cultures, considering the role of functional context, the relative cultural integration of substances, and factors relating to supply and availability. We then outline cultural influences on drug use, examining the role of norms, beliefs, values, expectations, and the symbolic role of substances in society. A discussion of wider cultural influences is provided, focusing on the impact of a range of social-structural factors on drug-taking behavior. We conclude by outlining the way these various cultural explanations may be related to one another.

DRUGS AND CULTURE

In this section we examine the place of drugs within culture. The way that substances are used, their relative integration into cultural contexts, and their availability all influence the way that such substances are employed and the harm (and benefit) that their use entails.

The Function of Drugs in Cultural Perspective

As our overview in Chapter 6 illustrates, most cultural groups use psychoactive drugs for a range of different purposes. Substances such as coffee, tea, kola, cocoa, tobacco, betel, qat, maté, coca, and pituri, for example, are used in pragmatic contexts to reduce fatigue, alleviate thirst and hunger, and to promote work. Any substance that has such properties (or is *believed* to have such properties) is likely to be valued by cultural groups. Most cultural groups also use drugs in social, recreational, and nutritional contexts. Psychoactive substances are widely used as medicines in cultures around the world. Indeed, it is hard to find a single example of a psychotropic drug that has not at some time, or in some culture, been employed for its (alleged or actual) therapeutic value. The ritual-religious use of drugs also emerges as a prominent context in many of the non-Western cultures, discussed in Chapter 6. Indeed, the use of drugs (especially hallucinogens) is often seamlessly interwoven into the spiritual life of individuals in many cultures. Two important questions that arise from a consideration of the functional contexts of drug use are (1) How do substances come to be employed in so many diverse contexts, even within the same cultural group? And (2) What are the implications of the context of drug use for drug-related harm?

In contemporary Western cultures, there is typically a fairly distinct line drawn between the different functional contexts of drug use. Substances that are used in recreational and social contexts are rarely accepted as legitimate therapeutic agents in medical domains. Indeed, there is often an explicit assumption that a substance that can be "enjoyed" should not also be employed as a medicine. The controversy surrounding the medicinal use of cannabis and the prescription of methadone (and especially heroin) illustrates these distinctions. Moreover, drugs are rarely used in ritual-religious contexts in Western society, although there are some exceptions here, such as the use of alcohol at Christian mass and in Judaic religious ceremonies and celebrations. In contrast, drug use by many cultural groups readily crosses these contextual boundaries, and what is noticeable from our overview in Chapter 6 is how the same drug is employed in multiple contexts within the same society. There is, after all, no logical (physiological) reason why a substance that enhances sociability or relieves fatigue should also be a valued agent in curing a diverse range of ailments, nor why it should necessarily be imbued with spiritual and symbolic significance. Why then do drugs permeate so many diverse spheres of existence for many cultural groups?

One possible explanation for the multi-functionality of drugs in various cultural contexts emphasizes their primary role in generating positive and alleviating negative psychological states (e.g., Horton, 1991). In short, individuals initially favor drugs because drugs make them feel good—at least in the short term. These substances consequently become sought after, and they acquire value in both economic and—because users garner status from their consumption—symbolic and social terms. Because of this value it seems natural to attribute the provision of such substances to the gods, and the offering of such substances to deities becomes an integral part of their use. Some of these substances, furthermore, have the capacity to generate profound shifts in states of consciousness that enable users to enter different worlds, which, in the absence of alternative explanatory accounts, are not surprisingly attributed to divine or spiritual forces. Any substance that tends to make individuals feel better and can be linked to spiritual domains is also likely to be popularly employed in medicinal contexts. In this way drugs come to permeate many aspects of cultural life and take on multiple meanings in an array of different contexts.

As a number of authors have noted, the context in which drugs are typically employed can exert powerful effects on the way that they are used and their potential for harm (e.g., Dobkin de Rios & Smith, 1977; Heath, 2000; Mäkelä, 1983). For example, in cultures where alcohol is primarily considered a food with important nutritional value, it may be consumed daily but generally in a moderate fashion (Heath, 2000; Room & Mäkelä, 2000). This reduces the risk for many alcohol-related problems that arise from acute intoxication, and may offer a range of psychological benefits as well (Peele & Brodsky, 2000). It has also been suggested that when drugs are used in culturally prescribed ways, they result in less harm than what is typically the case in Western contexts. In particular, when drugs are employed in predominantly ritual-religious contexts, it is argued, the risks for harm are reduced (Grob & Dobkin de Rios, 1992; Dobkin de Rios, 1990; Westermeyer, 1995). For example, Grob and Dobkin de Rios (1992) assert:

> Contemporary Western society . . . has acquired a destructive non-sacred use of drugs. The respect and reverence with which psychoactive sacraments have been used in tribal society has been abandoned. Drug initiation has become drug addiction. Circumscribed and protected rites have been forgotten, while frenetic and out-of-control drug use has proliferated. The sacred visions which served a socially enriching function have been lost. Repetitive, compulsive and habitual drug use, emerging from both individual and societal pathology has led to ever-increasing dangers to drug users and to society at large. (p. 135)

There are a number of reasons why the use of drugs in ritual-religious contexts is likely to reduce potential for harm. Substance use is typically under strict control, occurs infrequently, and there are proscriptions against use outside of strictly delineated contexts. The use of drugs for ritual-religious reasons, however, is not entirely without potential for harm. As outlined in Chapter 6, the use of eboka by the Fang has been linked to a number of deaths, and the regular consumption of narcotic snuff by Yanomamö males in order to communicate with the spirit world can contribute to aggression and violence (Chagnon, 1997). These are, though, fairly isolated examples, and the controlled use of drugs in various ritual-religious contexts—from the consumption of peyote during Native American worship to the use of sacramental wine by Jews—illustrates the idea that such use is largely unproblematic.

It is clear that the use of drugs in traditional contexts is not entirely problem-free. As discussed in Chapter 6, the use of qat, kava, and opium have all generated problems in areas where they have long been employed. However, by fostering implicit norms governing the use of drugs and delineating the functional contexts in which they may be employed, cultural groups may restrict some of the harms that arise from uncontrolled, recreational use.

Alien Poisons versus Culturally Integrated Substances

The way that different substances are integrated into cultural practices may also influence their potential for harm. More specifically, it has been suggested that novel substances, or "alien poisons," may prove to be especially deleterious (Westermeyer, 1995). Jaffe (1983) sums up these ideas:

> It seems that when drug use is integrated into the social fabric, it is viewed as a problem only in extreme situations, such as when it constitutes a significant health hazard or causes work inefficiency. In contrast, where, in the same societies, drugs are used outside the historically (and hence, socially) accepted patterns, the deviant pattern is often associated with criminality, health hazards, and non-productiveness of the users. (p. 104)

The use of many psychoactive substances is prescribed in specific contexts. Their use may be mandatory, or simply encouraged, but such use often forms an integral component of many social activities. The use of beer among the West African Koyfar provides a nice example of the way substances can become integrated within a diverse array of cultural contexts. According to Netting (1964), "The Koyfar make, drink, talk, and think about beer. It is a focus of cultural concern and activity . . . " (p. 376). Beer consumed at celebratory events, like harvest time, provides a medium of social exchange, is given in reward for valued behavior, extracted as punishment for disobeying the rules, and is offered to the gods in numerous ceremonial contexts. Even the marking of time is based on the brewing cycle of beer. Netting concludes that there are no drinking problems among the Koyfar, and others have also pointed to the relative absence of problems that arise for culturally integrated substances (e.g., Westermeyer, 1995).

In contrast, substances that are relatively novel to cultural groups or are consumed in novel ways may invoke greater levels of harm, as their use is only loosely controlled (if at all), and the effects of the drug are not well understood (see also Chapter 5). This "law of alien poisons" (Schenk, 1956) has been used to explain the problems experienced with alcohol by Native Americans and indigenous Australians (e.g., Frank, Moore, & Ames, 2000), who prior to European contact had little experience with alcoholic beverages. Reports that kava has become a substance of abuse among indigenous Australians, in contrast to its largely problem-free consumption in traditional contexts, has also been explained in terms of the novelty of the substance and the lack of culturally prescribed channels for use (Gregory & Cawte, 1988; although see Clough, Burns, & Mununggurr, 2000). Becker (1967) has developed a similar idea in order to explain the higher incidence of "psychotic reactions" to cannabis and LSD early in their history of use in American society. Individuals who are inexperienced in the effects of these drugs and lack an experienced culture of users to draw on interpret their subjective experiences as evidence that they are "losing their minds." As individuals learn to understand that the drug effects are only temporary, and there emerges an experienced group of fellow users who can provide guidance, these adverse reactions decline.

Although the way that substances are integrated into cultural contexts can influence the way that they are used in various ways, a number of caveats are in order. First, harmful ways of consuming drugs may also have a long history and be quite integrated into some cultural contexts. Patterns of "fiesta drinking," for example, found among a number of cultural groups, such as those in Mexico, are often well entrenched in society even though they are the context for high rates of violence, aggression, and other problems (e.g., Medina-Mora, Borges, & Villatoro, 2000; Peréz, 2000). Indeed, both tobacco and alcohol have been firmly entrenched in Western cultural contexts while causing significant levels of harm for individuals and society. Second, novel substances do not necessarily generate harm. The use of alcohol by New Zealand Maori, for instance, who were naïve to its effects, was largely unproblematic after its initial introduction, certainly in comparison to the problem drinking that emerged among indigenous Australians and Native Americans (Hutt, 1999).

However, novel substances are often *perceived* as more dangerous, especially if they are used only by a minority, and the harm of culturally entrenched substances may be overlooked even if such harm is substantial. Responses to cannabis use in Western society, thus, are more critical than they are to alcohol, despite little evidence that the former is more "dangerous" than the latter. The general conclusion is that the details in the way that drugs are used within different cultural groups play an important role in their potential for harm—culturally integrated substances may typically lead to fewer problems and novel drugs result in more harm, but this is not inevitably the case.

Production, Supply, and Availability

During the "war on drugs" in the late 1980s, President Bush illustrated the putative ubiquity of illicit substances during a televised speech by holding up a bag of crack cocaine that he claimed was "seized a few days ago in a park across the street from the White House" (cited in Reinarman & Levine, 1997). As it later transpired, Bush's desire to employ this locally acquired prop had resulted in a farcical chain of events that involved federal drug agents *persuading* a reluctant dealer to sell them the drug in Lafayette Park across from the White House—a location the dealer had no idea how to find (Reinarman & Levine, 1997). In fact, the difficulty of finding anyone to purchase crack from in the vicinity of the White House underscores the point that drug availability varies considerably both across and within cultures. In one study, for example, individuals living in the most disadvantaged neighborhoods were more than five times more likely to be offered cocaine than those in more advantaged neighborhoods (Crum, Lillie-Blanton, & Anthony, 1996). Given that individuals from minority backgrounds are more likely to live in poorer environments, explanations for cultural differences in patterns of drug use should not ignore the role of availability.

For some cultural groups, certain drugs are simply easier to obtain and cheaper to purchase than others. For example, someone living in Christchurch, New Zealand, would find it extremely hard to develop a crack cocaine habit even if they were resolutely determined to do so. Cocaine is simply difficult to obtain in many parts of New Zealand and is prohibitively expensive to purchase. An individual might pass half a dozen alcohol retailers on their way to work in Christchurch, but the purchase of cocaine would require a determined search. By contrast, someone living in El Barrio in East Harlem, New York, is constantly exposed to dealers selling crack and powder cocaine, heroin, and various other substances. They might encounter such dealers in the stairwell of their apartment building or see them on the street on their way to work (Bourgois, 1995). Individuals who live in Christchurch are overwhelmingly Caucasian, whereas those residing in East Harlem are likely to be African American or Hispanic (especially Puerto Rican). Even without considering a range of other relevant factors, sheer availability alone dictates that African Americans and Puerto Ricans will be more likely to use crack cocaine than Caucasian New Zealanders.

As we pointed out in Chapter 6, both historically and cross-culturally, the use and abuse of psychoactive substances is related to both their availability and their price. Availability not only influences overall levels of use, but also the *way* that drugs are used. Many indigenous Australian communities, for example, are located long distances from alcohol outlets, and supplies are thus irregular. These features tend to promote periods of abstinence punctuated by episodes of heavy drinking, as supplies are rapidly used up when obtained. In general, it is important not to ignore the economic and political factors that shape patterns of substance use (Singer, 1986, 2001). As Singer (1986) notes, the alcohol and tobacco industries in the twentieth century have exerted profound effects on who uses these substances as they have continued to search for new markets and new ways to market their products. The production, supply, and availability of drugs are influenced by social and cultural factors that can differentially affect different cultural groups in terms of rates of substance use and subsequent drug-related problems. The reason why opium dependence is a problem in Southeast Asia, whereas the smoking of cocaine paste is more prevalent in Andean cultures, for example, is not related in any obvious way to differences in norms, values, or beliefs, but rather is a direct consequence of the proximity to opium and coca cultivation and production in these different regions.

CULTURE AND DRUGS

The importance of social norms, values, beliefs, and expectations in explaining patterns of substance use and substance-related problems is well recognized. At one level, these kinds of explanatory accounts are psychological in nature: they refer to the cognitions that individuals have, and how their beliefs about what is accepted behavior influence their subsequent drug-using practices. However, the *content* of social norms, values, beliefs, and explanations is patterned according to specific cultural contexts. Indeed, these are the very features that distinguish (in part) cultural groups from one another. Moreover, the process of *acquiring* these culture-specific characteristics is moderated by an individual's engagement in that culture and identification with other cultural groups. Social norms, beliefs, expectations, and the process of socialization, therefore, can be understood as culture-level explanations, especially if the goal is to explicate why cultural groups *differ* in their drug-using practices. Before addressing these approaches, however, we consider the possibility that ethnic differences in patterns of drug use might be the result of genetic differences.

Genetic Factors

In the past few decades, as in many other areas of medical science, there has been growing interest in the role of genetic factors in substance abuse and dependence. Whereas in the past, research on the heredity of substance abuse was limited to twin studies that examined the presence or absence of substance use problems, the recent mapping of the human genome has opened possibilities for more detailed investigations at the genetic level. However, despite advances in genetic research, the exact role of genes in the development of substance use disorders remains uncertain. While impressive progress has been made in the study of genetic diseases in which a discrete gene or set of genes causes the disease, progress in the area of substance dependence has been substantially slower due to its more complex genetic origins (Crabbe & Phillips, 1999).

Substance use disorders appear to run in families. For example, studies have found that sons of alcohol-dependent fathers were four times more likely than sons of non-alcohol-dependent fathers to develop alcohol dependence, even when they had been adopted out at birth (Hesselbrock, Hesselbrock, & Epstein, 1999). Similarly, twin studies indicate a higher level of concordance for alcohol dependence among monozygotic as compared to dizygotic twins (McGue, 1999; Pihl, 1999). One study, which examined data from the Swedish temperance board register, reported concordance rates of 47.9% for monozygotic twins and 32.8% for dizygotic twins, indicating that at least part of the variance in alcohol disorders is genetic in origin (Kendler, Prescott, Neale, & Pederson, 1997). Other studies that have examined large numbers of male twins have reported very similar findings for alcohol dependence (e.g., Prescott & Kendler, 1999) and for other substance use disorders (Tsuang, Lyons, Eisen, et al., 1996). Although these studies are not without their problems (see Heather & Robertson, 1997; Margolis & Zweben, 1998), taken together, data from adoption and twin studies provide support for the proposition that genes do influence the development of substance use disorders.

Although evidence for the heritability of psychological and behavioral traits *within* cultures cannot inform us about the role of genetic factors *between* cultural groups, it is plausible to suggest that specific genes may contribute to substance use problems and may vary in their expression among different ethnic groups. Indeed, one of the best-studied relations between genetic factors and substance use disorders has been used to explain ethnic differences in the prevalence of alcohol problems. This program of research has focused on genes that code for the liver enzyme aldehyde dehydrogenase (ALDH), which plays a critical role in the metabolization of alcohol. Research has indicated that the presence of a particular allele (ALDH2*2) produces a deficiency of ALDH2, which appears to be protective against alcohol problems by allowing the build-up of acetaldehyde, leading to an unpleasant reaction to alcohol that can include symptoms of nausea, sweating, dizziness, and palpitations (Goldman, 1993; McGue, 1999). The presence of the ALDH2*2 allele varies across ethnic groups: from near zero in Europeans, Native Americans, and Africans, to 30–50% in Northeast Asian populations (McGue, 1999).

A number of studies have found an association between the presence of the ALDH2*2 allele and reduced risk for alcohol abuse and dependence (e.g., Higuchi, Matsushita, Murayama, Takagi, & Hayashida, 1995; Neumark, Friedlander, Thomasson, & Li, 1998; Wall, Shea, Chan, & Carr, 2001). This relationship appears to be particularly robust for individuals who are homozygous for the ALDH2*2 allele (i.e., have two copies), and such individuals have virtually no risk for alcohol dependence (Wall et al., 2001). Although it appears, on the basis of these results, that genetic factors can potentially explain important cultural differences in alcohol use between individuals of Northeast Asian ancestry and other ethnic groups, the influence of specific genes also appears to be modified by cultural factors. For instance, in a study by Higuchi and colleagues (Higuchi, Matsushita, Mazeki, Kinoshita, Takagi, & Kono, 1994), the protectiveness of the ALDH2*2 allele in Japanese populations was examined over time. This study indicated that the protective effects decreased dramatically over time as Japanese people have increased their acceptance and consumption of alcohol. It seems that as alcohol use has further permeated Japanese culture, the negative physical effects of its ingestion have become less influential. An individual who previously may have avoided or limited his or her alcohol use due to these effects may now ignore these and focus instead on the social context, which may encourage and even reward drinking behavior.

In general, we should not ignore the possibility that ethnic differences in substance use may in part be the result of physiological differences that have a genetic basis. Lin and Poland (1995), for example, detail a number of cross-ethnic differences in drug metabolism that are likely to be influenced by genetic factors. However, such factors are likely, at best, to play only a partial role in explaining cultural differences. Given that patterns of drug use vary in important ways over time in the same culture and may be influenced by such factors as migration and acculturation, it is unlikely that any simple causal relationship between genetic factors and drug use can explain the significant differences that are found between ethnic groups. More generally, the extent of genetic influences is unclear, for genes are always seen as risk factors rather than straightforward determinants of substance-related problems. Even in the case of psychological disorders with strong genetic loadings, such as schizophrenia and bipolar affective disorder, the genetic history simply represents a particular amount of risk for developing the disorder. Hence, in order to understand the exact role of heredity one must understand how it interacts with environmental variables such as prevailing patterns of norms, values, and beliefs regarding psychoactive substances.

Norms, Values, and Roles

Social norms are often invoked to account for cultural differences in substance use because they define what are, and what are not, accepted patterns of behavior for individuals within specific social groups. Norms are often linked to values, although as Elster (1999) points out, values tend to reflect *individual* commitments to certain ways of thinking and behaving, which may be influenced by group-level norms. Social norms can also dictate the *roles* that individuals are expected to fulfill within society, and may delineate the boundaries for what is deemed acceptable behavior for different individuals within cultural groups. Norms, values, and roles are especially relevant for explaining patterns of drug use, because virtually no culture is indifferent to the psychological and behavioral states of its group members, which are obviously influenced by the ingestion of psychoactive substances. Indeed, often complex and frequently contradictory sets of norms and values govern *what* are acceptable drugs to take, *who* are allowed to take them, *where* and *when* the drugs should be consumed, and what *behaviors* that arise from their consumption might be allowed.

The social regulation of alcohol use cross-culturally provides an especially instructive example. Many cultural groups proscribe outright the consumption of alcohol to all individuals, virtually regardless of context. Muslims, Mormons, some Protestant sects, and AA members are just some examples here, although the reasons for proscription are somewhat different in each case. Of course, social norms proscribing alcohol use are not necessarily rigidly adhered to by all members of these different cultural groups. Rates of alcohol use by Muslims in Israel, Jordan, and Palestine, for example, are much higher than would be anticipated given the fairly clear rejection of alcohol in Islamic law (Weiss, Sawa, Abdeen, & Yanai, 1999).

Many cultures also have norms that, while allowing alcohol use, strongly condemn excessive consumption or drunkenness. Norms prescribing moderate drinking in Jewish culture are probably the best-known example here (Glassner, 1991; Straussner, 2001a), although similar norms against immoderate drinking are found in Italian, Chinese, and French cultures (Heath, 2000; Li & Rosenblood, 1994; Marinangeli, 2001). Again, the way these norms manifest in individual patterns of drinking is moderated by within-group factors. Recently, young Italians in some regions have been consuming more alcohol than usual, with a concomitant rise in alcohol-related problems (Marinangeli, 2001), and American-born Chinese tend to consume more alcohol than Asian-born Chinese (Li & Rosenblood, 1994). Russian Jews who have immigrated to Israel were also found in one study to have higher rates of alcohol use than other Jewish Israelis—in part, perhaps, because of culturally accepted patterns of heavy drinking in Russia (Rahav, Hasin, & Paykin, 1999). The higher rates of alcohol consumption by Caucasians in comparison to African Americans in the United States has also been linked to norms relating to alcohol use

(Herd, 1994, 1997; Harper & Saifnoorian, 1991). Specifically, it has been suggested that there is a historical link between sobriety and African American civil rights, based on the idea that heavy drinking is a handicap to aspirations of freedom and equality. Studies also demonstrate that both African American men and women have less permissive drinking norms than do Caucasians (Herd, 1994, 1997), which for women at least are related to higher rates of abstinence and lower levels of alcohol problems.[1]

Perhaps one of the most robust cross-cultural norms that influence drinking behavior relates to women. In virtually all countries, alcohol consumption by women is less accepted than it is by men (Wilsnack, Vogeltanz, Wilsnack, & Harris, 2000). In some cultures, female drinking is strongly disapproved of, and women with alcohol problems in Nigeria (Ikuesan, 1994) and Lesotho (Mphi, 1994) are heavily stigmatized and face divorce, economic marginalization, and social ostracism. Norms against alcohol use by women in other countries may not be as strict as in these two African nations, but in such diverse cultures as Japan (Gotoh, 1994, Hendry, 1994), China (Kua, 1994), Mexico (Medina-Mora, 1994), and Peru (Pacurucu-Castillo, 1994), the use of alcohol is less acceptable for women than for men. In part, this seems to reflect the idea that drinking, and especially drunkenness, is incompatible with traditional female roles relating to home and family.[2] These— seemingly cross-cultural—differences in social norms regarding alcohol use have been used to explain the lower prevalence of alcohol use and alcohol-related problems in women described in Chapter 3. Of course, as Wilsnack et al. (2000) have argued, there are also biological differences between men and women (e.g., in the metabolization of alcohol) that contribute to these gender disparities, and social norms may amplify or dampen biological differences depending on specific cultural contexts.

Among some cultural groups there are also norms that *prescribe* drinking, and individuals who do not drink, or even who drink lightly, are viewed as deviant. For example, in New Zealand, the use of alcohol in many social contexts is essentially obligatory—especially for young men. Individuals who refuse to drink may be subject to subtle— and not so subtle—disapproval from group members in the form of jokes, critical comments, and even violence (Paton-Simpson, 2001). Cultural norms also can influence the way that alcohol is consumed in different social contexts. The practice of "standing rounds" or "shouting," where individuals take turns to pay for all the group's drinks, encourages patterns of heavy alcohol consumption (O'Dwyer, 2001; Paton-Simpson, 2001). Indeed, for many cultural groups, periodic heavy drinking and extreme drunkenness, usually in the context of sporadic celebratory events, is culturally normative (see Heath, 2000; Peréz, 2000; MacAndrew & Edgerton, 1969).

In summary, social norms can influence whether, when, where, and how alcohol may be consumed (Heath, 2000), with important implications for levels of alcohol use and alcohol-related harm. Moreover, these cultural differences in norms regarding alcohol use can also influence what are considered to be alcohol problems, how such problems arise, and how seriously they are taken (Schmidt & Room, 1999; see also Chapter 8). Social norms can also influence the consumption of other psychoactive substances in important ways. For example, whereas the use of cannabis is essentially normative for adolescents and young adults in many Western societies (Parker et al., 1998), it is still viewed as unacceptable among most demographic groups. The use of ecstasy and other drugs, as we have seen, is also the norm for individuals who participate in dance culture, but not for those outside this cultural group. Understanding the way that social norms influence drug use is important, because it opens up possibilities for intervening in ways that can minimize drug-related harm, although *changing* social norms may prove to be difficult to accomplish.

Beliefs, Expectations, and Concepts

The way that individuals behave after consuming psychoactive substances varies depending on the social and cultural context. The consumption of alcohol, for example, is often related to instances of aggression and violence. In Mexican drinking fiestas, drunkenness and violence—especially toward women—are common occurrences (Peréz, 2000). The same appears to be the case for tribes in the Papua New Guinean Highlands (Dernbach & Marshall, 2001), and the link between drinking and violence is also familiar in Western contexts (Bushman & Cooper, 1990; Parker & Auerhahn, 1998). However, this relationship is by no means inevitable. As we noted in Chapter 6, the Camba of Eastern Bolivia, despite imbibing voluminous quantities of high-proof alcohol, exhibit few if any instances of overt aggression and violence (Heath, 1991a). Likewise, the Yuruna Indians of the Amazon consume large quantities of alcohol made from fermented manioc root, but rather than becoming aggressive, violent, or disinhibited at all, simply withdraw into themselves (MacAndrew & Edgerton, 1969). It appears, as Mandelbaum (1965) has summarized, "the behavioral consequences of drinking alcohol depend as much on a people's idea of what alcohol does to a person as they do on the physiological processes that take place" (p. 282). These profound cross-cultural differences in the behavioral consequences of alcohol consumption led MacAndrew and Edgerton (1969) to conclude that drunken comportment was essentially the product of culturally shared *beliefs* about the effects of alcohol on behavior, rather than the consequence of alcohol per se.

The importance of beliefs relating to alcohol's effects are combined, argued MacAndrew and Edgerton (1969), with cultural norms that prescribe what is acceptable behavior after consuming alcohol, to explain cultural differences in drunken comportment. They argued that while drunkenness in many societies takes the form of a "time out" from normal social roles, there is also a "within limits" clause, which specifies the norms relating to drunken behavior. MacAndrew's and Edgerton's thesis offered a profound challenge to purely pharmacological theories of alcohol's effect on human behavior and has been hugely influential, although it has not gone without criticism (see Critchlow, 1986; Room, 2001). Psychologists, for example, have explored in detail the link between alcohol *expectancies* and subsequent behavior. This voluminous body of research clearly supports the idea that an individual's belief about the effects of a substance can shape their subsequent responses in ways that can predict subsequent patterns of use (see Goldman, Del Boca, & Darkes, 1999; Kirsch, 1997; Stacy, Widaman, & Marlatt, 1990; Vogel-Sprott & Fillmore, 1999, for reviews).

A number of studies have elucidated the relationship between beliefs and expectations about the effects of drugs and subsequent patterns of use. Research, for example, indicates that more positive drug-related expectancies are associated with higher rates of drug use for a variety of substances, including alcohol, tobacco, cocaine, and cannabis (Brandon, Juliano, & Copeland, 1999; Goldman, Del Boca, & Darkes, 1999; Schafer & Brown, 1991). Furthermore, interventions that focus on modifying expectancies about the effects of drugs such as alcohol can lead to a reduction in subsequent levels of consumption (Kirsch, 1997). In support of MacAndrew's and Edgerton's theory, expectancies have been shown not only to influence subsequent patterns of use, but also to affect behavioral *responses* to drug use (Vogel-Sprott & Fillmore, 1999). For example, in one study, individuals who expected their performance on a cognitive task to be more impaired by alcohol actually performed more poorly even when they were given a placebo that was believed to be alcohol (Fillmore, Carscadden, & Vogel-Sprott, 1998). Research has thus led to the identification of a number of different types of drug-related expectancies; there are expectancies about receiving a drug, the effects of a drug, and about the consequences of these effects (Vogel-Sprott & Fillmore, 1999). Expectancies will also change over time as a person gains more experience with a substance. For instance, Brandon, Juliano, and Copeland (1999) report an association between expectancies and smoking at all stages of use, including initiation, maintenance, cessation, and relapse.

Expectancy theory provides a point of convergence between a range of quite different etiological variables: developmental factors, individual experiences, and cultural-historical contexts. Clearly culture-specific beliefs and expectations can influence subsequent patterns of use and can provide potential explanations for cultural *differences* in the prevalence of drug use and drug-related problems (e.g., Marin, 1996; Teahan, 1988). For example, whereas cannabis has been described by some as a substance that reduces motivation and industry in Western cultures, it is used for just the opposite reason by workers on Jamaican sugar cane plantations, who believe it promotes productivity (Dreher, 1983).[3] Cultural influences on the *content* of drug experiences are also illustrated by the way that the visions experienced by users of hallucinogens are strongly influenced by prevailing cultural beliefs. Fernandez (1990), for example, has commented on the "remarkable stereotyping of the vision experience" (p. 251) by the Fang after consumption of *Tabernathe iboga*, and Reichel-Dolmatoff (1990) has explored a similar phenomenon among Turkano after ingesting yajé *(Banesteriopsis caapi)*. Not all studies, however, have found a relationship between expectancies and drug use, and more research is needed to elucidate the potential *causal* role of beliefs and expectations on subsequent patterns of drug use (Jones, Corbin, & Fromme, 2001).

More general beliefs about the benefits and harms of drugs can also impact on patterns of use in different ways depending on the cultural context. Warnings about the harm of smoking, for example, are less widely disseminated in developing nations than they are in Western cultures, thereby reducing the effectiveness of one important preventative measure. Cultural groups also differ widely in their beliefs about the harm of drinking alcohol and taking other drugs during pregnancy. Whereas the deleterious prenatal effects of alcohol are widely recognized in most Western societies (Randall, 2001), in other cultural groups alcohol is believed to be beneficial to the developing fetus. Indeed, in many African cultures, beer is not only prescribed to pregnant mothers but is given to infants as a supplement to milk (Heath, 2000). The prevalence of these different beliefs can, of course, influence gender differences in drinking patterns in various ways, especially as in many Western societies women are advised not to drink *any* alcohol, even if they *might* become pregnant.

Beliefs and expectations can not only influence whether individuals take psychoactive substances and the way that those drugs are taken, but can also affect the nature of drug-related problems such as addiction. As Peele (1987, 1989) and others (e.g., Schaler, 2000) have argued, the belief that individuals with drug problems have no control over their drug-taking behavior is likely to foster such uncontrolled patterns of use. Cultural beliefs about the nature of drug addiction can thus influence subsequent levels of addiction in society if many people believe that they have no control over their use of alcohol and other drugs. Baumeister, Heatherton, and Tice (1994) clearly draw these links between culture, beliefs about self-control, and addiction when they state, "It is obvious that self-regulation depends heavily on cultural factors. Among these are beliefs about self control" (p. 253). Thus "the parallel rise in addictive behaviors may be similarly fuelled by the belief that people cannot control their desires for drugs and alcohol" (p. 251). In summary, cultural differences in the way that drugs are used, their subsequent effects, and the incidence of drug-related harm may be influenced in important ways by beliefs, expectations, and concepts that are themselves the product of social learning in different cultural contexts.

Socialization and Social Identity

Beliefs, norms, values, and expectations are the products of a process variously called "social learning," "socialization," or "enculturation." Social learning can be conceptualized as a general theory of human behavior (Maisto, Carey, & Bradizza, 1999). Oetting et al. (1998), for example, assert, "Primary socialization theory . . . proposes that essentially all human behaviors are learned behaviors or have major components that are learned" (p. 2079). Individuals learn social norms, values, beliefs, and practices through imitation, modeling, and observational learning. Certain behaviors are reinforced either directly or indirectly, while others are not. Important sources for social learning include family, school, peers, and the media, although the relevance of these will vary in different cultural contexts (Oetting et al., 1998; White, Bates, & Johnson, 1991).

One historical illustration of the role of social learning in patterns of drug use is provided by the development of heavy and problematic drinking by Native Americans and indigenous Australians in response to the widespread dissemination of alcohol by European colonists. Although this pattern of heavy drinking to the point of intoxication, and subsequent aggression, violence, and sexual licentiousness, differed from "mainstream" European practices of alcohol use, it resembled the way alcohol was used by many of the individuals that indigenous people would have had frequent contact with. In Australia, drinking to excess and engaging in violent behavior while drunk was a cultural norm for many European colonists and convicts, who, after months in the bush, would "knock down the cheque" at the local pub (Brady, 1990). A similar pattern of "frontier drinking" characterized many colonists' use of alcohol in America (Frank et al., 2000). As Frank et al. (2000) summarize:

> Up to the end of the 19th century, Indians were exposed to persistent modeling of antisocial behavior associated with frequent high-dose drinking by soldiers, *coureurs des bois* (fur traders), and subsequently cowboys and miners—notably, all self-selected communities of men, away from their families and from the reach of alcohol policies and other forms of social control. (p. 348)

The influence of social learning on the use of alcohol and other drugs has also been the subject of a number of empirical studies. Experimental research has demonstrated that individuals can be "taught" to respond to alcohol in different ways (Zack & Vogel-Sprott, 1997), and the use of alcohol and other drugs by parents has been shown to predict substance use by their children (Epstein, Botvin, Baker, & Diaz, 1999; Hops, Andrews, Duncan, Duncan, & Tildesley, 2000). Children from one-parent families also appear to be at a risk for the harmful use of alcohol and other drugs, perhaps in part through a weakening of parental influences (Hops et al., 2000; Jenkins & Zunguze, 1998).

Numerous studies have also demonstrated that adolescents and young adults who have friends who use drugs, or approve of drug use, are themselves more likely to use them (e.g., Epstein et al., 1999;

Jenkins & Zunguze, 1998; Tani, Chavez, & Deffenbacher, 2001). However, as Bauman and Ennett (1996) have pointed out, these studies rarely tease apart the different causal pathways that might lead to these findings (although see Krohn, Lizotte, Thornberry, Smith, & McDowall, 1996). Do individuals who have friends who use drugs *become* drug users themselves, or do people *select* friends who share their drug-taking predilections? The popular notion of "peer pressure" as a reason why young people take drugs has also been challenged. Parker et al. (1998), for example, found in their study that most of their young participants denied that peer pressure was a factor influencing their drug-taking behavior. Of course they could be lying or simply be unaware of such influences, but critically, as Borsari and Carey (2001) have recently argued, there is a need to unpack the notion of peer pressure in more detail. They suggest that peer pressure encompasses various kinds of influence: overt offers of drugs, modeling, and social norms that might influence the use of drugs in different ways. However, what is clear is that social processes can influence patterns of drug use: for example, who one interacts with can be an important predictor of what kinds of drugs are likely to be taken and how they are used.

What are the implications of socialization practices for explaining *cultural* differences in patterns of drug use? The theoretical linkages here are fairly clear. Individuals in different cultural groups are exposed to different sources of socialization, be they families, friends, communities, or the culture at large. For example, the low rates of alcohol use by Asian Americans compared to Caucasians is likely to be due, in part, to the low exposure to various risk factors: less drinking models in the family, fewer peers who drink, and less exposure to beliefs about the positive rather than the negative effects of alcohol (Keefe & Newcomb, 1996). Likewise, moderate alcohol use among Jews has been explained, in part, in terms of strong family role models for moderate, controlled drinking and insulation from non-Jewish peer networks (Glassner, 1991). Children in France and other "wet cultures" are also socialized into moderate drinking patterns by being offered (watered down) wine with meals at an early age, and learning cultural norms regarding the use of alcohol with food (Heath, 2000). There also might be important cultural differences in *general* socialization practices, not specifically related to alcohol and other drugs, which can influence patterns of use (e.g., Catalano, Morrison, Wells, Gillmore, Iritani, & Hawkins, 1992).

It is important to recognize, however, that the influence of cultural group membership on patterns of substance use is strongly affected by the nature and extent of cultural identification and the relative importance of different sources of socialization (Oetting et al., 1998). These issues become especially relevant in multicultural societies where multiple cultural groups coexist with varying degrees of integration. The extent to which an individual's drug use is influenced by cultural norms, beliefs, and expectations depends on their degree of identification with that group. Moreover, the process of acculturating to mainstream cultural norms, values, and practices may itself give rise to psychological problems that can influence substance use and abuse in various ways. One idea, prominent in early research, was that the process of acculturation was *necessarily* stressful, and the concept of "acculturation stress" or "culture shock" was employed to capture these psychological difficulties (Berry, 1998; Horton, 1991). Certainly there is some empirical support for the idea that acculturation might lead to an increase in the use of alcohol and other drugs. Caetano (1987a, 1987b), for instance, found a positive association between acculturation and drinking for Hispanics in U.S. society, although this relationship appeared to be much stronger for women. In an emergency room study, Cherpitel (1992) found that acculturation in a sample of Hispanics was related to positive Breathalyzer readings, and other studies have also reported an association between acculturation and alcohol use in Hispanics (e.g., Marin & Posner, 1995).

However, these findings can be equally plausibly interpreted as reflecting adaptation to American norms for drinking rather than as a result of stress associated with acculturation. More generally, the notion of acculturation itself has been criticized by a number of authors as unhelpful and misleading (e.g., Gutmann, 1999). This does not mean that exploring cultural identification is irrelevant to understanding patterns of substance use; rather, attention needs to be directed toward the details, on an individual basis. More specifically, cultural identification with multiple groups needs to be established, the nature of those groups (whether peer, family, or community) elucidated, and the drug-related norms, beliefs, and expectations held by those groups ascertained. Migrants to the United States and other countries, for instance, are at risk for developing drug-related problems along with other psychological disorders (Westermeyer, 1995, 1996c; Burfield, Sundquist, & Johansson, 2001). However, the extent of this risk depends on the context of their migration (e.g., whether forced or voluntary), the length of time spent in their new location, age, and the levels of drug use in their country of origin.

In furthering our understanding of the relationship between cultural identification and drug use, it is also important to examine the symbolic role that drugs can play in affirming group identity. As we described in Chapter 5, the use of drugs historically and cross-culturally has been associated with many different social movements. Examples here include the use of peyote in the Native American Church, cannabis use by the Rastafari Bretheren, and the poly-drug explorations characteristic of the hippie movement (see Knipe, 1995). The use of substances may also provide key markers that delineate membership in one group from another. The use of ecstasy may be one mark of identification with dance culture, for example, although it probably does not explicitly demarcate in-group from out-group. By contrast, Mars (1987) describes how different styles of drinking clearly delineate regular membership in longshore gangs in Newfoundland:

> Regular men drink in taverns close to the wharf; they sit with their regular workmates and drink beer: outside men, even though working on the same wharves, usually drink in the open air or sit in parked cars and drink rum or wine in smaller groups. . . . We can see how styles of drinking not only reflect basic differences between two groups of men but how they contribute to and reaffirm these differences. (p. 91)

The use of illicit drugs in Western society may also reflect the rejection of mainstream values and norms and allegiance to alternative political economies. Collison (1996) describes how drug use and drug dealing in Britain can be one way of developing a positive self-identity, especially for males with little opportunity for "making it" within mainstream society. Bourgois (1995) explores a similar theme in his detailed ethnographic account of crack dealing in El Barrio, East Harlem. As Caesar, one of the Puerto Rican crack dealers with whom Bourgois spent time, asserts:

> That's right my man! We is real vermin lunatics that sell drugs. We don't wanna be part of society. . . . We have no regard for nothing. The new generation has no regard for the public bullshit. We wanna make easy money, and that's it. . . . we're in a rebellious state. We rather evade taxes; make quick money; and just survive. (p. 131)[4]

More generally, disenfranchised groups have played a major part in the drug trade, whether through cultivation of drug crops or through their production, distribution, and sale (Westermeyer, 1999).

SOCIAL-STRUCTURAL FACTORS

In the previous two sections we have explored a range of cultural explanations for substance use that draw primarily on the place of drugs within cultures and cultural orientations toward the use of drugs. Cultural differences in patterns of drug use can also be accounted for by considering a range of social-structural factors that do not relate to drug use per se, but affect the way that drugs are used. The social organization of society and factors relating to power, oppression, marginalization, poverty, and discrimination have all been advanced as potential explanations for patterns of drug use and drug-related problems. These kinds of explanations can be clearly located at the cultural-historical level of analysis as they refer to macro-level properties of social groups (and the interactions of social groups), which reflect contingent social histories.

Social Organization, Social Control, and Power

The idea that the social organization of society might influence drug use was expounded by Field (1991) in an early cross-cultural study of drunkenness. A number of relationships were found between levels of drunkenness and organizational features of society. Drunkenness was more common among hunter-gatherer than agricultural societies; and *sobriety* was related to patrilocal residence, presence of a bride-price, collective ownership of property, and settled villages (rather than nomadism). Overall, Field's results seemed to suggest that more stratified, traditional, and controlled societies have lower incidences of drunkenness. A similar theme has been developed by Dobkin de Rios and Smith (1977), who argue that *social control* over drug use increases as societies become less egalitarian and more hierarchical in nature. The sharp contrast between the rigid control of psychoactive substances in Aztec society and the more informal social proscriptions found in most indigenous Amerindian cultures is one illustration of this difference. Unfortunately, a systematic evaluation of these ideas has not been attempted. In part this is because of the difficulty of teasing apart other relevant factors that are likely to be related to social organization and that might influence patterns of drug use in important ways. However, it is plausible to suggest that more socially stratified societies are likely to foster comparably more rigid forms of social control, as social and political elites have vested interests in maintaining social order, economic growth, and worker productivity (Room & Mäkelä, 2000).

One illustration of this theme has been offered by Bourgois (2000), who has recently characterized American policies toward opiate users as primarily concerned with social control. One of the few harm-reduction strategies employed (although somewhat irregularly) in the United States is methadone maintenance. Although methadone maintenance can be an effective way of reducing problems relating to heroin dependence (e.g., Rao & Schottenfeld, 1999), Bourgois also suggests that it is often "experienced as a hostile and/or arbitrary forum for social control and enforced dependency among street addicts" (p. 171). The contrast between heroin users, who are referred to as "criminals" or "deviants," and those enrolled in methadone maintenance, who are described as "patients" or "clients," emphasizes the role of policy in maintaining carefully delineated social roles for drug users (Bourgois, 2000). A continuing reluctance in the United States to develop federally funded needle exchange or heroin maintenance programs underscores these differences and reflects the powerlessness of heroin users whose personal preferences (and the harm they generate) are subordinate to policies of social control (see Singer, 2001). Mandatory drug treatment and drug testing in some contexts are other visible manifestations of drug-related control in society.

Historically, the use of drugs to promote work, trade, and social relations has been an important tool in European colonialism. As Jankowiak and Bradburd (1996) have argued, drug use has been *encouraged* among indigenous populations as an effective tool of control and subordination. This is clearly evident in the relations between European colonists and the indigenous peoples of North America, Australia, and New Zealand. Native Americans, for example, traded rum for much-valued furs and skins. This practice was encouraged by colonists, as demand for alcohol, unlike other commodities such as blankets or guns, was unceasing (Mancall, 1995). Moreover, by engaging Native Americans in the social and economic nexus of European mercantile relations, it was hoped that the "natives" would become integrated into "civilized" European society. Alcohol was thus an important tool, which, as Mancall (2000) asserts, "played a key role in the efforts to colonize British America" (p. 205). A similar conclusion has been drawn regarding the role of alcohol in the "rum economy" of colonial Australia. As in America, alcohol was traded for a variety of goods and services, including the sexual favors of Aboriginal women (Langton, 1993; Saggers & Gray, 1998). "Alcohol was," Langton (1993) avers, "consciously or unconsciously, used by the British as a device for seducing the Aboriginal people to engage economically, politically and socially with the colony" (p. 201). This process of assimilation was perhaps less insidious in New Zealand, where there was considerable variation in demand for alcohol among different groups of Maori (Hutt, 1999). Maori were encouraged to accumulate debts for alcohol and other commodities, however, which they would subsequently have to meet by selling land (Saggers & Gray, 1998).

Importantly, these forms of social control and the power differentials they reflect may impact in different ways on different cultural groups. The relative powerlessness of women in many cultures, for example, with strong social norms against female drinking, may contribute to the harm that arises if women do develop alcohol problems (Ikuesan, 1994; Mphi, 1994). The consequences of powerlessness, social control, and oppression are also relevant in understanding drug use by ethnic minorities in multicultural societies, who are influenced in various ways by mainstream policies. A similar theme might be explored in reference to the use of illicit substances by some groups of adolescents. Their preferred drugs of choice—cannabis, amphetamines, and ecstasy—are deemed dangerous not only to individual users but also to society. Individuals who choose to reject warnings against their use face potentially punitive responses from society, despite any overwhelming evidence that these drugs are more harmful than those considered acceptable by social and political elites.

The Minority Experience: Marginalization, Poverty, Prejudice, and Social Change

One of the most striking findings that emerged from our review of cultural differences in patterns of drug use and drug-related harm in Chapter 6 is that in the United States, Hispanics and in particular African Americans are overrepresented in statistics relating to most measures of drug-related harm. Differences in the reported prevalence of drug use seem unable to explain these findings, although it may be, as some have argued (e.g., Brownsberger, 1997), that national surveys fail to provide representative measures of ethnic differences in the use of illicit drugs. If the various kinds of harm associated with the use of drugs are related to factors such as neighborhood disadvantage, stress, poverty, and discrimination, then because minority groups tend to be differentially affected by these factors, they can potentially account for the cultural disparities in drug-related problems that are found.

Most ethnic minority groups in Western nations such as the United States, Great Britain, Australia, Canada, and New Zealand are at a disadvantage in terms of education level, employment, income, social stress, health, and mortality. In the United States, for instance, the mean family income for Hispanics, African Americans, and Native Americans is substantially lower than that for Caucasians, and the percentage of persons living below the poverty line is significantly higher (Waters & Eschbach, 1995). The relationship between income inequality and mortality has been well established (e.g., McLaughlin & Stokes, 2002); poverty, segregation, and powerlessness have deleterious effects on health for minorities in the United States (e.g., LaVeist, 1993). The links between neighborhood disadvantage, stress, crime, and drug use have also been well established. For example, in a study of neighborhoods in Columbus, Ohio, Krivo and Peterson (1996) found support for the idea that extreme disadvantage is related to levels of crime. Furthermore, in this study, the disparities between Caucasian and African American levels of crime could be explained (although not entirely) by the overrepresentation of African Americans in disadvantaged neighborhoods. Similarly, a relationship between drug use and neighborhood disadvantage was found in a recent study with a sample of 1,101 adults living in Detroit (Boardman, Finch, Ellison, Williams, & Jackson, 2001).

One prominent theoretical model that can be employed to account for these findings is based on the idea that substance use is one way of coping with stress (e.g., Greeley & Oei, 1999; Rhodes & Jason, 1990). The experience of living in impoverished environments, with high levels of crime and unemployment, contributes to greater levels of stress, which can be temporarily relieved by the use of psychoactive drugs. These problems are likely to be especially prevalent among minority groups, who are more likely to be exposed to a wide range of social and environmental stressors.[5] As Scheir, Botvin, and Miller (1999) summarize for adolescents, "minority youth may face a unique landscape of developmental risk stemming from poverty, urban crowding, and discrimination, all of which may encourage deviant behavior" (p. 23). These environments are likely to encourage harmful patterns of drug use, in line with the idea that the use of alcohol and other drugs in order to regulate *negative* emotions tends to be related to detrimental outcomes (e.g., Cooper, Frone, Russell, & Mudar, 1995). One especially relevant form of stress experienced by minority groups is related to discrimination and prejudice. In one recent study, for example, around half of all African Americans reported being exposed to major lifetime discrimination (Kessler, Mickelson, & Williams, 1999). A positive association was also found between discrimination and mental health problems, although this could not explain ethnic differences in mental health outcomes. The idea that exposure to a wide range of stressful life experiences is an important component of substance-related problems has been characterized as one feature of "oppression illness" (Singer, 2001; Baer, Singer, & Susser, 1997). The combined forces of poverty, social stress, marginalization, discrimination, and prejudice result, it is argued, in a sense of powerlessness and helplessness that can be temporarily relieved through the ingestion of psychoactive drugs (Singer, 2001). According to Bourgois (1995), "Substance abuse in the inner city is merely a symptom—and a vivid symbol—of deeper dynamics of social marginalization and alienation" (p. 2) (see also Agar & Reisinger, 2001).

The cluster of factors that relate to the minority experience may thus partially mediate the relationship between ethnicity and drug-related harm. For example, socially and economically disadvantaged individuals have limited access to health care and are thus likely to use emergency rooms in different ways than do more affluent individuals. They are, furthermore, more likely to have other health problems, have less social and economic resources with which to cope with substance abuse, and be exposed to additional hazards compared with those who are more advantaged (Brownsberger, 1997; Murphy & Rosenbaum, 1997). The use of drugs, therefore, may be more likely to show up in emergency room statistics, affect other health problems, and prove more difficult to control for disadvantaged ethnic minorities. This mediational model for ethnic differences in drug-related problems, however, has yet to be fully and rigorously evaluated. Studies often find that some ethnic differences remain after controlling for relevant sociodemographic variables such as unemployment, poverty, and discrimination, suggesting that other factors may also be involved (e.g., Kessler et al., 1999; Leischow, Ranger-Moore, & Lawrence, 2000).

Can this combination of social structural factors—poverty, oppression, stress, marginalization, and discrimination—also account for the dramatic ethnic disparities in drug-related arrests and incarcerations described in Chapter 6? A number of authors have argued that at least part of these discrepancies can be explained in terms of racially biased sentencing practices (Free, 1997; Lusane, 1994; Tonry, 1994). For instance, sentences for crack cocaine in the United States are significantly more severe than those for powdered cocaine—the law equates 1 gram of the former with 100 grams of the latter. With the return of federal mandatory minimum penalties in 1984, possession of 5 grams of crack cocaine could result in a five-year prison term. Given that African Americans are more likely to use crack cocaine than Caucasians, the average minimum sentence increases dramatically due to these legal changes (Free, 1997).

Brownsberger (2000) suggests, however, that these sources of discrimination cannot fully account for the ethnic disparities in drug-related arrests and incarcerations. One factor that can plausibly explain differences in arrest rates is that African Americans and Hispanics are overrepresented among drug users and drug dealers, especially for more vigorously enforced substances like cocaine and heroin. However, as discussed in Chapter 6, there is no really reliable evidence that can address this possibility. Certainly, high rates of poverty and unemployment and the absence of licit sources of income encourage engagement in underground drug economies for minorities with limited employment options (Bourgois, 1995).[6] Moreover, street dealing, which is more visible and more targeted by law enforcement officers, is more prevalent in high-poverty areas where minority groups are overrepresented, possibly increasing the risk for arrest. Furthermore, "racial profiling" by predominantly Caucasian narcotic officers may increase the targeting of ethnic minorities, leading to higher rates of arrest. One recent study, however, found that these various factors could explain only part of the ethnic discrepancies in drug-related arrests, and the author concluded with the suggestion that there is a "need to look beyond the existing families of explanations in order to understand racial/ethnic disproportionality of incarceration for drug dealing" (Brownsberger, 2000, p. 359). The fact that ethnic differences for drug-related crime are far greater than those for other sorts of offenses suggests the need to examine other factors that are specific to drug use and drug dealing.

Bourgois (1995), in his detailed study of crack dealing in El Barrio, East Harlem, provides one example of how cultural values, historical change, and social-structural factors interact to provide a framework for understanding patterns of drug use among immigrant Puerto Ricans. First, the restructuring of the global economy over the past thirty years, which has resulted in the wide-scale loss of entry-level manufacturing jobs in the United States, has disproportionately affected ethnic minority groups such as Puerto Ricans, who typically lack the educational resources to obtain work in other sectors. These changes have wrought their greatest impact on men, who can no longer fulfill their traditional role as providers. The jobs that *are* available occur primarily in the service sector. However, as Bourgois (1995) explains, "Obedience to the norms of high-rise, office-corridor culture is in direct contradiction to street culture's definitions of personal dignity—especially for males who are socialized not to accept public subordination" (p. 115). The only viable way of earning income and maintaining respect and dignity—central values in Puerto Rican culture—is to engage in the underground economy of drug dealing. Drug dealing and drug use by Puerto Ricans in El Barrio, therefore, represent the confluence of both macro-level (the restructuring of the American economy) and micro-level (oppression, marginalization, discrimination) social-structural factors, with culturally based norms relating to self-respect and masculine identity.

As this example illustrates, although social-structural factors are often important in understanding cultural patterns of substance use and substance-related problems, there is a need to consider how such factors interact with cultural norms, beliefs, expectations, and socialization practices. We examine how such an integrated cultural explanation might look in the next section.

INTEGRATING CULTURAL EXPLANATIONS

In this chapter we have discussed a wide array of cultural explanations that have been employed to account for the differences (and similarities) in patterns of substance use and abuse among different cultural groups. One critical issue, of both theoretical and practical relevance, relates to the relative *importance* of these different kinds of explanation. Are the differences in the prevalence of alcohol-related problems between Native Americans and Caucasians the result of difference in cultural norms, beliefs, and expectations, or do they stem from social structural factors relating to marginalization, poverty, and discrimination? Do gender differences in drug use arise primarily from expectations about the social roles of men and women, or are they the result of economic, political, or even biological factors? Do young aficionados of dance culture consume more ecstasy than do middle-aged individuals because of different patterns of socialization with peers, or does this difference arise from historical changes in the avail-ability of drugs, or even the meaning and nature of adolescence and young adulthood? Our answers to these questions have profound implications for understanding the causes of substance-related prob-lems, and the development of prevention, treatment, and public policy initiatives. We suggest here, drawing on a distinction made in Chapter 1, that the full range of cultural and social-structural explanations are typically *relevant* in answering these questions, but some kinds of explanation are more *salient* in specific cases.

For example, in explaining the low rates of alcohol problems among Jewish people, it appears likely that factors relating to social norms, values, and expectancies and how these arise through social-ization with family and peers are most salient, although other social-structural factors may well be relevant. In contrast, in explaining the overrepresentation of African Americans and Hispanics in emergency room statistics and drug-related arrests, social-structural factors relat-ing to poverty, marginalization, oppression, and discrimination are likely to be more salient, although cultural norms and socialization are also probably relevant. Establishing causal primacy in these and other cases, however, is difficult because the various factors outlined in this chapter interact in complex and dynamic ways. Economic and political contexts, for example, influence and constrain the social learning of norms, values, beliefs, and expectations, which are related to the way that drugs are subsequently employed.

In order to illustrate how different kinds of cultural explanation may interact, we explore in more detail the factors influencing the use of drugs, especially alcohol, by indigenous Australians. Indigenous Australians are at a greater risk for alcohol-related problems, have sig-nificantly higher rates of alcohol-related mortality, and have more alcohol-related health and social problems than do non-indigenous Australians (Brady, 2000; Hunter, 1992; Saggers & Gray, 1998). The abuse of inhalants, kava, and other substances has also been noted (e.g., Brady, 1992; Carroll, Houghton, & Odgen, 1998). Why do these differences between indigenous and non-indigenous Australians exist? In Table 7.1 we provide a list of potential explanations that have been

Table 7.1   Explanations for the High Rates of Alcohol and Other Drug
Problems Among Indigenous Australians

Form of Explanation	Details
Alien poison theory	Absence of alcohol prior to European colonization resulted in a lack of understanding about its effects and how to use it.[a] For kava[b]
Background cultural factors	(a) Hunter-gatherer lifestyles foster a pattern of immediate consumption, which manifests itself in bingeing on alcohol and other drugs[c] (b) Autonomy is a valued idea among indigenous Australians, and there is a belief in the individual right to pursue activities, including drinking, without overt control from others[d]
Availability	Sporadic availability of alcohol and kava in remote communities encourages patterns of binge consumption[c] Unavailability of drug alternatives leads to the use of solvents by indigenous Australian adolescents[g,h]
Norms, beliefs, and expectations	The belief that individuals who are intoxicated are not wholly responsible for their actions encourages aggressive and violent behavior when drunk[d,i]
Symbolic value of drinking	(a) The use of alcohol is associated with citizenship and equality because of laws against indigenous Australian drinking[e] (b) Drinking and drunkenness used as a symbol of resistance to domination by European culture[a]
Social learning	Indigenous Australians learned harmful patterns of drinking from European colonists,[f] which perpetuate in subsequent generations through socialization
Experience of colonialism	The experience of oppression, economic and political marginalization, discrimination, loss of culture, and disruption to local communities created high levels of "culture

(Continued)

Table 7.1   (Continued)

Form of Explanation	Details
	shock," "anomie," and stress, which could be self-medicated through the use of alcohol[e]
Social structural factors	Ongoing marginalization, oppression, and discrimination, high levels of unemployment, ill health, and other such factors contribute to continuing high levels of substance use and abuse[e]

SOURCES: Based on ideas from:

[a]Kahn et al., 1990
[b]Gregory & Cawte, 1988
[c]Gerrard, 1988
[d]Brady, 1990
[e]Saggers & Gray, 1998
[f]Brady, 1992
[g]Dinwiddie, 1994
[h]Burns et al., 1995
[i]MacAndrew & Edgerton, 1969

offered by various authors, and that have often been employed in combination (see Kahn et al., 1990; Saggers & Gray, 1998, for summaries of these various explanations).

Most of these explanations are likely to have some relevance in explaining patterns of Aboriginal drug use, but some are more salient than others. For example, as Saggers and Gray (1998) argue, the novelty of alcohol for indigenous Australians probably played a fairly limited role in contributing to harmful patterns of use and is a less relevant explanation for *current* alcohol-related problems. Some of the other explanations are salient in terms of accounting for harmful patterns of alcohol use, but not for other substances. Although, for example, social learning and peer interaction play an important role in inhalant abuse among indigenous Australian adolescents (e.g., Burns, D'Abbs, & Currie, 1995; Carroll et al., 1998), social learning is not derived from Caucasian models, as early drinking patterns were. We should also recognize that indigenous Australians represent a diverse collection of cultural groups, and therefore some explanations may be more salient for some communities but not for others (Kahn et al., 1990). Likewise,

Figure 7.1   An Integrated Model of the Role of Cultural Factors in Substance Use

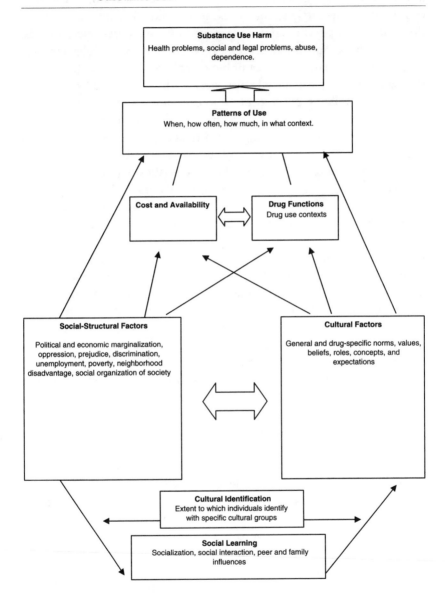

some explanations may be more salient for men than for women, and for adolescents rather than adults.

In Figure 7.1 we provide an outline of an integrated model of cultural explanations for substance use and abuse, which details the dynamic interrelationships among various kinds of cultural and social structural factors. Before we discuss this model in detail, however, a couple of caveats are in order. First, this is a model of *cultural* explanations; although psychological level accounts are incorporated (beliefs, expectations, socialization processes), we ignore other relevant psychological explanations and omit biological perspectives entirely. This does not mean these factors are necessarily irrelevant, but rather reflects their relative unimportance in explaining *cultural differences* in the ways that drugs are used and abused. Second, the model is cross-sectional in nature, illustrating the interaction of factors at a given point in time. The ways in which these dynamics play out obviously have historical and developmental characteristics that need to be considered. Bearing these points in mind, we examine how this general model of cultural explanations can be employed to explain the relations between indigenous Australians and psychoactive substances.

When the first fleet landed in Australia in 1788, a relatively novel substance—alcohol—was introduced into the existing cultural experiences of indigenous Australians, who had occupied the continent for more than 40,000 years. Although there were important intergroup differences, cultural norms regarding the ingestion of food and drink among indigenous Australians emphasized sharing and immediate consumption. These general cultural factors subsequently influenced patterns of alcohol use that typically involved drinking until supplies ran out. Exposure to the use of alcohol primarily occurred in the context of heavy patterns of consumption by Caucasian colonists, often involving bouts of intoxicated aggression. Consequently, as noted earlier, alcohol-specific norms and beliefs were learned commensurate with these role models as a result of such interactions. General cultural beliefs that emphasized tolerance and respect for individual autonomy probably interacted with these learning experiences to contribute to a heavy pattern of sporadic consumption, often accompanied by harmful outcomes such as aggression and violence.

Social-structural factors also impacted on socialization practices, most dramatically via the forced relocation of thousands of indigenous Australian children, who were taken from their parents and put in various homes and institutions (Read, 1999). The effects of this brutal forced assimilation on patterns of substance abuse and dependence have not been systematically detailed, although the frequent lack of positive parenting, role models, and cultural anomie can be plausibly related to drug problems in later life. Social-structural factors in the guise of ongoing oppression, marginalization, and discrimination, and their consequences in the form of poverty, unemployment, and health problems can also both directly, and indirectly, be related to patterns of substance use and drug-related problems. For example, the prohibition of alcohol use imposed by colonists on indigenous Australians, and which lingered well into the twentieth century, limited supplies, which encouraged rapid consumption of high-proof alcohol and contributed to alcohol-related harm (Brady, 2000; Saggers & Gray, 1998). These prohibitions also made alcohol a symbol of equality and citizenship to indigenous Australians, which in turn affected levels of cultural identity and adherence to indigenous values, beliefs, and norms. For example, in a strange but telling loophole in legal restrictions on the sale of alcohol, indigenous Australians who demonstrated their assimilation into European culture—by, for example, serving in the armed forces or dissolving tribal affiliations—ceased to be "Aborigine" and were thus exempted from the liquor laws (Brady, 1990; Langton, 1993). The intermittent availability of alcohol in many Aboriginal communities has also influenced patterns of use in different ways—sometimes reducing levels of alcohol consumed, but also contributing to harmful patterns of use and the consumption of other substances, notably kava and inhalants.

The relative importance of these different explanations, as we suggested earlier, depends on the kind of substance consumed, the community considered, gender, age, and other factors. But in sum, the model we provide here offers a general framework for understanding the way that various different cultural factors interact to produce patterns of use and abuse. Importantly, cultural differences in the use of drugs can be accounted for by considering how the various factors play out in the context of different cultural groups. Given suitably rigorous methods of operationalizing these various important factors, it should also be possible to explore the importance of the various pathways in specific cases using the resources of methodological tools such as structural equation modeling.

SUMMARY

It is clear that the way that drugs are used and the harm that they generate vary in important ways depending on a variety of biological, psychological, and cultural-historical factors. However, in order to explain why different cultural groups vary in the drugs that they use, how such substances are employed, and the harm (and benefit) that they generate, we need to draw on multiple explanatory accounts drawn primarily from a cultural-historical level of analysis. In this chapter we have provided an overview of the various explanations that have been offered from this perspective. Our focus has shifted from the place of drugs within cultures (their functions, integration, and availability), through cultural orientations to the use of drugs (norms, values, beliefs, and expectations), to the influence of wider social structural factors (social organization, oppression, marginality, discrimination, and so on). We concluded by drawing these various kinds of cultural explanation into an integrated framework that highlighted the dynamic reciprocity of different perspectives in explaining patterns of substance use and abuse. However, which of these factors or combinations of factors might be considered the most salient needs to be addressed on a case-by-case basis.

NOTES

1. For men, however, Herd (1994) found that more severe alcohol-related problems were experienced by African Americans compared to Caucasians.

2. See Room (1996) for a more nuanced discussion of how gender roles and drinking are influenced by different social contexts and male-female interactions.

3. Dreher's (1983) empirical study found that heavy smokers of cannabis (more than three cigars a day every day) produced an equal amount of sugar cane as nonsmokers.

4. Although as Bourgois (1995) clearly relates, there is a *desire* by the crack dealers he talked to in El Barrio to obtain legal jobs in mainstream society, but simply a lack of opportunity. Dealing drugs becomes, therefore, not only a way of earning a living, but also of obtaining respect and developing an alternative identity.

5. Interestingly, there appears to be important ethnic differences in the etiology of substance abuse. Caucasian substance abusers typically have significantly higher rates of psychopathology than either Hispanics or African Americans, suggesting that environmental factors such as those relating to unemployment, poverty, and discrimination are more relevant in the development of substance abuse disorders in the latter two groups (Roberts, 2000).

6. Drug dealing, however, is not necessarily the lucrative business it is sometimes made out to be, and like many occupations the amount that is earned depends very much on one's place in the social hierarchy (see Caulkins, Johnson, Taylor, & Taylor, 1999). Unreliable income, coupled with poor and often dangerous working conditions, with the ever-present risk of arrest, makes the sale of illicit drugs very much a second-best option for many individuals (Bourgois, 1995).

8

Conceptualizing and Treating Substance Use Problems: A Cultural-Historical Perspective

INTRODUCTION

Classification schemes for mental disorders have shown substantial variation during the past 100 years. Diagnostic categories have been removed, added, and revised in significant ways. For example, slaves who absconded from their masters were said to be afflicted with "drapetomania," children could suffer from "childhood masturbation disorder," and women might endure "lack of vaginal orgasm" (Wakefield, 1992). Of course, it is not the disorders themselves that have arisen only to disappear with the passing of time, but it is our *perception* of what constitutes a mental disorder that has changed. Mental disorders are in part *social constructions*, which are influenced in important ways by specific social and cultural contexts (see Thakker, Ward, & Strongman, 1999).

Other disorders, such as depression and schizophrenia, have occupied a more enduring place in our taxonomies of mental illness, although the way we have conceptualized and treated these disorders has undergone substantial change. There is some sense of progress in these developments. Although there is still much to learn about the etiology of schizophrenia and the most effective treatments for this disorder, our current therapeutic initiatives can be viewed as an advance over the potpourri of treatment options—insulin coma, ECT, prolonged narcosis, psychosurgery—that were in vogue in the early part of the twentieth century (Shorter, 1997). The nature and existence of mental disorders also varies in important ways cross-culturally. Some authors, for instance, have identified more than 180 so-called culture-bound syndromes, which are restricted to specific cultural contexts (Simons & Hughes, 1993). Moreover, despite the universalist assumptions of the DSM-IV, many disorders such as schizophrenia and depression manifest in quite different ways in different cultures (Thakker & Ward, 1998; Thakker et al., 1999).

The historical and cross-cultural variability of mental disorders indicates that our current conceptions of substance abuse and dependence may themselves be the product of cultural-historical contingencies (Room, 1985). That is not to say that our current views are *wrong*; merely that there are, and have been, quite different ways of conceptualizing exactly what substance-related problems are and how best to deal with them. Understanding the historical development of concepts relating to drug problems, and especially drug dependence, can shed light on our current understanding of these issues. Further illumination can be gained by exploring cross-cultural differences in the understanding of substance-related problems. Moreover, examining the range of treatments that have been provided for drug problems during the past 200 years puts our current therapeutic initiatives in perspective.

THE PRE- AND EARLY HISTORY OF ADDICTION

People have been using psychoactive substances, in some form or another, for at least 4,000 years (see Chapter 4). Given the harm that can arise from the use of drugs, it would be surprising if ideas about substance *abuse* were an entirely modern phenomenon. Indeed, as we noted in Chapter 4, concerns about excessive drinking were not uncommon in ancient Rome. Moreover, Jellinek (1976) suggests that many of the features of alcohol abuse recognized today were understood by Roman physicians. Furthermore, the habit-forming properties of opium and the concept of tolerance were also recognized in Greek and Roman societies (Scarborough, 1995). Despite these antecedents, however, the modern concept of drug addiction as a disease characterized by physiological components (tolerance and withdrawal) and behavioral impairments (especially loss of control) can be located, it has been argued, in the development of ideas at the end of the eighteenth century (Levine, 1979, 1984).

For most of the seventeenth and eighteenth centuries in America, alcohol was viewed as "the goodly creature of God," and although consumption was heavy, it was perceived as unproblematic (Rorabaugh, 1979). Drinking itself was viewed as an integral part of daily existence, although excessive drunkenness was condemned as a sin or moral vice. A similar situation held in England, although the gin epidemic of the eighteenth century had clearly shown the harm that alcohol could cause. This "world without addiction" (Levine, 1979, p. 474), however, was swiftly eclipsed at the close of the eighteenth century, due in large part to the ideas of the Englishman Thomas Trotter and the American Benjamin Rush.

In 1802,[1] Thomas Trotter published *An Essay, Medical, Philosophical, and Chemical, on Drunkenness, and its Effects on the Human Body*, in which he clearly stated that the "habit of drunkenness was a disease"; moreover, he viewed such a state as a "disease of the mind" (cited in Porter, 1987, p. 199). In this work Trotter systematically organized what was currently known about drunkenness—its course, its short- and long-term effects, and its prevention and treatment (Grant, 1984). For Trotter there was an urgent need to relocate the view of habitual drunkenness from that of a sin, or a vice, to the idea that it was a medical condition that needed to be treated (Porter, 1985). Contemporaneously with Trotter, Benjamin Rush, a signer of the Declaration of Independence and so-called father of American psychiatry, forwarded the idea that chronic drunkenness was a disease to be treated rather than a vice to be condemned. In 1784, Rush published his influential pamphlet, *The Effects of Ardent Spirits upon the Human Mind and Body*, in which, like Trotter, he characterized drunkenness as a "disease."[2] In this tract, Rush outlined—in often graphic detail—the various physical and psychological consequences of chronic drunkenness, from fetid breath and gout to memory impairments and madness. Most important, Rush located the problems squarely with alcohol itself (or rather with spirits—he excluded wine, beer, and cider). "Every man is in danger of becoming a drunkard," he asserted, "who is in the habit of drinking ardent spirits" (Rush, 1784). It is alcohol (or ardent spirits) itself that is addictive, and any individual who consumes too much will be prey to its poisonous effects. Crucially, Rush enunciated a view that emphasized that, in addition to the diseases that *arise* from chronic drunkenness, the *process* of excessive drinking was itself a disease, and the only cure was abstinence: "It [the drinking of ardent spirits] forms an unnecessary, artificial, and very dangerous appetite; which, by gratification, like the desire for sinning, in the man who sins, tends continually to increase" (Rush, 1784).

Other important developments in the concept of alcohol addiction were occurring in Europe in the first half of the nineteenth century. In 1819, the Russian-German physician von Brühl-Cramer published his influential monograph, translated as *On Dipsomania and a Rational Therapy* (Kielhorn, 1996). Von Brühl-Cramer, like Trotter and Rush, characterized excessive alcohol use as a disease, which he labeled *trunksucht*, or *dipsomania*.[3] Dipsomania was conceived as an involuntary, compulsive desire for alcohol, brought about by regular consumption, which could take various courses that von Brühl-Cramer labeled continuous, remittent, intermittent, and periodic, presaging to some extent Jellinek's (1960) famous Greek letter typology (Kielhorn, 1996). The consequences of this disease, von Brühl-Cramer averred, involved both physical and psychological degeneration. It could, however, be cured, although only, as he presciently observed, if the patient *desired* to be relieved of his problem. *Delirium tremens* was also described in the early part of the nineteenth century by Thomas Sutton, and the term "alcoholism" was coined by the Swedish physician Magnus Huss in 1842—although Huss's concept referred to the *consequences* of excessive alcohol use rather than its cause (Sournia, 1990).

From a modern perspective, the crucial development that occurred in the early part of the nineteenth century was the belief that habitual heavy drinking constituted a disease rather than a sin or vice. Although habitual drunkenness was identified as being associated with various physical and psychological impairments, the critical conceptual development was the idea that it arose as a *result* of impaired control over drinking. Moreover, such a view implied that excessive drinking was a medical problem, amenable to treatment rather than—or as well as—punishment. Although this "discovery of addiction" has been located in the work of Rush and Trotter in the late eighteenth and early nineteenth centuries (Levine, 1979, 1984), other scholars have argued that similar ideas had been promulgated at an earlier date (Porter, 1985; Warner, 1992). Both Porter and Warner suggest that the idea of drunkenness as a disease characterized by loss of control was already in place in the early eighteenth century or earlier, well before Trotter and Rush's influential formulations. Warner (1994b), for instance, suggests that "Benjamin Rush was less an innovator in advancing the notion of addiction than the last great voice in a tradition already 150 years old" (p. 685). And Porter (1985) asserts:

> The formulation of the disease concept of alcoholism was not the inspiration of a single pioneer. It formed part of a wider arena of consciousness, extending far beyond physicians into pressure groups, the lay public, and indeed the drunkards too. . . . What was new was not the concept of the chronic drunkard, but the strategies for dealing with the beast. (p. 393)

More recently, Ferentzy (2001) has suggested a compromise between the ideas of Levine and those of Porter and Warner in this dispute over origins. Although many of the aspects of the early eighteenth century conception of chronic drunkenness as a disease have antecedents in earlier works, Ferentzy suggests that they only come together in a complete form in the work of Trotter and Rush. And, as suggested by Porter (1985), the social context was more sympathetic to the idea of habitual drunkenness as a disease in the early eighteenth century than at earlier times (Ferentzy, 2001). However, regardless of its precise origins, it is clear that the modern conception of addiction as a disease—characterized especially by loss of control—is no more than 200–300 years old (e.g., Warner, 1992).

Social attitudes toward drinking and alcohol problems in the nineteenth century were also changing, reflected most visibly in the emergence of temperance groups like the Washingtonians and the Women's Christian Temperance Union. These groups were to have an important influence not only on the way that alcohol was used, but also, ultimately, on how it was controlled. Alcohol in the nineteenth century, partly as a result of the proselytizing of the temperance societies, was increasingly seen as a prominent cause of poverty, violence, disease, insanity, and racial degeneration (Bynum, 1984; Gutzke, 1984; McCandless, 1984). For instance, "intemperance" in Victorian Britain was blamed for up to nine-tenths of all insanity (McCandless, 1984).

Theories of "racial deterioration" under alcohol's solvent effects were also widely promulgated (Bynum, 1984; Gutzke, 1984). It was believed, for example, that the morbid craving for alcohol described in the work of Rush could be passed on to offspring, creating a lineage of "drunkards" (Bynum, 1984).

Professional associations formed alongside the many temperance groups in the nineteenth century. The Association for the Study of Inebriety was launched in the United States in 1877, and a similar organization—the Society for the Study and Cure of Inebriety—was started in Britain in 1884 (Berridge, 1990). The view of "inebriety" or "dipsomania" as a chronic disease with physiological changes caused by the use of alcohol and requiring treatment was clearly articulated by the members of these organizations. Norman Kerr, for example, in his inaugural address to the Society for the Study and Cure of Inebriety in 1884, stated that inebriety was an "intractable disease" that "for the most part has a physical origin" as "the result of the operation of natural law, of the physiological and pathological action of an irritant narcotic poison on the brain and nervous system" (pp. 14–15, reprinted in Berridge, 1984, p. 3). The appropriate approach to this disease, therefore, was not moral condemnation, but instead medical treatment, involving abstinence from alcohol.

Whereas the disease concept of alcoholism had emerged early in the nineteenth century, a full-fledged view of addiction to other drugs was only developed, by analogy with alcohol, late in the same century (Acker, 1993; Parssinen & Kerner, 1980). Certainly there were earlier understandings of the habit-forming properties of substances such as tobacco and opium; however, dependence on these substances was typically viewed as a moral rather than a medical matter (Berridge, 1985). No doubt one reason for this reluctance to label addiction to drugs other than alcohol as a medical problem was the fact that most cases of dependence in the nineteenth century were induced by physicians themselves. Edward Levinstein, in his book *The Morbid Craving for Morphia*, published in 1875, made an important contribution to the idea of drug addiction as a disease when he characterized a pattern of uncontrollable desire for morphine. However, whereas the disease concept of alcoholism held sway over other perspectives, the idea that addiction to opiates and other drugs could also be a disease had to jostle with views that characterized such (nonmedical) use as "a vice" or "a form of moral insanity" (Parsinnen & Kerner, 1980).

TREATMENT FOR ALCOHOL AND
DRUG PROBLEMS IN THE NINETEENTH CENTURY

One of the important implications of the emerging disease concept of alcoholism (and, later, addiction to other drugs) was that chronic drunkenness and drug addiction could—and should—be treated. The development of treatment for alcoholism was also profoundly shaped by the various temperance societies that proliferated in the nineteenth century. William White (1998), in his exhaustive history of addiction treatment in the United States, provides an excellent overview of these developments, and we draw heavily on his work in this section. One important early development in the history of addiction treatment was the appearance of mutual aid organizations like the Washingtonians, who would create an exemplar of alcoholism treatment that was to be repeated, with modifications, during the course of the next 150 years. Formed in 1840, the Washingtonians preached total abstinence from alcoholic beverages—including spirits, wine, and cider—and soon attracted a large number of converts. The core ideas of the Washingtonian program involved public confession, mutual aid and the sharing of experiences, and non-alcoholic entertainment—features of course that were to characterize Alcoholics Anonymous (AA) just under a century later. Despite considerable early support—more than 600,000 people signed their pledge for abstinence—the Washingtonian movement had essentially run its course by 1845 (White, 1998). In the social environment of mid-century America, with its widespread support for temperance values, many other mutual aid groups, societies, and drinking clubs flourished, such as "The Sons of Temperance," "The Order of Good Templars," and "Osgood's Reformed Drinkers Club." These various organizations shared many similarities: the emphasis on mutual support, often charismatic leaders (and trappings of cults or religious groups), and the unswerving belief in the need for total abstinence (White, 1998).

Alongside these various mutual aid societies, there also emerged dedicated "inebriate asylums," which had their origins in the sanatoriums, insane asylums, and reform schools that were widespread in America in the first half of the nineteenth century. Benjamin Rush had advocated the use of such institutions, where inebriates could be removed from the source of their disease and have the opportunity to recover by receiving specialized medical treatment. By 1878, more than 30 of these institutions had opened in the United States, and by the close of the nineteenth century they numbered in the hundreds (White, 1998). Similar establishments were also founded in Britain, where the key emphasis of treatment lay in the seclusion of "inebriates," away from the harmful influences of alcohol. Treatment primarily was oriented around good food, exercise, religious instruction, and—for the poorer clients—work therapy (Berridge, 1990). Comparable regimes held sway in American institutions, with local idiosyncrasies such as hydrotherapy (in the form of steambaths, wet packs, body sponging, and the like), moral suasion, and induced aversion[4] (White, 1998). How successful were these inebriate asylums in curing their patients from chronic drunkenness? From this distance it is hard to know. Berridge (1990) reports that in Britain cure rates of around 30% were claimed, although there was little in the way of after-care or patient follow-up. Reported success rates in America typically ranged higher—from 33% to 63%—although the criteria for what constituted a "cure" varied substantially (White, 1998).[5]

Perhaps the most controversial treatment for alcohol and other drug problems in the nineteenth century was to be found in the Keeley Institutes, first opened in 1879. Dr. Leslie Keeley believed that alcohol and drug addiction were fundamentally biological problems requiring physical solutions. The cure came in the form of Keeley's "Double Chloride of Gold," which, it was claimed, restored the addicts' poisoned cells to their former healthy state. This cure proved extraordinarily popular; by 1920 more than half a million individuals with alcohol and drug problems had taken the Keeley cure in more than 100 Keeley Institutes in the United States and in Europe. Indeed, the Keeley Institutes claimed a 95% or higher success rate (White, 1998). The pharmacological constituents of the "gold cure" were never revealed (although they apparently did not contain gold) and were presumably of little genuine therapeutic value. However, as Heather and Robertson (1997) point out, two important lessons can be drawn from this episode in treatment history: "First, the popularity of a cure for alcoholism may bear little relationship to its scientific validity. Secondly, the story of Keeley's cure shows how powerful is the attraction of a simple and undemanding solution to the problem of alcoholism" (p. 26).

Other physical treatments were also widely used in the nineteenth century. In Britain and the United States, drug treatments included the use of bromides, ammonia, opium, morphine, and chloral hydrate, which could be taken in a medical context or obtained via mail order (Berridge, 1990). Indeed, a large market for "miracle cures" flourished in the nineteenth century, although many a cure for inebriety actually contained substantial quantities of alcohol. More outlandish—to modern readers at least—therapies included water cures, electrotherapies, spinal puncture, insulin injections, and massage treatments (White, 1998).

The history of treatment for addiction to other drugs followed a similar course to that of alcohol, although treatment options were never as widespread and tended to focus on physical cures. Levinstein advocated a "cold turkey" regime for morphine addicts: forced seclusion accompanied by warm baths, chloral hydrate, and alcohol. Other treatments also focused primarily on managing withdrawal symptoms and bringing about a cessation of opiate use. Various drugs were employed to facilitate these goals, including hyoscine, codeine, cannabis, belladonna, and, as Freud enthusiastically urged, cocaine (Acker, 1993; White, 1998; Parsinnen & Kerner, 1980). Spas, sanatoriums, and other similar institutions were also established that offered to cure individuals from addiction to a wide variety of drugs, and that combined a range of physical treatments with seclusion and social support. As was the case for alcohol, a sizeable industry hawking nostrums for opiate addiction emerged in the nineteenth century, although such homely sounding remedies as "Carney Common Sense Opiate Cure" and "St. Anne's Morphine Cure" often contained significant amounts of morphine (White, 1998, p. 69). Despite similarities in the conceptualization and treatment of dependence on alcohol and other drugs in the nineteenth century, views of drug addiction in the twentieth century were to be more profoundly shaped by the rapidly changing legal environment of drug use.

THE CHANGING FACE OF
DRUG ADDICTION: 1914–1960

Although by the end of the nineteenth century the idea that addiction to drugs like cocaine and morphine could be considered a disease was widely accepted, this perspective was to change significantly during the course of the next two decades, with important implications for treatment. Ernest Bishop had advanced an "autoimmune" theory of addiction in the early part of the twentieth century, based on the physiological changes that occur in response to morphine use. However, many still maintained that drug addiction was essentially a vice. This latter view was to gain ascendancy during the next few decades, due, in no small part, to important legislative changes in the use of drugs.

The introduction of the Harrison Narcotic Act in 1914, in particular, was to have profound implications for the conceptualization and treatment of drug problems in the twentieth century. By making the use of opiates and cocaine illegal, except through legitimate medical channels, the Harrison Narcotic Act effected a transformation of drug addicts in the United States from patients to criminals in the space of less than a decade (Acker, 1993; Parsinnen & Kerner, 1980). In the United States, individuals who were addicted to opiates could still obtain regular supplies from physicians, but only in ever-reducing amounts. By 1922, even this tapering supply was stemmed, and prescription of any narcotics became a criminal offense. Indeed, between 1914 and 1938 some 25,000 physicians were indicted for illegal prescriptions and about 3,000 went to jail for this offense (White, 1998). The situation was somewhat different in Britain, where the medical establishment managed to maintain control over the prescription of opiates and vigorously resisted attempts to renounce this right. For instance, calls to ban heroin prescription in 1955 met with stern opposition from physicians and members of the Society for the Study of Addiction (Berridge, 1990). Throughout the century, a distinctly pragmatic and medical approach to (illicit) drug use in Britain helped to set it apart from developments across the Atlantic, where punitive measures have been more favored (MacGregor & Smith, 1998).

Etiological accounts of drug addiction in the 1920s, in contrast to earlier theories, emphasized the role of psychological factors. Addiction was viewed in many quarters as a kind of neurosis arising from personality defects. Lawrence Kolb was one prominent advocate of this view. He argued that drug addicts had pre-existing psychological deficits, characterized by feelings of inadequacy, which were assuaged by the use of narcotics like heroin and cocaine (Acker, 1993). "Addiction was in effect," Acker (1993) notes, viewed as "a kind of deviance" (p. 201).

Given the emergence of this stigmatizing notion of addiction and constraints on legal supplies of opiates, available treatment options were limited and were predominantly directed at isolation and detoxification. The idea, derived from public health models, that addicts should be quarantined so as to stem the spread of addiction was prominent in both Britain and America (Berridge, 1990; White, 1998). In the United States, from 1913 on, a number of public health clinics were opened to treat drug addiction. Typical methods involved the gradual reduction of opiates augmented with the use of a range of other substances—from scopolamine and chloral hydrate to cannabis and castor oil. However, by 1925 these facilities were shut down, not to reopen for another four decades, leaving a meager range of options for those desiring treatment (White, 1998). In the interim, several "narcotic farms" were established—at Lexington in 1935 and Fort Worth in 1938. Described as a combination of "hospital, farm, and prison" (Fernandez, 1998, p. 107), treatment at one of these institutes entailed gradual detoxification, convalescence, and rehabilitation. The success of these institutions, however, appears to have been limited, with studies suggesting that more than 90% of individuals relapsed to addiction within a year of treatment (White, 1998, p. 125).

Other mid-century developments in the treatment of drug dependence included the emergence of the multidisciplinary "Minnesota model" in the late 1940s, therapeutic communities such as Synanon in the early 1950s, and Narcotics Anonymous in 1953. However, it was the ideas of Vincent Dole and Marie Nyswander that were to exert the greatest impact on the understanding and treatment of drug addiction during this period. As Courtwright (1997a) has argued, Dole, a metabolic disease specialist, and Nyswander, a psychiatrist, played an important role in attempts to shift the concept of addiction back within a resolutely medical framework. Rather than viewing drug addiction as arising from character deficits, as the prominent sociopathic model suggested, Dole and Nyswander argued that it was essentially a biological problem with origins in "neurological susceptibility." Thus it was proposed that drug addicts "needed narcotics in a visceral way, the way a diabetic needed insulin" (Courtwright, 1997a, p. 259). It followed from this view that abstinence was an inappropriate therapeutic goal and that maintenance on drugs was the most viable option. Methadone—a long-acting synthetic opioid—appeared to be the ideal substance: it could be administered at fairly wide intervals, reduced craving for heroin, and helped to allow the addict to lead a relatively normal life. Despite considerable early resistance from the Bureau of Narcotics, methadone maintenance became an important treatment option in America from the mid-1960s and continues to be one of the few "harm-minimization" approaches endorsed by American drug policy.

The illegality of drugs like heroin, cocaine, and cannabis and the persistence of harsh penalties for their sale and use (in the United States at least) continue to have important effects on social attitudes toward drug use and the range of treatment options that are available. The idea that dependence on illicit substances is essentially a legal rather than a medical matter is still influential and has retarded the introduction of harm-reduction measures like needle exchange programs and safe injecting rooms. Incarceration of drug users—some of whom may be dependent on heroin, cocaine, or other drugs—also does little to encourage treatment and perpetuates the view of drug addiction as a moral rather than medical issue. Attitudes toward alcohol and alcohol problems, however, were to take a quite different form in the twentieth century.

THE ALCOHOLISM MOVEMENT

In the early part of the twentieth century, the disease model of alcoholism was ascendant. Physiological approaches to alcoholism, prominent in the early part of the twentieth century, however, had to compete with an increasing array of psychological perspectives. Psychodynamic theories, for instance, flourished in the 1920s and 1930s, as Freud's ideas gained increasing recognition in the United States. Alcoholism, from a psychoanalytic perspective, was viewed as arising from a fixation on the oral stage of psychosocial development, and treatment involved the usual methods of psychoanalysis: recovering repressed memories, working through conflicts, and the like. Aversion therapies, based on ideas drawn from theories of classical conditioning, also appeared in the first half of the twentieth century, and various agents—including apomorphine, electric shocks, and antabuse—were employed (Berridge, 1990; White, 1998).

Perhaps the most influential development in the alcohol field that occurred in the first half of the twentieth century was the introduction of Alcoholics Anonymous, or AA. The story of AA has been told many times, so we will simply outline the main themes here. Born from the serendipitous meeting of two alcoholics—William Wilson and Robert Smith—in 1933, AA emerged as a mutual aid self-help group, which through a combination of public confession, social support, and strict adherence to the "twelve steps" aimed to initiate and maintain sobriety. The core idea of AA is that alcoholism is a disease: a chronic biological disorder characterized by loss of control over drinking, which can only be cured by abstinence.[6] Early formulations of alcoholism, drawing on the work of William Silkworth, suggested that some individuals had an "allergy to alcohol," and contemporary accounts make comparisons between alcoholism and diseases like diabetes (Edwards, 2000; White, 1998). In institutional terms, AA has been a phenomenal success. By 1993, it was estimated that AA had more than 2 million members in more than 100 countries around the world (DuPont & McGovern, 1994). Although in many respects similar to the mutual aid organizations that flourished in nineteenth century, one crucial difference is that AA supports the idea that alcohol addiction arises from individual susceptibility to alcohol rather than, as in Rush's formulation, the consequence of alcohol use per se.

AA, the National Council of Alcoholism, and the Yale Center for Alcohol Studies formed the nucleus of what is known as the "alcoholism movement" in the middle of the twentieth century (Levine, 1984). The ideas of E. M. Jellinek were to prove influential in this movement, as he forwarded—or some would say "rediscovered"—a disease concept of alcoholism that was based on the core theme that alcohol addiction arose due to uncontrollable cravings for alcohol[7] (Page, 1997). The emphasis in the early stages of the alcoholism movement was very much on alcoholism or alcohol addiction per se rather than on the broader range of alcohol-related problems. As P. B. Page (1997) argues, this focus arose for predominantly pragmatic reasons. If the movement highlighted a subset of alcohol-related problems, suffered by only a small number of individuals, neither the liquor industry, which was recovering from the Prohibition drought, nor the public, equally unsympathetic to prohibitionist ideas, would be offended.

Jellinek, however, was also interested in the wide range of problems that might arise from the use of alcohol. After a stint with the World Health Organization, Jellinek (1960) incorporated social, cultural, and economic factors into his disease model of alcoholism and highlighted the limitations of an approach that focused on the narrow confines of alcohol problems in a North American context. Jellinek, for instance, displayed a broad understanding of the rich and complex diversity of drinking patterns in different cultures and how such patterns could give rise to different sorts of problems. In this latter period, alcoholism was defined as *"any use of alcoholic beverages that causes any damage to the individual or society"* (Jellinek, 1960, p. 35). This definition, Jellinek admitted, was vague, but it embraced the idea that alcoholism is a genus with many different species (see Table 8.1). Jellinek urged that "the student of alcoholism should emancipate himself from accepting the exclusiveness of the picture of alcohol as propounded by Alcoholics Anonymous" (p. 38). According to Jellinek, the gamma form of alcoholism was the most prevalent one found in the United States,

Table 8.1   Alcoholism and Its Species

Type of Alcoholism	Description
Alpha alcoholism	A non-progressive psychological dependence or reliance on alcohol that does not lead to loss of control but that contravenes social norms and may impair work and interpersonal relations.
Beta alcoholism	Heavy drinking, without either physical or psychological dependence, which may reflect the social norms of a culture but which leads to health problems such as cirrhosis of the liver and early mortality.
Gamma alcoholism	Alcoholism in which tolerance, "adaptive cell metabolism," withdrawal, and loss of control are involved. This form has the worst prognosis and may lead to severe health and interpersonal problems.
Delta alcoholism	Involves tolerance, "adaptive cell metabolism," and withdrawal, although the ability to control intake remains. The form of drinking that gives rise to this species may be socially normative.
Epsilon alcoholism	Periodic heavy or excessive drinking.

SOURCE: Jellinek (1960), pp. 36-40

and individuals with this form were most likely to attend AA. Delta alcoholism was common in the wine-drinking culture of France, where regular consumption of alcohol occurs throughout the day, but is socially accepted and creates little in the way of obvious problems. Epsilon alcoholism, Jellinek suggested, was to be found in some Latin American societies where a "fiesta" pattern of drinking prevails, characterized by occasional but heavy alcohol consumption. Jellinek's typology thus reflects a shift in emphasis from a narrow, parochial conceptualization of alcoholism to embrace the full spectrum of alcohol-related problems that might occur in different cultural contexts.

CONTEMPORARY DEVELOPMENTS

A comprehensive analysis of developments in the classification, etiology, and treatment of alcohol and drug problems from the 1960s is beyond the scope of this historical overview. However, we briefly trace the evolution of diagnostic categories for alcohol and drug disorders and indicate the range of etiological accounts and treatment approaches that have been forwarded in the past 40 years. Perhaps the most important theme that emerges from developments in addiction science at the end of the twentieth century is one of diversity: There is widespread agreement that multiple perspectives are required to understand the rich complexity of substance-related problems. Our understanding of what underlies drug problems, as we have seen, has variously embraced psychological, biological, and moral perspectives during the course of the past 200 years. Approaches to treatment have been similarly diverse, with psychological measures favored at some times and biological methods at others. This plurality of approaches and methods is clearly evident in contemporary developments, which embrace a wide range of different etiological theories and treatment options.[8]

The multifactorial nature of substance use problems is also captured in the development of diagnostic concepts during the past 40 years. In the 1950s, "alcoholism" and "drug addiction" were categorized in both the ICD and the DSM under "personality disorders," reflecting the idea that such problems could be best thought of in psychological or social terms. Indeed, the DSM-I grouped alcoholism and drug addiction with sexual deviations and antisocial and dyssocial reactions under the umbrella of "sociopathic personality disturbances" (Nathan, Skinstad, & Langenbucher, 1999; Room, 1998a; Sellman, 1994). In the DSM-II, however, alcoholism became a disorder in its own right, although still grouped with sexual deviations and personality disorders. Three subtypes of alcoholism were defined in the DSM-II and ICD-8: episodic excessive drinking, habitual excessive drinking, and alcoholic addiction (which included the presence of withdrawal symptoms). In the 1960s and 1970s there was a shift from the use of the term "addiction" to that of "dependence." This change occurred initially for other drugs and somewhat later for alcohol. In the DSM-III and ICD-9, alcohol and drug dependence were separated from alcohol and drug abuse for the first time (Sellman, 1994). The DSM-III diagnosis for dependence favored physiological criteria such as tolerance and withdrawal. This was revised in the DSM-IV to embrace a range of criteria, including physiological, psychological, and behavioral phenomena, which brought it into line with the criteria in the ICD-10 (see Chapter 2).

Conceptualizations of alcohol and drug disorders in the early twenty-first century, therefore, combine both psychological and physiological components, and distinctions are drawn based on the severity of problems experienced. In some respects these contemporary classification schemes share many features with those offered in the nineteenth century. The concept of "inebriety," for instance, also included the central features of craving and compulsion, and was distinguished from "dipsomania," which is perhaps closest to the modern-day category of "alcohol abuse." There are also points of continuity in distinguishing the chronic *effects* of alcohol and drug consumption from the problems that underlie continued use. However, as Room (1998b) points out, current concepts of dependence and abuse are narrower than those envisaged by Jellinek (1960) in his Greek-letter taxonomy, and questions have been raised regarding their cross-cultural applicability (see "Culture and Classification" following).

Contemporary formulations of substance abuse and dependence, therefore, embrace psychological, social, and biological factors; etiological accounts at the end of the twentieth century display a similar diversity. In a recent overview of theories of addiction, for example, West (2001) notes the diverse range of perspectives that encompass such varied phenomena as neurotransmitter systems, cognitive mechanisms, attachment processes, peer relationships, and social arrangements. Some authors have suggested that there has been a swing back to the primacy of biological explanations for substance use disorders in the late twentieth century (e.g., Acker, 1993; Courtwright, 1982). However, most scholars recognize the importance of multiple etiological factors that traverse different levels of analysis. Although, as we pointed out in Chapter 1, many contend that their perspective is the most *important* one.

Approaches to treatment are equally diverse. For instance, someone who is diagnosed as suffering from alcohol dependence has a range of quite distinct options available to them. They might, for instance, be referred to a twelve-step group like AA and find themselves sharing their life story with a group of other individuals suffering from alcohol problems, admitting that they are powerless over alcohol, and attempting to obtain strict sobriety. Or, they might engage in a cognitive-behavioral treatment program, in which they are taught social and interpersonal skills along with self-control training that might allow them to maintain "controlled drinking." Finally, they could be prescribed naltrexone by their physician, which reduces their craving for alcohol by blocking opioid receptors. Moreover, they may receive these treatments, and others, as either inpatient or outpatient, and over

Table 8.2   Treatments Old and New: A Selection

Nineteenth Century[a]	Twentieth Century[b]
Mutual aid societies and reform clubs	AA and other twelve-step groups
Inebriate homes and asylums (social support, work and recreation, moral suasion, detoxification, religious instruction, drug abstinence, etc.)	Inpatient treatment and therapeutic communities (detoxification, drug abstinence, social skills training, motivation, etc.)
Drug treatments (e.g., hyoscine, chloral hydrate, morphine, "gold cures")	Pharmacotherapies (e.g., disulfiram, naltrexone, methadone)
Managed withdrawal and detoxification	Cognitive behavior therapy
Religious conversion	Network therapy
Hydrotherapy	
Aversion therapies	

[a]This list is based on the ideas of White (1998).
[b]This list is based on the ideas of Ott, Tarter, & Ammerman (1999).

varying lengths of time. They may further receive a combination of these different treatments, either simultaneously or sequentially.

As illustrated in Table 8.2, the range of treatments available in the late twentieth century shares many similarities with those on offer 100 years ago, although there are also important differences. Persistent themes in the treatment of substance-related problems include the role of social support and mutual aid, pharmacological interventions, and the availability of inpatient facilities. New psychosocial interventions such as cognitive-behavior therapy have, however, been introduced, and contemporary drug treatments are based on a much better understanding of the physiological nature of drug dependence. The diversity of treatment options available reflects the multiple causal paths underlying substance use problems. Given the rough equivalence, in terms of treatment efficacy, of many of these options (e.g., Miller, 1998a; Moyers & Hester, 1999; Project MATCH Research Group, 1997), they also suggest the role of non-specific factors, such as those relating to therapist characteristics, client motivation, and self-healing processes. The realization that many individuals apparently "cure themselves" from drug-related problems (Price et al., 2001; Finney, Moos, & Timko, 1999) further complicates our understanding of how treatment might be best achieved—although it also offers some tantalizing leads (see Chapter 9).

CULTURE AND CLASSIFICATION

In an insightful article, Room (1985) suggests that there are three ways of considering the relationship between sociocultural factors and drug dependence. First, dependence can be taken as a given, and we can examine the way that cultural variables such as social norms, values, beliefs, and expectations influence its nature and course (as we did in Chapter 7). Second, cultural factors can be understood as representing part of the *concept* of dependence; that is, dependence might be "seated" in culture, just as it might be in psychology or physiology. Third, and most radically, one can challenge the very notion of dependence itself and question its cross-cultural validity. On this view, dependence might be viewed as a social construction—a reality bound only by cultural-historical context (Room, 1985).

A classification system attempts to carve nature at its joints. That is, it endeavors to capture a reality that endures through space and time. Thakker and Ward (1998), for example, suggest that the DSM-IV, despite its avowed atheoretical stance, follows a biomedical model of mental disorder that assumes universalism. Although a sample of culture-bound syndromes are included in the DSM-IV, these tend to be presented in a way that highlights their similarity to more readily recognizable disorders. Thus, the Japanese culture-bound syndrome *taijin kyofusho*, characterized by an excessive fear of offending others through socially inappropriate behavior (Kirmayer, 1991), is viewed as a cultural variation of social phobia. However, although this interpretation is plausible, a more radical alternative also exists in which "cultural factors are not merely an overlay of variance upon uniform patterns of psychopathology" (Thakker et al., 1999, p. 852) but are, instead, an integral component of the disorder itself. Even if both social phobia and taijin kyofusho, for instance, are related to, say, universal human fears of social exclusion, they arise due to the unique understanding of what this means in different cultural contexts (Thakker & Durrant, 2001).

Anthropological research has clearly illustrated that different *kinds* of substance use problems arise in different cultural contexts. By adopting a narrow definition of what constitutes such problems, potentially important harm might be ignored or downplayed (Room, 1984). Cross-cultural variation in the conceptualization of substance use problems like alcoholism are clearly illustrated in a study of Korean and American university students by Cho and Faulkner (1993). After participants read a vignette depicting the drinking behavior of "Mr. Kim," significantly more American than Korean students believed that this individual was an "alcoholic." Moreover, although both groups agreed that "drinking every day" and "lack of control over drinking" were reasons to believe that someone is an alcoholic, the American students were more likely to endorse the importance of social and interpersonal problems in this diagnosis than were the Korean participants. Cho and Faulkner (1993) argue that these differences reflect the social acceptance of diminished responsibility that occurs with heavy drinking in Korea but not in America. The authors conclude that "the American disease concept of alcoholism and the scales used to diagnose it have limited cross-cultural validity and that cultural factors should not be ignored in the study, diagnosis, and treatment of alcohol problems" (p. 692).

The most ambitious attempt to evaluate cross-cultural differences in the understanding of alcohol and other drug problems was undertaken as part of the WHO's collaborative cross-cultural applicability (CAR) study (Gureje, Vazquez-Barquero, & Janca, 1996; Room et al., 1996; Schmidt & Room, 1999). This study involved nine different cultures[9] chosen for their diversity in social norms regarding the use of drugs, especially alcohol. A number of important findings emerged regarding the different ways that the ICD-10 diagnostic criteria for alcohol abuse and dependence were understood in the different cultural contexts. Differences emerged in the way that the different diagnostic criteria were interpreted, how problematic they were considered, and the threshold at which they were viewed as problems.

The concepts of tolerance and withdrawal, which comprise "physiological dependence" in the ICD-10, were recognized across all the samples, although there were important differences in the way that they were understood. For instance, at several sites, including Athens and Seoul, the idea of a hangover was not clearly differentiated from that of withdrawal, and the concept of tolerance was variously conceived as the ability to *endure* the effects of alcohol (e.g., in Greece, Turkey, Mexico) and a specific "immunity" to the effects of drinking (in Korea). Moreover, the concept of tolerance had positive connotations in many of the cultures, as it was associated with learning how to drink and being able to drink without showing the effects of intoxication (Schmidt & Room, 1999; Room et al., 1996).

There were also important variations in the understanding of the *psychological* components of the dependence concept. The crucial idea of impaired control over drinking, for instance, was recognized everywhere, but the understanding of this concept showed important variations. In several cultures the idea of impaired control was understood to refer to the *consequences* of drinking, while in others it conformed more closely to the ICD-10's conception as a *cause* of excessive alcohol consumption. At several sites (Korea and Nigeria), the idea of impaired control was also seen as a positive aspect of drinking, and losing control was viewed as the *reason* why individuals drink.

The threshold at which patterns of drinking were viewed as problematic also showed considerable cross-cultural variation in this study. In Bangalore, India, for instance, an individual who consumed about two bottles of beer every couple of months met three of the diagnostic criteria for alcohol dependence: he reported tolerance to alcohol's effects, he continued to drink despite objections from family, and he wanted to stop his drinking but could not (Room et al., 1996). In general, concepts of alcohol dependence and other alcohol-related problems were most similar in those cultures with similar orientations toward alcohol use, but were often quite different where cultural engagements with alcohol varied. Moreover, the Western conception of alcohol dependence did not map onto the understanding found in other cultures in a way that lends credence to the idea that alcohol dependence—as defined by the ICD-10 at least—is a universal mental disorder. Schmidt and Room (1999) conclude, "The findings of this study suggest that the ICD criteria for dependence—which were developed and first operationalized within the narrow band of cultural variation represented by Anglo-American societies—do not easily cross particular kinds of cultural boundaries" (p. 460), and "there is a clear need for sustained attention to these cultural variations arising at the symptom level in future work in international nosology and cross-cultural epidemiology" (pp. 460–461).

The CAR study also included the assessment of cultural differences relating to the use of other drugs in addition to alcohol, although this was a less prominent part of the research. The main finding was that a much lower threshold of impairment was employed by respondents to determine if drug use was problematic. This is not surprising, given that in most cultures the use of drugs other than alcohol is socially and legally proscribed. There were, however, some exceptions to this general finding. For example, the use of cannabis was considered normal in Ankara and Mexico, and in some contexts in India. It is interesting that, because of the association of cannabis with religious contexts in India, the "giving up of alternate activities" to consume cannabis was seen in a positive light, as indicative of forgoing worldly pleasures to obtain spiritual enlightenment (Gureje, Vazquez- Barquero, & Janca, 1996).

IMPLICATIONS

What can we conclude from this historical and cross-cultural review of the conceptualization, etiology, and treatment of substance-related problems? One central and unavoidable conclusion is that what constitutes a drug problem, and the nature of that problem, is profoundly shaped by cultural and historical contexts. Individuals have used and continue to use a variety of different psychoactive substances in a diversity of ways, at different times, and in different cultures. Some of these patterns of use have been conceptualized as problems. The concept of addiction as a disease, for instance, characterized by craving and loss of control, appears to be a product of a specific set of social circumstances that arose in Britain and the United States just over 200 years ago (Levine, 1979; 1984). The idea of impaired control, for example, as a central feature of addiction makes sense only in a cultural context where self-control over the use of substances is a valued attribute (Room, 1985). Moreover, the whole concept of self as an autonomous agent separate from its manifestation in action, it has been argued, is a product of social developments in early modern Europe (e.g., Baumeister, 1987). Furthermore, as we have seen, the concept of loss of control is understood in different ways cross-culturally and is not universally viewed as problematic.

From this perspective, the idea of addiction that emerged in the nineteenth century was not a medical discovery akin to the identification of the bacterial origin of pneumonia, but rather was a social construction wrought from a particular cultural-historical milieu. The adoption of this perspective does not entail, of course, the denial of the physiological reality of such phenomena as withdrawal or tolerance, although they may be manifest and understood in different ways in different cultural contexts (Room et al., 1996). Nor does it obviate the acceptance that the problems that individuals experience with drugs are real, important, and potentially in need of treatment. Moreover, there clearly *have* been advancements in our understanding of the *effects* that drugs can have—such as the link between smoking and lung cancer—that have created new and real examples of drug-related problems. Other substance use problems, such as drunk driving, are also clear and unequivocal, although they owe their origin to social changes in transportation rather than to newly discovered harms of drinking.

Whether a given pattern of substance use *constitutes* a problem is strongly influenced by cultural context. Whether that pattern of use is *experienced* as a problem is also shaped by prevailing norms, values, and expectations regarding substance use and acceptable behavior, which vary in important ways cross-culturally. For instance, in Western societies, an individual who consumes two or three glasses of wine every evening after work would not typically be viewed as having a substance use problem. If, by contrast, that individual was to sniff a couple of packets of heroin every evening, most people would view such use as problematic, even if the harm caused by such use (in terms of the impact on health, social, and work obligations, and so on) was similar to that for alcohol. As the results of the CAR study indicated, the threshold at which a given pattern of use constituted abuse or dependence is strongly influenced by the *kind* of substance employed— although there is little pharmacological rationale for these distinctions. Current concepts of addiction are also likely to impact on the way that individuals *experience* their use of drugs and when such use might be deemed problematic. The idea that loss of control is a central feature of dependence on alcohol and other drugs might, in fact, foster such beliefs among cultural groups where this idea is widely accepted. For instance, after, but not before, Rush's influential and widely read for-mulation of alcohol addiction, there was a sharp increase in confes-sional literature testifying to the experience of involuntary loss of control that Rush had described (Levine, 1978). Likewise, the wide-spread belief in the disease model of alcoholism among Native Americans can be viewed, in part, as one reason why loss of control is central to their pattern of drinking, and moderation is rarely counte-nanced as an appropriate response to alcohol problems. As we eluci-dated in Chapter 7, beliefs and expectations regarding the effects of drugs can influence subsequent patterns of use in important ways.

Our understanding of what underlies substance use problems has also changed in important ways during the course of the past 200 years. Perhaps the most dominant theme in the history of etiological accounts of drug problems is the way that they have vacillated among biological, psychological, and social (including moral) perspectives. This enduring tension between biological and psychological approaches has also been noted for mental health problems in *general* (e.g., Porter, 1997). The historical trajectory of these different approaches, however, has varied somewhat depending on the kind of drug concerned, and often multiple theories have coexisted at any given time. At the beginning of the twenty-first century, there appears to be no resolution in favor of any one perspective, and addiction is variously characterized as a chronic disease with clear biological origins, a problem of self-regulation, and the result of specific social and political contexts. Indeed, these different approaches are not necessarily mutually exclusive (although to be compatible some modifications are probably required to each perspective), and the most plausible—and widely recognized—idea is that no one account can provide all the answers to what causes substance use problems.[10]

The history of treatment for substance use problems also forces us to consider the idea that no one approach is likely to prove efficacious in ameliorating such problems. Although we may view with distaste and amusement such methods as "hydrotherapy" or Keeley's "Double Chloride of Gold," it is clear that the history of treatment for substance use problems is not a story of how we have advanced from the dark uncertainty of the past into the glorious illumination of the present era. Rather, history suggests a patchwork of treatment options and treatment contexts, some ineffectual, others dangerous, a fair few of modest value, but none perfect. As Martensen (1994) notes, despite many important developments, the treatments of today do not look that different from those that were employed 150 years ago. Indeed, it is somewhat sobering to reflect that the most sophisticated products of psychological science or the latest pharmacological agents fare, in general, no better than the seemingly atheoretical methods of AA (e.g., Moyers & Hester, 1999; Project MATCH, 1997). Indeed, some studies of "natural recovery" suggest that many individuals recover from substance use problems without the benefits of formal treatment at all (e.g., Finney, Moos, & Timko, 1999; Sobell, Cunningham, & Sobell, 1996; Chapter 9).

One should, of course, never second-guess science. However, we view as somewhat overoptimistic the suggestion that we are at the edge of a breakthrough in the treatment of addiction that might "*dramatically* reduce drug abuse in the twenty-first century" (Leshner, 1999b, p. 23, italics added). Certainly, there have been no "revolutions" in the treatment of substance use problems during the past 200 years, as there have, say, for bacterial infections, rheumatoid arthritis, tuberculosis, or even schizophrenia (see Le Fanu, 1999). The sheer variety of different treatments that are currently on offer also contrasts with the way that other medical problems are treated. For instance, it would be odd, to say the least, if an individual suffering from cancer was given the option of chemotherapy *or* group counseling, and was told that each was pretty much as effective as the other.

There are two traps for the unwary in drawing implications from cultural and historical comparisons. The first is to assume that the ideas and practices of other times and other places are oddities—more items of amusement than instruction—that simply underscore the superiority of our own methods and beliefs. The second is to conclude that the ideas from different times and places are all equal in their validity—different in content maybe, but not in their truth value. Neither of these approaches is satisfactory in evaluating the rich complexity of our understanding of substance use and abuse throughout history and across cultures. We certainly have advanced our understanding of the etiology of substance use problems in important ways in the past 100 years, although we are far from an "ideally complete" explanatory account. Moreover, our current concepts of dependence and abuse may have limited cross-cultural applicability, but they still have considerable pragmatic value in various cultural contexts. However, we need also to recognize that our understanding, conceptualization, and treatment of substance use problems are influenced in profound ways by cultural-historical factors.

NOTES

1.   Although originally written in 1788.

2.   All quotes from Rush (1784), online version: www.druglibrary.org/schaffer/History/temptract/00050001_tif4.gif

3.   The terminology employed in the nineteenth century to refer to alcohol problems is somewhat confusing, as labels such as "habitual drunkenness," "dipsomania," "alcoholism," "inebriety," and "the liquor habit" were all employed. In general, the term "inebriety" was used to refer to the disease underlying compulsive drinking, and has its closest correspondence in the DSM-IV and ICD-10 to "alcohol dependence." "Dipsomania" tended to be used to indicate patterns of heavy or "binge" drinking, and "alcoholism" was more frequently used to refer to the *effects* of chronic alcohol consumption on physical and psychological health (Berridge, 1990; White, 1998). Similar distinctions were drawn between "morphinism," which referred to the long-term effects of morphine use, and "morphinomania," which identified the compulsion to continue use (Parsinnen & Kerner, 1980).

4.   White (1998) describes such measures, known as the "Swedish Treatment," as follows:

Patients staying at the sanatorium were encouraged to drink all of the whiskey they wished. In fact, that is all they could drink—whiskey, whiskey-saturated coffee, whiskey-saturated tea, and whiskey-saturated milk. All meals and snacks, regardless of fare, were saturated with whiskey. Patients wore whiskey-sprayed clothes and slept in whiskey-saturated sheets. The goal was to satiate and sicken the appetite for alcohol and leave one begging for water. (p. 39)

5. Although it is easy to dismiss these findings as the result of unsophisticated methods, they do show similarities to the figures reported from contemporary studies. For instance, Miller, Walters, & Bennett (2001) suggest, on the basis of a recent review of outcome studies, that "about a third of clients remain asymptomatic during the year following a single treatment event. The remaining two thirds show, on average, large and significant decreases in drinking and related problems" (p. 211).

6. Although as White (1998) points out, despite clear adherence to a disease perspective, AA focuses as much on psychological and spiritual defects or problems as it does on biological ones.

7. Jellinek made the distinction between "alcohol addiction," which was the result of uncontrolled cravings for alcohol, and "alcoholism," which referred to the physical and psychological effects of chronic alcohol use (Page, 1997).

8. This plurality of perspectives does not, of course, imply that particular individuals necessarily endorse a wide range of etiological factors or treatment options. Rather, viewed from a global perspective, there appear to be numerous—often quite distinct—approaches that coexist and that provide accounts of often equal explanatory value.

9. The nine sites examined in this study were Ankara, Turkey; Athens, Greece; Bangalore, India; Flagstaff, Arizona, USA (Navajo nation); Ibaden, Nigeria; Jebel, Romania; Mexico City, Mexico; Santander, Spain; and Seoul, South Korea (Room et al., 1996).

10. We strongly disagree, therefore, with the idea that "major scientific advances have *revolutionized* our understanding of drug abuse and addiction" (Leshner, 1999, p. 22, italics added). If the concept of a scientific "revolution" is understood as the overthrow of previous theories with new ones that provide us with greater explanatory understanding of the relevant phenomenon (e.g., Thagard, 1992), then it is clear (to us at least) that no such revolution has occurred.

9

Prevention, Treatment, and Public Policy: An Integrated Perspective

INTRODUCTION

A number of different approaches have been employed to reduce the impact and incidence of drug-related problems in society. These approaches can be conveniently, if somewhat imperfectly, categorized in terms of the primary focus and target of the intervention strategy. A number of initiatives, for instance, are directed at reducing the *demand* for psychoactive substances. Demand-reduction strategies include (1) drug education, which primarily aims to reduce and delay initiation into drug use and prevent the transition to regular use; and (2) treatment programs directed at individuals with substance use disorders. Other approaches are aimed mainly at reducing the *supply* of drugs. For instance, legal restrictions on the sale and purchase of drugs, criminal sanctions, and law enforcement activities such as crop eradication and interdiction are designed to limit the availability of drugs. Also, some legal measures are aimed at attenuating demand for drugs by raising costs—as the result of either taxation or prohibition. All of these strategies can be characterized as aimed primarily at reducing the *use* of drugs. Harm-minimization strategies, such as methadone maintenance and needle exchange programs, in contrast, are mainly directed at reducing the *harm* associated with drug use, while not necessarily influencing overall levels of use.

MacCoun and Reuter (2001) have cogently argued that the aim of drug policy should be "total harm reduction," where total harm is the product of total drug use multiplied by the average harm per drug use episode. Total harm, therefore, can be reduced either by decreasing the number of users in society or by reducing the harm associated with use, or both. In this chapter we discuss the range of approaches that have been employed to reduce drug-related harm, including prevention strategies, treatment, legal sanctions and restrictions, and harm-minimization approaches. Although an exhaustive review of these approaches is beyond the scope of this chapter, we aim to illustrate how theoretical approaches drawn from different levels of analysis (see Chapter 1) may be relevant to the development and implementation of effective intervention strategies.

PREVENTION

Broadly speaking, prevention efforts encompass a range of strategies designed to reduce the prevalence of drug use in society, or, ideally, to prevent it from occurring at all. More narrowly, prevention typically refers to initiatives aimed at delaying the onset of drug use and preventing the transition from initial use to regular use to abuse and dependence (Pentz, 1999). One important component of prevention efforts, which we will focus on in this section, is drug education. Drug education, in its widest sense, aims to change beliefs, expectations, norms, values, and behaviors in ways that reduce drug use and drug-related harm.

It is widely accepted that substance use problems are the result of multiple etiological factors. Efforts to prevent substance abuse, therefore, should also ideally employ multiple approaches (Botvin & Kantor, 2000; Jansen, Glynn, & Howard, 1996; Johnson, Farquhar, & Sussman, 1996). In practice, however, prevention efforts focus on a range of psychosocial and cultural variables: beliefs and expectations regarding drugs, social norms and values, peer and familial relations, and cultural and community factors. Biological approaches, although prominent in etiological accounts of substance use and substance use disorders, are rarely employed in the context of prevention (leaving aside their role in treatment contexts).

Drawing on research relating to the genetic epidemiology of substance use disorders, some researchers have, however, suggested that prevention efforts might specifically target those individuals who—because of their genetic history—are at greater risk for substance use problems (e.g., Merikangas & Avenevoli, 2000). In principle this approach might prove valuable through the targeting of individuals who are most likely to suffer from drug-related harm. However, in practice, there are a number of problems with this approach to prevention. First, although substance use disorders do tend to run in families, genetic variables only represent one risk factor for the development of drug problems. Individuals who may be targeted by such an approach, though, may interpret their genetic vulnerability in more determinative ways that may in fact *contribute* to subsequent drug problems—for example, by fostering the idea that once drugs are used, abuse and dependence are inevitable. Second, there is the possibility that those individuals who are identified as having a genetic susceptibility for the development of substance use problems may be denied insurance or be singled out in other harmful ways (see Kitcher, 1996, for an especially thoughtful discussion of these general issues). Third, all targeted programs (including those that are guided by cultural or environmental risk factors) face the problem of stigmatizing individuals who are branded as "likely" to develop drug problems even before they have occurred.

These sorts of problems are also likely to limit the scope of putative vaccines for substance use disorders, which are currently being developed for cocaine (Cohen, 1997; Fox, 1997). In principle, a biological preventative that "immunizes" against substance use problems by making drug use unpalatable may appear to be the ideal public health initiative. However, in practice, even setting aside safety issues, there are profound moral questions that would need to be addressed, because the introduction of such a vaccine would create the potential for coercion, stigmatization, and the erosion of civil liberties (Cohen, 1997). In sum, despite their important role in understanding the etiology of substance use problems, biological approaches may continue to play a limited role in prevention efforts.

Indeed, most approaches to prevention have focused on psychosocial and cultural factors, especially in the domain of drug education. Although the development of evidence-based education programs is a relatively recent phenomenon, drug education initiatives have a long history. Beck (1998) in his historical review of drug education in the

United States, divides such approaches into three categories: "Just Say No," "Just Say Nothing," and "Just Say Know." By the turn of the twentieth century, some form of "temperance instruction" was mandated in American public schools. This instruction typically took the form of injunctions against *any* use of alcohol, tobacco, or other drugs and used scare tactics to get this message across.

Instructing students about the potential dangers of drug use, backed by the latest "scientific" findings, formed the basis of these early drug education efforts. Following Prohibition in the United States, a "Just Say Nothing" approach prevailed. Alcohol and tobacco were no longer primary targets for drug education, and it was believed that any reference to drug use might arouse curiosity and therefore encourage use. In the 1970s, however, alternative approaches began to be introduced that focused on the presentation of credible information about drug use and drug-related harm in order for individuals to make rational, informed choices about drug use (Beck, 1998). Despite the introduction of these "Just Say Know" approaches to drug education, "Just Say No" perspectives have remained an important component of American drug policy, although primarily for political reasons rather than any overwhelming evidence of their efficacy in reducing drug use and drug-related problems. Indeed, in the past 20 years a significant body of evidence has accumulated about what does and what does not work in drug education (see Midford, 2000; Pentz, 1999; White & Pitts, 1998, for reviews).

Programs that focus primarily on changing knowledge, delivered in a didactic fashion, or that target self-esteem appear to be of negligible value (Pentz, 1999). The widely used Project DARE, which involves uniformed police officers delivering hard-hitting lectures promoting abstinence from drug use, has been shown to be similarly ineffective (Ennett, Tobler, Ringwalt, & Flewelling, 1994). Although evaluating the efficacy of drug education programs is hampered by methodological limitations, problems in the fidelity of program implementation, and different measures of success, a number of approaches have been shown to be of value (Midford, 2000; White & Pitts, 1998).

Programs that tend to be effective in reducing substance use and substance use problems address a number of relevant individual, social, and cultural factors. An example of a successful program is Botvin's Life Skills Training approach, which provides accurate knowledge about drugs and drug effects, targets attitudes and norms regarding drug use, teaches skills for resisting peer and social influences, and addresses general self-management and social skills (Botvin & Kantor, 2000). Life Skills Training is a school-based program delivered during 15 class periods, with booster sessions in subsequent years. Research suggests that this program has been effective in preventing alcohol, tobacco, and marijuana use and has significant lasting effects (Botvin & Kantor, 2000; Botvin, Baker, Dusenbury, Botvin, & Diaz, 1995). It is important that the generic nature of this program and others like it allows for the recognition that multiple factors influence drug use and addresses substance use issues in the context of wider social, developmental, cultural, and environmental contexts.

Community-based and mass media prevention programs, which target wider audiences, have also been shown to have some success in reducing substance use problems, although there is considerable variability in their effectiveness. For instance, a number of studies have demonstrated the efficacy of anti-smoking advertising in reducing tobacco use, although the success of such initiatives is typically obtained in concert with other measures such as taxation and community programs (e.g., Goldman & Glantz, 1998; Mudde & De Vries, 1999; Sly, Hopkins, Trapido, & Ray, 2001). One recent example of a successful anti-smoking advertising program is the Florida "truth" campaign, which has demonstrated a reduced risk for youth smoking initiation in individuals exposed to the anti-smoking messages (Sly, Hopkins, Trapido, & Ray, 2001). The effectiveness of this campaign was due to a number of factors: the use of modern marketing tools, detailed research on what approaches were most likely to influence youth smoking behavior, and the effective targeting of youth through the use of magazines and mobile trucks at raves, concerts, and other youth events (Hicks, 2001). Critically, rather than focusing on the manifold harm of smoking and telling youths to "say No" to tobacco, the campaign was directed at exposing the manipulative and duplicitous nature of tobacco companies. If, it was argued, one of the primary reasons that young people start smoking is to affirm their independence, then strategies that tell young people what to do would be less effective than those that undermine that independence by portraying the choice to smoke as simply part of the marketing plan of the tobacco industry. The lesson here is that prevention efforts must address the reasons that individuals use drugs and the function of drug use in their lives.

In sum, although the effects of drug education programs are often small, they have clearly shown to be valuable in reducing drug use and drug-related problems. As Midford (2000) summarizes, "The drug education literature does indicate that soundly conceptualized and rigorously implemented programmes can influence drug-using behavior and that comprehensive provisions of such programmes is likely to produce a net social cost saving to society" (p. 444). Some important questions remain, however, about how such programs might be targeted toward specific individuals or adapted to particular social and cultural contexts.

Cultural Issues

In Chapter 7 we identified a number of cultural factors that influence patterns of drug use. Cultural groups differ in their drug-specific norms and values, their beliefs and expectations about the effects of drugs, and their experience of a range of social-structural factors such as poverty, discrimination, and marginalization, which subsequently affect drug use and drug-related harm. If cultural factors permeate the etiology of substance use problems, then it makes good theoretical sense to incorporate cultural elements in our efforts to *prevent* the harmful use of drugs.

Culturally focused education programs, for instance, can be achieved in a number of ways. Material from existing programs may be modified so as to include culturally relevant examples and role models, in appropriate language, and delivered by culturally competent researchers (e.g., Botvin & Kantor, 2000). Education programs may also be tailored to incorporate culture-specific elements. For instance, prevention programs targeted at African American youth might include material devoted to Afrocentric values of community and spirituality and discussions of African American history (e.g., Chipungu, Hermann, Sambrano, Nistler, Sale, & Springer, 2000). Programs can also target culture-specific beliefs regarding drugs. For example, May (1986) suggests that in addressing alcohol problems among Native Americans, there is a need to provide information that counters fatalistic beliefs about alcohol use and the inevitability of alcohol problems in the Native American community. Finally, if part of the reason that ethnic minorities are overrepresented in measures of drug-related harm relates to such factors as poverty, unemployment, and marginalization, then prevention efforts need to address these issues in a systematic fashion. In addition to providing knowledge and teaching peer resistance and social skills, it is necessary to create viable alternatives to drug use and drug dealing in minority communities.

However, despite considerable theoretical support for the development and implementation of culture-specific prevention initiatives (e.g., Segal, 1995), there has been little systematic empirical evaluation of their efficacy (White & Pitts, 1998). In one recent study that aimed to reduce HIV risk among ethnic minority drug users, there were no significant differences between a culturally targeted intervention and a standard intervention (Dushay, Singer, Weeks, Rohena, & Gruber, 2001). Research carried out using Botvin's Life Skills Training approach to drug education has also shown little difference between a standard and a culturally tailored version, although follow-up data have shown stronger effects for the culturally targeted program for minority youth (Botvin, Schinke, Epstein, Diaz, & Botvin, 1995). In another recent study by Chipungu et al. (2000), an education program that incorporated Afrocentric principles and values was rated as more likeable and more important by African American youth than a similar program that did not, although the effects on measures of actual drug use were not included.

Clearly there is a need for more systematic research in the evaluation of culture-specific drug prevention programs. Given that the impact of education on subsequent drug-taking behavior is typically small, additional gains from culturally targeted programs may be hard to achieve. However, programs that incorporate cultural elements and that are implemented in culturally relevant ways in a community context may increase their potential for success. There is also a continuing need to systematically address inequalities in society that may contribute to drug problems among ethnic minorities, however intractable these may seem.

In sum, prevention programs ideally need to address drug use in a holistic fashion, and should be targeted toward creating alternative "lifeways" that do not entail the harmful use of psychoactive substances. Programs tend to emphasize the prevention of *any* drug use as the gold standard for how they should be evaluated, but given that experimental drug use appears to be a "normal" component of adolescence (e.g., Shedler & Block, 1990), efforts to manage *harmful* patterns of use should be given more consideration. Although the factors underlying successful drug education programs appear to be general in nature, there is substantial room for the development of culture-specific elements that are tailored toward the needs of specific social and ethnic groups.

ASSESSMENT

Individuals who present to addiction specialists with alcohol and other drug problems are a heterogeneous group of clients. Not only do the nature and severity of their problems vary, but how they come to be involved in treatment contexts also may differ in important ways. Many individuals will be seeking treatment of their own volition, but others will be there because of the problems their use of drugs has created for family, friends, employers, and the state. These factors, in combination with the intrinsically complex nature of substance use problems, necessitates a comprehensive assessment, usually involving a team of psychiatrists, clinical psychologists, social workers, and addiction counselors (Clark, 1999).

Recommended assessment procedures, moreover, are multimodal in nature and involve biological, psychological, and social components. We will not outline in detail here all the relevant domains that need to be assessed. However, they will ideally include an evaluation of the history of the present problems and past substance use; medical and psychiatric histories; social, developmental, family, and occupational histories; and an assessment of mental and physical health (Clark, 1999). The common co-occurrence of substance use problems with mental health disorders such as depression, bipolar disorder, and antisocial personality disorder (e.g., Kessler et al., 1997; Strakowski & DelBello, 2000; Swendsen & Merikangas, 2000) means that the careful assessment of psychiatric comorbidity is especially important. Furthermore, if possible, it is helpful to understand whether substance use disorders are primary or secondary to other mental health problems (Compton et al., 2000), as this evaluation has important implications for treatment strategies. The prevalence of psychiatric comorbidity varies among different cultural groups in the United States. African Americans are much less likely to have co-occurring mental health problems than are Caucasians, suggesting there may be culture-specific pathways to substance use disorders (Roberts, 2000).

Standard assessment procedures that involve biological, psychological, and social components also need to be expanded to include cultural-historical factors. For instance, the use of orthodox scoring instruments for alcohol problems may fail to encompass the full diversity of such problems if they are based on a narrow conceptualization of alcohol abuse and dependence (Baxter, Hinson, Wall, & McKee,

1998). As we have discussed in Chapter 8, many of the concepts employed in the DSM-IV diagnostic criteria for alcohol abuse and alcohol dependence are understood in different ways by different cultural groups (Room et al., 1996; Schmidt & Room, 1999). There is a need, therefore, to determine whether the terms employed are understood in similar ways by different clients. It is also important to be sensitive to threshold issues. A pattern of drug use that is viewed as problematic by an addiction specialist working within an Anglo-American framework may not necessarily be viewed as such by clients from other cultural backgrounds.

In order to overcome these problems, it is essential to take a "cultural history" from clients whenever there is reason to believe that cultural differences may play a relevant role in assessment procedures (Westermeyer, 1995a). A cultural history will include, among other factors, the degree of cultural identification with relevant ethnic groups, migration/immigration status, family structure and social roles, encounters with prejudice and discrimination, language issues, and degree of substance enculturation (e.g., what substances were employed in the home or community; acceptance of different substances) (Straussner, 2001b; Westermeyer, 1995a). Which features of this cultural history will prove important will depend on the cultural origin of the client concerned. For instance, the role of family and social support networks may be especially relevant for many clients, and will therefore need to be carefully assessed (e.g., Marinangeli, 2001).

The process of assessment also needs to be carried out in a culturally sensitive fashion. There are many relevant issues here, but it is important to recognize cultural differences in such factors as the relative stigmatization of substance use disorders, variations in interpersonal style, and acceptance of self-disclosure. In Indian cultures, for instance, as Sandhu & Malik (2001) note, psychological problems tend to be heavily stigmatized, so emphasizing the somatic aspects of substance use problems may be more appropriate, especially in the initial stages. Also, intimate topics relating to sexual functioning are best avoided when working with Indian clients until a comfortable working relationship has been established. Issues relating to cultural differences in personal boundaries, nonverbal communication, acceptance of confrontation, and so forth all need to be taken into account. Knowledge of a client's culture, language, and orientation to substance use are important in these contexts.

We also suggest that fundamental issues relating to the notion of self as a unique product of biological, psychosocial, and cultural components need to be addressed. In particular, it is important to establish just *why* someone is using a specific substance, what benefits they obtain from that use, and in what context use occurs. That is, there is a need to establish what the role and function of drug use is in that individual's life. If, for example, the use of a drug, despite problems, is an integral component of the social life of the individual concerned or is employed for self-medicinal reasons (say, to cope with oppression, poverty, and marginalization), then abstaining from use will represent only a small part of what needs to be addressed in treatment. The individual's own unique understanding of what underlies substance use problems also needs to be evaluated. If an individual believes in a disease model of addiction, for instance, this will influence the kind of treatment option that they may prefer and what the acceptable outcomes of treatment might be.

In short, a comprehensive assessment must consider all four components of the integrated model that we presented in Chapter 1. Which components might be considered the most salient, however, will vary on an individual basis. For ethnic minorities, for instance, cultural-historical issues may be the most salient factors that need to be assessed, if only because they are likely to differ from those of the addiction specialist. For long-term heavy drinkers or individuals dependent on opiates, biological factors might be most salient, as the most pressing issues may be related to health concerns, detoxification, and managing withdrawal symptoms.

TREATMENT

What should we consider as "treatment" for substance use problems? Understood narrowly, treatment involves the use of biological and/or psychosocial interventions that eliminate (or substantially reduce) the symptoms associated with substance abuse or dependence. The broader view of substance use problems, which we urged in Chapter 2, however, suggests that "harm-reduction" strategies, such as heroin maintenance and needle exchange programs should also be considered as treatment. They are, after all, reducing or eliminating the problems associated with substance use, even if they do not specifically address the core issue of substance *dependence*. We should also recognize that many—perhaps most—individuals who experience substance use problems essentially "cure" themselves of these problems, without any professional involvement. We discuss "natural recovery" from substance use problems and harm-reduction strategies later in the chapter, however, and concentrate in this section on treatment that focuses on reducing levels of drug use.

Another important issue relates to the *goals* of treatment. Should individuals be expected to abstain entirely from drug use to count as "cured," or at least "in remission"? Views on this issue vary substantially depending on the treatment modality employed and the beliefs of individual practitioners and clients. However, again drawing on a broader view of what constitutes substance use problems, we suggest that any "significant" reduction in the harm associated with drug use should count as a "success," even if this does not entail complete abstinence. Indeed, returning to "normal" substance use (where what is normal is culturally defined) should be considered as much a successful treatment outcome as complete abstinence, which may, depending on the substance in question, be *ab*normal in specific cultures. Bearing these points in mind, in this section we discuss the use of different treatment approaches. We focus first on biological and psychosocial interventions, and then discuss a number of important treatment issues raised by a cultural-historical perspective. We conclude with some suggestions about treatment from a more holistic point of view, focusing on the function of substance use in individual lives.

Biological and Psychosocial Treatment Approaches

Treatment options typically encompass a variety of different biological, psychological, and social approaches. Although different methods are sometimes used in isolation, they are often used in combination with one another. Treatment of alcohol problems may involve the use of drugs such as benzodiazepines to aid detoxification and to alleviate withdrawal symptoms (Gallant, 1999). Biological approaches aimed at preventing relapse of alcohol problems include the use of a range of drugs such as naltrexone, disulifram, acamprosate, and buspirone (Gallant, 1999; Schuckit, 1996b). The use of drug treatments for alcohol, however, has been subject to criticism (e.g., Moncrieff & Drummond, 1997; Hughes & Cook, 1997). Schuckit (1996b), for instance, in a review of pharmacotherapies for alcohol use disorders, concluded, "There are no pharmacological treatments for alcoholism rehabilitation for which long-term, appropriately controlled evaluations have indicated that routine use is justified" (p. 674). More generally, however, pharmacotherapies for alcohol problems are effective only when used in conjunction with a comprehensive treatment program that also involves psychosocial interventions (Moyers & Hester, 1999).

Psychological and social treatment methods also include a plethora of alternative approaches, including cognitive-behavior therapy, social skills training, family therapy, twelve-step facilitation approaches (e.g., AA), and motivational enhancement therapy. A review of the efficacy of these, often very different, approaches is beyond the scope of this chapter. However, broadly speaking, most of these methods appear to have some success (Miller, 1998a; Moyers & Hester, 1999). Miller, Waters, and Bennett (2001), for instance, in a recent review of the efficacy of alcohol treatment in the United States, concluded:

> After a single treatment episode, roughly one client in four will abstain from alcohol throughout the first year, which is the period of highest risk for return to drinking. In addition, about 1 in 10 will moderate the quantity and frequency of their drinking to remain free of alcohol-related problems in the same 1-year period. In combination, these unambiguously positive outcomes account for about one third of treated cases. (p. 218)

Treatment for other substances, such as heroin, cocaine, cannabis, and nicotine, also involves a variety of different biological, psychological, and social approaches. The salience of each kind of approach, however, varies depending on the drug in question. A number of viable pharmacological interventions, for instance, have been developed for opiate dependence, including buprenorphine, naltrexone, LAAM, and methadone (see Ling, Huber, & Rawson, 2001; Tucker & Ritter, 2000, for reviews). However, no pharmacotherapies have yet shown to be effective in the treatment of cocaine or cannabis dependence (O'Brien, 1996). As is the case with the treatment of alcohol, psychosocial interventions will typically be employed in conjunction with drug treatments (where they are available) for dependence on other substances. A more important role for drugs, however, occurs in the context of managing detoxification and withdrawal from a variety of substances such as opiates and cocaine. The use of biological approaches in essentially harm-reduction contexts, such as methadone maintenance and nicotine replacement, is discussed later in the chapter.

The effectiveness of a wide range of quite different treatment approaches has raised important issues about what it is that facilitates recovery from substance use problems (Edwards, 2000a; Miller, 1998a). Clearly, no pharmacological agent has been devised (as yet) that can "fix" or "cure" what may be occurring at a neurobiological level and that, as has been argued by some, underlies addictive disorders (e.g., Leshner, 1997). Indeed, the fact that such a variety of treatments with divergent methods and theoretical underpinnings can be—at least modestly—efficacious points to the role of nonspecific factors in recovery from drug problems.

Perhaps one way of accounting for the modest success of a variety of different treatment approaches is to suggest that substance use problems are heterogeneous in nature, and some treatments work better for some individuals or some problems than do others. Across treatments, success tends to even out as different methods attract different clients with different kind of problems. However, despite the conceptual plausibility of this suggestion, the results from Project MATCH provided very little support for the idea of client-treatment matching (see Project MATCH Research Group, 1997; Project MATCH Research Group, 1998). Project MATCH involved the assessment of three treatment approaches for alcoholism—twelve-step facilitation therapy, cognitive-behavior therapy, and motivational enhancement therapy—involving 1,726 patients at more than 30 treatment agencies in the United States. Clients were randomly assigned to the three treatment approaches at nine different sites, and a number of specific client-treatment matching hypotheses were evaluated, based on prior research. Although all three treatment methods proved (roughly equally) effective in reducing alcohol-related problems, virtually none of the specific a priori matching hypotheses were upheld. One notable exception emerged at the three-year follow-up. Individuals with social support networks that supported drinking did better when assigned to twelve-step facilitation therapy than did those who were assigned to motivational enhancement therapy (Longabaugh, Wirtz, Zweben, & Stout, 1998). Despite this important finding, it was concluded that "the results suggest that triaging clients to individual therapy, at least based on the attributes and treatments studied in Project MATCH, is not a compelling requirement for treatment success as previously believed" (Project MATCH Research Group, 1999, p. 33).

We appear to be left with the somewhat perplexing conclusion that many different treatments appear to work reasonably well with a wide range of different individuals.

In the next two sections, we first challenge this general finding by discussing the potential relevance of cultural factors in the treatment process. We then endorse the non-specific nature of treatment by considering the role of natural recovery before describing a more holistic conception of what "treatment," broadly conceived, appears to facilitate.

Cultural Issues

Most treatment options, as we outlined earlier, involve biological and psychosocial interventions. However, it is also important to recognize the role of cultural factors in the treatment process. As we discussed at length in Chapter 7, individuals from different cultural groups have different beliefs, norms, values, and expectancies regarding the use of drugs that might influence treatment in important ways. Moreover, we need to address the issue of whether standard treatment methods are appropriate for individuals from a diverse range of cultural backgrounds, or if cultural-specific treatment programs are more effective.

It is important to recognize first, however, that there are significant cultural differences in the availability of and access to treatment services. Barriers to treatment may be pragmatic in nature: ethnic minorities may have less time or opportunity to seek treatment because of less flexible work commitments, lack of available child care, cost, and so forth. Other impediments to seeking treatment may reflect cultural differences in how treatment is *perceived* (Baxter et al., 1998; Westermeyer, 1995). Among cultural groups in which alcohol and other drug problems are heavily stigmatized, for example, treatment may be avoided. For instance, Japanese individuals may be extremely reluctant to seek treatment for drug problems because these bring shame on the entire family (Matsuyoshi, 2001). Similarly, women with substance use problems may be less likely to approach treatment providers because drug problems are typically more stigmatizing for women than for men. For ethnic minorities who have been exposed to prejudice and discrimination, there may be a lack of trust in treatment services, especially for illicit drug problems. For instance, African Americans and Hispanics in the United States tend to be reluctant to become involved in methadone maintenance programs because they are often viewed as a method of control and oppression rather than treatment (Baxter et al., 1998; Bourgois, 2000).

Once in treatment, a variety of culturally relevant factors need to be taken into account. Cultural differences in norms, values, beliefs, and expectations regarding drug use need to be assessed. That is, a clear picture of an "individual's explanatory model of substance abuse" (Terrell, 2001, p. 90) needs to be obtained. For instance, belief in the disease model of alcohol dependence, with its emphasis on loss of control and individual susceptibility, is widespread among Native Americans. Treatment options, thus, might favor AA, the philosophy of which is commensurate with these beliefs. There is some suggestion that AA programs are less appropriate for Native Americans (see Weaver, 2001; Westermeyer, 1996b). However, a modified form of AA that incorporates elements of Native American culture is believed to be more acceptable (Westermeyer, 1995).[1] Generally speaking, there has been a call for more "culturally competent" treatment that takes into account the beliefs and values of clients from diverse cultural backgrounds (see Baxter et al., 1998; Castro et al., 1999; Straussner, 2001b). The matching of clients to practitioners, and clients to treatments, are two ways that culturally appropriate treatment might be delivered. There is also recognition that cultural elements are not just ones that need to be *accommodated* in treatment, but they in fact may form an integral *component* of the treatment process itself. For instance, Rowe and Grills (1993) assert that for African Americans:

> The central treatment issues involve empowering African-Americans to alter the fundamental cultural-political power imbalance that informs the superior position (institutionally, ideologically, and structurally) that persons of European ancestry currently maintain, and emphasizing African-centered ideas, methods, and values in the development of drug abuse treatment and recovery. (p. 26)

The reaffirmation of cultural values (and the rejection of the values of the "dominant culture"), according to this point of view, become the way individuals might overcome problems with alcohol and other drugs.

In order to achieve this vision of "cultural recovery," there has been a call for the development of more programs dedicated specifically to the treatment of ethnic minorities that incorporate core elements of cultural belief systems. For instance, treatment programs for New Zealand Maori with alcohol and other drug problems have focused on indigenous ideas of "wellness," which embrace physical, mental, social, and spiritual components. The development of Maori self-identity and fostering connections with *whanau* (family) and *iwi* (tribes) are integral components of these treatment initiatives (Huriwai et al., 2001; Sellman, Huriwai, Ram, & Deering, 1997).

Culture-specific treatments may embrace a wide variety of different methods. In North America, for instance, alternatives to mainstream treatment programs for Native Americans include sweat lodges and the peyote ceremony of the Native American Church. Hill (1990), for example, describes the emergence of peyotism as an effective way of reducing drinking problems among the Nebraska Winnebago at the turn of the twentieth century. Participation in the peyote ceremony is one of the central features of the peyote religion. Such ceremonies involve all-night meetings, with prayer, meditation, singing, and the ingestion of peyote. Belonging to the peyote religion also involved the rejection of certain practices, including the use of tobacco and alcohol. Although we shouldn't ignore the possibility that the pharmacological properties of peyote contributed to the success of peyotism in reducing alcohol problems (e.g., see Mangini, 1998, for a comprehensive review of the use of hallucinogens in the treatment of alcohol problems), as Hill notes, it is likely that the psychosocial and spiritual features of the movement were most important. Specifically, involvement in the peyote ritual included the formal renunciation of alcohol, the creation of new alcohol-free social networks, the development of alternative activities, and the use of recovered drinkers as role models.

The way that alcohol problems may be overcome through cultural means is nicely illustrated in a long-term study of alcohol use in San Pedro Chenalhó, a highland township in Chiapas, Mexico (Eber, 2001). In this community, in the 1970s and 1980s, alcohol was employed in social, ritual, and medicinal contexts. However, in part as a result of poverty and social marginalization, the use of alcohol also resulted in a number of problems. Even more tumultuous change in the 1990s led to the emergence of a movement against alcohol by members of the community, characterized by the need to forge an independent social identity and to take control of their lives. Abstinence has thus become a symbol of self-affirmation among these people: "Efforts to heal themselves of problem drinking are inseparable from both their personal paths to honor and respect and their collective efforts to construct a more democratic society" (Eber, 2001, p. 259).

These efforts resemble similar attempts by Native Americans and indigenous Australians to develop dry communities that encourage positive identification with traditional values, in part through a rejection of alcohol and its association with colonial dominance and oppression. Of course, the substantial challenge for Native Americans, indigenous Australians, and other indigenous groups is to develop constructive ways of dealing with alcohol (and other drugs) within the midst of multicultural societies for which alcohol is a ubiquitous, culturally approved, and institutionally ingrained substance.

The idea of culture *as* treatment, however, has not gone without criticism (e.g., Brady, 1995). Brady suggests that an emphasis on cultural issues may narrow the options for recovery for ethnic minorities by reinforcing specific views about the nature of substance use problems. Moreover, some traditional values and beliefs may actually hinder the recovery process. For instance, the cultural importance of autonomy and the reluctance to tell others what they should do, for indigenous Australians, may impede the ability to instigate change. Furthermore, by focusing on culture-specific treatments, Brady (1995) suggests, more general pathways to recovery may be downplayed or ignored. Perhaps most important, there is a need to provide careful evaluations of culture-specific treatment programs in order to establish what features (if any) of these methods are effective. Unfortunately, despite many promising findings, methodologically rigorous assessments of culturally based treatment initiatives are lacking (Gray, Saggers, Sputore, & Bourbon, 2000; Saggers & Gray, 1998).

Although we would suggest that a focus on purely "cultural" elements in treatment is important—if in need of more rigorous evaluation—we should not ignore the importance of social-structural factors. For instance, Gray et al. (2000), in a review of approaches to treating alcohol and drug problems among indigenous Australians, conclude, "There is a need to redress the fundamental inequalities faced by Aboriginal people" (p. 20). As long as the pervasive and enduring prejudice, discrimination, marginalization, and oppression of ethnic minorities in multicultural societies persist, strategies for reducing substance use problems will remain limited. The creation of meaning and the fostering of cultural identity will be seriously hampered in social environments in which minorities are impoverished or have few life options, positive role models, or viable aspirations. Attending to social-structural inequalities, therefore, is crucial to the alleviation of much of the harm related to the use of drugs, especially by ethnic minority groups.

Natural Recovery

It is also important to appreciate that many individuals successfully overcome substance use problems without recourse to formal treatment. It is well recognized that the use of drugs (especially illicit ones) tends to decline as individuals get older (Bachman et al., 1996). This phenomenon, referred to as "maturing out," is attributed to a number of factors, such as the incompatibility of continued drug use with new roles and responsibilities relating to work and family. The idea that people can recover from substance use problems without treatment, however, is less well accepted. Indeed, the existence of "natural recovery" appears to challenge the prominent view that addiction is a chronic relapsing disorder, which gets progressively worse unless treated.

However, a growing number of studies suggest that such natural recovery, even from quite severe drug problems, is a common phenomenon (e.g., Burman, 1997; Granfield & Cloud, 1996; Sobell, Cunningham, & Sobell, 1996; Sobell, Sobell, & Toneatto, 1991). For instance, Sobell et al. (1996), in a survey study of the general population in Canada, found that more than 75% of their participants who had recovered from an alcohol problem for more than one year had done so without treatment. Moreover, many individuals reported that they had returned to moderate drinking, rather than maintaining strict abstinence. Many studies that have investigated natural recovery from substance use problems have methodological limitations, which restrict the drawing of strong conclusions (see Sobell, Ellingstad, & Sobell, 2000, for a comprehensive review). However, what is clear is that the phenomenon of natural recovery from problems with a wide range of different drugs is real, and worthy of further investigation. Indeed, Edwards (2000c) suggests that "natural recovery is the only recovery," with "treatment conceived at best simply the skilful business of nudging and supporting self-determined change" (p. 747).

How is such recovery achieved without treatment, and why do people change? The influential "stages of change" model (Prochaska, DiClemente, & Norcross, 1992) provides one way of understanding the *process* by which people overcome their substance use problems. According to the authors of this model, individuals move through five stages—precontemplation, contemplation, preparation, action, and maintenance—in changing their addictive behaviors. Whether this model accurately reflects the way that individuals recover from substance use problems is, however, a question in need of further research. Sobell et al. (2000), for instance, report that a number of studies suggest that many individuals who quit their use of drugs do so without a protracted process of change. The reasons *why* individuals change their harmful patterns of substance use are varied. Some of the most important reasons given include health concerns, social and family problems, employment difficulties, and economic problems (Sobell et al., 2000).

The reasons for changing patterns of substance use are probably similar across different cultural groups, although there may be important cultural differences as well. In an ethnographic study of "giving away the grog" among Australian Aborigines, Brady (1993) found many of the same reasons—such as health, social, financial, and family problems—that have been reported in other studies. However, Quintero (2000), in a study of "aging out" of problem drinking among Native Americans, suggests that some of these familiar reasons may unfold in a culturally specific manner. In particular, for Navajo men who were drinking heavily in their twenties, settling down and having children is one important reason for change. Quintero (2000) suggests that:

> Navajo men frame changes in their drinking behaviors with culturally important modes of meaning. The traditional Navajo ideals of a good life associated with home, family, and the accumulation of valued possessions, and beauty and harmony, are all predicated on temperance. (p. 1043)

The importance of family and social roles in instigating change is especially relevant to the substance use problems experienced by African American and Hispanics in inner-city communities. Because such problems are more likely to center on illicit drug use, a large number of young African American and Hispanic men end up spending time in prison. This forced removal from the community contributes to a breakdown in traditional family structures, skews sex ratios, and leads to the erosion of relationship commitment among men and consequently to a high number of single-parent families. Social norms relating to fatherhood and family roles, as a consequence, have changed, perhaps removing some of the factors that can contribute to natural recovery among men. To curb such social changes, attention must be paid to the factors that allow them to occur.

An Holistic View of Treatment

Drawing on the brief review of treatment and natural recovery from substance use problems presented, we suggest that the central feature in overcoming such problems relates to changes in self-concept.

Returning to our model outlined in Chapter 1, these changes reflect the confluence of biological, psychosocial, and cultural elements. In short, changes in drug-taking behavior represent altered ways of conceptualizing the self in relation to drugs in particular, and more generally, to other areas of life functioning. Different components of the self-system, though, may be more salient in these changes, depending on individual circumstances. The rejection of old drug-using social groups in favor of new abstinent ones, for instance, and the reaffirmation of cultural identity highlight the links between cultural-historical variables and the self. Forgoing drugs because of beliefs about their deleterious effects on health and intrapersonal functioning, by contrast, emphasizes the relation between the self and psychosocial variables. Some individuals may also give up drugs through the use of pharmacological interventions, which may check the "biological pull" of drugs on self-initiated behaviors, thus highlighting the paths between biological variables and the self. Of course, often all four components will be important in understanding the process of change that individuals go through.

The nature of these changes may be radical in nature, involving a systematic transformation of the self. The therapeutic interventions characteristic of AA, the peyote cult, and many instances of natural recovery may reflect such wholesale changes. The individual in these cases in effect becomes a "new" person: he or she sheds his or her former substance-using identity, social networks, and physiological relations to the drug and becomes biologically, psychosocially, and culturally a new individual. Often, however, changes are more subtle in character. Individuals with emerging health problems as a result of a history of heavy alcohol use, for example, may decide that such patterns of use are incompatible with the image they have of themselves as competent individuals, and thus cut down the amount that they use. They have now become a "moderate drinker" and have shed their identity as a "heavy drinker," but the changes wrought in their lifestyle and their relations to others have not altered dramatically. In short, there are many pathways to change, although we suggest that they all critically involve a change in the self-system.

Many of these general themes have been explored by others. Edwards (2000a), for instance, provides a list of what he suggests are the "mysterious essences of treatment." These factors include the belief that change is possible and the motivation to proceed with change, the development of support networks, and the instigation of new ways of living (see also Miller, 1998b). How important these different elements are will depend on the individual concerned. They are also likely to manifest in different ways among individuals from different cultural groups. Spicer (2001), for instance, explores how recovery from alcohol problems among Native Americans involves the realization that "alcohol is incompatible with the way of life that is proper to Indian people" (p. 232). Native Americans who abuse alcohol are faced with a form of cognitive dissonance: Alcohol is inimical to traditional cultural values, and yet they (as Native Americans) continue to drink in harmful ways. The resolution of this intrapersonal conflict may take the form of the rejection of alcohol and the reaffirming of cultural identity. As Spicer (2001) summarizes, "Transformations of the self and its relationship to core symbols in a particular cultural system of meaning appear to lie at the heart of how people are restored to wholeness following their problematic involvements with alcohol" (p. 238).

In understanding how individuals can recover from substance use problems and what needs to be done to facilitate such changes, it is also important to consider the functions that drug use serves in their lives. That is, the critical question—Why do people use drugs?—that we have addressed from various perspectives throughout this book needs to be engaged in the context of treatment. Drawing on the evolutionary perspective outlined in Chapter 3, for instance, we can recognize that because drugs offer powerfully rewarding experiences, which push the right "evolutionary buttons," they will remain an attractive alternative for many people. Substance abuse, argues Nesse (1994, p. 346), is not a disease to be treated, but rather an "intrinsic human tendency" to be managed in the most effective way possible. If part of the great appeal of many psychoactive drugs is in their ability to generate positive emotional experiences and to alleviate negative ones (at least in the short term), then one plausible tactic for intervention is to examine the strategies that people employ to get "natural" satisfaction out of life experiences.

By examining rewarding experiences that have evolutionary relevance, such as social interaction, close relationships, physical exercise, sex, and so forth, a clearer picture can be obtained of why some people are drawn to the "artificially" rewarding experiences offered by drugs. As Nesse and Berridge (1997) make clear, general strategies that increase a person's ability to get "normal" satisfaction out of life experiences should be viewed as an *essential*, not merely an adjunctive, feature of treatment. The findings reviewed earlier, that marriage, parenthood, gainful employment, and rewarding social relationships are all related to a decline in drug use, underscore the importance of meaningful life experiences and responsibilities in the context of prevention and treatment of drug problems.

If part of the reason that people consume drugs, or consume certain types of drugs, is related to an innate need for the experience of altered states of consciousness (ASC), then, as Weil (1986, 1990) makes clear, alternative methods for generating ASC should be seen as a critical part of any intervention strategy. "The overall goals of drug treatment," Weil (1990, p. 1107) states, "are to encourage people to satisfy their needs for ASC in less destructive ways." More generally speaking, what McPeake, Kennedy, and Gordon (1991) term "Altered States of Consciousness Therapy" should become a more prominent treatment approach. Weil suggests that the controlled use of psychoactive drugs may be one legitimate strategy in managing drug problems. However, he believes, in the long run, the generation of altered states via other means is likely to prove more effective. Other, less harmful methods of creating ASC include meditation, biofeedback, relaxation, self-hypnosis, and breathing techniques. Indeed, a body of evidence suggests that Transcendental Meditation (TM) has proven to be an effective method for treating substance abuse problems (e.g., Staggers, Alexander, & Walton, 1994; Sharma, Dillbeck, & Dillbeck, 1995; Gelderloos, Walton, Orme-Johnson, & Alexander, 1991).

For example, in a review of 24 studies that used TM, Gelderloos et al. (1991) found that this method compares favorably to traditional treatment programs in treating substance abuse problems. TM methods appeared to be especially efficacious in relapse prevention, possibly because they aim to offer something of value in place of drug taking. The efficacy of TM is probably related to a variety of factors, which include the reduction of psychological stress; the enhancement of psychological well-being, self-esteem, and life meaning; and the alteration of important physiological processes such as heart rate and blood pressure. These various therapeutic avenues may be related more generally to the adaptive mechanisms that promote psychological health via ASC. No doubt there are also important changes occurring in the levels of various neurotransmitters, which may be implicated in the effectiveness of meditation in treating substance abuse problems. Of course, meditation requires a reasonable level of investment on a client's behalf, and may not be an appropriate method for all individuals with substance abuse problems.

Perhaps most important, an evolutionary perspective urges the importance of examining the function that drugs perform in the lives of individuals with substance use problems. For instance, as Pomerleau (1997) outlines in her informative discussion of nicotine addiction, clinicians need to be sensitive to the underlying problems in their client's lives that they may be trying to manage by using drugs. Pomerleau argues that people often use nicotine to manage other problems in their lives, such as depression and anxiety. If such management is effective within the context of an individual's life, then one possible "treatment" option may involve the replacement of smoking by nicotine delivered via less health-threatening channels.

It is clear that there is much to learn about treatment and about how people recover from substance use problems. However, by adopting a broader perspective on the nature of substance use, by considering the range of different problems that individuals might have, and by locating the process of change in the context of an individual's self-system, a clearer picture might be established.

LEGAL SANCTIONS, REGULATIONS, AND RESTRICTIONS

The control of psychoactive substances through the imposition of sanctions, regulations, and restrictions is an enduring theme in the history of drugs (see Chapters 4 and 5). Drug control is also a feature of many "traditional" cultural groups, although in such cases it is often achieved through the use of informal social sanctions rather than overt legal measures (Westermeyer, 1996a). In contemporary Western societies, efforts at drug control encompass a range of approaches, including taxation, limits on availability, outright prohibition, interdiction, and drug crop eradication.

For licit substances such as alcohol and tobacco, efforts to reduce drug use and drug-related harm typically involve raising prices, restricting promotion, and limiting supply through restrictions on sale and availability. What evidence we have suggests that many of these initiatives are effective in reducing drug use and drug-related harm. Efforts to limit the promotion of tobacco, for instance, have been effective in reducing use, although only when they target multiple forms of media (Slade, 2001). Despite claims to the contrary from tobacco industries, tobacco marketing is effective in recruiting new smokers, and tobacco companies have specifically targeted youth in their marketing programs (Pollay, 2000). However, whereas 27 countries have enacted complete bans on tobacco advertising, claims that such restrictions inhibit freedom of speech have hampered such initiatives in the United States, where tobacco advertisements still appear in various forms of media (Gostin, 2002; Kagan & Nelson, 2001). Other strategies such as taxation, age limits, and limiting the availability of alcohol and tobacco also have been shown to be effective in reducing levels of use. As we note in our historical review of drug use in Chapters 4 and 5, taxation on drugs has been a popular form of generating revenue for governments. However, raising prices through taxation is also effective in reducing the demand for substances such as tobacco, and hence their levels of use (e.g., Chaloupka, Wakefield, & Czart, 2001).

It is important to recognize that the kinds of restrictions and regulations outlined impact in different ways on different social groups within society. For instance, increasing the price of alcohol and tobacco is most effective at reducing use by youth, lower socioeconomic groups, and heavy users (Chaloupka & Wechsler, 1997; Marmot, 1997; Townsend, Roderick, & Cooper, 1994). However, little research seems to have addressed the impact of different policy initiatives on cultural differences in alcohol and tobacco use, although the way such policies are implemented show considerable cross-national variability. For example, despite the overwhelming evidence that high taxation rates are effective in reducing the prevalence of smoking, the United States taxes tobacco at low rates in comparison to international standards (Chaloupka et al., 2001). For instance, whereas the average price in U.S. dollars per packet of cigarettes in the United States is $1.94, the equivalent cost in Australia is $4.85, and in Denmark it is $5.20 (Kagan & Nelson, 2001).

The use of alcohol and tobacco is related to many problems in society that various regulations and restrictions have been shown to reduce. The cultural embeddedness of these substances, however, and powerful vested interests (i.e., alcohol and tobacco companies) in their continued use tend to restrict the strength of measures designed to reduce their consumption. The use of restrictions, regulations, and sanctions for alcohol and tobacco provide a striking contrast to the measures used to curb the use of other drugs, such as cocaine, heroin, and cannabis. This difference is especially noticeable in the United States, which not only has some of the weakest tobacco and alcohol control policies in the developed world but also has the strongest and most punitive approaches to the reduction of illicit drug use.

The rationale for drug prohibition is straightforward, although as MacCoun and Reuter (1996) elucidate, the effects of drug laws on drug use are complex and involve multiple pathways. By imposing strict sanctions on the sale and use of drugs such as cocaine, heroin, and cannabis, drug use should in theory be reduced because of the fear of arrest and imprisonment. Drug prohibition may also reduce drug use by making such use socially unacceptable and by limiting drug availability and hence raising prices to unaffordable levels. The imposition and enforcement of strict penalties on the sale and use of drugs are coupled with efforts to control the flow of these substances through interdiction and control strategies in source countries (MacCoun & Reuter, 2001).

Efforts to reduce drug use through prohibition form the cornerstone of American drug policy, and are prominent methods used by other countries, typically attracting far more government resources than either prevention or treatment initiatives (Reuter, 2001; Wodak & Moore, 2002). Given their importance, how effective are such methods at reducing drug use and drug-related harms? Surprisingly, this is a difficult question to answer, as there has been little in the way of systematic empirical evaluation of the efficacy of prohibition, interdiction, and other such control measures (Reuter, 2001). Such efforts do probably reduce, or at least limit, the prevalence of illicit drug use in society (MacCoun & Reuter, 2001); however, as many authors have noted, the implementation of drug policy, American-style, also contributes to drug-related problems in important ways (e.g., Heath, 1992; Nadelmann, 1989; Reuter, 2001; Ryan, 1998). These problems are many and varied: Prohibition entails substantial financial investment through law enforcement activities; incarcerates thousands of individuals at significant personal cost; fosters often violent criminal activity among drug users, dealers, and traffickers; contributes to the spread of drug-related diseases such as AIDS; restricts legitimate medical uses of illicit drugs; and in general erodes civil liberties and contributes to the decline of many urban communities. Critically, drug prohibition as it is currently enacted in the United States impacts in harmful ways on ethnic minority groups. As noted in Chapter 6, African Americans and Hispanics are grossly overrepresented in drug arrest and incarceration statistics. Indeed, in some communities, more than a quarter of young African American men have convictions for drug dealing (Saner, MacCoun, & Reuter, 1995), a phenomenon with multiple deleterious effects on ethnic minority communities.

Rehearsing these critiques of American drug policy, of course, does not provide us with ready solutions. However, it is important to recognize that contemporary policy responses are the result of specific cultural-historical trajectories, which in the United States (and elsewhere—see Manderson, 1993; Wodak & Moore, 2002, for a critique of Australian drug policy) have been profoundly shaped by prejudicial attitudes toward drug use by ethnic minority groups (see Jensen & Gerber, 1998; Chapters 4–7). Certain drugs in American society, in short, have been the object of moral condemnation, out of all proportion to the actual harm that they generate. In this sense, drug prohibition can be viewed as a cultural-historical construction rather than as a rational response to enduring social problems (see Heath, 1992; Jensen & Gerber, 1998).

Policy responses toward alcohol and tobacco provide an interesting contrast to responses toward illicit substances in the United States. Whereas the use, sale, and promotion of one set of potentially harmful substances is defended as a fundamental civil right, the use and sale of another set of potentially harmful substances is condemned as criminal activity and is subject to punitive responses. This schism in drug policy is also manifest in the international arena, as Sugarman (2001) clearly elucidates:

> During the 1980s in particular, the United States took a position on tobacco products that dramatically opposed its position on other drugs. The "war on drugs" that sought to keep other nations' products out of the United States was matched by an equally strong war to force other countries to open up their markets to our tobacco products. (p. 258)

Inconsistencies in policy responses toward psychoactive substances are further reinforced once another class of drugs is included: prescription substances. Throughout the period when the "war on drugs" was at its height in American society, profits on prescription medicines (of which about a quarter are "psychoactive") skyrocketed. More than 22 million Americans, for instance, have used Prozac alone, and some sources estimate that 15% of children have been prescribed Ritalin (Shenk, 1999). Although the use of these substances may occur through legitimate channels and have real value in medicinal terms, they are also associated with a number of costs, including abuse and dependence.

If drug prohibition is responsible for much of the harm that arises from the use of psychoactive substances, what alternative regimes are available, and are they likely to deliver more acceptable outcomes? Two main alternatives to drug prohibition have been suggested: legalization and decriminalization. Despite historical precedents, the outright legalization of all currently licit psychoactive substances has few supporters, except among libertarians (e.g., Szasz, 1998). Support for the selective legalization of cannabis, however, is more widespread (e.g., Wodak & Moore, 2002). The legalization of drugs would certainly reduce the systemic violence endemic under prohibition and of course would eliminate the harm associated with arrest and incarceration for drug use and drug dealing. The likely effects of legalization on patterns of use, however, are largely unknown. The critical question is whether such reductions in harm under legalization would be offset by a dramatic increase in the use of currently illicit substances, with a concomitant rise in other problems such as abuse and dependence (MacCoun & Reuter, 2001). Western nations' experience with the legalization of drugs in the nineteenth century provides little support either way (although see Courtwright, 1998). Certainly there were high levels of dependence on substances such as morphine and cocaine when they were legal and freely available. However, knowledge of the harm these substances can cause is more widespread in contemporary society, and it is unlikely that the same kinds of individuals (mainly middle-class women) would experience problems under legalization in the twenty-first century, although others (predominantly young men) certainly would.

In a sense, speculation on the likely effects of the outright legalization of drugs is not especially fruitful, because in current social and political environments it is extremely unlikely that any Western nation will experiment with such changes. The decriminalization, or more accurately *depenalization* of drugs, however, is a potentially more realizable option (MacCoun & Reuter, 2001). By retaining laws against the sale and supply of drugs, but lifting sanctions on personal use (or treating such use in the manner of a civil misdemeanor with a small fine), some drug-related problems such as arrest, incarceration, and restriction on civil liberties are attenuated. By removing the fear of prosecution or police harassment, individuals with drug problems, and perhaps especially ethnic minorities, may be less reluctant to engage in treatment and other control initiatives. Depenalization, however, does not remove the black market in illicit drugs and the violence that often accompanies it, especially in the United States.

Unlike the legalization option, there are several recent precedents to draw on in examining the likely effects of depenalization on levels of drug use and drug-related harm. Such harm includes the deleterious effects on individuals of receiving criminal convictions, the expense of maintaining law enforcement activities for cannabis use, and disrespect for cannabis laws, perhaps undermining the value of other legislation (Lenton, 2000). The Netherlands, Italy, Spain, and several states in Australia have all depenalized the use of cannabis (MacCoun & Reuter, 2001). By doing so, much of the harm associated with cannabis *prohibition* may be reduced. Of course, cannabis is not a completely benign substance, so potential reductions in harm as a result of decriminalization must be placed against whatever costs, such as increase in use, that arise from such moves (Hall, 1997). However, the *use* of cannabis appears to be relatively unaffected by changes in its legal status. Although it is hard to obtain precise information about use-related harm in those places that have decriminalized cannabis possession, certainly overall prevalence of cannabis use does not seem to have increased (see Donnelly, Hall, & Christie, 2000; MacCoun & Reuter, 2001).

Finding the right balance of restrictions, regulations, and sanctions is a difficult task. Effective policy initiatives, ideally, should be evidence-based and directed at attenuating the total harm related to drug use, rather than simply attempting to reduce levels of use. It is also important to address the cultural-historical assumptions underlying current drug policy. For instance, there is growing support for the idea that there is a need in the United States to shift from criminal to public health perspectives on the use and control of illicit substances. A middle way, thus, between punitive prohibition and outright free market legalization would be to adopt a harm-minimization perspective.

HARM REDUCTION

An expanded view on the nature of substance use problems encourages a broader perspective on how such problems may be reduced or eliminated. The fact that the human nervous system has evolved in a manner that makes many psychoactive drugs powerfully rewarding, the ubiquity of such substances in nature (and in the laboratory), and the diverse psychosocial and cultural uses to which such substances are put strongly indicate that the complete eradication of drugs is an unreasonable and unreachable goal. Drugs will not go away; therefore, we must develop the most appropriate way of managing the problems associated with their use. In short, harm-reduction and harm-minimization policies should be at the forefront of policy options for managing drug-related problems.

As Roberts and Marlatt (1999) elaborate, a harm-reduction approach provides an alternative to both moral/criminal and medical/disease perspectives on substance use problems. A harm-reduction orientation is pragmatic in nature and operates within a broad public health approach to individual and social harms. The core features of harm reduction involve an acceptance that substance use occurs, and will continue to occur, while attempting to minimize the problems that may result from such use. The philosophy of harm reduction is thus in sharp contrast to policy approaches that advocate that the decline of any drug use—via reductions in supply or demand—should be the central criterion for "success" (Erickson & Butters, 1998). In principle, there are many strategies that might reduce the harm associated with drug use—from the provision of safe detention shelters for drunk individuals to the use of nicotine patches. However, in practice, three programs receive the most attention: needle and syringe exchange, methadone maintenance, and heroin prescription. We shall discuss each of these harm-reduction strategies in turn.

The costs associated with intravenous drug use are numerous. They include the risk of overdose, infection, the spread of diseases like hepatitis and AIDS, and criminal prosecution. At least some of these costs, in principle, can be attenuated through the ready, legal availability of clean needles and syringes. Unsafe injection practices, such as the sharing of needles and syringes and the use of common water to mix drugs, may thus be reduced (Page, 1997). Needle and syringe exchange programs (NEPs) have a relatively long history in European countries such as Britain, the Netherlands, Denmark, and Switzerland. In other nations, such as Italy and Spain, syringes are available at pharmacists, and their possession is not illegal (MacCoun & Reuter, 2001).

In sharp contrast to this situation in Europe, NEPs have had limited government support in the United States. The paucity of effective programs, it is argued, not only contributes to drug-related harm but also selectively disadvantages minorities, for whom such harm tend to be concentrated (Singer, 2001). Most evaluations of NEPs suggest that they are effective in reducing risky behaviors. However, as Page (1997) suggests, there are often important methodological limitations in most outcome studies that restrict the drawing of firm conclusions.

It is significant that there is no evidence that the ready availability of clean needles and syringes increases either the use of injectable opiates or the harm associated with such use. There is evidence, however, that the *illegality* of needles and syringes contributes to risky drug-using practices (Page, 1997). Page concludes, though, that for such programs to be effective they must address the social conditions in which intravenous drug use is prevalent and incorporate ideas and support from community members.

Another harm-reduction strategy that has been employed in Europe but has found little favor in the United States is the prescription of injectable opiates to individuals dependent on heroin. In Britain, the prescription of heroin has a long history, and heroin maintenance has also been trialed in Switzerland. In principle, by providing unadulterated heroin in a controlled environment, with clean syringes and needles (or via other routes such as smoking), much of the harm associated with heroin use may be decreased. However, this approach has received criticism from some sources (e.g., Zador, 2001). In particular, it is suggested that the system is expensive to maintain, may delay abstinence by users, allows diversion of licit sources of heroin to the black market, and sends "inappropriate" messages about the acceptability of drug use (see Carnwath, 2001, for a defense of this practice). Perhaps most important, though, there simply has not been an adequate evaluation of the "British system" that can inform debate in a meaningful way (Strang, 2001; Zador, 2001).

The recent Swiss trial using heroin prescription, however, has provided some relevant data, which generally indicate positive outcomes in terms of retention in treatment, employment, and mental health. The participants in this study were all long-term heroin users (10 years or more), and most were unemployed, so the positive outcomes were especially noteworthy. Specifically, at six months, 82% of participants were still in treatment, and the retention rate at 18 months was 69% (Klingemann, 1998). These figures compare favorably to the typically high drop-out rates for most treatment programs for heroin addiction. Moreover, the illicit use of other drugs declined during the course of the study, and there were improvements in social and occupational functioning (Klingemann, 1998). However, as MacCoun and Reuter (2001) note, the absence of participant randomization and the lack of control groups render these promising findings in need of further support.

Perhaps the most widespread and certainly most widely accepted form of harm reduction is methadone maintenance. Methadone is a long-acting synthetic opioid that reduces craving for heroin and other opiates (Rao & Schottenfeld, 1999). When administered in appropriate doses and in combination with psychosocial interventions, methadone can be an effective method of treating opiate dependence. As with NEPs and prescribed heroin, methadone maintenance is used because it can reduce the harm associated with intravenous drug use. Most studies of methadone programs have reported positive outcomes in terms of reductions in heroin use, improved social and occupational functioning, and reduced criminal behavior (e.g., Gossop et al., 1997). Problems with methadone programs typically include high drop-out rates, the use of other drugs such as alcohol, benzodiazepines, and cocaine, and there are concerns over their cultural appropriateness. The persistence of methadone programs, however, is significant, and they play an important role in reducing drug-related harm, even in the United States, where harm-reduction strategies typically find less political support. Replacement strategies are, it should be noted, effective only in reducing the harm associated with drug use for substances like opiates, which, unlike alcohol or tobacco, do not cause major health problems with long-term use.

Critics of harm-reduction approaches (e.g., DuPont, 1996) suggest that such measures typically result in an increase in substance use by "sending the wrong message" that the use of drugs is OK. However, despite DuPont's denial of evidence that clearly contradicts this assertion, most studies do not suggest that drug use increases significantly as a result of harm-reduction initiatives (MacCoun & Reuter, 2001). Indeed, it appears that some critics of harm-reduction approaches are more informed by moral perspectives on drug use than by a rational assessment of costs and benefits. For instance, DuPont (1996) asserts:

> There are many harm reductionists who would teach kids to smoke pot and use hallucinogens responsibly. Is that really a good idea? I think it is beyond scary. Kids are better served by learning the dangers of drug use. They need to know that drug use is unacceptable and will be punished, including not only the drugs that are illegal for adults, but those that are legal for adults but illegal for youth, tobacco and alcohol. Harm reduction is incremental surrender in the war against drug use in the name of reasonableness, tolerance, and sophistication. (p. 1940)

Unfortunately, such a view fails to accord with reality. For the many reasons outlined in this book, individuals will continue to use a variety of drugs, along with engaging in various other potentially harmful activities such as playing contact sports, sunbathing, driving cars, eating fast food, and so forth. This view is also inconsistent with the available evidence that posits the real benefits that can accrue from harm-reduction programs such as needle and syringe exchange and cannabis decriminalization. Finally, sending the message that drug use is "unacceptable and will be punished" provides a moral view of drug use, which many individuals in society simply do not accept (although others of course do). It is extremely difficult to ground the idea that the use of any psychoactive substance is morally wrong within most accepted approaches to moral theory (see Husak, 1992).

Harm-reduction strategies are, however, not always successful, and their implementation may in fact contribute to greater levels of drug-related harm. For instance, in response to credible and widely disseminated information about the health consequences of smoking, tobacco companies have developed a number of putatively less harmful methods of tobacco use (Berridge, 1999; Warner, 2001). Such alternatives in the past have included low-tar and low-nicotine brands, and recent initiatives include the development of cigarette-like nicotine delivery systems such as Eclipse and Premiere in the 1980s and 1990s. Without doubt, such alternatives have contributed to higher rates of smoking-related harm by reducing the number of individuals who might have quit smoking (Warner, 2001). However, we shouldn't dismiss the possibility of tobacco harm-reduction strategies, and nicotine replacement therapy products such as gum, patches, and nasal sprays have been effective in increasing cessation from smoking, especially in conjunction with psychosocial interventions (Ockene, Kristeller, & Donnelly, 1999). The value of such products for long-term nicotine maintenance, however, is less clear, and there is concern that the ready availability of such products may give individuals, especially youth, the illusion that smoking cessation is easily accomplished (Melanie Wakefield—personal communication).

CONCLUSION

In *Othello*, Shakespeare nicely captures the attitude toward alcohol in the early modern period as a benign or good substance that could be *used* badly. Cassio, bemoaning his foolish acts of violence after having been plied with alcohol by Iago, declaims, "O Strange! Every inordinate cup is unblest, and the ingredience is a devil." Iago replies,

"Come, come, wine is a good familiar creature, if it be well used; exclaim no more against it" (Shakespeare, 1622/1992, 2.3.300). Given its integration into all parts of daily life, alcohol itself was as little to blame for excessive intoxication as food was for gluttony. One enduring theme in the history of drugs is their ambivalent status in society. One the one hand, they are often praised as medical agents, lauded in social, recreational, and pragmatic contexts, and imbued with ritual and religious significance. On the other hand, it is widely recognized that drugs have the potential for significant harm, and they have been demonized as agents of social and moral decay. Our equivocal attitudes toward these substances are no accident—psychoactive drugs, through their actions on the central nervous system, have the capacity to modify or transform the self, in both harmful and beneficial ways.

In Shakespeare's day, new drugs were starting to appear in European society—coffee, tea, tobacco, and distilled liquor—that would supplement more familiar substances such as, beer, wine, and opium. These new substances were welcomed and feared—praised as medicines and condemned as poisons. In the past 400 years we have added a huge range of new drugs to this list, and it is to be expected that this process of accumulation will continue over the next few centuries. New substances are likely to be developed in the chemist's laboratory with increasingly subtle and targeted sites of action that are able to moderate emotional, psychological, and behavioral states in ways that will be valued by some individuals and reviled by others. How we respond to these new developments, along with the persistence of more familiar substances, will have profound implications for substance-related harm in society.

Throughout this book we have urged a view of drug use that emphasizes the importance of context. It is critical to examine why drugs are employed and the functions that they serve in people's lives. In order to reduce the harms caused by drugs in society, it is necessary to accommodate drug use in less harmful ways, to promote the development of social norms, values, and beliefs that foster abstinence or moderate use, and to create alternatives that can replace the role of drugs in people's lives. These tasks are not easy, but an inclusive approach to drugs that addresses cultural-historical determinants along with biological and psychological factors, is likely to prove fruitful.

NOTE

1.   It has often been suggested that AA is less appropriate for individuals from ethnic minorities or for women than it is for Caucasian males. Certainly, some of the features of AA, such as group confession and its spiritual overtones, may be less acceptable to some cultural groups. However, in one recent evaluation it was found that both women and ethnic minorities were as likely to participate, and to remain involved in AA, as were Caucasian males (Hillhouse & Fiorentine, 2001).

References

Abaka, E. (2000). Kola nut. In K. F. Kiple & K. C. Ornelas (Eds.), *The Cambridge world history of food* (684–692). Cambridge: Cambridge University Press.

Abel, E. L. (1980). *Marijuana: The first twelve thousand years.* New York: Plenum Press.

Abel, S. (1997). Cannabis policy in Australia and New Zealand. *Drug and Alcohol Review, 16,* 421–428.

Abrahamsen, A. A. (1987). Bridging boundaries versus breaking boundaries: Psycholinguistics in perspective. *Synthese, 72,* 355–388.

Acker, C. J. (1993). Stigma or legitimation? A historical examination of the social potential of addiction disease models. *Journal of Psychoactive Drugs, 25,* 193–205.

Acker, C. J. (1995). From all purpose anodyne to marker of deviance: Physicians' attitudes towards opiates in the US from 1890 to 1940. In R. Porter & M. Teich (Eds.), *Drugs and narcotics in history* (114–132). Cambridge: Cambridge University Press.

Agar, M., & Reisinger, H. S. (2001). Open marginality: Heroin epidemics in different groups. *Journal of Drug Issues, 31,* 729–746.

Akil, H., Owens, C., Gutstein, H., Taylor, L., Curran, E., & Watson, S. (1998). Endogenous opioids: Overview and current issues. *Drug and Alcohol Dependence, 51,* 127–140.

Alexander, B. K. (1990). The empirical and theoretical bases for an adaptive model of addiction. *Journal of Drug Issues, 20,* 37–65.

Allen, S. L. (1999). *The devil's cup: Coffee, the driving force in history.* New York: Soho Press, Inc.

Alper, K. R., Lotsof, H. S., Frenken, G. M. N., Luciano, D. J., Bastiaans, J. (1999). Treatment of acute opioid withdrawal with ibogaine. *American Journal on Addictions, 8,* 234–242.

Anderson, P. (1995). Alcohol and the risk of physical harm. In H. D. Holder & G. Edwards (Eds.), *Alcohol and public policy: Evidence and issues* (82–113). Oxford: Oxford University Press.

Andersson, M. (1994). *Sexual selection.* Princeton, NJ: Princeton University Press.

Andritzky, W. (1989). Sociopsychotherapeutic functions of ayahuasca healing in Amazonia. *Journal of Psychoactive Drugs, 21,* 77–89.

Anslinger, H., & Cooper, C. (1937). Marijuana: Assassin of youth. *American Magazine*, July. Reprinted in S. R. Belenko (Ed.), *Drugs and drug policy in America: A documentary history* (145–147). Westport, CT: Greenwood Press.

Anthony, J. C., Warner, L. A., & Kessler, R. C. (1994). Comparative epidemiology of dependence on tobacco, alcohol, controlled substances, and inhalants: Basic findings from the National Comorbidity Survey. *Experimental and Clinical Psychopharmacology, 2,* 244–268.

Antze, P. (1987). Symbolic action in Alcoholics Anonymous. In M. Douglas (Ed.), *Constructive drinking: Perspectives on drink from anthropology* (149–181). New York: Cambridge University Press.

Arnett, J. J. (1992). Reckless behavior in adolescence: A developmental review. *Developmental Review, 12,* 339–373.

Arnett, J. J. (1998). Learning to stand alone: The contemporary American transition to adulthood in cultural and historical context. *Human Development, 41,* 295–315.

Atran, S. (1990). *Cognitive foundations of natural history: Towards an anthropology of science.* Cambridge: Cambridge University Press.

Baasher, T. (1981). The use of drugs in the Islamic world. *British Journal of Addiction, 76,* 233–243.

Bachman, J. G., Johnston, L. D., & O'Malley, P. M. (1990). Explaining the recent decline in cocaine use among young adults: Further evidence that perceived risks and disapproval lead to reduced drug use. *Journal of Health and Social Behavior, 31,* 173–184.

Bachman, J. G., Johnston, L. D., & O'Malley, P. M. (1998). Explaining recent increases in students' marijuana use: Impacts of perceived risks and disapproval, 1976 through 1996. *American Journal of Public Health, 88,* 887–892.

Bachman, J. G., Johnston, L. D., O'Malley, P. M., & Humphrey, R. H. (1988). Explaining the recent decline in marijuana use: Differentiating the effects of perceived risks, disapproval, and general lifestyle factors. *Journal of Health and Social Behavior, 29,* 92–112.

Bachman, J. G., Johnston, L. D., O'Malley, P. M., & Schulenberg, J. (1996). Transitions in drug use during late adolescence and young adulthood. In J. A. Graber, J. Brooks-Gunn, & A. C. Paterson (Eds.), *Transitions through adolescence: Interpersonal domains and context* (111–140). Mahwah, NJ: Lawrence Erlbaum Associates.

Baer, H. A., Singer, M., & Susser, I. (1997). *Medical anthropology and the world system: A critical perspective.* Westport, CT: Bergin & Garvey.

Balick, M. J. & Cox, P. A. (1996). *Plants, people, and culture: The science of ethnobotany.* New York: Scientific American Library.

Baridon, P. (1973). A comparative analysis of drug addiction in 33 countries. *Drug Forum, 2,* 335–365.

Baron-Cohen, S. (Ed.) (1997), *The maladapted mind: Classic readings in evolutionary psychopathology.* Hove, East Sussex: Psychology Press.

Barr, A. (1995). *Drink: A social history.* London: Pimlico.

Bauman, K. E. & Ennett, S. T. (1996). On the importance of peer influence for adolescent drug use: Commonly neglected considerations. *Addiction, 91,* 185–198.

Baumeister, R. F. (1987). How the self became a problem: A psychological review of historical research. *Journal of Personality and Social Psychology, 52*, 163–176.

Baumeister, R. F., Heatherton, T. F. & Tice, D. M. (1994). *Losing control: How and why people fail at self-regulation.* San Diego: Academic Press.

Baxter, B. E., Hinson, R. E., Wall, A-M., & McKee, S. A. (1998). Incorporating culture into the treatment of alcohol abuse and dependence. In S. S. Kazarian & D. R. Evans (Eds.), *Cultural clinical psychology: Theory, research, and practice* (215–245). New York: Oxford University Press.

Beauvis, F., Oeting, E. R., Wolf, W., & Edwards, R. W. (1989). Native American youth and drugs, 1976–1987: A continuing problem. *American Journal of Public Health, 79*, 634–636.

Bechtel, W. (1986). The nature of scientific integration. In W. Bechtel (Ed.), *Integrating scientific disciplines* (3–52). The Hague: Martinus Nijhoff.

Bechtel, W., & Abrahamsen, A. (1993). Interfield connections and psychology. In H. V. Rappard, P. J. VanStrien, L. P. Mos, & W. J. Baker (Eds.), *Annals of Theoretical Psychology, 9*, 125–141.

Beck, J. (1998). 100 years of "Just Say No" versus "Just Say Know": Reevaluating drug education goals for the coming century. *Evaluation Review, 22*, 15–45.

Becker, H. S. (1953). Becoming a marihuana user. *American Journal of Sociology, 59*, 235–243.

Becker, H. S. (1967). History, culture and subjective experience: An exploration of the social basis of drug-induced experiences. *Journal of Health and Social Behavior, 8*, 163–176.

Ben-Yehuda, N. (1986). The sociology of moral panics: Towards a new synthesis. *Sociological Quarterly, 27*, 495–513.

Berlin, B., Breedlove, D., & Raven, P. (1973). General principles of classification and nomenclature in folk biology. *American Anthropologist, 74*, 214–242.

Berridge, V. (1984). Editorial: The centenary issue. *British Journal of Addiction, 79*, 1–6.

Berridge, V. (1985). Morbid cravings: The emergence of addiction. *British Journal of Addiction, 80*, 233–243.

Berridge, V. (1988). The origins of the English drug "scene" 1890–1930. *Medical History, 32*, 51–64.

Berridge, V. (1990). The Society for the Study of Addiction 1884–1988. *British Journal of Addiction, 85*, 983–1079.

Berridge, V. (1999). Histories of harm reduction: Illicit drugs, tobacco, and nicotine. *Substance Use and Misuse, 34*, 35–47.

Berridge, V., & Edwards, G. (1981). *Opium and the people: Opiate use in Nineteenth-Century England.* London: Allen Lane.

Berry, J.W. (1998). Acculturation and health: Theory and research. In S. S. Kazarian & D. R. Evans (Eds.), *Cultural clinical psychology: Theory, research, and practice* (39–57). New York: Oxford University Press.

Blum, K., Braverman, E. R., Holder, J. M., Lubar, J. F., Monastra, V. J., Miller, D., Lubar, J. O., Chen, T. J. H., & Comings, D. E. (2000). Reward deficiency syndrome: A biogenetic model for the diagnosis and treatment of impulsive, addictive, and compulsive behaviors. *Journal of Psychoactive Drugs, 32,* 1–68.

Blum, K., Cull, J. G., Braverman, E. R., & Comings, D. E. (1997). Reward deficiency syndrome. *American Scientist, 84,* 132–144.

Blum, K., Noble, E. P., Sheridan, P. J., Montgomery, A., Ritchie, T., Jagadeeswaran, P., Nogami, H., Briggs, A., Cohn, J. (1990). Allelic association of human dopamine D2 receptor in gene alcoholism. *Journal of American Medical Association, 263,* 2055–2060.

Boardman, J. D., Finch, B. K., Ellison, C. G., Williams, D. R., & Jackson, J. S. (2001). Neighborhood disadvantage, stress, and drug use among adults. *Journal of Health and Social Behavior, 42,* 151–165.

Booth, M. (1996). *Opium: A history.* London: Simon & Schuster.

Booth, P. B. (1997). E. M. Jellinek and the evolution of alcohol studies: A critical essay. *Addiction, 92,* 1619–1637.

Booth, P. G. (1990). Maintained controlled drinking following severe alcohol dependence—A case study. *British Journal of Addiction, 85,* 315–322.

Borsari, B., & Carey, K. B. (2001). Peer influences on college drinking: A review of the research. *Journal of Substance Abuse, 13,* 391–424.

Botvin, G. J., Baker, E., Dusenbury, L. D., Botvin, E. M., & Diaz, T. (1995). Long-term follow-up results of a randomized drug abuse prevention trial. *Journal of the American Medical Association, 273,* 106–112.

Botvin, G. J., & Kantor, L. W. (2000). Preventing alcohol and tobacco use through life skills training. *Alcohol Research and Health, 24,* 250–257.

Botvin, G. J., Schinke, S. P., Epstein, J. A., Diaz, T., & Botvin, E. M. (1995). Effectiveness of culturally focused and generic skills training approaches to alcohol and drug abuse prevention among minority adolescents: Two-year follow-up results. *Psychology of Addictive Behaviors, 9,* 183–194.

Bourgois, P. (1995). *In search of respect: Selling crack in El Barrio.* Cambridge: Cambridge University Press.

Bourgois, P. (2000). Disciplining addictions: The bio-politics of methadone maintenance and heroin addiction in the United States. *Culture, Medicine and Psychiatry, 24,* 165–195.

Bower, B. (1994). Ancient site taps into soldiers' brew. *Science News, 146,* 390.

Brady, M. (1990). Indigenous and government attempts to control alcohol use among Australian Aborigines. *Contemporary Drug Problems,* Summer, 195–220.

Brady, M. (1991). Psychoactive substance use among young Aboriginal Australians. *Contemporary Drug Problems,* Summer, 273–329.

Brady, M. (1992). Ethnography and understandings of Aboriginal drinking. *Journal of Drug Issues, 22,* 699–712.

Brady, M. (1993). Giving away the grog: An ethnography of Aboriginal drinkers who quit without help. *Drug and Alcohol Review, 12,* 401–411.

Brady, M. (1995). Culture in treatment, culture as treatment: A critical appraisal of developments in addictions programs for indigenous North Americans and Australians. *Social Science and Medicine, 41,* 1487–1498.

Brady, M. (2000). Alcohol policy issues for indigenous people in the United States, Canada, Australia and New Zealand. *Contemporary Drug Problems, 27,* 435–502.

Brandon, T. H., Juliano, L. M., & Copeland, A. L. (1999). Expectancies for tobacco smoking. In I. Kirsch (Ed.), *How expectancies shape experience* (263–299). Washington DC: American Psychological Association Press.

Brandt, A. M. (1990). The cigarette, risk, and American culture. *Daedalus, 119,* 155–176.

Breslau, N., Johnson, E. O., Hiripi, E., & Kessler, R. (2001). Nicotine dependence in the United States. *Archives of General Psychiatry, 58,* 810–817.

Brooke, C. (2000). Khat. In K. F. Kiple & K. C. Ornelas (Eds.), *The Cambridge world history of food* (671–684). Cambridge: Cambridge University Press.

Brown, D. E. (1991). *Human universals.* Philadelphia: Temple University Press.

Brown, T. N., Schulenberg, J., Bachman, J. G., O'Malley, P. M., & Johnston, L. D. (2001). Are risk and protective factors for substance use consistent across historical time? National data from high school classes of 1976 through 1997. *Prevention Science, 2,* 29–43.

Brownsberger, W. N. (1997). Prevalence of frequent cocaine use in urban poverty areas. *Contemporary Drug Problems, 24,* 349–371.

Brownsberger, W. N. (2000). Race matters: Disproportionality of incarceration for drug dealing in Massachusetts. *Journal of Drug Issues, 30,* 345–374.

Brunton, R. (1989). *The abandoned narcotic: Kava and cultural instability in Melanesia.* Cambridge, London: Cambridge University Press.

Buchanan, D. R. (1992). A social history of American drug use. *Journal of Drug Issues, 22,* 31–52.

Burfield, L. B., Sundquist, J., & Johansson, S. E. (2001). Ethnicity, self reported psychiatric illness, and intake of psychotropic drugs in five ethnic groups in Sweden. *Journal of Epidemiology and Community Health, 55,* 657–664.

Burman, S. (1997). The challenge of sobriety: Natural recovery without treatment and self-help groups. *Journal of Substance Abuse, 9,* 41–61.

Burns, C. B., D'Abbs, P., & Currie, B. J. (1995). Patterns of petrol sniffing and other drug use in young men from an Australian Aboriginal community in Arnhem Land, Northern Territory. *Drug and Alcohol Review, 14,* 159–169.

Bushman, B. J., & Cooper, H. M. (1990). Effects of alcohol on human aggression: An integrative research review. *Psychological Bulletin, 107,* 341–354.

Buss, D. M. (1995). Evolutionary psychology: A new paradigm for psychological science. *Psychological Inquiry, 6,* 1–49.

Buss, D. M. (1999). *Evolutionary psychology: The new science of the mind.* Boston: Allyn & Bacon.

Buss, D. M., Haselton, M. G., Shackelford, T. K., Bleske, A. L., & Wakefield, J. C. (1998). Adaptations, exaptations, and spandrels. *American Psychologist, 53,* 533–548.

Bynum, W. F. (1984). Alcoholism and degeneration in 19th century European medicine and psychiatry. *British Journal of Addiction, 79,* 59–70.

Byrnes, J. P., Miller, D. C., & Schafer, W. D. (1999). Gender differences in risk taking: A meta-analysis. *Psychological Bulletin, 125,* 367–383.

Caetano, R. (1987a). Acculturation and drinking patterns among U.S. Hispanics. *British Journal of Addiction, 82,* 789–799.

Caetano, R. (1987b). Acculturation, drinking and social setting among U.S. Hispanics. *Drug and Alcohol Dependence, 19,* 215–226.

Carnwath, T. (2001). In defense of the British system of injectable diamorphine prescription. *Addiction, 96,* 1405–1407.

Carroll, A., Houghton, S., & Odgers, P. (1998). Volatile solvent use among Western Australian adolescents. *Adolescence, 33,* 877–889.

Carroll, K. M., Rounsaville, B. J., & Bryant, K. J. (1994). Should tolerance and withdrawal be required for substance dependence disorders? *Drug and Alcohol Dependence, 36,* 15–22.

Carstairs, G. M. (1954). Daru and bhang: Cultural factors in the choice of intoxicant. *Quarterly Journal of Studies on Alcohol, 15,* 220–237.

Cassanelli, L. V. (1986). Qat: Changes in the production and consumption of a quasilegal commodity in northeast Africa. In A. Appadurai (Ed.), *The social life of things: Commodities in cultural perspective* (236–257). Cambridge: Cambridge University Press.

Castro, F. G., Proescholdbell, R. J., Abeita, L., & Rodriguez, D. (1999). Ethnic and cultural minority groups. In B. S. McCrady & E. E. Epstein (Eds.), *Addictions: A comprehensive guidebook* (499–526). New York: Oxford University Press.

Catalano, R. F., Morrison, D. M., Wells, E. A., Gillmore, M. R., Iritani, B., & Hawkins, J. D. (1992). Ethnic differences in family factors related to early drug initiation. *Journal of Studies on Alcohol, 53,* 208–217.

Caulkins, J. P. (1997). Is crack cheaper than (powder) cocaine? *Addiction, 92* 1437–1443.

Caulkins, J. P. (2001). Drug prices and emergency department mentions for cocaine and heroin. *American Journal of Public Health, 91,* 1446–1448.

Caulkins, J. P., Johnson, B., Taylor, A., & Taylor, L. (1999). What drug dealers tell us about their costs of doing business. *Journal of Drug Issues, 29,* 323–340.

Caulkins, J. P., & Reuter, P. (1998). What price data tell us about drug markets. *Journal of Drug Issues, 28,* 593–612.

Cawte, J. (1985). Psychoactive substances of the South Seas: Betel, kava and pituri. *Australian and New Zealand Journal of Psychiatry, 19,* 83–87.

Cawte, J. (1986). Parameters of kava used as a challenge to alcohol. *Australian and New Zealand Journal of Psychiatry, 20,* 70–76.

Chagnon, N. A. (1997). *Yanomamö* (5th ed.). Fort Worth: Harcourt Brace College Publishers.

Chaloupka, F. J., Wakefield, M., & Czart, C. (2001). Taxing tobacco: The impact of tobacco taxes on cigarette smoking and other tobacco use. In R. L. Rabin & S. D. Sugarman (Eds.), *Regulating tobacco* (39–72). Oxford: Oxford University Press.

Chaloupka, F. J., & Wechsler, H. (1997). Price, tobacco control policies and smoking among young adults. *Journal of Health Economics, 16,* 359–373.

Chen, K., & Kandel, D. B. (1995). The natural history of drug use from adolescence to the mid-thirties in a general population sample. *American Journal of Public Health, 85,* 41–47.

Chen, K., Scheier, L. M., & Kandel, D. B. (1996). Effects of chronic cocaine use on physical health: A prospective study in a general population sample. *Drug and Alcohol Dependence, 43,* 23–37.

Cherpitel, C. J. (1992). Acculturation, alcohol consumption, and casualties among United States Hispanics in the emergency room. *International Journal of the Addictions, 27,* 1067–1077.

Cherry, A. (2002a). Burma (Union of Myanmar). In A. Cherry, M. E. Dillon, & D. Rugh (Eds.), *Substance abuse: A global view* (1–21). Westport, CT: Greenwood Press.

Cherry, A. (2002b). Colombia. In A. Cherry, M. E. Dillon, & D. Rugh (Eds.), *Substance abuse: A global view* (51–75). Westport, CT: Greenwood Press.

Cheung, Y. W. (1990–1991). Ethnicity and alcohol/drug use revisited: A framework for future research. *International Journal of the Addictions, 25,* 581–605.

Childers, S. R., & Breivogel, C. S. (1998). Cannabis and endogenous cannabinoid systems. *Drug and Alcohol Dependence, 51,* 173–187.

Chipungu, S. S., Hermann, J., Sambrano, S., Nistler, M., Sale, E., & Springer, J. F. (2000). Prevention programming for African American youth: A review of strategies in CSAP's national cross-site evaluation of high-risk youth programs. *Journal of Black Psychology, 26,* 360–385.

Chisholm, J.S. (1993). Death, hope, and sex: Life history theory and the development of reproductive strategies. *Current Anthropology, 34,* 1-24.

Cho, Y. I., & Faulkner, W. R. (1993). Conceptions of alcoholism among Koreans and Americans. *International Journal of the Addictions, 28,* 681–694.

Chowdhury, A. N. (1995). Drug abuse and eco-stress adaptation. *Addiction, 95,* 19–20.

Clark, D. B. (1999). Psychiatric assessment. In P. J. Ott, R. E. Tarter, & R. T. Ammerman (Eds.), *Sourcebook on substance abuse: Etiology, epidemiology, assessment, and treatment* (197–212). Boston: Allyn & Bacon.

Clawson, P. L., & Lee, R. W. (1996). *The Andean cocaine industry.* London: MacMillan.

Clendinnen, I. (1991). *Aztecs: An interpretation.* Cambridge: Cambridge University Press.

Cloninger, C. R. (1999). Genetics of substance abuse. In M. Galanter & H. D. Kleber (Eds.), *Textbook of substance abuse treatment* (2nd ed.; 59–66). Washington DC: American Psychiatric Press.

Clough, A. R., Burns, C. B., & Mununggurr, N. (2000). Kava in Arnhem Land: A review of consumption and its social correlates. *Drug and Alcohol Review, 19,* 319–328.

Cohen, P. J. (1997). Immunization for prevention and treatment of cocaine abuse: legal and ethical implications. *Drug and Alcohol Dependence, 48,* 167–174.

Cohen, S. (1980). *Folk devils and moral panics: The creation of the mods and rockers* (2nd ed.). Oxford: Martin Robertson.

Collin, M. (1997). *Altered states: The story of ecstasy culture and acid house.* London: Serpents Tail.

Collins, R. L. (1995). Issues of ethnicity in research on the prevention of substance abuse. In G. J. Botvin, S. Schinke, & M. A. Orlandi (Eds.), *Drug abuse prevention with multiethnic youth* (28–46). Thousand Oaks, CA: Sage Publications.

Collins, R. L., Blane, H. T., & Leonard, K. E. (1999). Psychological theories of etiology. In P. J. Ott, R. E. Tarter, & R. T. Ammerman (Eds.), *Sourcebook on substance abuse: Etiology, epidemiology, assessment, and treatment* (153–165). Boston: Allyn & Bacon.

Collison, M. (1996). In search of the high life: Drugs, crime, masculinities and consumption. *British Journal of Criminology, 36,* 428–444.

Comer, J. (2000). Distilled beverages. In K. F. Kiple & K. C. Ornelas (Eds.), *The Cambridge world history of food* (653–663). Cambridge: Cambridge University Press.

Compton, W. M., Cottler, L. B., Phelphs, D. L., Abdallah, A. B., & Spitznagel, E. L. (2000). Psychiatric disorders among drug dependent subjects: Are they primary or secondary? *The American Journal on Addictions, 9,* 126–134.

Confessions of a middle–aged ecstasy eater. (2001). *Granta, 74,* Summer, 9–33.

Cooper, M. L., Frone, M. R., Russell, M., & Mudar, P. (1995). Drinking to regulate positive and negative emotions: A motivational model of alcohol use. *Journal of Personality and Social Psychology, 69,* 990–1005.

Cornell, S., & Hartmann, D. (1998). *Ethnicity and race: Making identities in a changing world.* Thousand Oaks, CA: Pine Forge Press.

Courtwright, D. T. (1982). *Dark paradise: Opiate addiction in America before 1940.* Cambridge, MA: Harvard University Press.

Courtwright, D. T. (1995). The rise and fall and rise of cocaine in the United States. In J. Goodman, P. E. Lovejoy, & A. Sherratt (Eds.), *Consuming habits: Drugs in history and anthropology* (206–228). London: Routledge.

Courtwright, D. T. (1997a). The prepared mind: Marie Nyswander, methadone maintenance, and the metabolic theory of addiction. *Addiction, 92,* 257–265.

Courtwright, D. T. (1997b). Morality, religion, and drug use. In A. M. Brandt & P. Rozin (Eds.), *Morality and health* (231–250). New York: Routledge.

Courtwright, D. T. (1998). Should we legalize drugs? History answers . . . no. In J. A. Schaler (Ed.), *Drugs: Should we legalize, decriminalize, or deregulate?* (83–92). New York: Prometheus Books.

Courtwright, D. T. (2001). *Forces of habit: Drugs and the making of the modern world.* Cambridge, MA: Harvard University Press.

Crabbe, J. C., Belknap, J. K., & Buck, K. J. (1994). Genetic animal models of alcohol and drug abuse. *Science, 264,* 1715–1723.

Crabbe, J. C., & Phillips, T. J. (1999). Genetics of alcohol and other abused drugs. *Drug and Alcohol Dependence, 51,* 61–71.

Crawford, V. (2002). The "homelie ." *History Today,* January, 40–41.

Critchlow, B. (1986). The powers of John Barleycorn: Beliefs about the effects of alcohol on social behavior. *American Psychologist, 41,* 751–764.

Crum, R. M., Lillie-Blanton, M., & Anthony, J.C. (1996). Neighborhood environment and opportunity to use cocaine and other drugs in late childhood and early adolescence. *Drug and Alcohol Dependence, 43,* 155–161.

Daly, J. W., & Fredholm, B. B. (1998). Caffeine—An atypical drug of dependence. *Drug and Alcohol Dependence, 51,* 199–206.

Darden, L., & Maull, N. (1977). Interfield theories. *Philosophy of Science, 44,* 43–64.

Davenport-Hines, R. (2001). *The pursuit of oblivion: A global history of narcotics 1500–2000.* London: Weidenfeld & Nicolson.

Dawkins, R. (1982). *The extended phenotype.* Oxford: Oxford University Press.

Dawkins, R. (1986). *The blind watchmaker*. New York: W. W. Norton.

Dawson, D. A. (1998a). Measuring alcohol consumption: limitations and prospects for improvement. *Addiction, 93*, 965–968.

Dawson, D. A. (1998b). Beyond Black, White and Hispanic: Race, ethnic origin and drinking patterns in the United States. *Journal of Substance Abuse, 10*, 321–339.

Dawson, D. A., & Room, R. (2000). Towards agreement on ways to measure and report drinking patterns and alcohol-related problems in adult general population surveys: The Skarpö Conference overview. *Journal of Substance Abuse, 12*, 1–21.

Dernbach, K. B., & Marshall, M. (2001). Pouring beer on troubled waters: Alcohol and violence in the Papua New Guinea Highlands during the 1980s. *Contemporary Drug Problems, 28*, 3–47.

De Smet, P. A. G. M. (1985). A multidisciplinary overview of intoxicating snuff rituals in the Western Hemisphere. *Journal of Ethnopharmacology, 13*, 3–49.

Dev, S. (1999). Ancient-modern concordance in Ayurvedic plants: Some examples. *Environmental Health Perspectives, 107*, 783–789.

Devlin, N. J., Scuffham, P. A., & Bunt, L. J. (1997). The social costs of alcohol abuse in New Zealand. *Addiction, 92*, 1491–1505.

Diamond, J. (1992). *The rise and fall of the third chimpanzee*. London: Radius.

Diamond, J. (1993). New Guineans and their natural world. In S. R. Kellert & E. O. Wilson (Eds.), *The biophilia hypothesis* (251–275). Washington, DC: Shearwater Books.

Dingle, A. E. (1980). "The truly magnificent thirst": An historical survey of Australian drinking habits. *Historical Studies, 19*, 227–250.

Dinwiddie, S. H. (1994). Abuse of inhalants: A review. *Addiction, 89*, 925–939.

Dobkin de Rios, M. (1990). *Hallucinogens: Cross-cultural perspectives*. Prospect Heights, IL: Waveland Press, Inc.

Dobkin de Rios, M., & Smith, D. E. (1977). Drug use and abuse in cross cultural perspective. *Human Organization, 36*, 14–21.

Dobkin de Rios, M., & Stachalek, R. (1999). The *Duboisia* genus, Australian Aborigines and suggestibility. *Journal of Psychoactive Drugs, 31*, 155–161.

Doll, R. (1998). The benefit of alcohol in moderation. *Drug and Alcohol Review, 17*, 353–363.

Doll, R., & Bradford Hill, A. (1954). The mortality of doctors in relation to their smoking habit. *British Medical Journal, 26*, 1451–1455.

Doll, R., Peto, R., Hall, E., Wheatley, K., & Gray, R. (1994). Mortality in relation to consumption of alcohol: 13 years' observations on male British doctors. *British Medical Journal, 309*, 911–916.

Donnelly, N., Hall, W., & Christie, P. (2000). The effects of the Cannabis Expiation Notice system on the prevalence of cannabis use in South Australia: Evidence from the National Drug Strategy Household surveys 1985–1995. *Drug and Alcohol Review, 19*, 265–271.

Dreher, M. C. (1983). Marihuana and work: Cannabis smoking on a Jamaican sugar estate. *Human Organization, 42*, 1–8.

Drew, L. R. H. (1990). Facts we don't want to face. *Drug and Alcohol Review, 9*, 207–210.

Drucker-Brown, S. (1995). The court and the kola: Wooing and witnessing in northern Ghana. *Journal of the Royal Anthropological Institute, 1*, 129–143.

Dudley, R. (2000). Evolutionary origins of human alcoholism in primate frugivory. *Quarterly Review of Biology, 75*, 3–15.

Dudley, R. (2002). Fermenting fruit and the historical ecology of ethanol ingestion: Is alcoholism in modern humans an evolutionary hangover? *Addiction, 97*, 381–388.

Dunbar, R. I. M. (1991). Foraging for nature's balanced diet. *New Scientist, 131*, 25–28.

Dunbar, R. I. M. (1995). *The trouble with science*. London: Faber & Faber.

DuPont, R. L. (1996). Harm reduction and decriminalization in the United States: A personal perspective. *Substance Use and Misuse, 31*, 1929–1945.

DuPont, R. L. (1997). *The selfish brain: Learning from addiction*. Washington DC: American Psychiatric Press.

DuPont, R. L., & McGovern, J. P. (1994). *A bridge to recovery: An introduction to 12-step programs*. Washington, DC: American Psychiatric Press.

Durrant, R., & Ellis, B. J. (2002). Evolutionary psychology: Core assumptions and methodology. In M. Gallagher & R. J. Nelson (Eds.), *Comprehensive handbook of psychology, Volume 3: Biological psychology*. New York: Wiley & Sons.

Durrant, R., & Haig, B. D. (2001). How to pursue the adaptationist program in psychology. *Philosophical Psychology, 14*, 357–380.

Dushay, R. A., Singer, M., Weeks, M. R., Rohena, L., & Gruber, R. (2001). Lowering the HIV risk among ethnic minority drug users: Comparing culturally targeted intervention to a standard intervention. *American Journal of Drug and Alcohol Abuse, 27*, 501–524.

Eber, C. (2001). "Take my water": Liberation through prohibition in San Pedro Chenalhó, Chiapas, Mexico. *Social Science and Medicine, 53*, 251–262.

Edwards, G. (2000a). *Alcohol: The ambiguous molecule*. London: Penguin.

Edwards, G. (2000b). Addiction treatment and the making of large claims. *Addiction, 95*, 1755–1757.

Edwards, G. (2000c). Editorial note: Natural recovery is the only recovery. *Addiction, 95*, 747.

Edwards, G., & Gross, M. M. (1976). Alcohol dependence: Provisional description of a clinical syndrome. *British Medical Journal, 1*, 1058–1061.

El-Bassel, N., Schilling, R. F., Irwin, K L., Faruque, S., Gilbert, L., Von Bargen, J., Serrano, Y., & Edlin, B. R. (1997). Sex trading and psychological distress among women recruited from the streets of Harlem. *American Journal of Public Health, 87*, 66–70.

el-Guebaly, N., & el-Guebaly, A. (1981). Alcohol abuse in ancient Egypt: The recorded evidence. *International Journal of the Addictions, 16*, 1207–1221.

Elster, J. (1999). *Strong feelings: Emotion, addiction, and human behavior*. Cambridge, MA: MIT Press.

Emboden, W. A. (1979). *Narcotic plants: Hallucinogens, stimulants, inebriants, and hypnotics, their origins and uses*. New York: Collier Books.

Emboden, W. A. (1981). Transcultural use of narcotic water lilies in ancient Egyptian and Maya drug ritual. *Journal of Ethnopharmacology, 3*, 39–83.

Ennett, S. T., Tobler, N. S., Ringwalt, C. L., & Flewelling, R. L. (1994). How effective is drug abuse resistance education? A meta-analysis of Project DARE outcome evaluations. *American Journal of Public Health, 84*, 1394–1401.

Epstein, J. A., Botvin, G. J., Baker, E. & Diaz, T. (1999). Impact of social influences and problem behavior on alcohol use among inner-city Hispanic and Black adolescents. *Journal of Studies on Alcohol, 60*, 595–604.

Erickson, P. G., & Butters, J. (1998). The emerging harm reduction movement: The de-escalation of the war on drugs. In E. L. Jensen & J. Gerber (Eds.), *The new war on drugs: Symbolic politics and criminal justice policy* (177–197). Highland Heights, KY: Academy of Criminal Justice Sciences.

Ervin, F. R., Palmour, R. M., Young, S. N., Guzman-Flores, C., Juarez, J. (1990). Voluntary consumption of beverage alcohol by vervet monkeys: Population screening, descriptive behavior and biochemical measures. *Pharmacology, Biochemistry and Behavior, 36*, 367–373.

Escohotado, A. (1996). *A brief history of drugs: From the stone age to the stoned age.* Rochester, VT: Park Street Press.

Evans, J. C. (1992). *Tea in China: The history of China's national drink.* New York: Greenwood Press.

Farrell, G. (1998). A global empirical review of drug crop eradication and United Nations' crop substitution and alternative development strategies. *Journal of Drug Issues, 28*, 395–436.

Federal Bureau of Investigation. (2000). *Crime in the United States: Uniform crime reports.* Washington, DC: U.S. Department of Justice.

Ferentzy, P. (2001). From sin to disease: Differences and similarities between past and current conceptions of chronic drunkenness. *Contemporary Drug Problems, 28*, 363–374.

Fernandez, H. (1998). *Heroin.* Center City, MN: Hazelden.

Fernandez, J. W. (1990). *Tabernathe iboga*: Narcotic ecstasies and the work of the ancestors. In P. T. Furst (Ed.), *Flesh of the gods: The ritual use of hallucinogens* (2nd ed.; 237–260). Prospect Heights, IL: Waveland Press Inc.

Field, N. (1992). The therapeutic function of altered states. *Journal of Analytical Psychology, 37*, 211–234.

Field, P. B. (1991). A new cross-cultural study of drunkenness. In D. J. Pittman & H. R. White (Eds.), *Society, culture, and drinking patterns re-examined* (32–61). New Brunswick, NJ: Rutgers Center of Alcohol Studies.

Fillmore, K. M. (2000). Is alcohol *really* good for the heart? *Addiction, 95*, 173–174.

Fillmore, M. T., Carscadden, J. L., & Vogel-Sprott, M. V. (1998). Alcohol, cognitive impairment and expectancies. *Journal of Studies on Alcohol, 59*, 174–179.

Finney, J. W., Moos, R. H., & Timko, C. (1999). The course of treated and untreated substance use disorders: Remission and resolution, relapse and mortality. In B. S. McCrady & E .E. Epstein (Eds.), *Addictions: A comprehensive guidebook* (30–49). New York: Oxford University Press.

Fleming, J., Watson, C., McDonald, D., & Alexander, K. (1991). Drug use patterns in Northern Territory Aboriginal communities 1986–1987. *Drug and Alcohol Review, 10*, 367–380.

Forsander, O. A. (1998). Dietary influences on alcohol intake: A review. *Journal of Studies on Alcohol, 59*, 26–31.

Forster, L. M. K., Tannhauser, M., & Barros, H. M. T. (1996). Drug use among street children in Southern Brazil. *Drug and Alcohol Dependence, 43,* 57–62.

Forsyth, A. J. M. (1996). Places and patterns of drug use in the Scottish dance scene. *Addiction, 91,* 511–521.

Forsyth, A. J. M., Barnard, M., & McKeganey, N. P. (1997). Musical preference as an indicator of adolescent drug use. *Addiction, 92,* 1317–1325.

Fox, B. S. (1997). Development of a therapeutic vaccine for the treatment of cocaine addiction. *Drug and Alcohol Dependence, 48,* 153–158.

Frank, B. (2000). An overview of heroin trends in New York City: Past, present and future. *Mount Sinai Journal of Medicine, 67,* 340–346.

Frank, J. W., Moore, R. S., & Ames, G. M. (2000). Historical and cultural roots of drinking problems among American Indians. *American Journal of Public Health, 90,* 344–351.

Free, M. D. (1997). The impact of federal sentencing reforms on African Americans. *Journal of Black Studies, 28,* 268–286.

French, L. A. (2000). *Addictions and Native Americans.* Westport, CT: Praeger.

French, R., & Power, R. (1998). A qualitative study of the social contextual use of alkyl nitrites (poppers) among targeted groups. *Journal of Drug Issues, 28,* 57–76.

Freud, S. (1884/1974). Über coca. In R. Byck (Ed.), *Cocaine papers* (49–73). New York: Stonehill.

Furst, P. T. (Ed.). (1990). *Flesh of the gods: The ritual use of hallucinogens.* Prospect Heights, IL: Waveland Press, Inc.

Furst, P. T. (1990). To find our life: Peyote among the Huichol Indians of Mexico. In P. T. Furst (Ed.), *Flesh of the gods: The ritual use of hallucinogens* (136–185). Prospect Heights, IL: Waveland Press, Inc.

Furst, P. T. (1995). "This little book of herbs": Psychoactive plants as therapeutic agents in the Badianus Manuscript of 1552. In R. E. Schultes & S. von Reis (Eds.), *Ethnobotany: Evolution of a discipline* (108–129). Portland, OR: Dioscorides Press.

Gable, R. S. (1993). Toward a comparative overview of dependence potential and acute toxicity of psychoactive substances used nonmedically. *American Journal of Drug and Alcohol Abuse, 19,* 263–281.

Galanter, M., & Kleber, H. D. (Eds.), (1999). *Textbook of substance abuse treatment* (2nd ed.). Washington, DC: American Psychiatric Press.

Gallant, D. (1999). Alcohol. In M. Galanter & H. D. Kleber (Eds.), *Textbook of substance abuse treatment* (2nd ed.; 151–165). Washington, DC: American Psychiatric Press.

Ganguly, K. K., Sharma, H. K., & Krishnamachari, K. A. V. R. (1995). An ethnographic account of opium consumers of Rajasthan (India): Socio-medical perspective. *Addiction, 90,* 9–12.

Gardner, E. L. (1999). Cannabinoid interaction with brain reward systems. In G. G. Nahas, K. M. Sutin, D. Harvey, & A. Stig (Eds.), *Marihuana and medicine.* (187–205). Totowa, NJ: Humana Press.

Geary, D.C. (2000). Evolution and proximate expression of human paternal investment. *Psychological Bulletin, 126,* 55-77.

Gelderloos, P., Walton, K. G., Orme-Johnson, D. W., & Alexander, C. N. (1991). Effectiveness of the transcendental meditation program in preventing and treating substance misuse: A review. *International Journal of the Addictions, 26*, 293–325.

Gerald, M. S., & Higley, J. D. (2002). Evolutionary underpinnings of excessive alcohol consumption. *Addiction, 97*, 415–425.

Gerrard, G. (1988). Use of kava in two Aboriginal settlements. In J. Prescott & G. McCall (Eds.), *Kava: Use and abuse in Australia and the South Pacific* (50–58). Kensington, NSW: National Alcohol and Drug Research Centre.

Giancola, P. R., & Tarter, R. E. (1999). What constitutes a drug of abuse? In R. T. Ammerman, P. J. Ott, & R. E. Tarter (Eds.), *Prevention and societal impact of drug and alcohol abuse* (21–28). Mahwah, NJ: Lawrence Erlbaum Associates.

Glantz, M. D., Weinberg, N. Z., Miner, L. L., & Colliver, J. D. (1999). The etiology of drug abuse: Mapping the paths. In M. D. Glantz & C. R. Hartel (Eds.), *Drug abuse: Origins and interventions*. Washington, DC: American Psychological Association.

Glassner, B. (1991). Jewish sobriety. In D. J. Pittman & H. R. White (Eds.), *Society, culture, and drinking patterns reexamined* (311–327). New Brunswick, NJ: Rutgers Center of Alcohol Studies.

Godfrey, C. (1997). Lost productivity and costs to society. *Addiction, 92*, S49–S54.

Goldman, D. (1993). Genetic transmission. In M. Galanter (Ed.), *Recent developments in alcoholism: Volume II*. New York: Plenum Press.

Goldman, L. K., & Glantz, S. A. (1998). Evaluation of antismoking advertising campaigns. *Journal of the American Medical Association, 279*, 772–777.

Goldman, M. S., Del Boca, F. K., & Darkes, J., (1999). Expectancy mediation of biopsychosocial risk for alcohol use and alcoholism. In I. Kirsch (Ed.), *How expectancies shape experience* (233–263). Washington, DC: American Psychological Association.

Goldstein, A. (1994). *Addiction: From biology to drug policy*. New York: W. H. Freeman & Co.

Goldstein, P. J., Ouellet, L. J., & Fendrich, M. (1992). From bags to skeezers: A historical perspective on sex-for-drugs behavior. *Journal of Psychoactive Drugs, 24*, 349–361.

Goodman, J. (1993). *Tobacco in history: The cultures of dependence*. London: Routledge.

Goodman, J. (1995). Excitantia: Or, how enlightenment Europe took to soft drugs. In J. Goodman, P. E. Lovejoy, & A. Sherratt (Eds.), *Consuming habits: Drugs in history and anthropology* (127–147). London: Routledge.

Gossop, M. (1995). Counting the costs as well as the benefits of drug control laws. *Addiction, 90*, 16–17.

Gossop, M., Griffiths, P., Powis, B., & Strang, J. (1992). Severity of dependence and route of administration of heroin, cocaine and amphetamines. *British Journal of Addiction, 87*, 1527–1536.

Gossop, M., Griffiths, P., Powis, B., & Strang, J. (1994). Cocaine: Patterns of use, route of administration, and severity of dependence. *British Journal of Psychiatry, 164*, 660–664.

Gossop, M. Marsden, J., Stewart, D., Edwards, C., Lehmann, P., Wilson, A., & Segar, G. (1997). The national treatment outcome research study in the United Kingdom: 6–month follow-up outcomes. *Psychology of Addictive Behaviors, 11*, 324–337.

Gostin, L. O. (2002). Corporate speech and the constitution: The deregulation of tobacco advertising. *American Journal of Public Health, 92*, 352–355.

Gotoh, M. (1994). Alcohol dependence of women in Japan. *Addiction, 89*, 953–954.

Gould, S.J. (1991). Exaptation: A crucial tool for evolutionary psychology. *Journal of Social Issues, 47*, 43–65.

Granfield, R., & Cloud, W. (1996). The elephant that no one sees: Natural recovery among middle-aged addicts. *Journal of Drug Issues, 26*, 45–61.

Grant, B. F. (1996). Prevalence and correlates of drug use and DSM-IV drug dependence in the United States: Results of the National Longitudinal Alcohol Epidemiologic Survey. *Journal of Substance Abuse, 8*, 195–210.

Grant, B. F., & Dawson, D. A. (1999). Alcohol and drug use, abuse, and dependence: Classification, prevalence, and comorbidity. In B. S. McCrady & E. E. Epstein (Eds.), *Addictions: A comprehensive guidebook* (9–29). New York: Oxford University Press.

Grant, M. (1984). Rereview of An Essay, Medical, Philosophical, and Chemical, on Drunkenness, and its Effects on the Human Body. *British Journal of Addiction, 79*, 121–122.

Gray, D., Saggers, S., Sputore, B., & Bourbon, D. (2000). What works? A review of evaluated alcohol misuse interventions among Aboriginal Australians. *Addiction, 95*, 11–22.

Greeley, J., & Oei, T. (1999). Alcohol and tension reduction. In K. E. Leonard & H. T. Blane (Eds.), *Psychological theories of drinking and alcoholism* (2nd ed.; 14–54). New York: Guilford Press.

Gregory, R. J., & Cawte, J. E. (1988). The principle of alien poisons: Contrasting psychopharmacology of kava in Oceania and Australia. In J. Prescott & G. McCall (Eds.), *Kava: Use and abuse in Australia and the South Pacific* (29–39). Kensington, NSW: National Alcohol and Drug Research Centre.

Griffiths, P., Gossop, M., Wickenden, S., Duntworth, J., Harris, K., & Lloyd, C. (1997). A transcultural pattern of drug use: Qat (khat) in the UK. *British Journal of Psychiatry, 170*, 281–284.

Grob, C., & Dobkin de Rios, M. (1992). Adolescent drug use in cross-cultural perspective. *Journal of Drug Issues, 22*, 121–138.

Grob, C. S., McKenna, D. J., Callaway, J. C., Brito, B. S. et al. (1996). Human psychopharmacology of Hoasca, a plant hallucinogen used in ritual context in Brazil. *Journal of Nervous and Mental Disease, 184*, 86–98.

Gual, A., & Colom, J. (1997). Why has alcohol consumption declined in countries of southern Europe? *Addiction, 92*, S21–S31.

Gureje, O., Vazquez-Barquero, J. L., & Janca, A. (1996). Comparisons of alcohol and other drugs: Experience from the WHO collaborative cross-cultural applicability research (CAR) study. *Addiction, 91*, 1529–1538.

Gusfield, J. R. (1991). *The culture of public problems: Drinking, driving and the symbolic order*. Chicago: University of Chicago Press.

Gutmann, M. C. (1999). Ethnicity, alcohol, and acculturation. *Social Science and Medicine, 48,* 173–184.

Gutzke, D. W. (1984). "The cry of the children": The Edwardian medical campaign against maternal drinking. *British Journal of Addiction, 79,* 71–84.

Hall, W. (1997). The recent Australian debate about the prohibition on cannabis use. *Addiction, 92,* 1109–1115.

Hanson, D. J. (1999). Historical overview of alcohol abuse. In R. T. Ammerman, P. J. Ott, & R. E. Tarter (Eds.), *Prevention and societal impact of drug and alcohol abuse* (31–45). Mahwah, NJ: Lawrence Erlbaum Associates.

Harper, F. D., & Saifnoorian, E. (1991). Drinking patterns among Black Americans. In D. J. Pittman & H. R. White (Eds.), *Society, culture, and drinking patterns re-examined* (327–337). New Brunswick, NJ: Rutgers Center of Alcohol Studies.

Hart, C. L., Smith, G. D., Hole, D. J., & Hawthorne, V. M. (1999). Alcohol consumption and mortality from all causes, coronary heart disease, and stroke: Results from a prospective cohort study of Scottish men with 21 years of follow up. *British Medical Journal, 318,* 1725–1729.

Hatsukami, D. K., & Fischman, M. W. (1996). Crack cocaine and cocaine hydrochloride: Are the differences myth or reality? *Journal of the American Medical Association, 276,* 1580–1588.

Hattox, R. S. (1985). *Coffee and coffeehouses: The origins of a social beverage in the medieval Near East.* Seattle: University of Washington Press.

Heath, D. B. (1989). The new temperance movement: Through the looking-glass. *Drugs and Society, 3,* 143–168.

Heath, D. B. (1990–1991). Uses and misuses of the concept of ethnicity in alcohol studies: An essay in deconstruction. *International Journal of the Addictions, 25,* 607–628.

Heath, D. B. (1991a). Drinking patterns of the Bolivian Camba (rev.). In D. J. Pittman & H. R. White (Eds.), *Society, culture, and drinking patterns re-examined* (62–77). New Brunswick, NJ: Rutgers Center of Alcohol Studies.

Heath, D. B. (1991b). Continuity and change in drinking patterns of the Bolivian Camba. In D. J. Pittman & H. R. White (Eds.), *Society, culture, and drinking patterns re-examined* (78–86). New Brunswick, NJ: Rutgers Center of Alcohol Studies.

Heath, D. B. (1994). Agricultural changes and drinking among the Bolivian Camba. *Human Organization, 53,* 357–361.

Heath, D. B. (1992). U.S. drug control policy: A cultural perspective. *Daedelus, 121,* 269–293.

Heath, D. B. (1999). Culture. In P. J. Ott, R. E. Tarter, & R. T. Ammerman (Eds.), *Sourcebook on substance abuse: Etiology, epidemiology, assessment, and treatment* (175–184). Boston: Allyn & Bacon.

Heath, D. B. (2000). *Drinking occasions: Comparative perspectives on alcohol and culture.* Brunner/Mazel: Taylor & Francis Group.

Heather, N., & Robertson, I. (1997). *Problem drinking* (3rd ed.) Oxford: Oxford University Press.

Helmer, J. (1975). *Drugs and minority oppression.* New York: The Seabury Press.

Hendry, J. (1994). Drinking and gender in Japan. In M. McDonald (Ed.), *Gender, drink, and drugs* (175–190). Oxford: Berg.

Herd, D. (1994). Predicting drinking problems among Black and White men: Results from a national survey. *Journal of Studies on Alcohol, 55,* 61–71.

Herd, D. (1997). Racial differences in women's drinking norms and drinking patterns: A national study. *Journal of Substance Abuse, 9,* 137–149.

Hernstein, R. J. (1990). Rational choice theory: Necessary but not sufficient. *American Psychologist, 45,* 356–367.

Hesselbrock, M. N., Hesselbrock V. M., & Epstein, E. E. (1999). Theories of etiology of alcohol and other drug use disorders. In B. S. McCrady & E .E. Epstein (Eds), *Addictions.* New York: Oxford University Press.

Hicks, J. J. (2001). The strategy behind Florida's "truth" campaign. *Tobacco Control, 10,* 3–6.

Higuchi, S., Matsushita, S., Mazeki, H., Kinoshita, T., Takagi, S., & Kono, H. (1994). Aldehyde dehydrogenase genotypes in Japanese alcoholics. *Lancet, 343,* 741–742

Higuchi, S., Matsushita, S., Murayama, M., Takagi, S., & Hayashida, M. (1995). Alcohol and aldehyde dehydrogenase polymorphisms and the risk for alcoholism. *American Journal of Psychiatry, 152,* 1219–1221.

Hill, E.M., & Chow, K. (2002). Life-history theory and risky drinking. *Addiction, 97,* 401–413.

Hill, E. M., & Newlin, D. B. (2002). Evolutionary approaches to addiction: Introduction. *Addiction, 97,* 375–379.

Hill, E. M., Ross, L. T., & Low, B. S. (1997). The role of future unpredictability in human risk-taking. *Human Nature, 8,* 287–325.

Hill, T. W. (1990). Peyotism and the control of heavy drinking: The Nebraska Winnebago in the early 1900s. *Human Organization, 49,* 255–265.

Hillhouse, M. P., & Fiorentine, R. (2001). 12–step program participation and effectiveness: Do gender and ethnic differences exist? *Journal of Drug Issues, 31,* 767–780.

Hirsch, E. (1995). Efficacy and concentration: Analogies in betel use among the Fuyuge (Papua New Guinea). In J. Goodman, P. E. Lovejoy, & A. Sherratt (Eds.), *Consuming habits: Drugs in history and anthropology* (88–102). London: Routledge.

Hops, H., Andrews, J. A., Duncan, S. C., Duncan, T. E. & Tildesley, E. (2000). Adolescent drug use development: A social interactional and contextual perspective. In A. J. Sameroff, M. Lewis, & S. M. Miller (Eds.), *Handbook of developmental psychopathology* (2nd ed.; 589–605). New York: Kluwer Academic.

Horton, D. (1991). Alcohol use in primitive societies. In D. J. Pittman & H. R. White (Eds.), *Society, culture, and drinking patterns re-examined* (7–31). New Brunswick, NJ: Rutgers Center of Alcohol Studies.

Hughes, J. C., & Cook, C. C. H. (1997). The efficacy of disulfiram: A review of outcome studies. *Addiction, 92,* 381–395.

Hughes, R. (1987). *The fatal shore: A history of the transportation of convicts to Australia, 1787–1868.* London: The Harvill Press.

Hugh-Jones, S. (1995). Coca, beer, cigars and yagé: Meals and anti-meals in an Amerindian community. In J. Goodman, P. E. Lovejoy, & A. Sherratt (Eds.),

Consuming habits: Drugs in history and anthropology (47–67). London: Routledge.

Hunt, G., & Barker, J. C. (2001). Socio-cultural anthropology and alcohol and drug research: Towards a unified theory. *Social Science and Medicine, 53,* 165–188.

Hunter, E. (1992). Aboriginal alcohol use: A review of quantitative studies. *Journal of Drug Issues, 22,* 713–731.

Huriwai, T., Robertson, P.J., Armstrong, D., & Huata, P. (2001). Whanaungatanga—A process in the treatment of Maori with alcohol and drug use related problems. *Substance Use and Misuse, 36,* 1033–1051.

Husak, D. N. (1992). *Drugs and rights.* Cambridge: Cambridge University Press.

Hutt, M. (1999). *Maori and alcohol: A history.* Wellington: Health Services Research Centre.

Ikuesan, B. A. (1994). Drinking problems and the position of women in Nigeria. *Addiction, 89,* 941–944.

Iverson, L. L. (2000). *The science of marijuana.* Oxford: Oxford University Press.

Jaffe, J. (1983). What counts as a drug problem? In G. Edwards, A. Arif, & J. Jaffe (Eds.), *Drug use and misuse: Cultural perspectives* (101–111). London: Groom & Helm.

James I (1616/1971). A counterblaste to tobacco. In, *The workes of the most high and mighty prince, James.* Hildesheim: Georg Olms Verlag.

Jankowiak, W., & Bradburd, D. (1996). Using drug foods to capture and enhance labor performance: A cross-cultural perspective. *Current Anthropology, 37,* 717–720.

Jansen, K. L. R. (2000). A review of the nonmedical use of ketamine: Use, users and consequences. *Journal of Psychoactive Drugs, 32,* 419–433.

Jansen, M. A., Glynn, T., & Howard, J. (1996). Prevention of alcohol, tobacco and other drug abuse. *American Behavioral Scientist, 39,* 790–807.

Jellinek, E. M. (1960). *The disease concept of alcoholism.* New Haven: Hillhouse Press.

Jellinek, E. M. (1976). Drinkers and alcoholics in ancient Rome. *Journal of Studies on Alcohol, 37,* 1718–1741.

Jenkins, J. E., & Zunguze, S. T. (1998). The relationship of family structure to adolescent drug use, peer affiliation, and perception of peer acceptance of drug use. *Adolescence, 33,* 811–822.

Jenkins, R. (1997). *Rethinking ethnicity: Arguments and explorations.* London: Sage Publications.

Jensen, E. L., & Gerber, J. (1998). The social construction of drug problems: An historical overview. In E. L. Jensen & J. Gerber (Eds.), *The new war on drugs: Symbolic politics and criminal justice policy* (1–23). Highland Heights, KY: Academy of Criminal Justice Sciences.

Jilek, W. G. (1989). Therapeutic use of altered states of consciousness in contemporary North American Indian dance ceremonials. In C. A. Ward (Ed.), *Altered states of consciousness and mental health: A cross-cultural perspective* (167–185). Newbury Park, CA: Sage Publications.

Johnson, C. A., Farquhar, J. W., & Sussman, S. (1996). Methodological and substantive issues in substance abuse prevention research. *American Behavioral Scientist, 39,* 935–942.

Johnston, L. D., O'Malley, P., & Bachman, J. G. (1996). National survey results on drug use from the monitoring the future study, 1975–1995. Washington DC: USGPO.

Jones, B. T., Corbin, W., & Fromme, K. (2001). Conceptualizing addiction: A review of expectancy theory and alcohol consumption. *Addiction, 96,* 57–72.

Jonnes, J. (1996). *Hep-cats, narcs, and pipe dreams: A history of America's romance with illegal drugs.* Baltimore: John Hopkins University Press.

Julien, R. M. (1998). *A primer of drug action* (8th ed.). New York: W. H. Freeman and Company.

Kagan, R. A., & Nelson, W. P. (2001). The politics on tobacco regulation in the United States. In R. L. Rabin & S. D. Sugarman (Eds.), *Regulating tobacco* (11–39). Oxford: Oxford University Press.

Kahn, M. W., Hunter, E., Heather, N., & Tebbutt, J. (1990). Australian Aborigines and alcohol: A review. *Drug and Alcohol Review, 10,* 351–366.

Kalix, P. (1992). Chewing khat, an old drug habit that is new in Europe. *International Journal of Risk and Safety in Medicine, 3,* 143–156.

Kandel, D. B. (1995). Ethnic differences in drug use: Patterns and paradoxes. In G. J. Botvin, S. Schinke, & M. A. Orlandi (Eds.), *Drug abuse prevention with multiethnic youth* (81–105). Thousand Oaks, CA: Sage Publications.

Kandel, D. B. (1998). Persistent themes and new perspectives on adolescent substance use: A lifespan perspective. In R. Jessor (Ed.), *New perspectives on adolescent risk behavior* (44-89). Cambridge: Cambridge University Press.

Kandel, D. B., & Chen, K. (1995). The natural history of drug use in a general population sample from adolescence to the mid-thirties. *American Journal of Public Health, 85,* 41–47.

Kandel, D. B., Chen, K., Warner, L. A., Kessler, R. C., & Grant, B. (1997). Prevalence and demographic correlates of symptoms of last year dependence on alcohol, nicotine, marijuana and cocaine in the U.S. population. *Drug and Alcohol Dependence, 44,* 11–29.

Kandel, D. B., & Yamaguchi, K. (1999). Developmental stages of involvement in substance use. In P. J. Ott, R. E. Tarter, & R. T. Ammerman (Eds.), *Sourcebook on substance abuse: Etiology, epidemiology, assessment, and treatment* (50–75). Boston: Allyn & Bacon.

Kaplan, H. I., & Sadock, B. J. (1998). *Synopsis of psychiatry* (8th ed.). Philadelphia: Lippincott Williams & Wilkins.

Karch, S. B. (1998). *A brief history of cocaine.* Boca Raton, FL: CRC Press.

Katz, S. H., & Voigt, M. M. (1986). Bread and beer: The early use of cereals in the human diet. *Expedition, 28,* 23–34.

Keefe, K., & Newcomb, M. D. (1996). Demographic and psychosocial risk for alcohol use: Ethnic differences. *Journal of Studies on Alcohol, 57,* 521–530.

Kellert, S. R., & Wilson, E. O. (Eds.) (1993). *The biophilia hypothesis.* Washington, DC: Shearwater Books.

Kendler, K. S., Prescott, C. A., Neale, M. C., & Pedersen, N. L. (1997). Temperance board registration for alcohol abuse in a national sample of Swedish male twins, born 1902–1949. *Archives of General Psychiatry, 54,* 178–184.

Kennedy, J. G. (1987). *The flower of paradise: The institutionalized use of the drug qat in North Yemen.* Dordrecht: D. Reidel Publishing Company.

Kessler, R. C., Crum, R. M., Warner, L. A., Nelson, C. B., Schulenberg, J., & Anthony, J. C. (1997). Lifetime co-occurrence of DSM-III-R alcohol abuse and dependence with other psychiatric disorders in the National Comorbidity Survey. *Archives on General Psychiatry, 54,* 313–321.

Kessler, R. C., McGonagle, K. A., Zhao, S., Nelson, C. B., Hughes, M., Eshleman, S., Wittchen, H., & Kendler, K. S. (1994). Lifetime and 12–month prevalence of DSM-III-R psychiatric disorders in the United States. *Archives on General Psychiatry, 51,* 8–19.

Kessler, R. C., Mickleson, K. D., & Williams, D. R. (1999). The prevalence, distribution, and mental health correlates of perceived discrimination in the United States. *Journal of Health and Social Behavior, 40,* 208–230.

Khantzian, E. J. (1995). Alcoholics Anonymous—Cult or corrective: A case study. *Journal of Substance Abuse Treatment, 12,* 157–165.

Khantzian, E. J. (1997). The self-medication hypothesis of substance use disorders: A reconsideration and recent applications. *Harvard Review of Psychiatry, 4,* 231–244.

Kielhorn, F-W. (1996). The history of alcoholism: Brühl-Cramer's concepts and observations. *Addiction, 91,* 121–128.

Kilham, C. (1996). *Kava: Medicine hunting in paradise.* Rochester, VT: Park St. Press.

Kirmayer, L. J. (1991). The place of culture in psychiatric nosology: Taijin kyofusho and DSM-III-R. *Journal of Nervous and Mental Disorder, 179,* 19–28.

Kirsch, I. (1997). Response expectancy theory and application: A decennial review. *Applied and Preventive Psychology, 6,* 69–79.

Kitcher, P. (1985). Two approaches to explanation. *Journal of Philosophy,* 633–637.

Kitcher, P. (1989). Explanatory unification and the causal structure of the world. In P. Kitcher & W. C. Salmon (Eds.), *Scientific explanation* (410–507). Minneapolis: University of Minnesota Press.

Kitcher, P. (1996). *The lives to come: The genetic revolution and human possibilities.* New York: Simon & Schuster.

Klingemann, H. (1998). Harm reduction and abstinence: Swiss drug policy at a time of transition. In H. Klingemann & G. Hunt (Eds.), *Drug treatment systems in an international perspective: Drugs, demons, and delinquents* (94–111). Thousand Oaks, CA: Sage Publications.

Klingemann, H., & Hunt, G. (Eds.) (1998). *Drug treatment systems in an international perspective: Drugs, demons, and delinquents.* Thousand Oaks, CA: Sage Publications.

Knipe, E. (1995). *Culture, society, and drugs: The social science approach to drug use.* Prospect Heights, IL: Waveland Press, Inc.

Kohn, M. (1992). *Dope girls: The birth of the British drug underground.* London: Granta Books.

Konuma, K., Shimizu, S., & Koyanagi, T. (1998). Societal control and the model of legal drug treatment: A Japanese success story? In H. Klingemann & G. Hunt (Eds.), *Drug treatment systems in an international perspective: Drugs, demons, and delinquents* (239–252). Thousand Oaks, CA: Sage Publications, Inc.

Koob, G. F., Caine, S. B., Hyytia, P., Markou, A., Parsons, L. H., Roberts, A. J., Schulteis, G., & Weiss, F. (1999). Neurobiology of drug addiction. In

M. D. Glantz & C. R. Hartel (Eds.), *Drug abuse: Origins and interventions* (161–190). Washington, DC: APA Press.

Koob, G. F., & Le Moal, M. (1997). Drug abuse: Hedonic homeostatic dysregulation. *Science, 278,* 52–58.

Kosten, T. R. (1998). Addiction as a brain disease. *American Journal of Psychiatry, 155,* 711–713.

Kreek, M. J., & Koob, G. F. (1998). Drug dependence: Stress and dysregulation of brain reward pathways. *Drug and Alcohol Dependence, 51,* 49–60.

Krivo, L. J., & Peterson, R. D. (1996). Extremely disadvantaged neighborhoods and urban crime. *Social Forces, 75,* 619–650.

Krohn, M. D., Lizotte, A. J., Thornberry, T. P., Smith, C., & McDowall, D. (1996). Reciprocal causal relationships among drug use, peers, and beliefs: A five-wave panel model. *Journal of Drug Issues, 26,* 405–428.

Kua, E. H. (1994). Chinese women who drink. *Addiction, 89,* 956–957.

La Barre, W. (1990). Hallucinogens and the shamanic origins of religion. In P. T. Furst (Ed.), *Flesh of the gods: The ritual use of hallucinogens* (2nd ed.; 261–279). London: George Allen & Unwin.

Langenbucher, J., Morgenstern, J., Labouvie, E., & Nathan, P. E. (1994a). Diagnostic concordance of substance use disorders in DSM-III, DSM-IV and ICD-10. *Drug and Alcohol Dependence, 36,* 193–203.

Langenbucher, J., Morgenstern, J., Labouvie, E., & Nathan, P. E. (1994b). Lifetime DSM-IV diagnosis of alcohol, cannabis, cocaine and opiate dependence: Six-month reliability in a multi-site clinical sample. *Addiction, 89,* 1115–1127.

Langton, M. (1993). Rum, seduction and death: "Aboriginality" and alcohol. *Oceania, 63,* 195–206.

LaVeist, T. A. (1993). Segregation, poverty and empowerment: Health consequences for African Americans. *Milbank Quarterly, 71,* 41–64.

Lebot, V., Merlin, M., & Lindstrom, L. (1992). *Kava: The pacific drug.* New Haven: Yale University Press.

Lee, M. A., & Shlain, B. (1985). *Acid dreams: The complete social history of LSD: The CIA, the sixties, and beyond.* New York: Grove Press.

Le Fanu, J. (1999). *The rise and fall of modern medicine.* London: Abacus.

Leischow, S. J., Ranger-Moore, J., & Lawrence, D. (2000). Addressing social and cultural disparities in tobacco use. *Addictive Behaviors, 25,* 821–831.

Lemert, E. M. (1958). The use of alcohol in three Salish tribes. *Quarterly Journal of Studies on Alcohol, 19,* 90–107.

Lemert, E. M. (1964). Forms and pathology of drinking in three Polynesian societies. *American Anthropologist, 66,* 361–374.

Lende, D. H., & Smith, E. O. (2002). Evolution meets biopsychosociality: An analysis of addictive behavior. *Addiction, 97,* 447–458.

Lenton, S. (2000). Cannabis policy and the burden of proof: Is it now beyond doubt that cannabis prohibition is not working? *Drug and Alcohol Review, 19,* 95–100.

Lenton, S., Boys, A., & Norcross, K. (1997). Raves, drugs and experiences: Drug use by a sample of people who attended raves in Western Australia. *Addiction, 92,* 1327–1337.

Leshner, A. I. (1997). Addiction is a brain disease, and it matters. *Science, 273*, 45–47.

Leshner, A. I. (1999a). Science is revolutionizing our view of addiction—and what to do about it. *American Journal of Psychiatry, 156*, 1–3.

Leshner, A. I. (1999b). We can conquer drug addiction. *The Futurist*, November, 22–25.

Levine, H. G. (1979). The discovery of addiction: Changing conceptions of habitual drunkenness in America. *Journal of Studies on Alcohol, 15*, 493–506.

Levine, H. G. (1984). The alcohol problem in America: From temperance to alcoholism. *British Journal of Addiction, 79*, 109–119.

Lewin, L. (1924/1974). Cocainism. In R. Byck (Ed.), *Cocaine papers* (239–251). New York: Stonehill.

Lewis-Williams, J. D., & Dowson, T. A. (1988). The sign of all times: Entoptic phenomena in Upper Paleolithic art. *Current Anthropology, 29*, 201–217.

Lewontin, R. C., Rose, S., & Kamin, L. J. (1984). *Not in our genes: Biology, ideology, and human nature.* New York: Pantheon.

Li, H. Z., & Rosenblood, L. (1994). Exploring factors influencing alcohol consumption patterns among Chinese and Caucasians. *Journal of Studies on Alcohol, 55*, 427–433.

Lin, K-M., & Poland, R. E. (1995). Ethnicity, culture, and psychopharmacology. In F. E. Bloom & D. J. Kupfer (Eds.), *Psychopharmacology: The fourth generation of progress* (1907–1917). New York: Raven Press Ltd.

Ling, W., Huber, A., & Rawson, R. A. (2001). New trends in opiate pharmacotherapy. *Drug and Alcohol Review, 20*, 79–94.

Lock, M. (1993). The concept of race: An ideological construct. *Transcultural Psychiatric Research Review, 30*, 203–227.

Longabaugh, R., Wirtz, P. W., Zweben, A., & Stout, R. L. (1998). Network support for drinking, Alcoholics Anonymous and long-term matching effects. *Addiction, 93*, 1313–1333.

Lovejoy, P. E. (1995). Kola nuts: The "coffee" of the central Sudan. In J. Goodman, P. E. Lovejoy, & A. Sherratt (Eds.), *Consuming habits: Drugs in history and anthropology* (103–125). London: Routledge.

Lusane, C. (1994). In perpetual motion: The continuing significance of race and America's drug crisis. *Chicago Legal Forum, 25*, 83–106.

Ma, G. X., & Shive, S. (2000). A comparative analysis of perceived risks and substance abuse among ethnic groups. *Addictive Behaviors, 25*, 361–371.

MacAndrew, C., & Edgerton, R. B. (1969). *Drunken comportment: A social explanation.* Chicago: Aldine.

MacCleod, M. J. (2000). Beer and ale. In K. F. Kiple & K. C. Ornelas (Eds.), *The Cambridge world history of food* (619–640). Cambridge: Cambridge University Press.

MacCoun, R. J., & Caulkins, J. (1996). Examining the behavioral assumptions of the National Drug Control Strategy. In W. K. Bickel & R. J. DeGrandpre (Eds.), *Drug policy and human nature: Psychological perspectives on the prevention, management, and treatment of illicit drug abuse* (177–197). New York: Plenum Press.

MacCoun, R. J., & Reuter, P. (2001). *Drug war heresies: Learning from other vices, times, and places.* Cambridge: Cambridge University Press.

MacDonald, D. (1996). Drugs in Southern Africa: An overview. *Drugs: Education, Prevention, and Policy, 3,* 127–144.

MacGregor, S., & Smith, L. (1998). The English drug treatment system: Experimentation or pragmatism? In H. Klingemann & G. Hunt (Eds.), *Drug treatment systems in an international perspective: Drugs, demons, and delinquents* (69–80). Thousand Oaks, CA: Sage Publications.

Maddux, J. F., & Desmond, D. P. (2000). Addiction or dependence? *Addiction, 95,* 661–665.

Maisto, S. A., Carey, K. B., Bradizza, C. M. (1999). Social learning theory. In K. E. Leonard & H. T. Blane (Eds.), *Psychological theories of drinking and alcoholism* (2nd ed.; 106–164). New York: Guilford Press.

Mäkelä, K. (1983). The uses of alcohol and their cultural regulation. *Acta Sociologica, 26,* 21–31.

Mancall, P. C. (1995). *Deadly medicine: Indians and alcohol in early America.* Ithaca: Cornell University Press.

Mancall, P. C. (2000). "The bewitching tyranny of custom": The social costs of Indian drinking in colonial America. In P. C. Mancall & J. H. Merrell (Eds.), *American encounters: Natives and newcomers from European contact to Indian removal—1500–1800* (195–215). New York: Routledge.

Mancall, P. C., Robertson, P., & Huriwai, T. (2000). Maori and alcohol: a reconsidered history. *Australian and New Zealand Journal of Psychiatry, 34,* 129–134.

Mandelbaum, D. G. (1965). Alcohol and culture. *Current Anthropology, 6,* 281–294.

Manderson, D. (1993). *From Mr Sin to Mr Big: A history of Australian drug laws.* Melbourne: Oxford University Press.

Manderson, D. (1999). Symbolism and racism in drug history and policy. *Drug and Alcohol Review, 18,* 179–186.

Mangini, M. (1998). Treatment of alcoholism using psychedelic drugs: A review of the program of research. *Journal of Psychoactive Drugs, 30,* 381–418.

Margolis, R. D., & Zweben, J. E. (1998). *Treating patients with alcohol and other drug problems: An integrated approach.* Washington, DC: American Psychological Association.

Marin, G. (1996). Expectancies for drinking and excessive drinking among Mexican American and non-Hispanic whites. *Addictive Behaviors, 21,* 491–507.

Marin, G., & Posner, S. F. (1995). The role of gender and acculturation on determining the consumption of alcoholic beverages among Mexican-Americans and Central Americans in the United States. *International Journal of the Addictions, 30,* 779–794.

Marinangeli, P. (2001). Italian culture and its impact on addiction. In S. L. A. Straussner (Ed.), *Ethnocultural factors in substance abuse treatment* (216–233). New York: Guilford Press.

Marmot, M. (1997). Inequality, deprivation and alcohol use. *Addiction, 92,* S13–S20.

Mars, G. (1987). Longshore drinking, economic security and union politics in Newfoundland. In M. Douglas (Ed.), *Constructive drinking: Perspectives from anthropology* (91–101). Cambridge: Cambridge University Press.

Marshall, M. (1987). An overview of drugs in Oceania. In L. Lindstrom (Ed.), *Drugs in Western Pacific societies* (13–49). Lanham, MD: University Press of America.

Marshall, M. (1991). The second fatal impact: Cigarette smoking, chronic disease, and the epidemiological transition in Oceania. *Social Science and Medicine, 33,* 1327–1342.

Marshall, M., Ames, G. M., & Bennett, L. A. (2001). Anthropological perspectives on alcohol and drugs at the turn of the new millennium. *Social Science and Medicine, 53,* 153–164.

Martensen, R. L. (1994). Alcoholism (JAMA 100 years ago . . . in perspective). *Journal of the American Medical Association, 272,* 1895–1896.

Marwick, A. (1989). *The nature of history* (3rd ed.). Chicago: Lyceum Books.

Matsuyoshi, J. (2001). Substance abuse interventions for Japanese and Japanese American clients. In S. L. A. Straussner (Ed.), *Ethnocultural factors in substance abuse treatment* (393–417). New York: The Guilford Press.

Matthee, R. (1995). Exotic substances: The introduction and global spread of tobacco, coffee, cocoa, tea, and distilled liquor, sixteenth to eighteenth centuries. In R. Porter & M. Teich (Eds.), *Drugs and narcotics in history* (24–51). Cambridge: Cambridge University Press.

Maxwell, J. C. (2001). Changes in drug use in Australia and the United States: Results from the 1995 and 1998 National Household Surveys. *Drug and Alcohol Review, 20,* 37–48.

Maxwell, N. (1984). *From knowledge to wisdom: A revolution in the aims and methods of science.* New York: Basil Blackwell.

May, P. A. (1986). Alcohol and drug misuse prevention programs for American Indians: Needs and opportunities. *Journal of Studies on Alcohol, 47,* 187–195.

McCandless, P. (1984). "Curses of civilization": Insanity and drunkenness in Victorian Britain. *British Journal of Addiction, 79,* 49–58.

McCauley, R. N. (1996). Explanatory pluralism and the co-evolution of theories in science. In R. N. McCauley (Ed.), *The Churchlands and their critics* (17–47). Cambridge, MA: Blackwell.

McCoy, A. W. (1992). *The politics of heroin: CIA complicity in the global drug trade.* New York: Lawrence Hill Books.

McDonald, D., & Jowitt, A. (2000). Kava in the Pacific Islands: A contemporary drug of abuse. *Drug and Alcohol Review, 19,* 217–227.

McElduff, P., & Dobson, A. J. (1997). How much alcohol and how often? Population based case-control study of alcohol consumption and risk of a major coronary event. *British Medical Journal, 314,* 1159–1164.

McGeorge, J., & Aitken, C. K. (1997). Effects of cannabis decriminalization in the Australian Capital Territory on University students' patterns of use. *Journal of Drug Issues, 27,* 785–793.

McGue, M. (1999). Behavioral genetic models of alcoholism and drinking. In K. E. Leonard & H. T. Blane (Eds.), *Psychological theories of drinking and alcoholism* (2nd ed.). New York: The Guilford Press.

McKenna, D. J., Luna, L. E., & Towers, G. N. (1995). Biodynamic constituents in ayahuasca admixture plants: An uninvestigated folk pharmacopoeia. In R. E. Schultes & V. Ries (Eds.), *Ethnobotany: Evolution of a discipline* (349–361). Portland, OR: Dioscorides Press.

McLaughlin, D. K., & Stokes, S. (2002). Income inequality and mortality in US counties: Does minority racial concentration matter. *American Journal of Public Health, 92,* 99–104.

McPeake, J. D., Kennedy, B. P., & Gordon, S. M. G. (1991). Altered states of consciousness therapy: A missing component in alcohol and drug rehabilitation treatment. *Journal of Substance Abuse Treatment, 8,* 75–82.

Measham, F., Parker, H., & Aldridge, J. (1998). The teenage transition: From adolescent recreational drug use to the young adult dance culture in Britain in the mid-1990s. *Journal of Drug Issues, 28,* 9–32.

Medina-Mora, M. E. (1994). Drinking and the oppression of women: The Mexican experience. *Addiction, 89,* 958–960.

Medina-Mora, M. E., Borges, G., & Villatoro, J. (2000). The measurement of drinking patterns and consequences in Mexico. *Journal of Substance Abuse, 12,* 183–197.

Merikangas, K. R., & Avenevoli, S. (2000). Implications of genetic epidemiology for the prevention of substance use disorders. *Addictive Behaviors, 25,* 807–820.

Midanak, L., & Room, R. (1992). The epidemiology of alcohol consumption. *Alcohol Health and Research World, 16,* 183–190.

Midford, R. (2000). Does drug education work? *Drug and Alcohol Review, 19,* 441–446.

Miller, M., & Draper, G. (2001). *Statistics on drug use in Australia 2000.* AIHW cat No. PHE 30. Canberra: Australian Institute of Health and Welfare.

Miller, W. E. (1997). Intoxicated lepidopterans: How is their fitness affected, and why do they tipple? *Journal of the Lepidopterists' Society, 51,* 277–287.

Miller, W. R. (1998a). Why do people change addictive behaviour? The 1996 H. David Archibald lecture. *Addiction, 93,* 163–172.

Miller, W. R. (1998b). Researching the spiritual dimensions of alcohol and other drug problems. *Addiction, 93,* 979–990.

Miller, W. R., Walters, S. T., & Bennett, M. E. (2001). How effective is alcoholism treatment in the United States? *Journal of Studies on Alcohol, 62,* 211–220.

Milton, K. (1987). Primate diet and gut morphology: Implications for hominid evolution. In M. Harris & E. B. Ross (Eds.), *Food and evolution: Toward a theory of human food habits* (93–117). Philadelphia: Temple University Press.

Miron, J. A., & Zwiebel, J. (1995). The economic case against drug prohibition. *Journal of Economic Perspectives, 9,* 175–192.

Moncrieff, J., & Drummond, C. (1997). New drug treatments for alcohol problems: A critical appraisal. *Addiction, 92,* 939–947.

Montagu, A. (1964). The concept of race in the human species in the light of genetics. In A. Montagu (Ed.), *The concept of race* (12–29). New York: The Free Press.

Morales, E. (1990–1991). Coca and cocaine in Peru: An international policy assessment. *International Journal of the Addictions, 25,* 295–316.

Moyers, T., & Hester, R. K. (1999). Outcome research: Alcoholism. In M. Galanter & H. D. Kleber (Eds.), *Textbook of substance abuse treatment* (2nd ed.; 129–135). Washington, DC: American Psychiatric Press.

Mphi, M. (1994). Female alcoholism problems in Lesotho. *Addiction, 89,* 945–949.

Mudde, A. N., & De Vries, H. (1999). The research and effectiveness of a national mass media-led smoking cessation campaign in the Netherlands. *American Journal of Public Health, 89,* 346–350.

Murphy, D., & Stich, S. (2000). Darwin in the madhouse: Evolutionary psychology and the classification of mental disorders. In P. Carruthers & A. Chamberlain (Eds.), *Evolution and the human mind: Modularity, language and meta-cognition* (62–92). Cambridge: Cambridge University Press.

Murphy, S. B., & Rosenbaum, M. (1997). Two women who used cocaine too much: Class, race, gender, crack, and coke. In C. Reinarman & H. G. Levine (Eds.), *Crack in America: Demon drugs and social justice* (98–113). Berkeley: University of California Press.

Musto, D. F. (1974). A study in cocaine. In R. Byck (Ed.), *Cocaine papers* (357–370). New York: Stonehill.

Musto, D. F. (1991). Opium, cocaine, and marijuana in American history. *Scientific American,* July, 20–27.

Musto, D. F. (1999). *The American disease: Origins of narcotic control* (3rd ed.). New York: Oxford University Press.

Nabuzoka, D., & Badhadhe, F. A. (2000). Use and perceptions of khat among young Somalis in a UK city. *Addiction Research, 8,* 5–26.

Nadelmann, E. A. (1989). Drug prohibition in the United States: Costs, consequences, and alternatives. *Science, 245,* 939–947.

Nahas, G. G. (1973). *Marihuana: Deceptive weed.* New York: Raven Press.

Nahas, G. G. (1976). *Keep off the grass.* New York: Readers Digest Press.

Nathan, P. E., Skinstad, A. H., & Langenbucher, J. W. (1999). Substance abuse: Diagnosis, comorbidity, and psychopathology. In T. Millon, P. H. Blaney, & R. D. Davis (Eds.), *Oxford textbook of psychopathology* (227–248). New York: Oxford University Press.

Nencini, P., & Ahmed, A. M. (1989). Khat consumption: A pharmacological review. *Drug and Alcohol Dependence, 23,* 19–29.

Nesse, R. M. (1990). Evolutionary explanations of emotions. *Human Nature, 1,* 261–289.

Nesse, R. M. (1994). An evolutionary perspective on substance abuse. *Ethology and Sociobiology, 15,* 339–348.

Nesse, R. M. (2002). Evolution and addiction. *Addiction, 97,* 470–471.

Nesse, R. M., & Berridge, K. C. (1997). Psychoactive drug use in evolutionary perspective. *Science, 278,* 63–66.

Netting, R. (1964). Beer as a locus of value among the West African Koyfar. *American Anthropologist, 66,* 375–384.

Neumark, Y. D., Friedlander, Y., Thomasson, H. R., & Li, T-K. (1998). Association of the ADH2*2 allele with reduced ethanol consumption in Jewish men in Israel: A pilot study. *Journal of Studies on Alcohol, 59,* 133–139.

Neve, R. J. M., Lemmens, P. H., & Drop, M. J. (1997). Gender differences in alcohol use and alcohol problems: Mediation by social roles and gender-role attitudes. *Substance Use and Misuse, 32,* 1439–1459.

Newlin, D. B. (2002). The self-perceived survival ability and reproductive fitness (SPFit) theory of substance use disorders. *Addiction, 97,* 427–445.

Newman, J. L. (2000). Wine. In K. F. Kiple & K. C. Ornelas (Eds.), *The Cambridge world history of food* (730–737). Cambridge: Cambridge University Press.

New Zealand Health Information Service (2001). *New Zealand drug statistics.* Wellington: Ministry of Health.

Norström, T. (2001). Per capita alcohol consumption and all-cause mortality in 14 European countries. *Addiction, 96,* S113–S128.

Obot, I. S. (2000). The measurement of drinking patterns and alcohol related problems in Nigeria. *Journal of Substance Abuse, 12*, 169–183.

O'Brien, C. P. O. (1996). Recent developments in the pharmacotherapy of substance abuse. *Journal of Consulting and Clinical Psychology, 64*, 677–686.

Ockene, J. K., Kristeller, J. L., & Donnelly, G. (1999). Tobacco. In M. Galanter & H. D. Kleber (Eds.), *Textbook of substance abuse treatment* (2nd ed.; 215–239). Washington, DC: American Psychiatric Press.

O'Dwyer, P. (2001). The Irish and substance abuse. In S. L. A. Straussner (Ed.), *Ethnocultural factors in substance abuse treatment* (199–215). New York: The Guilford Press.

Oetting, E. R., Donnermeyer, J. F., Trimble, J. E., & Beauvais, F. (1998). Primary socialization theory: Culture, ethnicity, and cultural identification. The links between culture and substance use IV. *Substance Use and Misuse, 33*, 2075–2107.

Olds, J., & Milner, P. M. (1954). Positive reinforcement produced by electrical stimulation of septal area and other regions of rat brain. *Journal of Comparative and Physiological Psychology, 47*, 419–427.

Olsen, E. (1992). Towards a new society. In G. W. Rice (Ed.), *The Oxford history of New Zealand* (254–285). Auckland: Oxford University Press.

O'Malley, P. M., Johnston, L. D., & Bachman, J. G. (1999). Epidemiology of substance abuse in adolescence. In P. J. Ott, R. E. Tarter, & R. T. Ammerman (Eds.), *Sourcebook on substance abuse: Etiology, epidemiology, assessment, and treatment* (14–32). Boston: Allyn & Bacon.

Ong, E. K., & Glantz, S. A. (2001). Constructing "sound science" and "good epidemiology": Tobacco, lawyers, and public relations firms. *American Journal of Public Health, 91*, 1749–1757.

Ott, J. (1993). *Pharmacotheon: Entheogenic drugs, their plant sources and history.* Kennewick, WA: Natural Products Co.

Pacurucu-Castillo, S. (1994). Drinking and drinking problems: Different stages of a fading taboo? *Addiction, 89*, 951–952.

Page, J. B. (1997). Needle exchange and reduction of harm: An anthropological view. *Medical Anthropology, 18*, 13–33.

Page, J. B. (1999). Historical overview of other abusable drugs. In R. T. Ammerman, P. J. Ott, & R. E. Tarter (Eds.), *Prevention and societal impact of drug and alcohol abuse* (47–63). Mahwah, NJ: Lawrence Erlbaum Associates.

Pandina, R. J., & Johnson, V. L. (1999). Why people use, abuse, and become dependent on drugs: Progress toward a heuristic model. In M. D. Glantz & C. R. Hartel (Eds.), *Drug abuse: Origins and interventions* (119–147). Washington, DC: American Psychological Association.

Panksepp, J., Knutson, B., & Burgdorf, J. (2002). The role of brain emotional systems in addictions: A neuro-evolutionary perspective and new "self-report" animal model. *Addiction, 97*, 459–469.

Pantellis, C., Hindler, C. G., & Taylor, J. C. (1989). Use and abuse of khat (*Catha edulis*): A review of the distribution, pharmacology, side effects and a description of psychosis attributed to khat chewing. *Psychological Medicine, 18*, 657–668.

Parascandola, J. (1995). The drug habit: The association of the word "drug" with abuse in American history. In R. Porter & M. Teich (Eds.), *Drugs and narcotics in history* (156–167). Cambridge: Cambridge University Press.

Paredes, A. (1975). Social control of drinking among the Aztec Indians of Mesoamerica. *Journal of Studies on Alcohol, 36,* 1139–1153.

Parker, H., Aldridge, J., & Measham, F. (1998). *Illegal leisure: The normalization of adolescent drug use.* London: Routledge.

Parker, R. N., & Auerhahn, K. (1998). Alcohol, drugs, and violence. *Annual Review of Sociology, 24,* 291–311.

Parssinen, T. M., & Kerner, K. (1980). Development of the disease model of drug addiction in Britain, 1870–1926. *Medical History, 24,* 275–296.

Paton-Simpson, G. (2001). Socially obligatory drinking: A sociological analysis of norms governing minimum drinking levels. *Contemporary Drug Problems, 28,* 133–177.

Pederson, W., & Skrondal, A. (1999). Ecstasy and new patterns of drug use: A normal population study. *Addiction, 94,* 1695–1706.

Peele, S. (1987). A moral vision of addiction: How people's values determine whether they become and remain addicts. *Journal of Drug Issues, 17,* 187–215.

Peele, S. (1989). *The diseasing of America: Addiction treatment out of control.* Lexington, MA: Lexington Books.

Peele, S., & Brodsky, A. (2000). Exploring psychological benefits associated with moderate alcohol use: A necessary corrective to assessments of drinking outcomes? *Drug and Alcohol Dependence, 60,* 221–247.

Pegram, T. R. (1998). *Battling demon rum: The struggle for a dry America, 1800–1993.* Chicago: Ivan R. Dee.

Pendergrast, M. (1999). *Uncommon grounds: The history of coffee and how it transformed the world.* New York: Basic Books.

Pentz, M. A. (1999). Prevention. In M. Galanter & H. D. Kleber (Eds.), *Textbook of substance abuse treatment* (2nd ed.; 535–545). Washington, DC: American Psychiatric Press.

Peréz, R. L. (2000). Fiesta as tradition, fiesta as change: Ritual alcohol and violence in a Mexican community. *Addiction, 95,* 365–373.

Perkins, K.A., Gerlach, D., Broge, M., & Grobe, J.E. (2000). Greater sensitivity to subjective effects of nicotine in nonsmokers high in sensation seeking. *Experimental and Clinical Psychopharmacology, 8,* 462–472.

Peters, H., & Nahas, G. G. (1999). A brief history of four millennia (B.C. 2000–A.D. 1974). In G. G. Nahas, K. M. Sutin, D. Harvey, S. Agurell, N. Pace, & R. Cancro (Eds.), *Marihuana and medicine* (3–7). Clifton, NJ: Humana Press. Inc.

Phillips, A. G., Blaha, C. D., Pfaus, J. G., & Blackburn, J. R. (1992). Neurobiological correlates of positive emotional states: Dopamine, anticipation and reward. In K. T. Strongman (Ed.), *International review of studies on emotion, Volume 2* (31–49). London: John Wiley & Sons.

Phillips, W. (1980). Six o'clock swill: The introduction of early closing in hotel bars in Australia. *Historical Studies, 19,* 250–265.

Phinney, J. S. (1996). When we talk about American ethnic groups, what do we mean? *American Psychologist, 51,* 918–927.

Picciotto, M. R. (1998). Common aspects of the action of nicotine and other drugs of abuse. *Drug and Alcohol Dependence, 51,* 165–172.

Pihl, R. O. (1999). Substance abuse: Etiological considerations. In T. Millon, P. H. Blaney, & R. D. Davis (Eds.), *Oxford textbook of psychopathology* (249–276). New York: Oxford University Press.

Pinker, S. (1997). *How the mind works.* London: Allen Lane.

Plant, S. (2000). *Writing on drugs.* London: Faber & Faber.

Pollay, R. W. (2000). Targeting youth and concerned smokers: Evidence from Canadian tobacco industry documents. *Tobacco Control, 9,* 136–147.

Pollock, N. J. (2000). Kava. In K. F. Kiple & K. C. Ornelas (Eds.), *The Cambridge world history of food* (664–670). Cambridge: Cambridge University Press.

Pomerleau, C. S. (1997). Co-factors for smoking and evolutionary psychology. *Addiction, 92,* 397–408.

Porter, R. (1985). The drinking man's disease: The "pre-history" of alcoholism in Georgian Britain. *British Journal of Addiction, 80,* 385–396.

Porter, R. (1987). *Mind-Forg'd manacles: A history of madness in England from the Restoration to the Regency.* London: Penguin.

Porter, R. (1997). *The greatest benefit to mankind: A medical history of humanity from antiquity to the present.* London: Harper Collins.

Prescott, C. A., & Kendler, K. S. (1999). Genetic and environmental contributions to alcohol abuse and dependence in a population-based sample of male twins. *American Journal of Psychiatry, 156,* 34–40.

Price, J. M. (1995). Tobacco use and tobacco taxation: A battle of interests in early modern Europe. In J. Goodman, P. E. Lovejoy, & A. Sherratt (Eds.), *Consuming habits: Drugs in history and anthropology* (165–185). London: Routledge.

Price, R. K., Risk, N. K., & Spitznagel, E. L. (2001). Remission from drug abuse over a 25–year period: Patterns of remission and treatment use. *American Journal of Public Health, 91,* 1107–1113.

Prince, R. (1982). Shamans and endorphins: Hypotheses for synthesis. *Ethos, 10,* 409–423.

Prochaska, J. O., DiClemente, C. C., & Norcross, J. C. (1992). In search of how people change: Applications to addictive behaviors. *American Psychologist, 47,* 1102–1114.

Proctor, R. N. (1997). The Nazi war on tobacco: Ideology, evidence, and possible cancer consequences. *Bulletin of the History of Medicine, 71,* 435–488.

Project MATCH Research Group. (1997). Matching alcoholism treatments to client heterogeneity: Project MATCH post-treatment drinking outcomes. *Journal of Studies on Alcohol, 58,* 7–29.

Project MATCH Research Group. (1998). Matching alcoholism treatments to client heterogeneity: Treatment main effects and matching effects of drinking during treatment. *Journal of Studies on Alcohol, 59,* 631–639.

Project MATCH Research Group. (1999). Comments on Project MATCH: Matching alcohol treatments to client heterogeneity. *Addiction, 94,* 31–69.

Puddey, I. B., Rakic, V., Dimmitt, S. B., & Beilin, L. J. (1999). Influence of pattern of drinking on cardiovascular disease and cardiovascular risk factors—A review. *Addiction, 94,* 649–663.

Pyörälä, E. (1990). Trends in alcohol consumption in Spain, Portugal, France, and Italy from the 1950s until the 1980s. *British Journal of Addiction, 85,* 469–477.

Quintero, G. (2000). "The lizard in the green bottle": "Aging out" of problem drinking among Navajo men. *Social Science and Medicine, 51,* 1031–1045.

Ragels, L. A. (2002). Is Alcoholics Anonymous a cult? An old question revisited. http://www.aadeprogramming.com/reclaim/oldquestion.html

Rahav, G., Hasin, D., & Paykin, A. (1999). Drinking patterns of recent Russian immigrants and other Israelis: 1995 National Survey Results. *American Journal of Public Health, 89,* 1212–1216.

Railton, P. (1981). Probability, explanation, and information. *Synthese, 48,* 233–256.

Ramsay, M., Baker, P., Goulden, C., Sharp, C., & Sondhi, A. (2001). *Drug misuse declared in 2000: Results from the British Crime Survey.* London: Home Office Research, Development and Statistics Directorate.

Ramstedt, M. (2001). Per capita alcohol consumption and liver cirrhosis mortality in 14 European countries. *Addiction, 96,* S19–S34.

Ramström, L. M. (1997). Prevalence and other world dimensions of smoking in the world. In C. T. Bolliger & K. O. Fagerström (Eds.), *The tobacco epidemic* (64–77). Basel: Karger.

Randall, C. L. (2001). Alcohol and pregnancy: Highlights from three decades of research. *Journal of Studies on Alcohol, 62,* 554–561.

Rao, S., & Schottenfeld, R. (1999). Methadone maintenance. In P. J. Ott, R. E. Tarter, & R. T. Ammerman (Eds.), *Sourcebook on substance abuse: Etiology, epidemiology, assessment, and treatment* (362–373). Boston: Allyn & Bacon.

Rasmussen, D. W., Benson, B. L., & Mocan, H. N. (1998). The economics of substance abuse in context: Can economics be part of an integrated theory of drug use? *Journal of Drug Issues, 28,* 575–592.

Read, P. (1999). *A rape of the soul so profound: The return of the stolen generations.* St. Leonards, NSW: Allen & Unwin.

Rehfisch, F. (1987). Competitive beer drinking among the Mambila. In M. Douglas (Ed.), *Constructive drinking: Perspectives on drink from anthropology* (135–145). New York: Cambridge University Press.

Rehm, J., & Sempos, C. T. (1995). Alcohol consumption and all-cause mortality. *Addiction, 90,* 471–480.

Reichel-Dolmatoff, G. (1990). The cultural context of an Aboriginal hallucinogen: *Banesteriopsis caapi.* In P. T. Furst (Ed.), *Flesh of the gods: The ritual use of hallucinogens* (84–114). Prospect Heights, IL: Waveland Press Inc.

Reinarman, C., & Levine, H. G. (1997). The crack attack: Politics and media in the crack scare. In C. Reinarman & H. G. Levine (Eds.), *Crack in America: Demon drugs and social justice* (18–49). Berkeley: University of California Press.

Reuter, P. (2001). Why does research have so little impact on American drug policy? *Addiction, 96,* 373–376.

Rhodes, J. E., & Jason, L. A. (1990). A social stress model of substance abuse. *Journal of Consulting and Clinical Psychology, 58,* 395–401.

Roberts, A. (2000). Psychiatric comorbidity in White and African-American illicit substance abusers: Evidence for differential etiology. *Clinical Psychology Review, 5,* 667–677.

Roberts, J. M. (1999). *Twentieth century.* London: Allen Lane.

Roberts, L. J., & Marlatt, A. G. (1999). Harm reduction. In P. J. Ott, R. E. Tarter, & R. T. Ammerman (Eds.), *Sourcebook on substance abuse: Etiology, epidemiology, assessment, and treatment* (389–399). Boston: Allyn & Bacon.

Robins, L. N., Helzer, J. E., Hesselbrock, M., & Wish, E. (1998). Vietnam veterans three years after Vietnam: How our study changed our view of heroin. In J. A. Schaler (Ed.), *Drugs: Should we legalize, decriminalize or deregulate?* (249–265). New York: Prometheus Books.

Robinson, T. E., & Berridge, K. C. (2001). Incentive-sensitization and addiction. *Addiction, 96,* 103–114.

Romelsjö, A. (1995). Alcohol consumption and unintentional injury, suicide, violence, work performance, and inter-generational effects. In H. D. Holder & G. Edwards (Eds.), *Alcohol and public policy: Evidence and issues* (114–142). Oxford: Oxford University Press.

Room, R. (1984). Alcohol and ethnography: A case of "problem deflation." *Current Anthropology, 25,* 169–191.

Room, R. (1985). Dependence and society. *British Journal of Addiction, 80,* 133–139.

Room, R. (1996). Gender roles and interactions in drinking and drug use. *Journal of Substance Abuse, 8,* 227–239.

Room, R. (1998a). Alcohol and drug disorders in the international classification of diseases: A shifting kaleidoscope. *Drug and Alcohol Review, 17,* 305–317.

Room, R. (1998b). Drinking patterns and alcohol-related social problems: Frameworks for analysis in developing societies. *Drug and Alcohol Review, 17,* 389–398.

Room, R. (2000). Measuring drinking patterns: The experience of the last half-century. *Journal of Substance Abuse, 12,* 23–33.

Room, R. (2001). Intoxication and bad behavior: Understanding cultural differences in the link. *Social Science and Medicine, 53,* 189–198.

Room, R., Janca, A., Bennett, L. A., Schmidt, L., & Sartorius, N. (1996). WHO cross-cultural applicability research on diagnosis and assessment of substance use disorders: An overview of methods and selected results. *Addiction, 91,* 199–220.

Room, R., & Mäkelä, K. (2000). Typologies of the cultural position of drinking. *Journal of Studies on Alcohol, 61,* 475–483.

Rooney, D. F. (1993). *Betel chewing traditions in South-East Asia.* Kuala Lumpur: Oxford University Press.

Rorabaugh, W. J. (1979). *The alcoholic republic.* New York: Oxford University Press.

Rowe, D., & Grills, C. (1993). African-centered drug treatment: An alternative conceptual paradigm for drug counseling with African-American clients. *Journal of Psychoactive Drugs, 25,* 21–33.

Rozin, P. (1996). Sociocultural influences on human food selection. In E. D. Capaldi (Ed.), *Why we eat what we eat: The psychology of eating* (233–263). Washington, DC: APA Press.

Rudgley, R. (1993). *The alchemy of culture: Intoxicants in society.* London: The British Museum Press.

Rugh, D. (2002). India. In A. Cherry, M. E. Dillon, & D. Rugh (Eds.), *Substance abuse: A global view* (101–115). Westport, CT: Greenwood Press.

Rush, B. (1784). The effects of ardent spirits upon the human body and mind. http://www.druglibrary.org/schaffer/History/temptract/00050001_tif4.gif

Ryan, K. F. (1998). Globalizing the problem: The United States and international drug control. In E. L. Jensen & J. Gerber (Eds.), *The new war on drugs: Symbolic politics and criminal justice policy* (141–156). Highland Heights, KY: Academy of Criminal Justice Sciences.

Sabbag, R. (1976). *Snowblind: A brief career in the cocaine trade.* New York: Bobbs-Merrill Company, Inc.

Saggers, S., & Gray, D. (1998). *Dealing with alcohol: Indigenous usage in Australia, New Zealand and Canada.* Cambridge: Cambridge University Press.

Salmon, W. C. (1985). Conflicting conceptions of scientific explanation. *Journal of Philosophy,* 651–653.

Sandhu, D.S., & Malik, R. (2001). Ethnocultural background and substance abuse treatment of Asian Indian Americans. In S. L. A. Straussner (Ed.), *Ethnocultural factors in substance abuse treatment* (368–392). New York: The Guilford Press.

Saner, H., MacCoun, R., & Reuter, P. (1995). On the ubiquity of drug selling among youthful offenders in Washington, DC, 1985–1991: Age, period, or cohort effect? *Journal of Quantitative Criminology, 11,* 337–362.

Scarborough, J. (1995). The opium poppy in Hellenistic and Roman medicine. In R. Porter & M. Teich (Eds.), *Drugs and narcotics in history* (4–23). Cambridge: Cambridge University Press.

Schafer, J., & Brown, S. A. (1991). Marijuana and cocaine effect expectancies and drug use patterns. *Journal of Consulting and Clinical Psychology, 59,* 558–565.

Schaler, J. A. (2000). *Addiction is a choice.* Chicago: Open Court.

Scheir, L. M., Botvin, G. J., & Miller, N. L. (1999). Live events, neighborhood stress, psychosocial functioning, and alcohol use among urban minority youth. *Journal of Child and Adolescent Substance Abuse, 9,* 19–50.

Schelling, T. C. (1992). Addictive drugs: The cigarette experience. *Science, 255,* 430–433.

Schenk, G. (1956). *The book of poisons.* London: Weidenfeld and Nicolson.

Schivelbusch, W. (1992). *Tastes of paradise: A social history of spices, stimulants, and intoxicants.* New York: Pantheon Books.

Schmidt, L., & Room, R. (1999). Cross-cultural applicability in international classifications and research on alcohol dependence. *Journal of Studies on Alcohol, 60,* 448–462.

Schuckit, M. A. (1996a). DSM-V: There's work to be done. *Journal of Studies on Alcohol, 57,* 469–470.

Schuckit, M. A. (1996b). Recent developments in the pharmacotherapy of alcohol dependence. *Journal of Consulting and Clinical Psychology, 64,* 669–676.

Schulenberg, J., O'Malley, P. M., Bachman, J. G., Wadsworth, K. N., & Johnston, L. D. (1996). Getting drunk and growing up: Trajectories of frequent binge drinking during the transition to young adulthood. *Journal of Studies on Alcohol, 57,* 289–304.

Schultes, R. E. (1990). An overview of hallucinogens in the Western hemisphere. In P. T. Furst (Ed.), *Flesh of the gods: The ritual use of hallucinogens* (2nd ed.). Prospect Heights, IL: Waveland Press Inc.

Schultz, W., Dayan, P., & Montague, P. R. (1997). A neural substrate of prediction and reward. *Science, 275,* 1593–1598.

Schumaker, J. F. (1990). *Wings of illusion: The origin, nature and future of paranormal belief.* Buffalo, NY: Prometheus Books.

Schumaker, J. F. (1991). The adaptive value of suggestibility and dissociation. In J. F. Schumaker (Ed.), *Human suggestibility: Advances in theory, research and application* (108–131). New York: Routledge.

Schumaker, J. F. (1995). *The corruption of reality: A unified theory of religion, hypnosis and psychopathology.* New York: Prometheus Books.

Segal, B. (1995). Prevention and culture: A theoretical perspective. *Drugs and Society, 8,* 139–147.

Self, D. W. & Nestler, E. J. (1998). Relapse to drug seeking: Neural and molecular mechanisms. *Drug and Alcohol Dependence, 51,* 49–60.

Sellman, D. (1994). Alcoholism: Development of the diagnostic concept. *Australian and New Zealand Journal of Psychiatry, 28,* 205–211.

Sellman, J. D., Huriwai, T. T., Ram, R. S., & Deering, D. E. (1997). Cultural linkage: Treating Maori with alcohol and drug problems in dedicated Maori treatment programs. *Substance Use and Misuse, 32,* 415–424.

Shaara, L., & Strathern, A. (1992). A preliminary analysis of the relationship between altered states of consciousness, healing, and social structure. *American Anthropologist, 94,* 145–160.

Sharma, H. K. (1996). Sociocultural perspective of substance use in India. *Substance Use and Misuse, 31,* 1689–1714.

Sharma, H. M., Dillbeck, M. C., & Dillbeck, S. L. (1994). Implementation of the transcendental meditation program and Maharishi Ayur-Veda to prevent alcohol and drug abuse among juveniles at risk. *Alcoholism Treatment Quarterly, 11,* 429–457.

Sharon, D. (1990). The San Pedro cactus in Peruvian folk healing. In P. T. Furst (Ed.), *Flesh of the gods: The ritual use of hallucinogens* (114–136). Prospect Heights, IL: Waveland Press, Inc.

Shedler, J., & Block, J. (1990). Adolescent drug use and psychological health. *American Psychologist, 45,* 612–630.

Shenk, J. W. (1999). America's altered states: When does legal relief of pain become illegal pursuit of pleasure? *Harper's,* May, 38–52.

Shepard, G. H. (1998). Psychoactive plants and ethnopsychiatric medicines of the Matsigenka. *Journal of Psychoactive Drugs, 30,* 321–332.

Sherratt, A. (1991). Sacred and profane substances: The ritual of narcotics in later Neolithic Europe. In P. Garwood, D. Jennings, R. Skates, & J. Toms (Eds.), *Sacred and profane.* Oxford: Oxford Committee for Archaeology.

Sherratt, A. (1995). Alcohol and its alternatives: Symbol and substance in pre-industrial cultures. In J. Goodman, P. E. Lovejoy, & A. Sherratt (Eds.), *Consuming habits: Drugs in history and anthropology* (11–47). London: Routledge.

Shorter, E. (1997). *A history of psychiatry.* Chichester: John Wiley & Sons.

Siegal, R. K., & Brodie, M. (1984). Alcohol self-administration by elephants. *Bulletin of the Psychonomic Society, 22,* 49–52.

Simons, R. C., & Hughes, C. C. (1993). Culture-bound syndromes. In A. C. Gaw (Ed.), *Culture, ethnicity, and mental illness* (75–99). Washington, DC: American Psychiatric Association.

Simpura, J. (1998). Mediterranean mysteries: Mechanisms of declining alcohol consumption. *Addiction, 93,* 1301–1304.

Singer, M. (1986). Toward a political economy of alcoholism: The missing link in the anthropology of drinking behavior. *Social Science and Medicine, 23,* 113–130.

Singer, M. (2001). Toward a bio-cultural and political economic integration of alcohol, tobacco and drug studies in the coming century. *Social Science and Medicine, 53,* 199–213.

Singh, Y. N. (1992). Kava: An overview. *Journal of Ethnopharmacology, 37,* 13–45.

Skog, O-J. (2001a). Alcohol consumption and mortality rates from traffic accidents, accidental falls, and other accidents in 14 European countries. *Addiction, 96,* S49–S58.

Skog, O-J. (2001b). Alcohol consumption and overall accident mortality in 14 European countries. *Addiction, 96,* S35–S47.

Slade, J. (2001). Marketing policies. In R. L. Rabin & S. D. Sugarman (Eds.), *Regulating tobacco* (72–111). Oxford: Oxford University Press.

Slade, J. S. (1989). The tobacco epidemic: Lessons from history. *Journal of Psychoactive Drugs, 21,* 281–291.

Sly, D. F., Hopkins, R. S., Trapido, E., & Ray, S. (2001). Influence of a counter-advertising media campaign on initiation of smoking: The Florida "truth" campaign. *American Journal of Public Health, 91,* 233–238.

Smith, E. O. (1999). Evolution, substance abuse, and addiction. In W. Trevathan, E. O. Smith, & J. J. McKenna (Eds.), *Evolutionary medicine* (375–405). New York: Oxford University Press.

Smith, W. D. (1995). From coffeehouse to parlor: The consumption of coffee, tea, and sugar in north-western Europe in the seventeenth and eighteenth centuries. In J. Goodman, P. E. Lovejoy, & A. Sherratt (Eds.), *Consuming habits: Drugs in history and anthropology* (148–164). London: Routledge.

Smyth, B. P., O'Brien, M., & Barry, J. (2000). Trends in treated opiate misuse in Dublin: The emergence of chasing the dragon. *Addiction, 95,* 1217–1223.

Sobell, L. C., Cunningham, J. A., & Sobell, M. B. (1996). Recovery from alcohol problems with and without treatment: Prevalence in two population surveys. *American Journal of Public Health, 86,* 966–972.

Sobell, L. C., Ellingstad, T. P., & Sobell, M. B. (2000). Natural recovery from alcohol and drug problems: Methodological review of the research with suggestions for future directions. *Addiction, 95,* 749–764.

Sobell, L. C., Sobell, M. B., & Toneatto, T. (1991). Recovery from alcohol problems without treatment. In N. Heather, W. R. Miller, & J. Greely (Eds.), *Self-control and the addictive behaviors* (198–242). Botany, NSW: Maxwell MacMillan Publishing Australia.

Sournia, J. C. (1990). *A history of alcoholism.* London: Basil Blackwell.

Spicer, P. (2001). Culture and the restoration of self among former American Indian drinkers. *Social Science and Medicine, 53,* 227–240.

Spillane, J. (1998). Did drug prohibition work? Reflections on the end of the first cocaine experience in the United States, 1910–1945. *Journal of Drug Issues, 28,* 517–538.

Spring, J. A., & Buss, D. H. (1977). Three centuries of alcohol in the British diet. *Nature, 270,* 567–573.

Spruit, I. P. (1999). Ecstasy use and policy responses in The Netherlands. *Journal of Drug Issues, 29,* 653–678.

Stacy, A. W., Widaman, K. F., & Marlatt, G. A. (1990). Expectancy models of alcohol use. *Journal of Personality and Social Psychology, 58,* 918–928.

Staggers, F., Alexander, C. N., & Walton, K. G. (1995). Importance of reducing stress and strengthening the host in drug detoxification: The potential offered by transcendental meditation. *Alcoholism Treatment Quarterly, 11,* 297–331.

Steele, C. M., & Josephs, R. A. (1990). Alcohol myopia: Its prized and dangerous effects. *American Psychologist, 45,* 921–933.

Sterelny, K. (1990). *The representational theory of mind.* Oxford: Basil Blackwell.

Sterk, C. E., Elifson, K. W., & German, D. (2000). Female crack users and their sexual relationships: The role of sex-for-crack exchanges. *Journal of Sex Research, 37,* 354–360.

Stevenson, M., Fitzgerald, J., & Banwell, C. (1996). Chewing as a social act: Cultural displacement and *khat* consumption in the East African communities of Melbourne. *Drug and Alcohol Review, 15,* 73–82.

Stewart, G. G. (1967). A history of the medicinal use of tobacco 1492–1860. *Medical History, 11,* 228–269.

Strakowski, S. M., & DelBello, M. P. (2000). The co-occurrence of biopolar and substance use disorders. *Clinical Psychology Review, 20,* 191–206.

Strang, J. (2001). Injectable opiate treatment—Feasible but for whom, how, and to what ends? *Addiction, 96,* 562–564.

Strang, J., Griffiths, P., & Gossop, M. (1997). Heroin smoking by "chasing the dragon": Origins and history. *Addiction, 92,* 673–683.

Straussner, S. L. A. (2001a). Jewish substance abusers: Existing but invisible. In S. L. A. Straussner (Ed.), *Ethnocultural factors in substance abuse treatment* (291–317). New York: The Guilford Press.

Straussner, S. L. A. (2001b). Ethnocultural issues in substance abuse treatment: An overview. In S. L. A. Straussner (Ed.), *Ethnocultural factors in substance abuse treatment* (3–28). New York: The Guilford Press.

Straussner, S. L. A. (Ed.). (2001c). *Ethnocultural factors in substance abuse treatment.* New York: The Guilford Press.

Strunin, L. (2001). Assessing alcohol consumption: Developments from qualitative research methods. *Social Science and Medicine, 53,* 215–226.

Substance Abuse and Mental Health Service Administration. (1999). *Mortality data from the Drug Abuse Warning Network, 1999.* Rockville, MD: Office of Applied Studies.

Substance Abuse and Mental Health Service Administration. (2000). Mortality data from the Drug Abuse Warning Network, 2000. Rockville, MD: Office of Applied Studies.

Substance Abuse and Mental Health Service Administration. (2001). *Summary of findings from the 2000 National Household Survey on Drug Abuse.* Rockville, MD: Office of Applied Studies, NHDSA Series H-13, DHHS Publication No. (SMA) 01–3549.

Sugarman, S. D. (2001). International aspects of tobacco control and the proposed WHO treaty. In R. L. Rabin & S. D. Sugarman (Eds.), *Regulating tobacco* (245–285). Oxford: Oxford University Press.

Suggs, D. N. (2001). "These young chaps think they are just men, too": Redistributing masculinity in Kgatleng bars. *Social Science and Medicine, 53,* 241–250.

Sulkunen, P. (1989). Drinking in France 1965–1979: An analysis of household consumption data. *British Journal of Addiction, 84,* 61–72.

Sullivan, R. J., Allen, J. S., Otto, C., Tiobech, J., & Nero, K. (2000). Effects of chewing betel nut (*Areca catechu*) on the symptoms of people with schizophrenia in Palau, Micronesia. *British Journal of Psychiatry, 177,* 174–178.

Sullivan, R. J., & Hagen, E. H. (2002). Psychotropic substance-seeking: Evolutionary pathology or adaptation? *Addiction, 97,* 389–400.

Swendsen, J. D., & Merikangas, K. R. (2000). The comorbidity of depression and substance use disorders. *Clinical Psychology Review, 20,* 173–189.

Swift, W., Copeland, J., & Lenton, S. (2000). Cannabis and harm reduction. *Drug and Alcohol Review, 19,* 101–112.

Szasz, T. S. (1985). *Ceremonial chemistry: The ritual persecution of drugs, addicts, and pushers.* Homes Beach, FL: Learning Publications.

Szasz, T. S. (1998). Drugs as property: The right we rejected. In J. A. Schaler (Ed.), *Drugs: Should we legalize, decriminalize, or deregulate?* (181–208). New York: Prometheus Books.

Tani, C. R., Chavez, E. L., & Deffenbacher, J. L. (2001). Peer isolation and drug use among white non-Hispanic and Mexican American adolescents. *Adolescence, 36,* 127–139.

Teahan, J. E. (1988). Alcohol expectancies of Irish and Canadian alcoholics. *International Journal of the Addictions, 23,* 1057–1070.

Terrell, D. (2001). The role of cultural cognition in substance abuse and alcoholism. In J. F. Schumaker & T. Ward (Eds.), *Cultural cognition and psychopathology* (81–95). Westport, CT: Praeger.

Thagard, P. (1992). *Conceptual revolutions.* Princeton, NJ: Princeton University Press.

Thakker, J., & Durrant, R. (2001). Culture and cognitive theory: Toward a reformulation. In J. F. Schumaker & T. Ward (Eds.), *Cultural cognition and psychopathology* (213–233). Westport, CT: Praeger.

Thakker, J., & Ward, T. (1998). Culture and classification: The cross-cultural application of the DSM-IV. *Clinical Psychology Review, 18,* 501–529.

Thakker, J., Ward, T., & Strongman, K. T. (1999). Mental disorder and cross-cultural psychology: A constructivist perspective. *Clinical Psychology Review, 19,* 843–874.

Thornton, M. (1998). The potency of illegal drugs. *Journal of Drug Issues, 28,* 725–740.

Tonry, M. (1994). Race and the war on drugs. *Chicago Legal Forum, 25,* 25–81.

Tooby, J., & Cosmides, L. (1990). The past explains the present: Emotional adaptations and the structure of ancestral environments. *Ethology & Sociobiology, 11,* 375–424.

Topik, S. C. (2000). Coffee. In K. F. Kiple & K. C. Ornelas (Eds.), *The Cambridge world history of food* (641–653). Cambridge: Cambridge University Press.

Tosh, J. (1991). *The pursuit of history: Aims, methods & new directions in the study of modern history* (2nd ed.). London: Longman.

Townsend, J. L., Roderick, P., & Cooper, J. (1994). Cigarette smoking by socio-economic group, sex, and age: Effects of price, income, and health publicity. *British Medical Journal, 309,* 923–926.

Trimble, J. E. (1990–91). Ethnic specification, validation prospects, and the future of drug use research. *International Journal of the Addictions, 25,* 149–170.

Trivers, R. L. (1972). Parental investment and sexual selection. In B. Campbell (Ed.), *Sexual selection and the descent of man: 1871–1971* (136–179). Chicago: Aldine.

Tsuang, M. T., Lyons, M. J., Eisen, S. A., Goldberg, J., True, W., Lin, N., Meyer, J. M., Toomey, R., Faroane, S. V., & Eaves, L. (1996). Genetic influences on DSM-III-R drug abuse and dependence: A study of 3372 twin pairs. *American Journal of Medical Genetics 67,* 473–477.

Tucker, T. K., & Ritter, A. J. (2000). Naltrexone in the treatment of heroin dependence: A literature review. *Drug and Alcohol Review, 19,* 73–82.

Tyrell, I. (1997). The U.S. prohibition experiment: Myths, history and implications. *Addiction, 92,* 1405–1409.

Vallee, B. L. (1998). Alcohol in the Western world. *Scientific American,* June, 62–67.

van de Wijngaart, G. F., Braam, R., deBruin, D., Fris, M., Maalsté, N. J. M, & Vergraeck, H. T. (1999). Ecstasy use at large-scale dance events in the Netherlands. *Journal of Drug Issues, 29,* 679–702.

van Fraassen, B. (1985). Salmon on explanation. *Journal of Philosophy,* 639–651.

van Ours, J. C. (1995). The price elasticity of hard drugs: The case of opium in the Dutch East Indies, 1923–1938. *Journal of Political Economy, 103,* 261–279.

Vogel-Sprott, M., & Fillmore, M. T. (1999). Expectancy and behavioral effects of socially used drugs. In I. Kirsch (Ed.), *How expectancies shape experience* (215–232). Washington, DC: American Psychiatric Association Press.

von Bibra, E. (1855/1995). *Plant intoxicants.* Rochester, VT: Healing Art Press.

von Gernet, A. (1995). Nicotian dreams: The prehistory and early history of tobacco in eastern North America. In J. Goodman, P.E. Lovejoy, & A. Sherratt (Eds.), *Consuming habits: Drugs in history and anthropology* (67–87). London: Routledge.

Wakefield, J. C. (1992). The concept of mental disorder: On the boundary between biological facts and social values. *American Psychologist, 47,* 373–388.

Walker, R. B. (1980). Tobacco smoking in Australia, 1788–1914. *Historical Studies, 19,* 267–285.

Wall, T. L., Shea, S. H., Chan, K. K., & Carr, L. G. (2001). A genetic association with the development of alcohol and other substance use behavior in Asian Americans. *Journal of Abnormal Psychology, 110,* 173–178.

Wallace, J. (1999). The 12-step recovery approach. In P. J. Ott, R. E. Tarter, & R. T. Ammerman (Eds.), *Sourcebook on substance abuse: Etiology, epidemiology, assessment, and treatment* (293–303). Boston: Allyn & Bacon.

Wallace, J. M., Bachman, J. G., O'Malley, P. M., & Johnston, L. D. (1995). Racial/ethnic differences in adolescent drug use. In G. J. Botvin, S. Schinke, & M. A. Orlandi (Eds.), *Drug abuse prevention with multiethnic youth* (59–81). Thousand Oaks, CA: Sage Publications.

Ward, C., & Kemp, S. (1991). Religious experiences, altered states of consciousness, and suggestibility: Cross culturally and historical perspectives. In

J. F. Schumaker (Ed.), *Human suggestibility: Advances in theory, research and application*. New York: Routledge.

Ward, R. (1992). *Concise history of Australia*. St Lucia, Queensland: Queensland University Press.

Warner, J. (1992). Before there was "alcoholism": Lessons from the medieval experience with alcohol. *Contemporary Drug Problems, 19,* 409–429.

Warner, J. (1994a). In another city, in another time: Rhetoric and the creation of a drug scare in eighteenth-century London. *Contemporary Drug Problems, 21,* 485–511.

Warner, J. (1994b). "Resolv'd to drink no more": Addiction as a preindustrial construct. *Journal of Studies on Alcohol, 55,* 685–691.

Warner, J. (1997). The naturalization of beer and gin in early modern England. *Contemporary Drug Problems, 24,* 373–402.

Warner, J., Her, M., Gmel, G., & Rehm, J. (2001). Can legislation prevent debauchery? Mother gin and public health in 18th-century England. *American Journal of Public Health, 91,* 375–384.

Warner, K. E. (2001). Reducing harm to smokers: Methods, their effectiveness, and the role of policy. In R. L. Rabin & S. D. Sugarman (Eds.), *Regulating tobacco* (111–143). Oxford: Oxford University Press.

Wasson, R. G. (1990). The divine mushroom of immortality. In P. T. Furst (Ed.), *Flesh of the gods: The ritual use of hallucinogens* (2nd ed.; 185–201). Prospect Heights, IL: Waveland Press, Inc.

Waters, M. C., & Eschbach, K. (1995). Immigration and ethnic and racial inequality in the United States. *Annual Review of Sociology, 21,* 419–446.

Weaver, H. N. (2001). Native Americans and substance abuse. In S. L. A. Straussner (Ed.), *Ethnocultural factors in substance abuse treatment* (77–96). New York: The Guilford Press.

Weil, A. (1986). *The natural mind: An investigation of drugs and the higher consciousness* (rev. ed.). Boston: Houghton Mifflin.

Weil, A. (1990). From theory to practice: The planned treatment of drug users. An interview with Andrew Weil. *International Journal of the Addictions, 25,* 1099–1125.

Weisburger, J. J., & Comer, J. (2000). Tea. In K. F. Kiple & K .C. Ornelas (Eds.), *The Cambridge world history of food* (713–720). Cambridge: Cambridge University Press.

Weiss, S., Sawa, G. H., Abdeen, Z., & Yanai, J. (1999). Substance abuse studies and prevention efforts among Arabs in the 1990s in Israel, Jordan and the Palestinian Authority: A literature review. *Addiction, 94,* 177–198.

West, R. (2001). Theories of addiction. *Addiction, 96,* 3–13.

Westermeyer, J. (1976). The pro-heroin effect on opium laws in Asia. *Archives of General Psychiatry, 33,* 1135–1142.

Westermeyer, J. (1981). Opium availability and the prevalence of addiction in Asia. *British Journal of Addiction, 76,* 85–90.

Westermeyer, J. (1991). Historical and social context of psychoactive substance disorders. In R. J. Frances & S. I. Miller (Eds.), *Clinical textbook of addictive disorders. The Guilford substance abuse series* (23–40). New York: The Guilford Press.

Westermeyer, J. (1995a). Cultural aspects of substance abuse and alcoholism: Assessment and management. *Psychiatric Clinics of North America, 18,* 589–604.

Westermeyer, J. (1995b). Beware the spread of heroin. *Addiction, 90,* 18–19.

Westermeyer, J. (1996a). Cultural factors in the control, prevention, and treatment of illicit drug use: The earthling's psychoactive trek. In W. K. Bickel & R. J. DeGrandpre (Eds.), *Drug policy and human nature: Psychological perspectives on the prevention, management, and treatment of illicit drug abuse* (99–124). New York: Plenum Press.

Westermeyer, J. (1996b). Alcoholism among New World peoples: A critique of history, methods, and findings. *American Journal on Addictions, 5,* 110–123.

Westermeyer, J. (1996c). Addiction among immigrants and migrants: Epidemiology and treatment. *American Journal on Addictions, 5,* 334–350.

Westermeyer, J. (1999). Cross-cultural aspects of substance abuse. In M. Galanter & H. D. Kleber (Eds.), *Textbook of substance abuse treatment* (2nd ed.; 75–89). Washington, DC: American Psychiatric Press.

White, D., & Pitts, M. (1998). Educating young people about drugs: A systematic review. *Addiction, 93,* 1475–1487.

White, H. R., Bates, M. E., & Johnson, V. (1991). Learning to drink: Familial, peer, and media influences. In D. J. Pittman & H. R. White (Eds.), *Society, culture, and drinking patterns re-examined* (177–198). New Brunswick, NJ: Rutgers Center of Alcohol Studies.

White, W. L. (1998). *Slaying the dragon: The history of addiction treatment and recovery in America.* Bloomington, IL: Chestnut Health Systems.

Wilbert, J. (1990). Tobacco and shamanistic ecstasy among the Warao Indians. In P. T. Furst (Ed.), *Flesh of the gods: The ritual use of hallucinogens* (2nd ed.; 55–84). Prospect, IL: Waveland Press, Inc.

Williams, G. C. (1966). *Adaptation and natural selection.* Princeton, NJ: Princeton University Press.

Williams, L., & Parker, H. (2001). Alcohol, cannabis, ecstasy and cocaine: Drugs of reasoned choice amongst young adult recreational drug users in England. *International Journal of Drug Policy, 12,* 397–413.

Wilsnack, R. W., Vogeltanz, N. D., Wilsnack, S. C., & Harris, T. R. (2000). Gender differences in alcohol consumption and adverse drinking consequences: Cross-cultural patterns. *Addiction, 95,* 251–265.

Wilson, E. O. (1984). *Biophilia.* Cambridge, MA: Harvard University Press.

Wislon, M., & Daly, M. (1985). Competitiveness, risk taking, and violence: the young male syndrome. *Ethology and Sociobiology, 6,* 59-73.

Wilson, M., Daly, M., & Gordon, S. (1998). The evolved psychological apparatus of human decision-making is one source of environmental problems. In T. Caro (Ed.), *Behavioral ecology and conservation biology* (501–523). New York: Oxford University Press.

Winant, H. (2000). Race and race theory. *Annual Review of Sociology, 26,* 169–185.

Winkelman, M. J. (1990). Shamans and other "magico-religious" healers: A cross-cultural study of their origins, nature, and social transformations. *Ethos,* 308–351.

Winkelman, M. J. (2001). Alternative and traditional approaches for substance abuse programs: A shamanic perspective. *International Journal of Drug Policy, 12,* 337–351.

Wise, R. A. (1988). The neurobiology of craving: Implications for the understanding and treatment of addiction. *Journal of Abnormal Psychology, 97,* 118–132.

Wise, R. A. (1998). Drug activation of brain reward pathways. *Drug and Alcohol Dependence, 51,* 13–22.

Wittig, M. C. W., Wright, J. D., & Kaminsky, D. C. (1997). Substance use among street children in Honduras. *Substance Use and Misuse, 32,* 805–827.

Wodak, A., & Moore, T. (2002). *Modernising Australia's drug policy.* Sydney: UNSW Press.

Young, A. M., Boyd, C., & Hubbell, A. (2000). Prostitution, drug use, and coping with psychological distress. *Journal of Drug Issues, 30,* 789–800.

Yuan, J-M., Ross, R. K., Gao, Y-T., Henderson, B. E., & Yu, M. C. (1997). Follow up study of moderate alcohol intake and mortality among middle aged men in Shanghai, China. *British Medical Journal, 314,* 18–23.

Zack, M., & Vogel-Sprott, V. (1997). Drunk or sober? Learned conformity to a behavioral standard. *Journal of Studies on Alcohol, 58,* 495–501.

Zador, D. (2001). Injectable opiate maintenance in the UK: Is it good clinical practice? *Addiction, 96,* 547–553.

Zahavi, A., & Zahavi, A. (1997). *The handicap principle: A missing piece of Darwin's puzzle.* New York: Oxford University Press.

Zias, J., Stark, H., Sellgman, J., Levy, R., Werker, E., Breuer, A., & Mechoulam, R. (1993). Early medical use of cannabis. *Nature, 363,* 215.

Zinberg, N. E. (1984). *Drug, set, and setting: The basis for controlled intoxicant use.* New Haven: Yale University Press.

Zuckerman, M. (1994). *Behavioral expressions and biosocial bases of sensation seeking.* Cambridge: Cambridge University Press.

Zuckerman, M. (1995). Good and bad humors: Biochemical bases of personality and its disorders. *Psychological Science, 6,* 325–332.

Zuckerman, M., & Kuhlman, D. M. (2000). Personality and risk-taking: Common biosocial factors. *Journal of Personality, 68,* 999–1029.

Author Index

Abaka, E., 135
Abdeen, Z., 167
Abeita, L., 122
Abel, E. L., 60, 66, 132
Abel, S., 85
Abrahamsen, A. A., 4
Acker, C. J., 80, 91, 196, 199, 200, 206
Agar, M., 181
Ahmad, A. M., 155n3
Akil, H., 42
Aldridge, J., 109, 151
Alexander, B. K., 52
Alexander, C. N., 237
Allen, J. S., 131
Alper, K. R., 136
Ames, G. M., 5, 102, 161
Anderson, P., 24
Andersson, M., 46
Andrews, J. A., 173
Andritzky, W., 141
Anslinger, H., 80
Anthony, J. C., 31, 32, 146, 162
Antze, P., 153
Armstrong, D., 123
Arnett, J. J., 46, 112
Atran, S., 54
Auerhahn, K., 169
Avenevoli, S., 218

Baasher, T., 132
Bachman, J. G., 19, 20, 46, 49, 85,
        86, 108, 112, 124, 233
Badhadhe, F. A., 149, 150
Baer, H. A., 181
Baker, E., 173, 220

Baker, P., 19, 45, 120
Balick, M. J., 55
Banwell, C., 149
Baridon, P., 99
Barker, J. C., 14, 15, 20, 125, 157
Barnard, M., 152
Baron-Cohen, S., 53
Barr, A., 40
Barros, H. M. T., 140
Barry, J., 87
Bastiaans, J., 136
Bates, M. E., 173
Bauman, K. E., 174
Baumeister, R. F., 172, 211
Baxter, B. E., 223, 229, 230
Bechtel, W., 4
Beck, J., 218, 219
Becker, H. S., 108, 161
Beilin, L. J., 25
Belknap, J. K., 9
Ben-Yehuda, N., 110
Bennett, L. A., 5, 10
Bennett, M. E., 215n5, 227
Benson, B. L., 5, 100
Berlin, B., 54
Berridge, K. C., 41, 43, 53, 75,
        77, 90, 196, 198, 200, 202,
        214n3, 236, 247
Berry, J. W., 175
Blackburn, J. R., 43
Blaha, C. D., 43
Blane, H. T., 5
Bleske, A. L., 36
Block, J., 46, 51, 222
Blum, K., 3, 53

Boardman, J. D., 180
Booth, M., 60, 65, 67, 75, 80, 95
Booth, P. G., 31, 34
Borges, G., 125, 161
Borsari, B., 174
Botvin, E. M., 220, 222
Botvin, G. J., 173, 180, 217, 219–220, 221, 222
Bourbon, D., 232
Bourgois, P., 163, 176, 178, 181, 182, 183, 190n4, 190n6, 229
Bower, B., 34
Boyd, C., 21
Boys, A., 151
Braam, R., 151
Bradburd, D., 178
Bradford Hill, A., 107
Bradizza, C. M., 172
Brady, M., 127, 173, 184, 186, 189, 232, 234
Brandon, T. H., 170, 171
Brandt, A. M., 107
Braverman, E. R., 3, 53
Breedlove, D., 54
Breivogel, C. S., 42
Breslau, N., 146
Breuer, A., 62
Brodie, M., 40
Brodsky, A., 25, 159
Broge, M., 50
Brooke, C., 23, 133
Brown, D., 35
Brown, F. A., 170
Brownsberger, W. N., 180, 181, 182
Brunton, R., 129
Bryant, K. J., 29
Buchanan, D. R., 113
Buck, K. J., 9
Bunt, L. J., 24
Burfield, L. B., 175
Burgdorf, J., 44
Burman, S., 233
Burns, C. B., 130, 161, 186
Burton, Robert, 68
Bushman, B. J., 169
Buss, D. M., 4, 36, 37, 61, 67, 101
Butters, J., 244

Bynum, W. F., 195, 196
Byrnes, J. P., 50

Caetano, R., 175
Caine, S. B., 41
Carey, K. B., 172, 174
Carnwath, T., 245
Carr, L. G., 165
Carroll, A., 184, 186
Carroll, K. M., 29
Carscadden, J. L., 171
Carstairs, G. M., 132
Cassanelli, L. V., 133, 134
Castro, F. G., 122, 123, 230
Catalano, R. F., 174
Caulkins, J. P., 86, 102, 118n4, 190n6
Cawte, J. E., 130, 131, 161, 186
Chagnon, N. A., 137, 160
Chaloupka, F. J., 239
Chan, K. K., 165
Chavez, E. L., 174
Chen, K., 20, 24, 112, 146
Chen, T. J. H., 3
Cherpitel, C. J., 175
Cherry, A., 131, 140
Cheung, Y. W., 122
Childers, S. R., 42
Chipungu, S. S., 221, 222
Chisholm, J. S., 47
Cho, Y. I., 208–209
Chow, K., 47
Chowdhury, A. N., 131
Christie, P., 243
Clark, D. B., 223
Clawson, P. L., 140
Clendinnen, I., 138, 139
Cloud, W., 233
Clough, A. R., 130, 161
Cohen, P. J., 218
Cohen, S., 110
Collin, M., 151
Collins, R. L., 5, 124
Collison, M., 176
Colom, J., 9
Comer, J., 70, 96, 130
Comings, D. E., 3, 53
Compton, W. M., 223

Cook, C. C., 226
Cooper, C., 80
Cooper, H. M., 169, 181
Cooper, J., 239
Cooper, M. L., 43
Copeland, A. L., 170, 171
Copeland, J., 85
Corbin, W., 171
Cornell, S., 121, 122
Courtwright, D. T., x, 33n2, 60, 74, 76, 77, 80, 81, 85, 86, 88n2, 91, 93, 94, 95, 97, 98, 100, 101, 108, 110, 111, 112, 118, 201, 206, 242
Cox, P. A., 55
Crabbe, J. C., 9, 164
Crawford, V., 68
Critchlow, B., 170
Crum, R. M., 162
Cull, J. G., 53
Cunningham, J. A., 213, 233
Curran, E., 42
Currie, B. J., 186
Czart, C., 239

D'Abbs, P., 186
Daly, J. W., 42
Daly, M., 47, 48
Darden, L., 4, 5
Darkes, J., 170
Davenport-Hines, R., x, 65, 76, 88n2, 92, 97
Dawkins, R., 36, 37
Dawson, D. A., 29, 45, 124, 144
Dayan, P., 44
De Smet, P. A. G. M., 137
De Vries, H., 220
deBruin, D., 151
Deering, D. E., 231
Deffenbacher, J. L., 174
Del Boca, F. K., 170
DelBello, M. P., 52, 223
Dernbach, K. B., 130, 169
Desmond, D. P., 30
Dev, S., 54
Devlin, N. J., 24
Diamond, J., 48, 54
Diaz, T., 173, 220, 222

DiClemente, C. C., 233
Dillbeck, M. C., 237
Dillbeck, S. L., 237
Dimmitt, S. B., 25
Dingle, A. E., 78, 83, 101, 103
Dinwiddie, S. H., 186
Dobkin de Rios, M., x, 22, 34, 46, 48, 51, 57, 70, 92, 127, 128, 135, 136, 137, 138, 139, 155n1, 155n2, 159, 177
Dobson, A. J., 25
Doll, R., 25, 107
Donnelly, G., 247
Donnelly, N., 243
Dowson, T. A., 34
Draper, G., 16, 18, 19, 25, 45
Dreher, M. C., 171, 190n3
Drew, L. R. H., 31
Drop, M. J., 46
Drucker-Brown, S., 135
Drummond, C., 226
Dudley, R., 40, 58
Dunbar, R. I. M., 55
Duncan, S. C., 173
Duncan, T. E., 173
Duntworth, J., 134
DuPont, R. L., 27, 203, 246
Durrant, R., 6, 36, 47, 208
Dusenbury, L. D., 220
Dushay, R. A., 222

Eber, C., 231
Edgerton, R. B., 120, 169, 170, 186
Edlin, B. R., 21
Edwards, G., 29, 61, 67, 75, 77, 81, 82, 90, 95, 114, 136, 203, 228, 233, 235
Eisen, S. A., 165
El-Bassel, N., 21
el-Guebaly, A., 64
el-Guebaly, N., 64
Elifson, K. W., 102
Ellingstad, T. P., 233
Ellis, B. J., 36, 47
Ellison, C. G., 180
Elster, J., 166
Emboden, W., 63, 137, 155n1

Ennett, S. T., 174, 219
Epstein, E. E., 164
Epstein, J. A., 173, 222
Erickson, P. G., 244
Ervin, F. R., 40
Eschbach, K., 123, 180
Escohatado, A., 88n2
Eshleman, S., 31
Evans, J. C., 70

Farquhar, J. W., 217
Farrell, G., 99, 100, 102, 131
Faruque, S., 21
Faulkner, W. R., 208–209
Federal Bureau of
    Investigation, 148
Fendrich, M., 102
Ferentzy, P., 195
Fernandez, H., 87, 136, 201
Fernandez, J. W., 135, 136, 171
Field, N., 141, 177
Field, P. B., 120
Fillmore, K. M., 25
Fillmore, M. T., 170, 171
Finch, B. K., 180
Finney, J. W., 207, 213
Fiorentine, R., 249n1
Fischman, M. W., 98
Fitzgerald, J., 149
Flewelling, R. L., 219
Forsander, O. A., 22
Forster, L. M. K., 140
Forsyth, A. J. M., 151, 152
Fox, B. S., 218
Frank, B., 87
Frank, J. W., 102, 161, 173
Fredholm, B. B., 42
Free, M. D., 182
French, L. A., 140
French, R., 152
Frenken, G. M. N., 136
Freud, S., 74
Friedlander, Y., 165
Fris, M., 151
Fromme, K., 171
Frone, M. R., 43, 181
Furst, P. T., x, 137, 139, 155n1, 155n5

Gable, R. S., 15
Galanter, M., 63
Gallant, D., 226
Ganguly, K. K., 131
Gao, Y-T., 25
Gardner, E. L., 42
Geary, D. C., 47
Gelderloos, P., 237
Gerald, M. S., 44
Gerber, J., 241
Gerlach, D., 50
German, D., 102
Gerrard, G., 186
Giancola, P. R., 14
Gilbert, L., 21
Gillmore, M. R., 174
Glantz, S. A., 49, 109, 220
Glassner, B., 167, 174
Glynn, T., 217
Godfrey, C., 24
Goldman, D., 165
Goldman, L. K., 49, 220
Goldman, M. S., 170
Goldstein, A., 41
Goldstein, P. J., 102
Goodman, J., 57, 68, 69, 71, 96, 101,
    107, 112, 138
Gordon, S., 48
Gordon, S. M. G., 237
Gossop, M., 87, 98, 132, 134, 246
Gostin, L. O., 239
Gotoh, M., 168
Gould, S. J., 37
Goulden, C., 19, 45, 120
Granfield, R., 233
Grant, B., 146
Grant, B. F., 29, 45
Grant, M, 193
Gray, D., 103, 130, 179, 184,
    186, 189, 232
Gray, R., 25
Greeley, J., 21, 180
Gregory, R. J., 130, 161, 186
Griffiths, P., 87, 98, 134, 149, 150
Grills, C., 230
Grob, C., 22, 46, 48, 51, 137, 159
Grobe, J. E., 50

Gross, M. M., 29
Gruber, R., 222
Gual, A., 9
Gureje, O., 209, 211
Gusfield, J. R., 112, 113
Gutstein, H., 42
Gutzke, D. W., 195, 196
Guzman-Flores, C., 40

Hagen, E. H., 38–40
Hall, E., 25
Hall, W., 243
Hanson, D. J., 61, 78, 79, 82
Harper, F. D., 168
Harris, K., 134
Harris, T. R., 10, 168
Hart, C. L., 25
Hartmann, D., 121, 122
Haselton, M. G., 36
Hasin, D., 167
Hatsukami, D. K., 98
Hattox, R. S., 68, 69, 92
Hawkins, J. D., 174
Hawthorne, V. M., 25
Hayashida, M., 165
Heath, D. B., 3, 22, 40, 46, 48, 83, 119,
    122, 133, 159, 167, 169, 172, 174,
    240, 241
Heather, N., 165, 198
Heatherton, T. F., 172
Helmer, J., 110
Helzer, J. E., 84
Henderson, B. E., 25
Hendry, J., 168
Herd, D., 168, 190n1
Hermann, J., 221
Hernstein, R. J., 118n5
Hesselbrock, M., 84
Hesselbrock, M. N., 164
Hesselbrock, V. M., 164
Hester, R. K., 207, 213, 227
Hicks, J. J., 220
Higley, J. D., 44
Higuchi, S., 165, 166
Hill, E. M., 35, 47, 49, 118n5
Hill, T. W., 231
Hillhouse, M. P., 249n1

Hindler, C. G., 133, 155n3
Hinson, R. E., 223
Hiripi, E., 146
Hirsch, E., 130
Holder, J. M., 3
Hole, D. J., 25
Hopkins, R. S., 220
Hops, H., 173
Horton, D., 158, 175
Houghton, S., 184
Howard, J., 217
Huata, P., 123
Hubbell, A., 21
Huber, A., 227
Hugh-Jones, S., 15, 70, 138
Hughes, C. C., 192
Hughes, J. C., 226
Hughes, M, 31
Hughes, R., 78, 103
Humphrey, R. H., 85
Hunt, G., 14, 15, 20, 125, 155n1, 157
Hunter, E., 184
Huriwai, T., 123, 231
Husak, D. N., 247
Hutt, M., 162, 179
Hyytia, P., 41

Ikuesan, B. A., 168, 179
Iritani, B., 174
Irwin, K. L., 21
Iverson, L. L., 84

Jackson, J. S., 180
Jaffe, J., 160
James I, 72
Janca, A., 10, 209, 211
Jankowiak, W., 178
Jansen, K. L. R., 152
Jansen, M. A., 217
Jason, L. A., 21, 180
Jellinek, E. M., 5, 65, 192–193, 194,
    203, 204, 206
Jenkins, J. E., 173, 174
Jenkins, R., 121, 122, 123
Jensen, E. L., 241
Jilek, W. G., 141
Johansson, S. E., 175

Johnson, B., 190n6
Johnson, C. A., 217
Johnson, E. O., 146
Johnson, V., 173
Johnson, V. L., 2
Johnston, L. D., 19, 20, 46, 85, 86, 124
Jones, B. T., 171
Jonnes, J., 15, 81, 84, 85, 86, 87, 98,
    99, 105
Jowitt, A., 129
Juarez, J., 40
Juliano, L. M., 170, 171
Julien, R. M., 14, 76, 86, 97, 155n2

Kagan, R. A., 239
Kahn, M. W., 186
Kalix, P., 133, 134, 150
Kamin, L. J., 121
Kaminsky, D. C., 140
Kandel, D. B., 20, 24, 45, 46, 112, 120,
    124, 146, 149
Kantor, L. W., 217, 220, 221
Karch, S. B., 73, 74
Katz, S. H., 34, 58, 64
Keefe, K., 174
Kellert, S. R., 54
Kemp, S., 141
Kendler, K. S., 31, 165
Kennedy, B. P., 237
Kennedy, J. G., 133
Kerner, K., 196, 199, 200, 214n3
Kessler, R. C., 31, 32, 146, 181, 223
Khantzian, E. J., 21, 52, 153
Kielhorn, F-W., 194
Kilham, C., 129
Kinoshita, T., 166
Kirmayer, L. J., 208
Kirsch, I., 170
Kitcher, P., 12n5, 218
Kleber, H. D., 63
Klingemann, H., 155n1, 245
Knipe, E., 155n1, 176
Knutson, B., 44
Kohn, M., 77
Kono, H., 166
Koob, G. F., 41, 43, 53
Kosten, T. R., 3

Krishnamachari, K. A. V. R., 132
Kristeller, J. L., 247
Krivo, L. J., 180
Krohn, M. D., 174
Kua, E. H., 168
Kuhlman, D. M., 50, 51

La Barre, W., 142, 155n4
Labouvie, E., 27
Langenbucher, J., 27
Langenbucher, J. W., 205
Langton, M., 179, 189
LaVeist, T. A., 180
Lawrence, D., 181
Le Fanu, J., 107, 213
Le Moal, M., 43, 53
Lebot, V., 128, 129
Lee, M. A., 93, 103
Lee, R. W., 140
Leischow, S. J., 181
Lemert, E. M., 120, 130
Lemmens, P. H., 46
Lende, D. H., 44
Lenton, S., 85, 151, 243
Leonard, K. E., 5
Leshner, A. I., 3, 31, 213, 215n10, 228
Levine, H. G., 110, 162, 193, 195, 203,
    211, 212
Levy, R., 62
Lewin, L., 73
Lewis-Williams, J. D., 34
Lewontin, R. C., 121
Li, H. Z., 167
Li, T-K., 165
Lillie-Blanton, M., 162
Lin, K-M., 166
Lindstrom, L., 128
Ling, W., 227
Lizotte, A. J., 174
Lloyd, C., 134
Lock, M., 123
Longabaugh, R., 228
Lostof, H. S., 136
Lovejoy, P. E., 134, 135
Low, B. S., 47, 118n5
Lubar, J. F., 3
Lubar, J. O., 3

Luciano, D. J., 136
Luna, L. E., 137
Lusane, C., 147, 148, 182
Lyons, M. J., 165

Ma, G. X., 86, 147
Maalsté, N. J. M., 151
MacAndrew, C., 120, 169, 170, 186
MacCoun, R. J., 23, 25, 61, 86, 104,
    105, 147, 217, 240, 242, 243, 244,
    245, 246
MacDonald, D., 132
MacGregor, S., 200
Maddux, J. F., 30
Maisto, S. A., 172
Mäkelä, K., 22, 145, 159, 178
Malik, R., 224
Mancall, P. C., 102, 178, 179
Mandelbaum, D. G., 170
Manderson, D., 109, 241
Mangini, M., 231
Margolis, R. D., 165
Marin, G., 171, 175
Marinangeli, P., 167, 224
Markou, A., 41
Marlatt, A. G., 244
Marlatt, G. A., 170
Marmot, M., 239
Mars, G., 176
Marshall, M., 5, 130, 169
Martensen, R. L., 213
Marwick, A., 61
Matsushita, S., 165, 166
Matsuyoshi, J., 229
Matthee, R., 60, 68, 71, 96, 99, 101,
    112, 114
Maull, N., 4, 5
Maxwell, J. C., 87
Maxwell, N., 12n4
May, P. A., 221
Mazeki, H., 166
McCandless, P., 195
McCauley, R. N., 5
McCoy, A. W., 83–84, 85, 99
McDonald, D., 129
McDowall, D., 174
McElduff, P., 25

McGonagle, K. A., 31
McGovern, J. P., 203
McGue, M., 164, 165
McKee, S., 223
McKeganey, N. P., 152
McKenna, D. J., 137
McLaughlin, D. K., 180
McPeake, J. D., 237
Measham, F., 109, 151, 152
Mechoulam, R., 62
Medina-Mora, M. E., 125, 161, 168
Merikangas, K. R., 52, 218, 223
Merlin, M., 128
Mickelson, K. D., 181
Midanak, L., 45
Midford, R., 219, 220–221
Miller, D., 3
Miller, D. C., 50
Miller, M., 16, 18, 19, 25, 45
Miller, N. L., 180
Miller, W. E., 40
Miller, W. R., 31, 207, 215n5, 227,
    228, 236
Milner, Peter, 41
Milton, K., 54
Miron, J. A., 100
Mocan, H. N., 5, 100
Monastra, V. J., 3
Moncrief, J., 226
Montagu, A., 121
Montague, P. R., 44
Moore, R. S., 102, 161
Moore, T., 240, 241, 242
Moos, R. H., 207, 213
Morales, E., 140
Morgenstern, J., 27
Morrison, D. M., 174
Moyers, T., 207, 213, 227
Mphi, M., 168, 179
Mudar, P., 43, 181
Mudde, A. N., 220
Mununggurr, N., 130, 161
Murayama, M., 165
Murphy, D., 53
Murphy, S. B., 181
Musto, D. F., 74, 75, 79, 84, 105, 108,
    109, 110, 113

Nabuzoka, D., 149, 150
Nadelmann, E. A., 240
Nahas, G. G., 66, 85
Nathan, P. E., 27, 205
Neale, M. C., 165
Nelson, C. B., 31
Nelson, W. P., 239
Nencini, P., 155n3
Nero, K., 131
Nesse, R. M., 41, 57, 236
Nestler, E. J., 43
Netting, R., 133, 160–161
Neumark, Y. D., 165
Neve, R. J. M., 46
New Zealand Health Information
    Service, 16–17, 18, 19, 45
Newcomb, M. D., 174
Newlin, D. B., 35, 44
Newman, J. L., 64
Nistler, M., 221
Norcross, J. C., 233
Norcross, K., 151
Norström, T., 9, 24

Obot, I. S., 125
O'Brien, M., 87, 227
Ockene, J. K., 247
Odgen, P., 184
O'Dwyer, P., 169
Oei, T., 21, 180
Oetting, E. R., 173, 175
Olds, James, 41–42
Olsen, E., 82
O'Malley, P. M., 19, 20, 46,
    85, 86, 124
Ong, E. K., 109
Orme-Johnson, D. W., 237
Ott, J., 155n1
Otto, C., 131
Ouellet, L. J., 102
Owens, C., 42

Pacurucu-Castillo, S., 168
Page, J. B., 67, 203, 215n7, 244
Palmour, R. M., 40
Pandina, R. J., 2
Panksepp, J., 44

Pantellis, C., 133, 134, 155n3
Parascandola, J., 33n1
Paredes, A., 139
Parker, H., 23, 109, 151,
    152, 169, 174
Parker, R. N., 169
Parsons, L. H., 41
Parssinen, T. M., 196, 199,
    200, 214n3
Paton-Simpson, G., 168, 169
Paykin, A., 167
Pedersen, N. L., 165
Pederson, W., 151, 152
Peele, S., 3, 25, 159, 172
Pegram, T. R., 78, 81, 82, 107
Pendergrast, M., 68, 69
Pentz, M. A., 217, 219
Peréz, R. L., 161, 169
Perkins, K. A., 50
Peters, H., 66
Peterson, R. D., 180
Peto, R., 25
Pfaus, J. G., 43
Phillips, A. G., 43
Phillips, T. J., 164
Phillips, W., 82
Phinney, J. S., 121, 122, 123
Picciotto, M. R., 42
Pihl, R. O., 7, 164
Pinker, Steven, 37
Pitts, M., 219, 222
Plant, S., 74
Poland, R. E., 166
Pollay, R. W., 239
Pollock, N. J., 129
Pomerleau, C. S., 21, 57, 238
Porter, R., 23, 80,
    193, 195, 212
Posner, S. F., 175
Power, R., 152
Powis, B., 98
Prescott, C. A., 165
Price, J. M., 72, 101, 112
Price, R. K., 31, 207
Prince, R., 142
Prochaska, J. O., 233
Proctor, R. N., 72

Proescholdbell, R. J., 122
Project MATCH Research Group,
    207, 213, 228
Puddey, I. B., 25
Pyörälä, E., 9

Quintero, G., 234

Ragels, L. A., 153
Rahav, G., 167
Railton, Peter, 9
Rakic, V., 25
Ram, R. S., 231
Ramsay, M., 19, 45, 120, 152
Ramstedt, M., 9, 24
Ramström, L. M., 18
Randall, C. L., 172
Ranger-Moore, J., 181
Rao, S., 178, 246
Rasmussen, D. W., 5, 100, 103
Raven, P., 54
Rawson, R. A., 227
Ray, S., 220
Read, P., 188
Rehm, J., 24
Reichel-Dolmatoff, G., 137, 171
Reinarman, C., 110, 162
Reisinger, H. S., 181
Reuter, P., 23, 25, 61, 86, 102, 104,
    105, 147, 217, 240, 242,
    243, 244, 245, 246
Rhodes, J. E., 21, 180
Ringwalt, C. L., 219
Risk, N. K., 31, 112
Ritter, A. J., 227
Roberts, A., 190n5, 223
Roberts, A. J., 41
Roberts, J. M., 62
Roberts, L. J., 244
Robertson, I., 165, 198
Robertson, P. J., 123
Robins, L. N., 84
Robinson, T. E., 43, 53
Roderick, P., 239
Rodriguez, D., 122
Rohena, L., 222
Romelsjö, A., 24

Room, R., 10, 27, 29, 45, 46, 124, 126,
    145, 159, 169, 170, 178, 190n2,
    192, 205, 206, 208, 209, 210, 211,
    215n9, 224
Rooney, D. F., 130, 131
Rorabaugh, W. J., 78, 82, 99, 193
Rose, S., 121
Rosenbaum, M., 181
Rosenblood, L., 167
Ross, L. T., 47, 118n5
Ross, R. K., 25
Rounsaville, B. J., 29
Rowe, D., 230
Rozin, P., 55
Rudgley, R., 34, 88n2, 130, 155n1
Rugh, D., 132
Rush, B., 193–194, 214n2
Russell, M., 43, 181
Ryan, K. F., 240

Sabbag, R., 86
Saggers, S., 103, 130, 179, 184, 186,
    189, 232
Saifnoorian, E., 168
Sale, E., 221
Salmon, W. C., 12n5
Sambrano, S., 221
Sandhu, D. S., 224
Sartorius, N., 10
Sawa, G. H., 167
Scarborough, J., 65, 193
Schafer, J., 170
Schafer, W. D., 50
Schaler, J. A., 3, 153, 172
Scheier, L. M., 24, 180
Schelling, T. C., 49, 108
Schenk, G., 161
Schilling, R. F., 21
Schinke, S. P., 222
Schivelbusch, W., 69, 88n2,
    92, 95, 112
Schmidt, L., 10, 169, 209, 210, 224
Schottenfeld, R., 178, 246
Schuckit, M. A., 27, 226
Schulenberg, J., 19, 46
Schulteis, G., 41
Schultes, R. E., 136, 137, 155n4

Schultz, W., 44
Schumaker, J. F., 142
Scuffham, P. A., 24
Segal, B., 222
Self, D. W., 43
Sellgman, J., 62
Sellman, D., 205, 231
Sempos, C. T., 24
Serrano, Y., 21
Shaara, L., 141
Shackelford, T. K., 36
Shakespeare, W., 248
Sharma, H. K., 131, 132
Sharma, H. M., 237
Sharon, D., 137
Sharp, C., 19, 45, 120
Shea, S. H., 165
Shedler, J., 46, 51, 222
Shenk, J. W., 241
Shepard, G. H., 137–138
Sherratt, A., 65, 66, 95
Shive, S., 86, 147
Shlain, B., 93, 103
Shorter, E., 192
Siegal, R. K., 40
Simons, R. C., 192
Simpura, J., 9
Singer, M., 5, 125–126, 163, 178, 181, 222, 244
Singh, Y. N., 128
Skinstad, A. H., 205
Skog, O. J., 24
Skrondal, A., 151, 152
Slade, J. S., 73, 96, 107, 238
Sly, D. F., 220
Smith, C., 174
Smith, D. E., 92, 159, 177
Smith, E. O., 38, 41, 44
Smith, G. D., 25
Smith, L., 200
Smith, W. D., 68, 69
Smyth, B. P., 87
Sobell, L. C., 31, 213, 233, 234
Sobell, M. B., 31, 213, 233
Sondhi, A., 19, 45, 120
Sournia, J. C., 60, 65, 78, 194
Spicer, P., 236

Spillane, J., 77, 99, 105
Spitznagel, E. L., 31, 112
Spring, J. A., 61, 67, 101
Springer, T., 221
Spruit, I. P., 151
Sputore, B., 232
Stachalek, R., 127, 128, 155n2
Stacy, A. W., 170
Staggers, F., 237
Stark, H., 62
Sterelny, K., 12n2
Sterk, C. E., 102
Stevenson, M., 149, 150
Stewart, G. G., 72, 73
Stich, S., 53
Stokes, S., 180
Stout, R. L., 228
Strakowski, S. M., 52, 223
Strang, J., 87, 98, 245
Strathern, A., 141
Straussner, S. L. A., 92, 146, 155n1, 167, 224, 230
Strongman, K. T., 6, 191
Strunin, L., 124–125, 126
Substance Abuse and Mental Health Services Administration, 13, 17, 18, 19, 24, 45, 143, 144, 145, 147, 148, 155n6
Sugarman, S. D., 241
Suggs, D. N., 133
Sulkunen, P., 9
Sullivan, R. J., 38–40, 131
Sundquist, J., 175
Susser, I., 181
Sussman, S., 217
Swendsen, J. D., 52, 223
Swift, W., 85
Szasz, T. S., 103, 118, 242

Takagi, S., 165, 166
Tani, C. R., 174
Tannhauser, M., 140
Tarter, R. E., 14
Taylor, A., 190n6
Taylor, J. C., 133, 155n3
Taylor, L., 42, 190n6
Teahan, J. E., 171

Terrell, D., 230
Thagard, P., 215n10
Thakker, J., 6, 191, 192, 208
Thomasson, H. R., 165
Thornberry, T. P., 174
Thornton, M., 100, 114
Tice, D. M., 172
Tildesley, E., 173
Timko, C., 207, 213
Tiobech, J., 131
Tobler, N. S., 219
Toneatto, T., 31, 233
Tonry, M., 147, 182
Topik, S. C., 68
Tosh, J., 61, 63
Towers, G. N., 137
Townsend, J. L., 239
Trapido, E., 220
Trivers, R. L., 46, 47
Tsuang, M. T., 165
Tucker, T. K., 227
Tyrell, I., 81, 82

Vallee, B. L., 22, 60, 64, 65, 67, 96
van de Wijngaart, G. F., 151
van Fraassen, B., 8
van Ours, J. C., 102
Vazquez-Barquero, J. L., 209, 211
Vergraeck, H. T., 151
Villatoro, J., 125, 161
Vogel-Sprott, M., 170, 171, 173
Vogeltanz, N. D., 10, 168
Voigt, M. M., 34, 58, 64
Von Bargen, J., 21
von Bibra, Ernst, 35
vonGernet, A., 71

Wadsworth, K. N., 46
Wakefield, J. C., 36, 191
Wakefield, M., 239
Walker, R. B., 72, 96, 101, 103, 107
Wall, A-M., 223
Wall, T. L., 165
Wallace, J., 153
Wallace, J. M., 124
Walters, S. T., 215n5, 227

Walton, K. G., 237
Ward, C., 141
Ward, R., 78
Ward, T., 6, 191, 192, 208
Warner, J., 67, 101, 105, 110, 114, 115, 116, 117, 195
Warner, K. E., 107, 247
Warner, L. A., 31, 146
Wasson, R. G., 137
Waters, M. C., 123, 180
Watson, S., 42
Weaver, H. N., 230
Wechsler, H., 239
Weeks, M. R., 222
Weil, A., 142, 237
Weisburger, J. J., 70
Weiss, F., 41
Weiss, S., 167
Wells, E. A., 174
Werker, E., 62
West, R., 7, 206
Westermeyer, J., 3, 91, 92, 95, 99, 105, 112, 131, 132, 149, 152–153, 159, 160, 161, 175, 177, 224, 229, 230, 238
Wheatley, K., 25
White, D., 219, 222
White, H. R., 173
White, W., 197–199, 200, 201, 202, 203, 207, 214n3, 214n4, 215n6
Wickenden, S., 134
Widaman, K. F., 170
Wilbert, J., 138
Williams, D. R., 180, 181
Williams, G. C., 36
Williams, L., 23
Wilsnack, R. W., 10, 168
Wilsnack, S. C., 10, 168
Wilson, E. O., 54
Wilson, M., 47, 48
Winant, H., 121–122
Winkelman, M. J., 141, 142
Wirtz, P. W., 228
Wise, R. A., 41, 42, 43
Wish, E., 84
Wittchen, H., 31
Wittig, M. C. W., 140

Wodak, A., 240, 241, 242
Wright, J. D., 140

Yamaguchi, K., 112
Yanai, J., 167
Young, A. M., 21
Young, S. N., 40
Yu, M. C., 25
Yuan, J-M., 25

Zack, M., 173
Zador, D., 245

Zahavi, A., 48
Zhao, S., 31
Zias, J., 62
Zinberg, N., 89, 108, 117
Zuckerman, M., 49, 50, 51
Zunguze, S. T., 173, 174
Zweben, A., 228
Zweben, J. E., 165
Zweibel, J., 100

Subject Index

Note: Page references followed by a
"t" indicate tables.

Abstinence movements (alcohol).
     See Temperance movements
Abuse, drug. *See* Drug abuse
Acculturation, 175
Adaptations, biological, 36–37
Addiction, 63
Addiction. *See also* Dependence
     contemporary concepts
          of, 204–208
     versus dependence, 29–30
     development of concept
          of, 192–196
     as disease, 193–196
     mid-twentieth century
          concepts of, 199–202
     role of beliefs in, 172
     versus use, 27
Alcohol, relation to other
     psychoactive drugs of, 15
Alcohol and drug studies. *See*
     Psychoactive drug studies
Alcohol use
     in ancient history, 64–65
     beliefs concerning effects of,
          169–170
     benefits of, 25
     colonialism and, 178–179
     control measures on (*See under*
          Control measures)
     cross-cultural concepts of,
          208–210
     degree of, 17
     for dietary reasons, 22

as disease, 83, 193–195, 196,
     202–204, 214n3
distillation practices and, 96
by ethnic group, 146t
harms of, 24
as legal, 59–60
in medieval period, 66–67
natural selection and, 40
opposition to, 77–79, 81–83, 107,
     167–168, 195
per capita, 16
pregnancy and, 171–172
social issues concerning, 83
social learning of, 173
by women, 168, 171–172
Alcoholics Anonymous (AA)
     as culture of recovery, 152–154
     and disease concept, 83, 202–204
     minorities and women in, 249n1
     as mutual aid group, 197
Alcoholism. *See also* Alcohol use: as
     disease
     alcoholism movement, 202–204
     concept of, 194
     types of, 204t
Alleles (ALDH enzymes), 165–166
Altered states of consciousness
     (ASC), 141–142, 237
American Surgeon General tobacco
     warning, 107
American Temperance Society, 78
Amphetamines, 97
Analysis
     biological, 1–5
     cultural-historical (*See* Cultural-
          historical analysis)

integrated model of, 6–10
levels of, 1–5
psychosocial, 1–5
role of questions in, 8
Anslinger, Harry, 80
Anti-saloon league, 79
Arrests. *See* Punitive measures
ASC. *See* Altered states of
consciousness
Assessment, 223–225
Association for the Study of
Inebriety, 196
Asylums, inebriate, 197–198
Attitudes. *See* Beliefs and
expectations; opposition to
under specific drugs; Social
factors
Australia, drug use in, 127–128, 130,
184–189
Availability, 98–100, 111, 162–163
Aversion therapies, 202
Ayahuasca, 137
Aztec society, 138–140

Balzac, Honoré de, 92
Banisteriopsis caapi, 137
Bayer and Company, 76
Beer
in ancient history, 64
earliest documentation of, 34
in Koyfar society, 160–161
Beliefs and expectations, 169–172
Betel, 130–131
Bhang, 132
Binge drinking, 17, 146t
Biological analysis, 1–5
Biophilia, 54
Bishop, Ernest, 199
Boggs Daniel legislation, 84
Brain, 40–44
Bureau of Narcotics, 201
Burroughs, William, ix
Bush, George H. W., 162

Caffeine use. *See also* Coffee
as legal, 59–60
prevalence of, 13

Camba society, 119
Cannabis
in ancient history, 66
in Asia, 132
bhang, 132
control measures on (*See under*
Control measures)
growth of, 84
in medieval period, 67–68
opposition to, 80–81, 84–85
use prevalence of, 18–19, 85
CAR (WHO cross-cultural
applicability) study, 209, 210
Charles II, King of England, 69
Chocolatl, 139
Choice, role in drug use of, 7
CIA (Central Intelligence Agency)
and drug trafficking, 83–84,
98–100, 103
and mind control, 93, 103
Classification systems. *See Diagnostic
and Statistical Manual of Mental
Disorders*; Diagnostic concepts;
*International Classification of
Diseases*
Club de haschischins, 92
Coca
in the Americas, 138
history of, 70, 73–74
Cocaine
benefits of, 74
crack, 97–98, 162–163
dependence on, 76–77
discovery of, 73–74
effects of, 97–98
growth in use of, 85–86
use prevalence of, 18–19
Coffee. *See also* Caffeine use
control measures on (*See under*
Control measures)
history of, 68–69
opposition to, 69
in social context, 92
Cohorts, influence on drug use of, 20
Coleridge, Samuel Taylor, 77
Colonialism, 178–179
Compulsion, 44

Control measures, 238–243. *See also*
    Social control; Taxes
    on alcohol, 64, 81–83, 167–168
    on cannabis, 80–81, 85
    on coffee, 69
    in gin epidemic, 115, 117
    harm caused by, 100, 113–114
    on opium, 79–80
    prevention (*See* Prevention)
    strategies of, 216–217
    on tobacco, 72
Cook, Captain, 128
Cooper, Courtney, 80
Cost-benefit analysis, 26
Crack. *See under* Cocaine
Craving, 43
Criminalization of drugs, 200. *See
    also* Decriminalization
    of drugs
Cultural-historical analysis, 1–5
    conceptual and methodological
        issues in, 121–126
    forms of explanation compared,
        185–186
    mistakes in, 214
Culture. *See also* Ethnic groups
    concept of, 121
    function of drugs in, 157–160
    integrated explanations
        involving, 183–189
    integration of drugs in, 160–162
    role in assessment of, 224
    role in prevention programs of,
        221–222
    role in treatment of, 229–232

Dance culture, 151–152
Dangerous Drug Act, 80
Datura, 136–137, 138–139
De Quincey, Thomas, ix, 77
Dealing, drug, 176, 182–183
Deaths, by ethnic group, 148t
Decriminalization of drugs, 242–243
Delacroix, Eugéne, 92
Delirium Tremens, 194
Demand-reduction strategies, 216
Demography, 45–51, 112

Dependence, 27–30. *See also*
    Addiction
    versus addiction, 29–30
    age group comparisons of, 32
    criteria for, 28–29
    evolutionary argument about,
        52–53
    gender differences in, 32
    prevalence of, 31–32
    rise in modern history of, 76–79
    terminology concerning, 205
    versus use, 31
*Diagnostic and Statistical Manual of
    Mental Disorders* (DSM), 26, 27,
    205, 208, 214n3, 224
Diagnostic concepts, 205–208. *See
    also Diagnostic and Statistical
    Manual of Mental Disorders;
    International Classification of
    Diseases*
    cultural variations in, 208–211
Dietary drug use, 22–23, 93
Dioscorides, 65
Disease concept, 83, 193–195, 196
Dispsomania, 194
Dole, Vincent, 201
Drug abuse, 26–32
    criteria for, 26–27
    by ethnic group, 148t
    evolutionary argument about,
        52–53
    versus harmful use, 27, 30
Drug dealing, 176, 182–183
Drug education programs, 218–221
    effectiveness of, 219–220
Drug policy, American, 239–241
Drug use. *See also use by name of drug*
    and abuse, 26–32
    addiction to (*See* Addiction)
    in Africa and Middle East,
        132–136
    age group comparisons of, 19–20,
        45–46
    in the Americas, 136–140
    in Asia, 130–132
    contexts of, 20–23
    cross-cultural nature of, 34–35

demographic effects on, 112
dependence on (*See* Dependence)
earliest evidence of, 34
early history of, 64–68
effect of knowledge on, 107
evolutionary perspective on,
    34–58
explanations of, 1–2
historical factors in, 89–118
illicit (*See* Illicit drug use)
in modern history, 68–79
in Oceania, 127–130
recreational (*See* Recreational
    drug use)
in twentieth century, 79–87
user characteristics, 81
Drugs
ambiguity of, 23
brain effects of, 40–44
and cultural integration,
    160–162
definition of, 14–15
functional contexts of, 90–93,
    157–160
harms and benefits of, 23–26
novel appearances of, 161–162
pharmacology of, 94–95
prescription, 241
public information about,
    108–109
DSM. *See Diagnostic and Statistical
    Manual of Mental Disorders*

Eboka, 135–136
Economic factors, 25, 101–103. *See
    also* Legislation; Taxes
Ecstasy (drug), 150–152
Emotions, and drug use, 40–44
Ethnic groups. *See also* Culture
concept of, 121–123
drug use in, 143–149
punitive measures and,
    147–148, 182
social factors in drug use for,
    179–183
Evolutionary explanations
as biological analysis, 4

integrated model, 54–57
nature and role of, 36–38
Exchange practices (trade), 102–103
Expectations and beliefs, 169–172
Explanations
determining factors in, 7–9
relevance versus salience of, 9–10
ultimate versus proximate, 36

Fleischl-Marxow, Ernst von, 74
Food, plants as, 54–55
Freud, Sigmund, 74, 199, 202

Gautier, Théophile, 92
Gender
and alcohol consumption, 45
and dependence prevalence, 32
gender roles, and drug use, 46
and sensation seeking, 50
Genetics
and drug abuse, 53, 164–166
and ethnic drug use patterns,
    165–166
and prevention measures, 218
George V, King of Austria, 82
Gin epidemic (Great Britain),
    114–117
Granta, 150

Hale Boggs legislation, 84
Hallucinogens
in the Americas, 136–138
use prevalence of, 18–19
Hammurabi, 64
Handicap principle, 48
Harm reduction strategies, 161–162,
    216–217, 243–247
Harmful use, 27, 30–31, 161–162
Harrison Narcotic Act, 79, 105, 200
Hemp. *See* Cannabis
Herodotus, 66
Heroin
addiction treatment for, 136 (*See
    also* Heroin prescription
    programs; Methadone
    maintenance)
early use of, 76

heroin chic, 87
methods of use of, 95
social control and, 178
use patterns of, 84, 87
use prevalence of, 18–19, 85
Heroin prescription programs, 245
Hippies, 92
Historical explanations, 60–63
Hoasca, 137
Hogarth, William, 115
Holmes, Sherlock, 77
Homer, 65
Hugo, Victor, 92
Huss, Magnus, 194
Hyoscine, 155n2
Hypodermic syringe, introduction
    of, 76

ICD. *See International Classification of
    Diseases*
Identification, cultural/social,
    175–176
Illicit drug use
    benefits of, 25–26
    harms of, 24–25
    prevalence of, 18–19
Incentive salience, 43–44
Indigenous Australians, drug use
    by, 184–189
Inhalants, 18–19
Integrated model, 6–10
    of cultural explanations, 187–189
    of evolutionary explanations,
        54–57
Interfield theories, 4–5
International Classification of Diseases
    (ICD), 26, 27, 205, 209–210,
    214n3

James I, King of England, 72
Jellinek, E. M., 203–204
Jones, John, 76
"Just say no" campaign, 85

Kava, 128–129
Keats, John, 77
Keeley Institutes, 198

Keeley, Leslie, 198
Kerr, Norman, 196
Kola nuts, 134–135
Kolb, Lawrence, 200
Koller, Carl, 74

Legalization of drugs, 242
Legislation, 104–106, 200
Levinstein, Edward, 196, 199
Life history theory, 47–51
Life Skills Training drug prevention
    program, 219–220, 222
LSD, in mind control
    experiments, 103

MADD (Mothers Against Drunk
    Driving), 83
Mariani, Angelo, 74
Marihuana Tax Act, 81, 110
Mather, Cotton, 72–73
Matsigenka society, 137–138
Maturing out, 233, 234
MDMA. *See Ecstasy*
Medicinal drug use, 20–21, 25, 91.
    See also under specific drugs
Medicine (profession), anti-opium
    trend in, 80
Men, young, 47–51
Mesolimbic dopaminergic system,
    43–44, 50
Methadone maintenance, 178, 201,
    245–246
Migrants, 149–150
Minnesota model, 201
Minorities. *See Ethnic groups*
Monardes, Nicholas, 73
Monitoring the Future study (MTF),
    15, 85
Moral panics, 110
Morning glory seeds, 139
Morphine
    discovery of, 75
    opposition to, 79
MTF. *See Monitoring the
    Future study*
Multiculturalism, and drug use,
    142–154

Mushrooms, 137, 138
Mutual aid groups, 197. *See also*
    Alcoholics Anonymous

Nahas, Gabriel, 85
Narcotic farms, 201
Narcotics Anonymous, 201
National Comorbidity Study, 31
National Council of
    Alcoholism, 203
National Household Survey on
    Drug Abuse (NHSDA),
    15, 26, 125
National Longitudinal Alcohol
    Epidemiological Survey, 45, 144
Native American Church, 92
Natural recovery, 212, 232–234
Natural selection, and drug use,
    38–40
Needle exchange programs (NEPs),
    244–245
Negative reinforcement, 42–43
NHSDA. *See* National Household
    Survey on Drug Abuse
Nicot, Jean, 73
Nicotine, discovery of, 73
Nicotine delivery systems, 247
Niemann, Albert, 73–74
Norms, cultural, 166–169
Nyswander, Marie, 201

Ololiuqui, 139
Opium
    in ancient history, 65
    in Asia, 131–132
    availability of, 98–99
    Burroughs and, ix
    control measures on (*See under*
        Control measures)
    De Quincey and, ix
    dependence on, 76, 77
    earliest documentation of, 34
    historical changes in use of, ix
    medicinal uses of, 74–75
    in medieval period, 67
    methods of use of, 95
    in modern history, 74–76

opposition to, 79–80
Othello, 247–248

Pacific Islands, drug use in, 128–130
Panics, moral, 110
Paraphernalia, 43
Peer pressure, 174
Peyote, 137, 139, 231
Pharmacology, 94–95
Pituri, 127–128
Plant chemicals, 38–39
Plants
    as food, 54–55
    knowledge of, 54–55
    psychoactive effects of, 55–57
Pliny, 65
Poisons and Pharmacy Act, 79
Policy, drug, 239–241
Political factors, 103, 125–126. *See
    also* Legislation
Positive reinforcement, 42–43
Posselt, Wilhelm, 73
Pragmatic drug use, 22, 93
Prejudice, racial, 109–110, 181
Prescription drugs, 241
Prevention, 217–222
    based on genetic history, 218
    culturally focused programs for,
        221–222
    drug education, 218–221
Price of drugs, 101–102
PRIDE (Parents Resource Institute
    for Drug Education), 85
Prohibition (movement),
    81–82, 100, 114
Project DARE, 219
Psychoactive drug studies,
    multidisciplinary nature
    of, 2, 3–5
Psychoactive drugs, definition of, 14
Psychosocial analysis, 1–5
Pulque, 139
Punitive measures, 104
    effect on treatment options of,
        201–202
    ethnicity and, 147–148, 182
Pure Food and Drug Act, 79

Qat, 133–134, 149–150

Race, concept of, 121–122
Racial prejudice, 109–110, 181
Rave culture, 151–152
Reagan, Ronald, 85
Recovery, natural, 212, 232–234
Recovery cultures, 152–154
Recreational drug use, 21, 81, 91–92
   growth of, 84
"Reefer Madness," 84
Reimann, Karl, 73
Reinforcement, 42–43
Reward systems
   description of, 41–43
   and drug abuse, 53
Risk-taking behavior, 47–50
Ritual-religious drug use, 22, 92–93
Rush, Benjamin, 73, 78, 193–194, 195,
   196, 197, 212

SADD (Students Against Drunk
   Driving), 83
Salience, incentive, 43–44
Santayana, George, 61
Self
   as central to recovery, 234–238
   role in assessment of, 224–225
   role in drug use of, 7
Self-medication, 21
Self-system, explanation of, 7
Sensation seeking, 49–50
Sentences, criminal. See Punitive
   measures
Setürner, Friedrich, 75
Sexual selection, 46–51
Shafer Commission, 84
Shakespeare, William, 247
Silkworth, William, 202
Sin taxes. See Taxes
Smith, Robert, 202
Smoking cessation, 247
Smoking Opium Exclusion Act, 79
Snuffs, 137
Social control, 177–179. See also
   Control measures
Social drug use, 21–22

Social factors, 106–113. See also
   Beliefs and expectations;
   Norms, cultural
   in minority drug use, 179–183
Social groups, concept of, 123–124
Social organization, 177
Socialization, 172–177
   alcohol use and, 173
   cultural comparisons of, 174
   of youth, 173–174
Society for the Study and Cure of
   Inebriety, 196
Society for the Study of
   Addiction, 200
Stages of change model, 233
Stevenson, Robert Louis, 74
Stimulus-response mechanisms,
   43–44
Stress
   of acculturation, 175
   of social disadvantage, 180–181
Subcultures, 123–124
Substances. See Drugs
Supply-reduction strategies, 216
Survey methods, 124–125
Surveys of drug use, 15–20
Sutton, Thomas, 194
Swan, Zachary, 86
Swedish treatment, 214n4
Syanon, 201
Sydenham, Thomas, 75
Synthetic substances, 96–97
Syringes. See Hypodermic syringe;
   Needle exchange programs

Tabernathe iboga, 135–136
Taft, William, 76
Taxes, 64, 101, 239
Tea, 70
Technological developments, 95–98
Temperance movements, 78–79,
   82–83, 195
TM. See Transcendental
   meditation
Tobacco use
   in the Americas, 138
   cessation of, 247

control measures on (*See under*
    Control measures)
by ethnic group, 147t
history of, 70–73
as legal, 59–60
"less harmful", 107, 247
for medicinal purposes, 71, 72
opposition to, 72–73, 106–107
prevalence of, 17–18
technological change and, 96
Tolerance, drug, 209
Transcendental meditation
    (TM), 237
Treatment, 225–238
    barriers to, 229
    biological and psychosocial,
        226–229
    in contemporary period, 206–207
    cultural issues in, 229–232
    diversity in, 212
    effectiveness of, 228
    holistic approach to, 234–238
    in mid-twentieth century,
        200–201
    in nineteenth and twentieth
        centuries compared, 207t
    in nineteenth century, 197–199
Trotter, Thomas, 78, 193
TSF. *See* Twelve-step facilitated
    (TSF) treatments

Twain, Mark, 74
Twelve-step facilitated (TSF)
    treatments, 152–154

United States, drug policy in,
    239–241

Vaccines, for drug use
    prevention, 218
von Brühl-Cramer (physician), 194

Washingtonians, 78, 195, 197
Water lilies, 137
WHO. *See* World Health
    Organization
Wilson, William, 202
Wine, in ancient history, 64–65
Withdrawal, drug, 209
Women's Christian Temperance
    Union, 79, 195
Wooten report, 84
World Health Organization (WHO),
    24, 203, 209
Wright, Hamilton, 110

Yajé, 137
Yale Center for Alcohol
    Studies, 83, 203
Young men, 47–51

About the Authors

Russil Durrant received his Ph.D. from the University of Canterbury, where he has recently completed a post-doctoral fellowship. He currently works at the Centre for Behavioral Research in Cancer, at the Cancer Control Research Institute in Melbourne, Victoria. His current research involves the design and evaluation of mass media tobacco prevention programs; his other research interests include evolutionary psychology, cultural psychology, and the social history of drug use.

Jo Thakker is a lecturer in clinical psychology at the University of Waikato in Hamilton, New Zealand. She received her Ph.D. from the University of Canterbury and has worked as a clinical psychologist in a variety of therapeutic contexts. Along with work in the substance abuse area, her research interests include cultural psychology and mental health issues in relation to migrants and refugees.